Thriving!

Third Edition

Thriving!

A Manual for Students in the Helping Professions

Third Edition

Lennis G. Echterling

Jack Presbury

Eric Cowan

A. Renee Staton

Debbie C. Sturm

Michele Kielty

J. Edson McKee

Anne L. Stewart

William F. Evans
James Madison University

Los Angeles | London | New Delhi
Singapore | Washington DC | Boston

Los Angeles | London | New Delhi
Singapore | Washington DC | Boston

FOR INFORMATION:

SAGE Publications, Inc.
2455 Teller Road
Thousand Oaks, California 91320
E-mail: order@sagepub.com

SAGE Publications Ltd.
1 Oliver's Yard
55 City Road
London EC1Y 1SP
United Kingdom

SAGE Publications India Pvt. Ltd.
B 1/I 1 Mohan Cooperative Industrial Area
Mathura Road, New Delhi 110 044
India

SAGE Publications Asia-Pacific Pte. Ltd.
3 Church Street
#10-04 Samsung Hub
Singapore 049483

Copyright © 2016 by SAGE Publications, Inc.

Printed in the United States of America

A catalog record of this book is available from the Library of Congress.

ISBN: 978-1-4833-4977-0

This book is printed on acid-free paper.

Acquisitions Editor: Kassie Graves
Editorial Assistant: Carrie Montoya
Production Editor: Veronica Stapleton Hooper
Copy Editor: Diane Wainwright
Typesetter: C&M Digitals (P) Ltd.
Proofreader: Ellen Howard
Indexer: Molly Hall
Cover Designer: Scott Van Atta
Marketing Manager: Shari Countryman

15 16 17 18 19 10 9 8 7 6 5 4 3 2 1

Contents

Preface xiv

CHAPTER 1 The Thriving Principles 1

HOW SHALL WE BEGIN? JEAN'S STORY 2

Use It—Don't Lose It! 4
Thriving 5
Pack Wisely 5
Make the Journey Your Destination 7

THE JOURNEY: A PARABLE 10

Have Traveling Companions 11

WORST PARENTS OF THE YEAR AWARD: JEN'S STORY 14

Keep Your Bearings 15

YOU'LL GO FAR IN LIFE: ANDREA'S STORY 17

EXERCISE 1.1. WHATCHA GONNA BE? A MAGIC MIRROR EXERCISE 19

Let the Trip Take You 19

I'M GOING IN. WANT TO JOIN ME? LENNIE'S STORY 21

Always Take the High Road 23
Summary 25
Resources 25
References 26

CHAPTER 2 Making Your Training Journey 28

WHY NOT ENJOY THE RIDE?: CATHY'S STORY 30

Being a Novice 31
Opening Rituals 32

EXERCISE 2.1. TRADITIONS: A REMINISCING
AND PLANNING EXERCISE   33

    Unlearning   35
    Communication   36
    Handling Personal Problems   37
    Keeping a Portfolio   38
    Dualistic Thinking   39

THE ONE: JUANITA'S STORY   39

    Perfectionism   40
    Keeping a Beginner's Mind   40
    Being an Apprentice   42
    Multiplistic Thinking   42

A DEER CAUGHT IN THE HEADLIGHTS: BILL'S STORY   43

    The "Sophomore Slump"   43

LEARNING FROM THE INSIDE OUT: TERESA'S STORY   44

    Your Relationships With Faculty   45
    Comprehensive Examination   46
    An Emerging Professional   47
    Relativistic Thinking   48
    Research Project   49
    Graduation and Commencement   51
    Summary   51
    Resources   51
    References   52

CHAPTER 3 Meeting Your Basic Needs   54
    Your Personal Hierarchy of Needs   56

A CONSTANT CHALLENGE: ELLEN'S STORY   57

    Basic Needs and Self-Actualization   58

EXERCISE 3.1. TAKE THAT JOB AND . . . A GUIDED
FANTASY EXERCISE   60

    Conducting a Needs Inventory   60

TOUCH THE SUN: RENEE'S STORY   61

EXERCISE 3.2. THE SEA STAR: A BALANCING EXERCISE   62

    Crafting a Balanced Life   63

WE HAVE NOTHING TO FEAR BUT . . . : BETH'S STORY   64

EXERCISE 3.3. YOUR NEEDS IN CONTEXT: A SYSTEMIC EXERCISE   64

Pathways to Balance 65
Housing 66
ADVENTURES IN SUBSIDIZED HOUSING LAND: CHRIS'S STORY 67
GIVING UP CITY LIFE TO FIT INTO A SMALL TOWN: DARA'S STORY 69
EXERCISE 3.4. IT TAKES A COMMUNITY: AN EXERCISE IN IMAGINATION 70
Financial Assistance 70
Wellness 74
KICKING AND SLEEPING: MARTIN'S STORY 76
Finding and Creating Perspective 77
THE ROAD FROM ORANGE CRACKERS TO RICE: ANNE'S STORY 77
EXERCISE 3.5. I'LL HAVE THE COMBO: MEETING MULTIPLE NEEDS 78
Summary 79
Resources 79
References 80

CHAPTER 4 Enhancing Your Academic Skills 82
MORE THAN I HAD BARGAINED FOR: BONNIE'S STORY 83
Hearts and Minds 84
Developing Critical Reflection Skills 86
Learning by Heart 87
Riding the Perturbation Wave 87
EXERCISE 4.1. THE BIRDCAGE: ENCOUNTERING OPPRESSION 89
Finding "The Zone" 90
Using the Zeigarnik Effect 91
The Core Academic Skills 92
Reading 92
EXERCISE 4.2. WHAT? SO WHAT? NOW WHAT? 95
I LEARNED HOW TO READ ALL OVER AGAIN: BRIAN'S STORY 95
Researching 96
EXERCISE 4.3. DOING A LITTLE DETECTIVE WORK 100
EXERCISE 4.4. CRITIQUING 100
Writing 101
LEARNING THE HARD WAY: SUSAN'S STORY 102
EXERCISE 4.5. WRITING TWICE-TOLD STORIES 104
EXERCISE 4.6. READING: A WRITING EXERCISE 104

EXERCISE 4.7. STRUCTURING: A WRITING EXERCISE   105

  Presenting   105

EXERCISE 4.8. PREPARING AND PRACTICING   110

EXERCISE 4.9. IMAGINING SUCCESS   111

EXERCISE 4.10. BREATHING   111

  Summary   111

  Resources   111

  References   112

CHAPTER 5 Mindfully Managing Stress   **114**

STRESSED OUT: BILL'S STORY   116

  Stress   117

    The Stress of Helping   118

    Distress   118

    Stressful Events   119

WHEN IT "HURTS GOOD": RACHEL'S STORY   119

  Responding to Stress   121

    Resting   122

    Eating Well   122

    Exercising   123

    Using Humor   123

    Relaxing, Refreshing, Renewing, and Revitalizing   124

    Seeking Professional Help   124

    Reflecting   124

    Managing Your Time   125

  Mindful Management of Stress   125

EXERCISE 5.1. STRESS FOR SUCCESS   127

EXERCISE 5.2. WAYS OF SAYING "NO" AND "YES!"   128

  Beyond Stress   129

    Resilience Under Stress   130

    Making Meaning of Stress   131

    Telling Your Story   131

EXERCISE 5.3. THE EMBRACING ATTITUDES:
A QUICK CHECK EXERCISE   132

  Thriving Under Stress   133

    Envisioning Your Goals   133

EXERCISE 5.4. MISSION: POSSIBLE: AN EXERCISE IN ENVISIONING   133

Using Your Strengths 134

EXERCISE 5.5. PANNING FOR GOLD: UNCOVERING STRENGTHS AND
RESOURCES 134

Connecting With Others 134

EXERCISE 5.6. THE SEA STAR II: A REVISITING EXERCISE 135

Stress and Character 136
Stress Into Strength 138
Summary 139
Resources 140
References 140

CHAPTER 6 Being With Others 143

BEING "PROCESSED": REBECCA'S STORY 144

What's in Your Backpack? 146
Self and Relationship 146
Exploring Your Relational Worldview 147

EXERCISE 6.1. VISITOR FROM ANOTHER PLANET: A GUIDED FANTASY 149

Growing in Relation 151
Mirrors 152

THE CHILDLIKE FEELING OF POSSIBILITY: ANTOINETTE'S STORY 153

The Counseling Qualities 153
Truth With a Capital T 155

EXERCISE 6.2. YOUR HARD-BELLY RESPONSE: A QUIZ 157

Giving and Receiving Feedback 157
Giving Helpful Feedback 158
The Johari Window 160

EXERCISE 6.3. GIVING AND RECEIVING FEEDBACK 160

Authenticity 161
Social Masks 161
Being and Seeming 162
Important People in Your Training 163
Mentors 163
Support Staff 166
Significant Others 166
Summary 168
Resources 169
References 170

CHAPTER 7 Exploring Yourself — 171

Make Personal Growth Your Goal — 171

THANKSGIVING LEFTOVERS: EDNA'S STORY — 172

Your Sense of Self — 173

EXERCISE 7.1. "I AM . . ." VERSUS "A COUNSELOR IS . . ." — 175

Ontological Security — 175

"I" and "Me" — 176

The Need for Personal Growth — 177

Being a "Do-Gooder" — 177

EXERCISE 7.2. THINGS I HOPE MY CLIENTS NEVER SAY:
AN AVERSION EXERCISE — 179

Consider Counseling for Yourself — 182

IT FEELS WEIRD FOR A COUNSELOR TO BE A CLIENT:
ROBERT'S STORY — 182

Allow Yourself to Mess Up — 183

Explore Your Assets — 184

Avoid the Groucho Paradox — 185

Assimilation and Accommodation — 186

Accommodating Information About Yourself — 187

Hold to Your Center — 188

Honor, but Modify, Your Style — 188

EXERCISE 7.3. TOWARD, AGAINST, OR AWAY? A MOVING EXERCISE — 189

Countertransference — 190

Getting Clear — 192

Finding Your Roots — 193

I NEED TO PAY ATTENTION TO WHO I AM: MICHELLE'S STORY — 194

Find the "I AM" Experience — 195

Summary — 195

Resources — 196

References — 197

CHAPTER 8 Becoming Neuro-Minded — 199

Neuroscience of Magic and Counseling — 200

Therapists, Minds, and Brains — 201

The Decade of the Brain — 202

Not as Hard as You Thought — 202

The Material Brain — 202

The Brain and Emotions — 204

There's No Place Like Home: Kiara's Story   206

  Promoting Neuroplasticity   207
    Attunement   208
A Valentine Gift of Attunement: Gene's Story   210

    What We Learned From a Monkey   211
    What Is Empathy?   212
    Optimal Emotional Arousal   213
     Necessary Self-Care   215
    Integration of Affect and Cognition   216
     The Hippocampus and Memory   216
     Amygdala and Hippocampus Collaboration   217
     The Right-Brain to Right-Brain Connection   219
    Co-Construction of Transformative Narratives   220
     Oxytocin   222
    Crap Detecting   223
  Summary   225
  Resources   226
  References   226

CHAPTER 9 Intervening in Crises, Traumas, and Disasters   230
  Fundamental Concepts   231
    Trauma and Crisis   231
    Resilience   232
  Intervention Principles   233
    LUV the Survivor   233
  Crisis Intervention Techniques   237
    Linking   238
    Making Meaning   239
    Regulating Emotions   240
    Moving On   241
  Preventing Suicide   243
  Disaster Intervention   247
Out of an Emergency, Something New Emerges:
  Lennie's Story   248

    Providing Psychological First Aid   249
  Mindfully Caring for Yourself   250
    When You Suffer a Loss   251
  Summary   253
  Resources   253
  References   254

CHAPTER 10 Thriving in Your Practicum and Internship   257

You Are Ready, Although You May Have Doubts   258

HOW OLD ARE YOU?: JERRA'S STORY   259

Preparing for Practicum: Who Are You?   260

BOUDOIR: GABRIELLE'S STORY   261

Your Practicum   262

Patience   263

Taking Pictures Along the Way   264

Internship   264

Choosing a Site   265

EXERCISE 10.1. REFRESHING YOUR MEMORY AND
PLOTTING YOUR COURSE: A DECISION-MAKING EXERCISE   266

Writing an Internship Agreement   266

Professional Liability Insurance   267

Competence   267

Informed Consent   268

Confidentiality   269

PUTTING IT ALL TOGETHER   269

Taking the High Road   271

Dual Roles   272

HIV: ERIC'S STORY   274

Making Rest Stops Along the Way   277

THESE POOR PEOPLE: NATHANIEL'S STORY   277

EXERCISE 10.2. FIRST THOUGHTS: AN EXPLORATORY EXERCISE   279

Stages in the Journey   281

Juggling   282

Making the Most of Your Internship   283

A Final Wish   284

Summary   284

Resources   284

References   285

CHAPTER 11 Launching Your Career   287

AROUND THE NEXT CORNER: BILL'S STORY   288

EXERCISE 11.1. LIFE SPAN TIME LINE   289

From Student to Professional   289

Exploring Your Values   290

EXERCISE 11.2. WHAT I TRULY WANT: A VALUES EXERCISE   290

   Exploring Your Roots   291

MY SACRIFICING, ADVENTUROUS ANCESTORS: MICHELE'S STORY   291

THE LEGACY OF MY PARENTS: GABE'S STORY   292

EXERCISE 11.3. CAREER GENOGRAM   293

  Using Your Resources   294

EXERCISE 11.4. INTERVIEWING TWO MASTERS: A JOURNAL EXERCISE   294

  Planning Your Career   295
    Being Intentional   295
    Becoming Professionally Involved   297
  Career Possibilities by Degree   298
    Careers With a Master's or EdS   298
    Careers With a Doctorate   300
  Conducting Your Search   301
    Where to Look for Jobs   301
    Successful Job Interviewing   302
  Your Career and Your Life   303
    Lifelong Learning   303
    Fitting In and Standing Out   304
    Think You're Not Creative?   306
    Clock-Watchers and Workaholics   307
    Leaving the Nest and Making Mistakes   307
  Summary   308
  One Final Point   309
  Resources   309
  References   310

Index   313

Preface

L earning to become a counselor is both an academically demanding and emotionally daunting process. Our purpose in writing this updated and expanded edition of our guidebook is to help counseling and therapy students not merely to survive their graduate education but actually to thrive. We have designed this book to serve as a supplement to other required texts in courses that introduce beginning graduate students to their professional identities. We have been heartened by the gratitude that many students have expressed to us for offering them such helpful advice in our previous editions. Our guidelines for thriving in one's graduate training are based on six important principles: come well prepared, live one's training, learn from others, explore oneself, be open to opportunities, and act with character.

Producing this new edition was like renovating an older home. We made major improvements, updated it with modern features, and even expanded it with new additions, but we also preserved the fundamental character and structural integrity of the original. So in each chapter of this new edition, we continue to explore a particular facet of succeeding in one's training and professional development. The format still includes inspirational quotes, engaging personal accounts of students' experiences, practical hints, hands-on suggestions, structured experiential learning activities, recommended resources, and relevant references. The tone of the book remains conversational, and we invite students to be actively involved as they read it.

However, for this edition, we also have significantly updated our material in every chapter because there has been a virtual explosion of exciting new research relevant to the education of counselors and therapists. Moreover, we added many more Internet resources that offer useful information and helpful assistance to graduate students in the helping professions. We also have given greater emphasis to the multicultural challenges and opportunities that counselors and therapists face in an increasingly diverse society.

In addition to these improvements throughout this edition, we have added two new chapters. Chapter 8 highlights the recent advances in the neuroscience of counseling and therapy. For decades, critics have pejoratively referred to counseling and therapy as warm-fuzzy, touchy-feely interventions that unlike psychopharmacology and other biological treatments lacked any scientific support for having any real impact on brain functioning. However, in recent years, neuroscience research has been uncovering clues that are solving some of the mysteries of the brain and discovering some of the mechanisms that make us tick. A fundamental understanding of neuroscience is now crucial for students of counseling and therapy, so this chapter is designed to be a brief introduction, or perhaps a refresher, on how we humans are wired.

Chapter 9 provides an introduction to the principles and basic techniques of crisis intervention, trauma counseling, and disaster response. In recent years, counselors and therapists have become increasingly active in serving vital roles as crisis interveners, providers of psychiatric emergency services, and members of disaster response teams. Accrediting bodies also have been requiring training programs to prepare students to perform these important functions. As a result, the greatest challenges students face in their training may involve dealing with these high-stakes situations. Nevertheless, in keeping with the overall theme of *Thriving!*, we highlight the resilience of the human spirit and the potential for posttraumatic growth, even under the direst of circumstances.

Like renovating a house, producing this edition has been a labor of love that involved the collaborative efforts of many talented individuals. We greatly appreciate the insightful comments of reviewers who provided helpful suggestions for enhancing our manuscript. The final version is much better as a result of their feedback. They include Chuck Reid at The University of Texas-Pan American, DeAnna Henderson at Alabama State University, Keith Klostermann at Medaille College, Kristi A. Gibbs at University of Tennessee at Chattanooga, Nina C. Martin at Vanderbilt University, and Ronica Arnold Branson at Jackson State University.

Finally, we wish to thank the countless students and colleagues who have enriched our personal and professional lives. In particular, we have been deeply touched by their countless gestures of support and encouragement throughout the process of creating this book. Our new edition reflects the excitement of embarking on a journey with fellow travelers who share the dream of thriving as students and professionals. Welcome aboard!

To our students, both current and past, who have taught us so much about thriving.

1

The Thriving Principles

The question is not how to survive, but how to thrive, with passion, compassion, humor, and style.

—Maya Angelou

Whether you have watched it or not, you have certainly heard of the immensely popular reality TV series *Survivor*. As you know, the show would involve dropping a group of castaways on a primitive island somewhere in the South Pacific or in a desolate spot in the Australian outback. Week after week, the contestants would have to suffer through ordeals—such as eating rats—that were hatched up by the program's producers. The castaways would hold tribal councils, scheme to form temporary alliances, vote contestants off the program, and compete with one another until only one lone survivor was left standing at the conclusion of the series.

No matter what kind of helping professional you aspire to become—counselor, psychologist, clinical social worker, therapist, or counselor educator—you first must complete an intensive and rigorous training program. We can guarantee you that whatever program you enter, you will sometimes feel as if you are a contestant on *Survivor*. Of course, instead of tribal councils, you will have committee meetings. Instead of foraging for berries, you will be subsisting on ramen noodles. And instead of enduring physical challenges, you will have tests, papers, and comprehensive examinations. In spite of these superficial differences, you will face ordeals and obstacles in your training that can be just as intimidating and challenging as anything on a reality TV show.

At times, you may feel so overwhelmed by the demands and so plagued with self-doubts that you wonder whether you will ever make it through the program. Quoting Winston Churchill, one former graduate student described those times as "full of blood, sweat, and tears." Whereas other trainees may seem to have the knack for picking up the skills almost effortlessly, you may feel that you have to struggle to master even the basics. As you face your first research methods test or your first client, you may wonder if you are even going to survive.

We also guarantee that as you progress through your training, you will regularly hear a certain phrase. Someone will say to you, with a heavy dose of irony, "Just think of this as a 'learning experience' for you." By themselves, these words typically suggest an opportunity for enrichment. However, the person's tone of voice, deep sigh, and shaking head strongly suggest that a frustrating, disappointing, and demanding time is in store for you. After a few of these difficult experiences, you may begin to suspect that there is a "no pain, no gain" philosophy of training in the helping professions. We believe, however, that the most productive "learning experiences" you encounter can actually be tremendously satisfying, fulfilling, and joyful.

In this chapter, we describe the principles that can help you do much more than just *survive* your training experiences. Following these principles can help you *thrive*—to succeed, flourish, and even enjoy your training with, as Maya Angelou said, "passion, compassion, humor, and style."

How Shall We Begin?

Jean's Story

I can remember vividly the first time I opened that door and stepped into the department as one of its newest and freshest counseling and psychotherapy trainees. I was so excited! Finally, after years of effort, I had fulfilled my long-standing dream of being accepted into a graduate program with a fine reputation. It was exactly what I wanted, and I couldn't have been happier. Of course, before applying, I had obsessively read all the information I could find about the program. It was credentialed, well known for its innovative methods, and respected for its commitment to professionalism. I had traveled to the campus, met with one of the professors, and even talked to several students. After all this research and preparation, I thought I had a pretty good idea of what I was getting into. Boy, was I wrong.

I had my rude awakening at my first class. Days before the semester began, I had bought all my textbooks and had even read several chapters ahead in each of them, diligently highlighting nearly every sentence I read. Back then, I had the delusion that learning took place only by a strange form of osmosis. Somehow, the knowledge contained in the sentence had to travel through the highlighter, up my arm, and finally into my brain. Of course, with this method, I was only turning my black-and-white textbooks into black-yellow-and-white textbooks. Somehow, though, the process seemed comforting to me in its familiarity. That's the way I had studied all through college, so I assumed that I would continue learning in the same tried-and-true way—by hunting for the absolute truth in a book and pouncing on it with my highlighter.

I came to that first class feeling eager, as well as a bit smug that I had already captured some truth in yellow. I was ready with my sharpened pencils, brand-new spiral-bound notebooks, and an academic year calendar in pristine condition. I found a desk in front, struck a pose of thoughtful attentiveness, and waited for the professor to enter the room and begin revealing the hidden truth that would make everything meaningful. My plan was to neatly write those messages down in my notebook and later high-light them all in that yellow shade of truth—just to be sure.

That's when it happened, when all my expectations were destroyed. My professor came in, asked us to form our desks into a circle, and sat down with us. That's the thing—she just sat there, smiling and looking at each of us with kind, but penetrating, eyes. What was her problem? Why didn't she begin lecturing?

Finally, one of the other students timidly raised her hand and asked, "Are you the professor?"

"Yes," she replied.

After a pause, the student reluctantly continued, "Well, isn't it time for us to start?"

"Yes, you're right," she answered. "How shall we begin?"

I was sitting there wondering, "What the hell is going on here? Is this woman playing some sadistic joke on us?"

Another student suggested, "Maybe we could introduce ourselves?"

"Sounds good!" the professor said. "Who would like to begin?"

It suddenly dawned on me that I was in new, uncharted territory here. I felt like Dorothy landing in Oz and telling Toto the obvious, "I don't think we're in Kansas anymore." I was disoriented but curious, anxious but intrigued, and a little dazed but ready to begin.

Use It—Don't Lose It!

> The essential of everything you do . . . must be choice, love, passion.
>
> —Nadia Boulanger

If you are already a trainee, your first experience may not have been as memorable for you as it was for the student who wrote this account, but you probably had some similar feelings. You are likely to find that training to become a counselor or therapist is dramatically different from your undergraduate education.

If you are at all familiar with the Harry Potter books and films, you know that Harry, Hermione, and Ron were constantly confronted with precarious and challenging situations in their adventures. However, no matter what the circumstance, they knew that they could rely on *The Standard Book of Spells* for the precise incantation they needed to successfully perform their magic. Our book offers neither spells nor magic wands. As mere muggles—people without magical powers—we can only provide you with useful tools to help you with your own adventures.

As you begin your training, you may sometimes think that you are embarking on a long and arduous journey with seemingly no end in sight. Although you will enjoy many aspects of your training, at times you will feel overwhelmed and disoriented. That is why we have conceived this book as a survival guide for you. Because you can feel lonely when you are lost and confused, this book is also like having a support group at hand. As you read it, you may find yourself recognizing the reactions of other students as similar to yours. At times, you may want to set aside this book to take some time to explore your own experiences. When you read the stories of other students, you may learn from their mistakes and feel encouraged by their successes. Finally, you can take advantage of the advice and tips from these fellow students as you forge your own training journey.

The earlier in your career training you read this book, the better. And be sure to keep it handy even after you have finished it. You may want to refer to it regularly throughout your training. When a training problem—or opportunity!—catches you off guard, you can refresh your memory and review strategies. In other words, use it—don't lose it. The book provides you with practical information and helpful hints on gaining the most from the experiences your training program has to offer.

Thriving

Life is either a daring adventure or nothing. To keep our faces toward change and behave like free spirits in the presence of fate is strength undefeatable.

—Helen Keller

As you enter your training program, you may have just completed your undergraduate education or you may be embarking on your second career path. You may be coming from an urban neighborhood in Los Angeles, a suburban community near Chicago, or a rural area in the Appalachian Mountains. Perhaps you are African American, White, Latino/a, Asian American, Native American, or an international student. However, no matter what your background or circumstances may be, you are joining with others who have one dream in common—to become a helping professional. As you make this training journey, which we describe in Chapter 2, you can thrive if you use the following simple principles.

Pack Wisely

What do you pack when you pursue a dream? And what do you leave behind?

—Sandra Sharp

The first principle of thriving involves meeting your basic needs and bringing along the resources you will require in your training. On any long journey, you will want to stock provisions, pack the right gear, prepare for emergencies, and travel light.

One resource you bring to your training is time. Unlike money, you cannot bank or buy time. You must learn to choose wisely how to spend the time you have available. One of the challenges you will face throughout your journey will be to balance the opportunities of your training program with other important aspects of your life (Brown, 2012).

Caring for your basic needs enables you to focus your energies on the personal and professional growth you can achieve in your training. In Chapter 3, we present useful information and guidelines for obtaining educational loans, applying for assistantships and scholarships, finding safe and affordable housing, taking care of your nutritional needs, and maintaining an active and healthy lifestyle.

Because you will be preparing to practice the craft of counseling and therapy, you will need to bring along some tools of the trade. Of course, a personal computer, notebooks, pens and pencils, a dictionary, the *Publication Manual of the American Psychological Association,* and other reference books are some of the essentials. While you are deciding what to take, keep in mind that how you use this gear is far more important than the equipment itself. For example, like some people in the helping professions, you may have technophobia, treating all electronic devices as predators ready to subdue and enslave humanity, which was the premise of *The Matrix* series of science fiction movies. As a result, you may not be taking full advantage of the computer in writing reports, doing presentations, conducting research, exploring resources, and communicating with others. On the other hand, you may be more of a technophile, such as Theodore Twombly, who fell in love with Samantha, a new, advanced operating system in Spike Lee's film *Her.* You may find yourself salivating over any new electronic device with all the latest "bells and whistles." In that case, keep in mind that these tools are only as good as your skill in using them. And don't forget that these devices are merely tools and not substitutes for actual life experiences. As a therapist in training, you want to include plenty of opportunities for having authentic, face-to-face encounters with real people and for relishing the natural world, which is, after all, our first play station. Watch out for becoming seduced by virtual worlds that rob you of the richness of immersing yourself into the real world.

Of course, a computer and reference books are examples of the obvious tools that you will be using. However, there are other resources you will want to bring to your training endeavors. These include your academic, time management, and stress management skills. Basic academic skills, such as reading and writing, do much more than just help you earn good grades. In fact, they are an indispensable part of being an effective professional helper. Reading allows you to broaden and enrich your own experiences by tapping into the minds of healers and thinkers throughout time and from around the world. Writing is a process in which you can give voice to your experiences, make your thoughts visible, and clarify your vague hunches by putting them into words. Keeping your curiosity alive, thinking critically about your assumptions, and thoughtfully examining current issues help you maintain your professional vitality throughout your career. In Chapter 4, we offer tips on improving your reading, writing, research, and presentation skills.

It is impossible to eliminate all the stressors you face in your training program. These challenges are a lot like Arnold Schwarzenegger's character in *The Terminator*—even when you successfully cope with one, you can almost hear it warning, "I'll . . . be . . . back." In fact, you will continue to deal with stressors throughout your professional career. Therefore, it is vital that you include stress management skills among the resources you pack for this journey (Kelly, 2005). In Chapter 5, you will explore specific tips for managing your time and using mindfulness and other practical techniques to handle the stressors that you will inevitably confront in your graduate and professional life.

Finally, do your best to travel light. If you are bringing a great deal of emotional baggage to your training, then it is hard to stay focused on the needs of your clients. One of the best ways to deal with your personal issues and to cope with the stresses of graduate school is becoming involved in your own counseling or therapy (Prosek, Holm, & Daly, 2013). Many training programs strongly recommend that their trainees engage in counseling, and they have developed resources to provide this service at little or no cost (Dearing, Maddux, & Tangney, 2005). It makes perfect sense for you to take advantage of this opportunity, even if it is not required. Being a client certainly is a powerful way to appreciate the risks, vulnerabilities, and pain that they face. More important, however, this level of involvement helps you learn to truly trust the process of counseling and therapy. Once you have been a client, you have no longer only read about or observed its benefits; you have encountered them personally. Besides, you will be encouraging others to engage in counseling and therapy; shouldn't you practice what you preach?

Make the Journey Your Destination

> To travel hopefully is a better thing than to arrive.
>
> —Robert Louis Stevenson

With many trips, getting there is half the fun, but when it comes to your personal and professional journey, the trip is *all* there is. You began this journey to become a counselor or therapist long before you entered a training program, and you will continue your journey long after you leave. The second principle of thriving involves the important point that just as life is not a rehearsal, neither is your training. From day one, your training is the real thing, not merely a rite of passage you have to endure to do counseling or therapy after graduation. You actually have chances to practice therapeutic principles in every facet of your training. Consider your helping skills to be like muscles that are strengthened by regular use.

In the 19th century, Horace Greeley extolled a "manifest destiny" in the United States by urging, "Go west." Joseph Campbell (1986), on the other hand, recommended, "Follow your bliss." In other words, your destiny is not found in a particular geographic territory. Instead, it lies in the joy you experience as you fulfill your potential, express your talents, follow your calling, and pursue your dreams *now*.

One of the biggest mistakes you can make on this journey is to view yourself as a customer and your program as merely a service station along the roadside. When you are truly learning, you are neither a passive recipient of training services nor only a consumer of educational goods. Instead, you are a dynamic, full, and equal participant in the learning endeavor (Corey & Corey, 2011).

Your teachers and supervisors will be expecting you to collaborate actively with them by always "bringing something to the table." In virtually every class and training experience, you will have an opportunity to practice the craft of counseling—the processes of encountering others, observing interpersonal dynamics, gathering information, conceptualizing, and taking action. You may participate in a structured exercise, respond to a video-recorded segment, act out a role play, or engage in some group task that demonstrates a principle you are studying. Actively participating in your readings means more than merely underlining or highlighting words. It means involving yourself by jotting down ideas and reactions in the margins, organizing the material into important concepts, critically evaluating the arguments, and talking about the readings before coming to class. It is only when you invest your whole self in these endeavors that you make the most of these learning opportunities. Many of your classes will be small and will have the format of a seminar, which literally means "seed plot." Do your part to tend these gardens so that the seeds will grow and be fruitful.

The depth and breadth of your program's curriculum reflect the high standards that trainers have set for you. Certainly, they expect that you will fulfill all the course requirements, but they also want you to extend yourself, to challenge yourself by pursuing knowledge and skills beyond the minimal course requirements. Coming to each class ready and willing to engage fully in the active, exciting process of learning is a great strategy for success, not only in school but also in your career.

Of course, you will also want to take full advantage of all the many enriching experiences that take place outside the classroom. During virtually any week of the academic year, you are likely to find an exciting array of talented artists, authors, scholars, and performers coming to your campus. Art exhibits, theater performances, poetry readings, invited lectures, musical performances, and films are just a few of the cultural opportunities you will have available—many of which are free to students. Reading has always been a solitary pursuit and so often carries the connotation of introversion or social awkwardness. However, recent findings in *Science* prove quite the opposite—namely, that the more good literature you read, the more empathetic and socially aware you become. Researchers Kidd and Castano (2013) found that reading literary fiction—narratives that explore the complex thoughts and emotions of multifaceted characters—actually enhanced the empathic abilities of participants. In contrast, randomly assigned participants who read selections from popular fiction with superficial, two-dimensional characters demonstrated no change in their empathy. So don't assume that only textbooks contribute to your therapeutic skills. Literary fiction, along with challenging films and plays with fully realized, complex characters, also offer multilayered, intricate case studies that can provide you with insights into the mysteries of the human mind and the dynamic undercurrents of intimate relationships.

In addition to enhancing their graduate education with meaningful experiences outside the classroom, truly successful counselors and therapists do not limit their professional development to those years in which they are immersed in their academic careers (Gayle, 2003). Whether you are a raw trainee or a seasoned professional, you need to recognize that you have two simple options: Either you can continue to grow personally and professionally by challenging yourself, or you can stagnate. Completing your training program with a curiosity about what makes people tick and a zest for discovery will guarantee that your learning will not end when you earn a diploma.

Curiosity is an intellectual attitude that celebrates taking the stance of not knowing, which is an essential quality of any successful therapist. You may find it particularly challenging to embrace not knowing. After all, aren't you attending graduate school, studying diligently, and earning your degree in order to become an *expert*? Setting aside that professional mask, stepping down from that expert pedestal to encounter your clients, to learn from them, and to bear witness to their journey of healing are daunting tasks. However, once you take these risks, you can become engaged in the lifelong endeavor of *becoming* truly therapeutic—not merely *performing* therapeutic techniques. As a result, you will see graduation as another step in the lifelong pursuit of professional mastery. One of the reasons that the counseling and therapy professions are so exciting is that the field is still in its infancy and is wide open for new breakthroughs. You can look forward to a long career of refining your skills, revising your thinking, and stretching the envelope.

Of course, you are familiar with Einstein's formula, $E = mc^2$. However, his friends recalled at his death that Einstein also had developed a formula, as simple and profound as its famous counterpart, for personal success in life: Personal Success = Work + Play + Not Bragging About Your Success (Calaprice, 2010). Einstein's formula sounds like good advice for almost anyone, especially if you are in training to help *others* achieve their personal success. Just remember: Your tires should always be inflated but your ego should not.

The Journey

A Parable

Kione was disappointed. The people were having a grand feast to honor the Great Chief, and entire clans were planning to attend. But Kione's village was located on the opposite end of the island. There was room in the village's lone outrigger canoe only for several local officials, four paddlers, and gifts. He begged his parents to allow him to go—after all, wasn't he named after the Great Chief himself? His father told him that there was not enough room.

"Besides," Kione's mother smiled when she asked him, "What present could you give the Great Chief?"

But Kione was determined to be a part of such a great occasion. He awoke just before dawn and, while the others were still sleeping, began the long trek to the Chief's village. He carried only some dried mullet and fruit wrapped tightly in a large cassava leaf, his bamboo knife, and a pouch containing his favorite seashell.

When the sun god was directly over his head, the boy stopped to eat beside a cool stream. As he was eating, an old man sat down beside him. Politely, Kione offered to share his meager fare with the stranger, who carefully consumed his portion. Thanking the boy, the old man said, "I want to offer you something in return, but all I have is my wisdom. People can be like a pack of monkeys—chattering, mimicking one another, and fighting for a better place in their pack. Or they can be like a pride of lions—sharing food, caring for one another, and protecting both the old and the young. You have been a lion with me. Can you be a lion surrounded by monkeys?" Kione did not know what the old man meant, but he politely thanked him for the advice and continued on his way.

In the early evening, Kione reached the village, full of music and revelers. He quietly joined the line of people waiting before the *bai* (council house) to offer their gifts. When his turn came, Kione bowed and solemnly handed his only treasure to the Chief, who showed it to everyone within sight and exclaimed rather loudly that this boy had brought a seashell to honor him! The crowd laughed uproariously, and Kione felt his face grow hot with shame. The laughter quickly subsided, however, as three distinguished-looking older women, moving quietly, gracefully, and majestically, gathered beside the Chief. They spoke quietly but intently to him while the festivities halted. Even the children and animals became quiet, for these women were very powerful—they decided who was to be chief and when it was time for a chief to be replaced. The women beckoned Kione to them and began asking him gentle questions about his village and his trip. After a few minutes, the trio went back to the Chief, spoke briefly, and moved back into the small group of elder women at the bai.

The Great Chief beckoned Kione to come and sit beside him. Then he announced in a humble voice, "This boy is a hero. He was willing to give us his only possession, but his long, hard journey here made his present the most magnificent gift of all."

The story has been told and retold throughout the years, and the message is always the same at the end. The gift *is* the journey.

Have Traveling Companions

> When we can share—that is the poetry in the prose of life.
>
> —Sigmund Freud

Every culture has its folk tales and myths that portray a heroic figure on a quest. No matter how talented and strong this protagonist may be, the person neither travels nor triumphs alone. Before the journey, the heroic figure may recruit traveling companions or, along the way, may encounter strangers who become comrades. In ancient Greece, Jason had the Argonauts. In *The Wizard of Oz*, Dorothy had the Cowardly Lion, Tin Man, and Scarecrow. Luke Skywalker of *Star Wars* had Obi-Wan Kenobi, Princess Leia, and Han Solo. And Frodo Baggins had Aragorn and Gandalf in *The Lord of the Rings*. As the journey progresses, these companions serve vital roles by giving guidance to the traveler, using special powers to help overcome obstacles, or offering useful gifts to provide physical and emotional sustenance.

Like the protagonists in those archetypal stories, you also will encounter others—peers, mentors, instructors, supervisors, and clients—who will have a profound impact on your training journey. The third principle of thriving in your program is being open to the resources that others offer you. This openness is essential because you cannot be trained as successfully, as completely, or even as joyfully on your own. Of course, you need to engage in the solitary work of reading, writing, reflecting, and studying if you expect to be successful in any training program. But to become an effective counselor or therapist, you also need to come together with others to engage in the collaborative work of observing, discussing, practicing, giving and receiving feedback, challenging, and encouraging one another.

Our society is one that emphasizes individual achievement and competition. In fact, most of your previous educational experiences probably reinforced a "do-it-yourself" approach to learning. Homework involved assignments that you completed on your own. Group activities, from elementary school spelling bees to high school debates, emphasized competition. Even your class ranking system translated into scholarship offers for those at the top and rejection letters for those at the bottom. In the education game, when there are winners, there have to be losers.

Because you were probably a successful student, it may be a challenge for you to participate in a program designed to train *helping* professionals—counselors and therapists who work effectively with others. Now your learning experiences will emphasize relating, listening, communicating, and collaborating. It may be hard for you to admit it, but it is absolutely true that you are not an island unto yourself in this kind of training—you cannot learn it all on your own.

As a matter of fact, such a collaborative approach to learning is closer to the roots of a true college experience. The word *college* comes from the same Latin word as *colleague—collega,* which means "one chosen to work with another." In other words, you need professors, supervisors, fellow learners, and clients to inform, inspire, prod, and even provoke you to refine your thinking, develop your skills, and make discoveries about yourself and others. For example, you will be receiving feedback from others on a regular basis. In every instance, you have the chance to be open to their observations, reactions, and suggestions. Just remind yourself that your mind is like a parachute—it works best when it is open.

Based on this principle of having traveling companions on your training journey, you have two daunting, but crucial, tasks. First, with each of your instructors, supervisors, fellow trainees, and clients, you need to develop a working relationship that is based on honesty, understanding, and acceptance (Burns, 2012). It is essential that you get to know, trust, and respect others if you are going to work well with them. Your second, but equally important, task is to do your part to contribute to developing your program into a true learning community. Instead of competing with one another for individual accolades, members of a learning community make a commitment to share information, insights, and ideas. They respect—and even value—different points of view. And they support one another in the formidable enterprise of becoming helping professionals. This way, *everybody* wins.

Because you learn by example, the heart of a training program is not the curriculum but its people. Actions do speak louder than words, so it is vital that you seek out professors and supervisors who exemplify the knowledge and skills you want to learn. You want to be with those whom you respect and admire, because the most important lessons in this line of work are not taught, but caught. Like chicken pox at a day care center, openness to feedback, commitment to helping, and curiosity about the human heart can be highly contagious. So take a close look at the people in a training program. What do you want to catch from them? Is it obvious that they are enthusiastic about training new professionals? Are they dedicated to the art of counseling and therapy? Do they have a sense of awe about the mysteries of the mind? Instead of looking for professors who merely spoon-feed simplistic answers, seek out those who truly educate by demonstrating their professionalism and who challenge you to do likewise. The counseling and therapy profession, like a fidgety kid, is never still—it is a living, breathing, kicking, and constantly evolving entity. Look for mentors and trainers who personify the kind of professional you want to become (Johnson & Huwe, 2002).

Of course, you can also serve as an example to others. You can demonstrate the fundamental helping attitudes of genuineness, compassion, and openness. You can practice the skills that you are developing. In class discussions, you can share your own discoveries and observations. Whatever the situation, you bring a wealth of experience and ideas to this training, and your colleagues will appreciate your generosity in sharing it. Keep in mind that your training program has changed in one important way since you applied to it—you are now a member of it! A vibrant, thriving training program, like the entire profession, is continually changing and growing as members like you contribute to its vitality. The African Mbuti have a ritualized song that is a wonderful example of what every learning community should aspire to achieve. In the song, individual singers are responsible for specific notes, but no one carries the entire melody. As a result, only the whole community can sing the song (Turnbull, 1990). You can follow the spirit of this song by adding your voice to your learning community. Practice making a difference by volunteering for committees, offering suggestions, and making your program a better one by the time you leave it.

As a member of this learning community, one of the essential tasks you need to perform unfailingly is to communicate with the other members. Of course, effective communication is important to any organization, but it is particularly essential to one that is dedicated to training counselors and therapists. Virtually every day, you will have opportunities to engage in all sorts of stimulating, intriguing, encouraging, and challenging interactions with your teachers, supervisors, and colleagues. In Chapter 6, we offer suggestions for ways you can connect with others in your program, broaden your experiences with diverse populations, and network with your future professional colleagues. We also explore how the personal changes you make will have an impact on your relationships with significant others, friends, and relatives.

Worst Parents of the Year Award

Jen's Story

You would have thought by the look on their faces that I had just handed them the award for "Worst Parents of the Year." They sat confused, hurt, and angry. On my left, my father was perched on his chair, waiting for me to give him a better explanation for all of this. To my right was my mother, fighting back tears as she struggled to understand what I had just told them. I was in the middle, feeling like this conversation I was having in my living room was just about the worst mistake I had ever made.

My intentions had been so noble, so heartfelt. I wanted to share with my parents my desire for a closer relationship with them. I wanted our conversations to reach beyond everyday chitchat and into depths of who we were. I wanted to know my parents as people, and I wanted the same from them in return. And why not? After the first three months in my counseling program, I was having conversations like this on a daily basis. My whole world was about sharing, listening, reflecting, and accepting the ideas of others. As classmates, we laughed together, cried together, and poured our souls out to one another. I thought for sure I could take home all the treasures I had learned and initiate the same experiences with my parents.

Unfortunately, as they say about baseball pitchers, my windup was great, but my delivery stunk. In my naïveté, I had assumed that because I had been living in a counselor's world, everyone else had been doing the same. I had forgotten that most people aren't having intimate discussions about the meaning of life on a daily basis. Therefore, when I brought my request to my parents, I chose words that had worked so well with my peers and professors. As you might think, their reactions were not what I had expected. They couldn't understand how, after all the love and support they had given me, I could ask for something more. How could I suggest that we were not close enough or that we didn't talk enough about the right things? The more I tried to explain, the unhappier they got. By the end of the conversation, I truly felt like I was speaking a different language. Needless to say, what started out as the perfect plan ended up as a complete failure. Or was it?

After I returned to school, strange things started happening. I began to get calls from my mom for no particular reason. My dad stopped asking me if I had gotten my oil changed and started inquiring what I wanted to do after graduation. E-mails began to appear from them, filling me in on how they were feeling about different things. I even went home out of the blue to spend the weekend with them.

What started out as a disaster turned into something amazing. I learned that we are all on a journey to find closeness with our loved ones, but not all of us go about it at the same pace. Those who are in training on a regular basis must resist the urge to carry those who prefer to walk. In this way, we will all feel comfortable when we reach the finish line.

Keep Your Bearings

> Our life's journey of self-discovery is not a straight line.
>
> —Stuart Wilde

The fourth principle of thriving is based on the fact that although you need company on your training journey, you also need time alone to check your bearings, process your experiences, and reflect on the discoveries you are making. As Paul Tournier (1957) explained, "The real meaning of travel . . . is the discovery of oneself" (p. 57). No matter what classes you take, the subject you are likely to learn most about is yourself. As a result, your training experiences will be like your fingerprints—uniquely your own.

You probably have access to information about your program's policies and procedures in your school catalog, program website, and student handbook. However, because embarking on any important journey is neither a certain nor an easy venture, you need to rely on more than this information to gain your bearings. As with any trip, you need to remember where you have been, determine where you are now, and envision where you are heading. In other words, you need to explore yourself in order to find the internal compass that can offer you a sense of direction, to develop a training time line and map, and to assess your progress regularly.

Keeping a journal is one excellent way to recollect important events, explore ideas, sort out reactions, and work through personal issues. Your journal then becomes a reservoir of discoveries, the place in which you face and answer your own questions by having an ongoing written conversation with yourself. You can use your journal to reflect on and tie together all your learning experiences: readings you encounter, relationships you establish, observations you make, and skills you practice.

At the very least, it is vital that you set aside personal time for yourself—to meditate, ponder, speculate, pray, relax, or simply *be*. Throughout your training, from your admissions interview to the commencement ceremony, you will have countless opportunities for personal growth and greater self-awareness. It is up to you to take full advantage of these opportunities and to make meaning of these experiences. You will find that the most important discoveries you make in your training—the greatest learning experiences you have—take place when you are truly open to looking at yourself.

Training programs repeatedly invite you to explore yourself, because in no other profession is the adage "know thyself" more important or more central. The many video recordings you will watch, the extensive feedback you will hear, and the countless occasions for introspection you will have can help you tremendously in knowing your most important tool as a counselor—yourself. However, the process is neither easy nor pain free. For example, you may begin a course on multiculturalism feeling pretty self-satisfied, confident that you do not have a racist or sexist bone in your entire body, only to discover quickly that you need to confront your own ethnocentrism and racism (Johnson & Lambie, 2013).

In life, it is sometimes tempting to stay right where you are, remaining in familiar territory, avoiding the troubling questions, and not breaking out of your routine. But just remember: If you have both feet firmly planted on solid ground, then you are not moving. You advance only when you lean forward enough to become momentarily imbalanced ... and then take a step. Simply put, progress involves constantly knocking yourself off balance and regaining it in a new position. Nobody can become a counselor or therapist without a spirit of adventure, without the willingness to try something different, take a few risks, and make lots of mistakes along the way. You might as well abandon any perfectionistic tendencies you may have, because they will do you no good in this field. There is an Inuit saying that expresses this spirit of adventure: "Only the air-spirits know what lies beyond the hills, yet I urge my team farther on" (Kent, 1996, p. 264).

As you engage in this process, remember to focus on your strengths, too. It is easy to ruminate on your mistakes, limitations, and blunders. If that is your inclination, then you are bound to be restless, troubled, and have many a sleepless night. Of course, all trainees occasionally feel demoralized. At these times, it may be helpful to remind yourself that you were selected for training because of your strengths, talents, and potential—and that you also chose to accept this challenge. So give yourself credit for having the chutzpah to think that you have what it takes to enter this tough and demanding profession.

You'll Go Far in Life

Andrea's Story

Like most graduate students, I've had my share of moments of self-doubt. There were times when I wondered how I ever got to graduate school in the first place. I sometimes believed that my acceptance to graduate school was a fluke and that I got in by the skin of my teeth. It was during one of these low points that I had what I consider a moment of clarity.

I was in one of my first graduate courses, and the professor was explaining to my class that his course was not part of the admissions process. I remember thinking, "Admissions process? What the heck is he talking about? What would this course have to do with the admissions process anyway?" Sensing our confusion, he went on to explain himself. He told us that his class was not designed to "weed out" any of us. He said that being accepted into graduate school was a difficult undertaking, but it was a task that we had already accomplished. He told us that he firmly believed that each and every one of us deserved to be there. He explained that he would expect a lot out of us because he believed that we were all quite capable. He concluded by telling us that as long as we were willing to work hard, he would do whatever he could to help us in our graduate careers. I left class that day feeling as though my professor had a personal investment in each and every one of us. I also knew that not living up to his expectations would result in my feeling as though I had personally let him down.

Reflecting on that particular class experience helped me to understand graduate school overall. I began to realize that it isn't about proving myself over and over again. I finally understood that everyone assumed that I deserved to be here. Furthermore, I realized that my professors were all willing to do whatever they could to help me succeed. And as I began to look around, I became aware of the feeling that they all had a personal investment in me.

(Continued)

(Continued)

On the last day of that particular class, my professor told me how much he had enjoyed having me in his class. I thanked him and told him that I had thoroughly enjoyed it. He went on to say that he knew that I would go far in life. Not being one to accept a compliment easily, I brushed his comment aside with a little bit of humor. Days later, though, I could not get his words out of my head. What did I ever do to deserve such a compliment?

This man, one of the most brilliant people I have ever met, believes that I am going to go far in life? Those words still echo in my mind at times, and I know that I will spend the rest of my life trying to do just that.

Of course, you are going to encounter roadblocks along the way in your training journey, but how you view them can turn these stumbling blocks into stepping-stones. It was during a particularly tough time that one student, Christine, found it helpful to give herself this motivational nudge: "If I look at challenges as only obstacles, then I'll have trouble handling them, but if I look at them as opportunities, I'll be enriched."

Another way to cope with this turmoil is to appreciate the humor in your situation, particularly if the joke is *yourself*—your own hang-ups, idiosyncrasies, limitations, and foibles. For example, during one class, when students were discussing their consultation projects, one participant, John, instead of presenting a successful experience, decided to talk about a session in which he "blew it." During a meeting with his consultees, John shared how he found himself making one mistake after another. His description of his frantic but futile attempts to salvage his image made the discussion a memorable learning experience. It was not only a hilarious story, but John's willingness to share his predicament was liberating for everyone in the class. They realized that they did not have to be perfect in their work and that they could safely talk about their mistakes with one another.

An important part of keeping your bearings is knowing where you are heading. Just remember that one of the simplest ways for you to achieve a goal is to envision it vividly. You will find that your vision of yourself as an emerging professional will help you to start acting as if you already have achieved that goal. All thriving counselors and therapists share certain fundamental qualities (Conyn & Bemak, 2005). First, they are committed to providing competent, caring, and ethical services. Second, they are professionals who engage in a lifelong process of learning and refining these helping skills.

Finally, they are actively involved in advancing the profession through research, innovation, training, or service. What particular kind of counselor or therapist do you want to become? To answer that question, you first must explore who you are *now*. In Chapter 7, we invite you to examine your belief system, your values, your paradigms, and your attitudes toward others who may differ significantly from you. We then follow with Chapter 8, which explores the inner universes of others and yourself from the perspective of the neurosciences. Recent findings are providing exciting documentation that counseling and therapy promote neuroplasticity and actually change brain functioning. You will come to appreciate how the empathic attunement of a therapeutic alliance provides the optimal chemical environment for creating new neural pathways—in both your client and yourself.

EXERCISE 1.1 Whatcha Gonna Be?

A Magic Mirror Exercise

The purpose of this guided imagery activity is for you to relax, reflect, and envision your future. Find a comfortable spot by yourself, away from distractions, and let yourself become mindful of the here and now. You may find yourself relaxing by lying down, closing your eyes, letting your muscles unwind, breathing more deeply and evenly, and allowing your mind to drift along. Once you are in a nice, peaceful state, imagine that you are about to step in front of a nearby magic mirror. Like any ordinary mirror, this one shows your reflection, but this magic mirror reflects how you will look and what you will do in the future. Now, go ahead and gaze into this magic mirror to see how you will appear when you have become a professional helper. Look carefully at your face. What does that expression communicate about the person you will become? Notice what you are doing. What skills are you demonstrating? What services are you providing? Pay attention to where you are in the future. Where are you working? Notice the other people around you. Who are your clients? Who are your colleagues? After you have completed this activity, use your journal to describe your vision of the future.

Let the Trip Take You

If you surrender to the wind, you can ride it.

—Toni Morrison

As you move along on your training journey, you will also discover that in spite of all your careful planning, you will find yourself being pulled in surprising directions. In *Travels with Charley,* John Steinbeck (1962) wrote, "We do not take a trip; a trip takes us" (p. 6). Your progress will build its own momentum, and you will find yourself taking the unexpected turn and discovering new territories. In your driver's education class, you probably learned not to slam on the brakes when you begin to skid on a slippery surface. Instead, as counterintuitive as it seemed, your best course of action is to steer in the direction of the skid. The same principle applies to your training. Let yourself be carried along by the flow of your discoveries and be open to the possibilities of your own transformation.

Learning is one of the most challenging, as well as most fulfilling, of life's adventures. As you examine ideas that may threaten your preconceived notions, as you grope along through your periods of confusion, and as you read, reflect, synthesize, speculate, and brainstorm, you will forge a new personal and professional identity. As a successful graduate, you will not be the same person who originally entered the training program. Along the way, you will gain a sense of self-efficacy, confidence, and trust in your own resources as a counselor or therapist (Vernarec, 2010). Eventually, during your years of supervision, you will develop your own internal supervisor.

By the time you complete your program, you will be more seasoned and have a greater insight into, and a deeper appreciation for, the clutter, confusion, and complexity of people's lives. Through this learning, you will acquire essential knowledge and develop valuable skills (Schaefle, Smaby, Maddux, & Cates, 2005). Moreover, at a fundamental level, you will transform yourself from a student into a professional. In other words, just as participating in counseling and therapy changes clients, becoming a helping professional changes *you.*

An important part of your training journey is preparing yourself to be a valuable resource in troubled times—especially during crises, traumas, and disasters that confront individuals, families, groups, and communities. Counselors and therapists now are serving vital roles as emergency service providers, crisis interveners, and members of disaster response teams. However, students consistently report that their overwhelming concerns, strongest doubts, and deepest apprehensions are that they are unprepared, both personally and professionally, to deal effectively with people in serious crisis situations. So in Chapter 9 we offer helpful hints for managing your own emotional stress and give guidance on how you can develop these essential competencies.

Chapter 10 helps you identify important sources of knowledge and emotional support to help you venture out, take risks, and grow in your practicum, field placement, or internship. These experiences give you the opportunity to translate your theoretical knowledge into effective clinical work and to gain confidence in yourself as an emerging professional.

I'm Going In. Want to Join Me?

Lennie's Story

Long after receiving my diploma, my friends from graduate school are still helping me learn the most important lessons of life—and death. Regularly, we still gather together for informal reunions. Sharing a beach house or a resort hotel for a weekend, we retell old stories, catch up on one another's lives, play together, and take delight in these special relationships that have aged so well and endured so long.

A couple of years ago, one of my dear friends from school was especially determined to attend our gathering. Stan had been dealing with cancer and was undergoing treatment that included radiation and chemotherapy—the whole poisonous works. Hit hard by the side effects, Stan was hairless, fatigued, and tormented with aches and pains, but he joined us for that weekend. In spite of his life-threatening illness, Stan was still Stan, a counselor who never lost his idealism, a former Eagle Scout who thrived on nature, and a fun-loving guy who was ready for any adventure. On our outings together over the years, Stan had always been willing to run in challenging races, hike steep mountain trails, and bodysurf the highest waves.

My final excursion with Stan on that weekend began with a slow and laborious walk from the house to the nearby beach. He had been a tall and graceful runner, so it was heartbreaking for me to see Stan moving so stiffly, swinging his arms in awkward arcs as his body lurched along. When he finally reached the water's edge, he gazed across the ocean's heaving surface and breathed deeply of the pungent, salty air. At that very moment, Stan became transformed. He flashed that mischievous grin I had seen so many times before and declared, "I'm going in. Want to join me?"

Before I knew it, we were both swimming on that late fall afternoon. For nearly half an hour, we rode the gently cascading waves, floated on our backs to watch seagulls swoop overhead, and let the powerful ocean current carry us along on its inevitable course. Together, we savored the experience of being immersed in the deep, dark, mysterious, living sea.

(Continued)

(Continued)

Three decades earlier, Stan and I had been immersed in graduate school, which had its own mysterious undercurrents, rhythms, tides, and surges. Stan was in a different program, but when we became friends, we found that we brought to our training a similar mixture of rough edges and potential, doubts and dreams, hang-ups and hopes. We told our life stories to one another, gave each other feedback on our work, and threw ourselves into heartfelt discussions that lasted late into the night. Once we solved to our satisfaction all the world's problems, revamped all the tired old theories with intriguing new concepts, and articulated the true meaning of life, we rejoiced by partying together. You won't find "parties well" on any checklist assessing graduate student performance, but Stan taught me how essential it was not only to work hard with your colleagues, but also to celebrate with them.

In spite of his love for sharing stories, debating issues, and telling jokes, Stan was an expert B.S. detector. Time after time, when I would find myself becoming inauthentic, spouting some counseling jargon, or acting the least bit pretentious, Stan would grimace and, without hesitation or diplomacy, give me his blunt two-word assessment. Then, my whole phony house of cards would begin to collapse, no matter how elaborate my self-deceptions. Even when I protested and argued, I knew in my heart that he was right, and it was only a matter of time before I would be answering his challenge to be my true self. In my graduate training, I was fortunate to have supervisors and mentors who could sense my defenses and invite me to set them aside, but their style had tact, subtlety, and discretion. I was truly blessed to also have a friend who may have been crude every now and then, but who always spoke to me straight from the heart.

After graduation, our careers took us in different directions. I entered academia, where I now train counselors. Stan went on to work with deeply troubled adolescents who were court-ordered into counseling. Although many other counselors burned out quickly in this setting, Stan continued to thrive year after year, keeping his idealism, working with integrity, and becoming a master counselor. He was at the peak of his powers and in the prime of his life when a routine medical examination found disturbing evidence of malignant and aggressive tumors.

However, alongside me on that October afternoon in the Atlantic Ocean, Stan was swimming with grace, laughing once again with gusto, and relishing his chance to feel in harmony with nature. The cancer seemed to be pacified, tamed—at least for the moment. Far off, the still ocean surface had a mirror-like sheen that melded imperceptibly into the sky. There was no horizon, no separation between the sea below and the heavens above. The whole universe seemed balanced, harmonious, and unified. When Stan and I finally emerged from the water, I looked down and noticed a nearly translucent pebble that the churning waves had polished over the centuries. I picked it up and put it in my pocket as a memento of our swim together.

I still have that pebble. In fact, I always carry it in my pocket. When my counseling work is particularly challenging, I find myself noticing that pebble by my side. It reminds me of important lessons that Stan taught me: Dive in, trust the process, go with the flow, and always remember that just like in graduate school, you are never truly all on your own.

Always Take the High Road

On life's journey . . . virtuous deeds are a shelter, wisdom is the light by day, and right mindfulness is the protection by night.

—Buddha

The final principle for thriving in your training recognizes that the helping professions are based on more than expert knowledge, technical skills, and self-awareness. They are also based on values. In fact, you cannot become a competent therapist or counselor unless you are also an ethical one (Pope & Vasquez, 2011). As an emerging professional trainee, you will sharpen your moral compass by learning your professional code of ethics and following it in *all* situations.

When you become a helping professional, you will have to comply with myriad state and federal laws, follow your profession's ethical standards, and observe the policies of your agency or school. As an enrolled student, you are expected to behave legally, ethically, and honorably in all your course work. Whenever you are unsure about what conduct is allowed by the law, the ethical standards of your profession, or the honor code of your university, immediately consult your academic advisor or supervisor. A violation can be grounds for failing a course and being expelled from the program.

Finally, taking the high road also means challenging yourself to maintain high professional standards. For example, you need to watch out for the temptation to merely impersonate Hollywood's version of a counselor or therapist—using jargon, spouting simplistic slogans, and blindly following the latest therapeutic fads. At times, you may find yourself being attracted to the certainty and confidence that this posturing seems to offer.

Randy, for example, was a beginning graduate student who found himself enamored of his expanding vocabulary of terms culled from courses on counseling theories, interpersonal dynamics, and diagnoses. At parties, he would liberally sprinkle these phrases throughout his conversations. Finally, one of his friends took Randy aside, gently pointed out these affectations, and told him how she missed the "real," unpretentious person she once knew. When he brought up this issue in his own therapy, Randy began to recognize how he was harboring serious doubts that he would ever be able to master the complex skills involved in being a professional helper. He discovered that he found some consolation, however superficial and brief, in at least talking like an expert.

Looking back on how she began her training, Zelda realized that she was counting on her professors to tell her exactly what to say to her clients. She had the notion that practicing good counseling and therapy could be reduced to following a script or relying on "chicken soup" inspirational maxims. But a supervisor challenged her to discover and develop her own therapeutic voice. Zelda remembered vividly how much she wrote in her journal that night about her doubts of ever becoming an effective therapist. As she read over her anguished journal entry, she realized that her words rang strong and true. Her voice, and no one else's, was emerging on her journal pages. With a sense of determination, Zelda wrote, "Hey, I'm here to become a therapist—not a ventriloquist's dummy!"

Of course, it is only natural to succumb to some of these temptations as you take on a professional identity. You are, after all, entering a tough, challenging, and nebulous line of work, so taking refuge in jargon, labels, and fads can be very appealing. However, you will come to realize that a true professional speaks and writes with clarity in order to enlighten—not to impress—others. A real helping professional avoids slapping on labels like a grocery clerk and, instead, recognizes the uniqueness and complexity of every client. Finally, a true counselor or therapist is one who thinks critically and develops a healthy skepticism regarding fads, misinformation, and biases in the field. Sure, as a helping professional, you may be softhearted toward people, but you also have to be hardnosed about the evidence needed to validate the effectiveness of therapy and counseling techniques. Taking the high road is not the easy way, but it is the only way if you plan to be a successful helping professional.

Chapter 11, the concluding chapter of our book, ironically deals with the themes of beginnings. With graduation, you undergo that dramatic transformation from a student to a professional who is launching a career and embarking on the next chapter of your life.

Summary

In this chapter, we presented six principles to follow on your training journey. Observing these guidelines will help you succeed not only as a student but also as a helping professional. The first principle is to pack wisely for the trip. Making provisions to meet basic needs and bringing along important resources are vital for your success. Second, make the journey your destination. Your training is not a rehearsal—it is an integral part of your lifelong commitment to professional development. The third principle of thriving is to have traveling companions. Be open to what your peers, mentors, instructors, supervisors, and clients can offer you because it is impossible to become a helping professional on your own. Fourth, keep your bearings. You will find that the most important discoveries you make in your training—the greatest learning experiences you have—take place when you are truly open to looking at yourself. Fifth, let the trip take you. Allow your progress to build its own momentum and you will find yourself taking the unexpected turn and discovering new territories. Finally, always take the high road. You cannot become a competent counselor or therapist unless you also become an ethical one.

Resources

One of the best ways to begin taking on a professional identity is to join the club. All professions have state, regional, and national organizations. Below is the information you need to contact six national associations in the helping professions. They have websites that provide excellent information regarding resources, training and employment opportunities, and current issues in the profession.

American Association for Marriage and Family Therapy

112 South Alfred Street
Alexandria, VA 22314–3061
703–838–9808
www.aamft.org

American Counseling Association

5999 Stevenson Avenue
Alexandria, VA 22304–3300
800–347–6647
www.counseling.org

American Mental Health Counselors Association
801 N. Fairfax St., Suite 304
Alexandria, VA 22314
800–326–2642
www.amhca.org

American Psychological Association
750 First Street, N.E.
Washington, DC 20002–4242
800–374–2721
www.apa.org

American School Counselor Association
1101 King Street, Suite 625
Alexandria, VA 22314
703–683-ASCA
www.schoolcounselor.org

National Association of Social Workers
750 First Street, N.E., Suite 700
Washington, DC 20002–4241
202–408–8600 or 800–638–8799
www.naswdc.org

References

Brown, C. S. (2012). Maximizing success in your graduate training. In P. J. Giordano, S. F. Davis, & C. A. Licht (Eds.), *Your graduate training in psychology: Effective strategies for success* (pp. 13–22). Thousand Oaks, CA: Sage.
Burns, S. R. (2012). Relationship issues: Peers, faculty, and families. In P. J. Giordano, S. F. Davis, & C. A. Licht (Eds.), *Your graduate training in psychology: Effective strategies for success* (pp. 33–39). Thousand Oaks, CA: Sage.
Calaprice, A. (2010). *The ultimate quotable Einstein.* Princeton, NJ: Princeton University Press.
Campbell, J. (1986). *The inner reaches of outer space: Metaphor as myth and as religion.* New York, NY: van der Marck.
Conyn, R. K., & Bemak, F. (Eds.). (2005). *Journeys to professional excellence.* Alexandria, VA: American Counseling Association.

Corey, M. S., & Corey, G. (2011). *Becoming a helper* (6th ed.). Stamford, CT: Cengage Learning.

Dearing, R. L., Maddux, J. E., & Tangney, J. P. (2005). Predictors of psychological help seeking in clinical and counseling psychology graduate students. *Professional Psychology: Research and Practice, 36,* 323–329.

Gayle, B. J. (2003). The graduate school experience: One faculty member's perspective. *Behavior Therapist, 26,* 245–247.

Johnson, J. M., & Lambie, G. W. (2013). Ethnic identity and social-cognitive maturity in a multicultural group experience. *Counselor Education and Supervision, 52,* 193–206. doi:10.1002/j.1556–6978.2013.00037.x

Johnson, W. B., & Huwe, J. M. (2002). *Getting mentored in graduate school.* Washington, DC: American Psychological Association.

Kelly, M. M. (2005). Psychological adaptation to graduate school: How to smell the roses while burning the midnight oil. *Behavior Therapist, 28,* 57–59.

Kent, R. (1996). *N by E.* Middletown, CT: Wesleyan University Press.

Kidd, D. C., & Castano, E. (2013). Reading literary fiction improves theory of mind. *Science, 342*(6156), 377–380. doi:10.1126/science.1239918

Pope, K. S., & Vasquez, M. J. T. (2011). *Ethics in psychotherapy and counseling* (4th ed.). Hoboken, NJ: Wiley.

Prosek, E. A., Holm, J. M., & Daly, C. M. (2013). Benefits of required counseling for counseling students. *Counselor Education & Supervision, 52,* 242–254. doi:10.1002/j.1556–6978.2013.00040.x

Schaefle, S., Smaby, M. H., Maddux, C. D., & Cates, J. (2005). Counseling skills attainment, retention, and transfer as measured by the Skilled Counseling Scale. *Counselor Education and Supervision, 44,* 280–292.

Steinbeck, J. (1962). *Travels with Charley.* New York, NY: Bantam Books.

Tournier, P. (1957). *The meaning of persons.* New York, NY: Harper & Row.

Turnbull, C. (1990). Luminality: A synthesis of subjective and objective experience. In R. Schechner & W. Appel (Eds.), *By means of performance* (pp. 50–81). New York, NY: Cambridge University Press.

Vernarec, E. (2010, October). The confidence factor. *Counseling Today, 53,* 36–41.

2

Making Your Training Journey

When one travels, the first step is the beginning of the arrival.

—Seng-Chao

Our task is to make ourselves architects of the future.

—Jomo Kenyatta

Over 500 years ago in Florence, a young artist discovered a giant marble block that had been abandoned for decades. Other sculptors considered it to be ruined, but Michelangelo looked within the stone and saw something beautiful. In fact, he believed that every block of stone had a statue inside it, and it was the job of the sculptor to discover it. By chipping away everything that was not the statue, Michelangelo created the masterpiece *David* (Hibbard, 1974).

As a student of counseling and psychotherapy, you face a similar challenge—seeing and actualizing the counselor that is emerging from within yourself. This process is neither easy nor painless. In fact, your training may sometimes feel as if your professors and supervisors are chipping away at you. However, if you remain committed to exploring yourself, accepting feedback, and practicing your skills, you can sculpt yourself into a successful and effective counselor. Throughout your professional career, you are always in the process of *becoming*, while recognizing that you will never fully achieve, your full potential as a master counselor and therapist.

On a lighter note, one of our colleagues described his journey to earning his doctorate degree as one of taking on the character of each of the Seven Dwarfs. "At the start of my training," he said, "I felt so naïve and shy that I was Dopey and Bashful. By the second year, I felt so sick, exhausted, and frustrated with everything that I was either Sneezy, Sleepy, or Grumpy. Finally, when I got my PhD, I was thrilled that I was at last both Doc and Happy."

Although our friend offered this description as merely a cute story, you can expect to undergo profound transformations in your own identity. Whether you pursue a master's, educational specialist, or doctoral degree, you take on distinct roles as you make your way through a program. These roles include novice, apprentice, and emerging professional. This chapter is organized according to the three roles that you assume as you chart your course along your training journey.

Your journey includes important milestones—such as orientation, practicum, comprehensive examination, internship, capstone experiences, and graduation—that mark the crucial turning points you face along the way (Giordano, Davis, & Licht, 2013). In this chapter, we describe the process of becoming a counselor or therapist as you proceed through your training program's rites of passage. In many ways, the milestones involved in becoming a helping professional parallel your own growth from child-hood into adulthood. Just as children learn to crawl before they can walk, you learn basic theories and techniques before you can practice complex therapeutic interventions. And just as children discover and explore their unique sense of self as they grow and mature, you also learn about your-self, forging a new identity that emerges and crystallizes at each stage of your own development.

Mark Young (2013) described the successful completion of graduate training as a personal journey with identifiable developmental stages in your ways of thinking about counseling and therapy—from dualistic through multiplistic to relativistic thinking. Keep in mind that these developmental stages refer only to general trends in one's journey to become a counselor. As you have matured, your ways of thinking about life, people, and the world in general have become complex, nuanced, and sophisticated, but you are now exploring new territory, so your ways of thinking in this specific intel-lectual domain need time to develop. This stage model can provide you with a useful framework for reflecting on your own training journey. But do not view this developmental process as a simple sequence of steps that you take one at a time. In reality, your development involves much ebb and flow, and at any point in your training, you incorporate elements from all three stages, even though one may dominate.

In the following sections, in addition to offering practical advice about handling the nuts and bolts of completing your training requirements, we also suggest ways you can thrive at each stage of your professional development. For example, by creating a portfolio, keeping a journal, and using rituals, you can facilitate your own growth, document your achievements, celebrate your progress, and foster a sense of community with your colleagues.

Why Not Enjoy the Ride?

Cathy's Story

At the end of this semester, I'm going to be graduating. Of course, I'm excited about finishing up and a little nervous about finding a job. While I'm pretty busy completing my internship and sending out resumes, at times I've found myself just skimming through the journals I've written over the past three years. It reminds me of when I was a senior in high school. I was excited about all the changes in my life, but I also had a need to look through my yearbooks and relive a little of my earlier high school days.

I'm not sure why, but my reactions to my journals have gone through an incredible change. When I used to read over my entries right after writing them, I would often feel embarrassed and supercritical. I would think to myself, "Those words don't capture my experiences at all. They're so lame, superficial, and trite!" Now when I read over those same entries that I had written at the start of my training, I feel like I'm encountering another person.

Like an indulgent older sister, I now am quick to forgive this person's mistakes, find her awkward phrases endearing, and am charmed by her naïve views. In fact, I feel protective of her, wanting to offer her some nurturance and encouragement, saying something like, "You go, girl!" I'm proud of how that person hung in there through some tough times.

I haven't really counted, but I bet that the number of words I wrote in an entry was a pretty good measure of the turmoil I was in at the time. Last year, there were lots of entries about my comps. I was so afraid that I was going to fail that exam! One week, I had spent every free minute in the library doing this marathon review of all the comps material. When I finally finished studying, I was convinced that there was no way that I could pass.

When I came home that night, my partner innocently asked me about my day, and the next thing I remember is sobbing uncontrollably in her arms, saying that it was no use because passing was impossible. She was great—she didn't give me any silly reassurances or inspirational slogans. She just stayed there with me until I was ready to move on to making a plan of action. Reading that journal entry reminded me of just how lucky I've been to have her and others in my life.

I'm at a different place now—more confident of myself, more seasoned, and on my way to becoming a good counselor. As I reread what I've just written, I recognize that my words still don't capture fully what I'm experiencing right now, but I'm a lot more tolerant and charitable toward myself than I used to be. Sure, I haven't arrived—I still have a long way to go, but why not enjoy the ride?

Being a Novice

A dream [is] the bearer of a new possibility, the enlarged horizon, the great hope.

—Howard Thurman

When you were offered admission into your training program, you probably felt a thrilling combination of excitement and worry, eagerness and apprehension (Kersting, 2005). And no matter how old you may be as you start your training, what responsibilities you have had in the past, and what lessons you already have learned in your life, you are in many ways a novice in this new endeavor. When you were considering possible graduate programs, you gathered information on a variety of programs before narrowing your choices and making a final commitment to a particular program (Norcross & Sayette, 2014). Now, as a beginning graduate student and one of the newest members of this learning community, you need to become even more informed of your program's policies, requirements, curriculum options, and procedures. In fact, it is likely that you have access to an overwhelming amount of data. Just sifting through it all, along with skimming through your new textbooks, can leave you confused and intimidated, reaffirming just how little you actually do know—and just how much you still need to learn. But take it easy on yourself. Your basic goal as a novice is to embark successfully on your training journey.

In Chapter 4, we describe in detail how you can enhance your abilities to perform well academically. In the meantime, we invite you to focus on the broader themes of your novice experience: becoming oriented, learning the basics, connecting with others, and becoming fully involved in the training process (McAuliffe & Eriksen, 2011). As you participate in your beginning courses, you begin to develop a foundation—the basic knowledge, skills, and attitudes—necessary for you to move into the apprenticeship phase of your training.

When you first become a novice, you may feel like a kid who has just climbed up the ladder to the high diving board for the first time. You may think that everyone is looking at you, while you stand up there wondering what in the world you were thinking when you decided to make this dive. A belly flop would be painful enough, but to add insult to injury, everyone would see you fail so spectacularly. Well, if you want to thrive in your training, your best option is to go ahead and dive right into this new endeavor.

To help you leap into your training and succeed as a novice, just remember the thriving principles: Come well prepared, live your training, learn from others, explore yourself, be open to opportunities, and always act with integrity. In the following section, we discuss how you can use rituals to engage deeply in your training experiences right from the start.

Opening Rituals

Rituals are ceremonial activities that give expression to beliefs, values, and concepts. Baptisms, bar mitzvahs, Hindu samsaras, vision quests, walkabouts, and marriage ceremonies are only a few of the countless religious and cultural rituals that mark major turning points in people's lives. Many counselors, especially those who work with couples and families, also have found that rituals can be powerful intervention techniques (Becvar & Becvar, 2013). Rituals in graduate school can enrich your own training experience, strengthen your sense of community, celebrate your accomplishments, and give voice to your program's fundamental mission (McKee, Smith, Hayes, Stewart, & Echterling, 1999).

All counseling programs have orientation meetings or social gatherings to welcome new students and mark the beginning of a new academic year. These opening rituals are nice ways to introduce everyone to one another and to familiarize newcomers with the workings of their new community. For example, recognizing the emotional and bonding power of rituals, the James Madison University Counseling Programs has carried out an annual initiation ceremony for over 20 years. The ceremony has involved faculty and students forming a circle, lighting candles, declaring personal goals, and pledging support to one another. However, even if your program does not offer any initiation ceremony, you can develop your own ritual to mark this special occasion.

EXERCISE 2.1 Traditions

A Reminiscing and Planning Exercise

Rituals that are repeated become traditions. In this exercise, we invite you first to think about two important traditions that have already enriched your life. Select one tradition that is closely connected to your family life and another that reflects your religious or cultural heritage.

Spend a little time reminiscing about each tradition. What were the circumstances? Who was involved? What was your role? When you're ready, go ahead and describe each tradition.

Looking back on these traditions, write about the meaning they hold for you now.

FAMILY

Tradition:

_____

_____

Meaning:

_____

_____

_____

_____

_____

RELIGION OR CULTURE

Tradition:

_____

_____

(Continued)

(Continued)

Meaning:

_____

_____

_____

_____

_____

   The second part of this exercise is a planning task. Think of a ritual that you would like to make a tradition connected with your training. It could be a personal ritual that only you would perform, a family ceremony that involves your relatives, or a community activity that includes everyone in the program. Describe the activity and explore its meaning for you.

TRAINING

Tradition:

_____

_____

Meaning:

_____

_____

_____

_____

_____

   We encourage you to perform an individual or shared initiation ritual at the start of your training and at the start of every academic year. Describe your experience in your training journal so that you can refer to it each year to reflect on your progress. Such an initiation ritual, like the morning ritual of taking a shower, can be an invigorating and awakening experience. Besides, you may be surprised by the powerful emotions and meaningful discoveries that your ritual can evoke.

Unlearning

To attain knowledge, add things every day. To attain wisdom, subtract things every day.

—Lao Tsu

You must unlearn what you have learned.

—Yoda

You are not a "tabula rasa," a blank slate, when you enter your graduate training program. In fact, you come with years of personal experiences and cultural socialization that have created in you many fundamental assumptions about the world. You also have been involved in countless occurrences of being "helpful." These untold transactions have crystallized into rules that govern your way of behaving with others without your full realization. Such ingrained habits as giving advice, being agreeable, and fixing problems often are deep-seated in students who want to become professional therapists or counselors. However, these habits can interfere with such essential counseling skills as active listening, empathic understanding, noting discrepancies, and being immediate. In addition to learning these new skills, you therefore need to unlearn old automatic responses—such as sympathizing, caretaking, and rescuing—that sabotage therapeutic effectiveness with your clients.

Because your "helpful" habits are so entrenched, they will be as tenacious as dandelions that return in a garden that had been thoroughly weeded; therefore, abandoning these familiar, automatic responses takes persistence and determination on your part. Just like a counseling client, you are embarking on the challenging process of giving up the familiar to embrace the new. Expect that your professors and supervisors will shake up some of your preconceptions about how to be helpful. When you encounter one of these conflicting notions, your first reaction may be to hunker down and resist—just like many clients. The advantages of your old ideas of helping seem patently obvious to you, and these new concepts may be counterintuitive. Nevertheless, we invite you to open yourself up to each new idea, to view the therapeutic process from this new lens—as if you were at the optometrist's office, mulling over the question, "Is it better now?"

In your basic skills training, you quickly learn that counseling is not algebra, where you solve for X. The wonderful insight that you may have found so helpful in your own life may come across as glib, superficial, or irrelevant to a client. There's an old joke about the scout who resolutely led an old lady across the street only to discover that she had not wanted to cross it in the first place. Therapists are not in the business of earning merit badges. Simply veneering the new skills over the old habits will not complete the process, so it is not unusual for your graduate education to involve both learning new skills and unlearning old habits that sabotage effective counseling.

Communication

If you are to thrive in your new learning community, you need to be in communication with others. As you have heard so many times, communication is a two-way street. Be ready to do your part to be both an active listener and an open communicator in your program. Stay in touch. Keep your program administrators up to date on your current postal address, telephone number, and e-mail address. Be sure to let people know what is on your mind. Both you and the program will be the better for it.

Most training programs have developed a number of ways for their members to share information, ideas, and feedback with one another.

Newsletters. A program newsletter provides an overview of recent developments and a preview of upcoming events. It may, for example, introduce you to new members, update you on the accomplishments of students and faculty, and announce program changes. It also offers information on important deadlines, meetings, and conferences.

When you receive a newsletter, take some time to jot down immediately the important dates and times in your calendar; then keep the most recent edition handy in case you need to refer to it. It is a valuable tool to help you stay up to date and involved. Also, feel free to suggest items for inclusion in your program's newsletter.

Texts and E-Mails. Texting and e-mailing have become great ways to communicate quickly and easily with others. As you know, texting is especially fast and effective when your message is simple. You can send a text anytime and anywhere—as long as you have your phone handy. With longer messages, you can use e-mails to share information about employment possibilities, social events, or other opportunities. Of course, e-mail messages are useless if you don't check your account. If you want to keep in touch, check and use your e-mail regularly.

Bulletin Boards. Even the most high-tech programs still have plenty of bulletin boards in the halls for posting hard copies of announcements, job opportunities, brochures, and other information. Check these boards regularly, and use them to post interesting and useful information.

Program Committee Meetings. All training programs have regular meetings to review procedures, develop policies, and address concerns. Most programs include student representatives as members of these committees. We encourage you to consider volunteering to be a student representative at these meetings. It is a great way to see how the organization operates and to participate in the planning process.

Meetings With Your Adviser. Every graduate student has an assigned faculty adviser, and you should be meeting regularly with yours. Consider your adviser as a ready and reliable source of information and support. Yes, of course, your faculty adviser is a busy person, but remember that advising is an integral part of teaching—and an essential resource for you.

Progress Reviews. One accreditation standard is that the faculty must review the overall progress each student is making every semester. Near the end of each semester, you can also conduct your own review by taking some time to think about all that you have discovered, learned, and experienced during the semester. Record these reflections in your journal and write your ideas for making continued progress. The end of the semester is an especially busy time, but reviewing your progress and planning your future will be time well spent!

Participation in Formal Assessment Procedures. All graduate training programs have developed several formal assessment procedures in order to obtain your feedback and suggestions. In your courses, your faculty members will ask you to assess their teaching performance and class activities. We encourage you to offer constructive feedback and practical suggestions when faculty and supervisors request your assessment of training experiences. You will also complete assignments and take tests to evaluate the effectiveness of the program in achieving the learning outcomes that are essential for the practice of counseling and therapy. Your faculty members will aggregate these data, discuss the assessment results in their meetings, and modify the courses, curricula, and policies to improve the overall effectiveness of the training program.

Handling Personal Problems

Because you were selected for admission from among many candidates, you will likely do well in your training and make satisfactory progress throughout the program. Of course, you will encounter the inevitable speed bumps that slow your progress, but those are merely brief hindrances to your positive momentum. However, it is also possible that at some point in your training, you could face serious academic or personal difficulties. If these difficulties threaten to impair your performance as a trainee, you have the responsibility to take positive steps to address these concerns. You can pursue several practical, specific strategies, such as taking a remedial course, repeating a course, entering personal counseling or therapy, or taking a leave of absence.

If you are dealing with concerns that seem overwhelming, talk to your adviser about your options. In Chapter 3, we explore in detail how to deal with the stressors of graduate training, and in Chapter 6 we elaborate on the value of participating in your own personal counseling or therapy. There is no need for you to struggle through your training like one of the walking wounded. Take care of yourself, and seek help at the first sign of any impairment.

Keeping a Portfolio

A portfolio is a collection of your work that tells the story of your efforts, progress, and achievement in your training. As part of their evaluation procedures, many programs now require students to assemble certain materials into a portfolio (Cobia et al., 2005). However, even if your program does not require a portfolio, we encourage you to begin one in order to take advantage of its many benefits.

Your portfolio offers a composite picture of your professional development. It allows you to demonstrate what you know in a way that reflects the complexity of particular topics and how you have integrated your skills and knowledge to create useful counseling tools. There are no cookbook recipes for what goes into your counseling portfolio. In fact, you can include different items in your portfolio depending on how you're going to be using it. For example, if you need it to document your progress or to evaluate the effectiveness of your program, then certain materials will be required. However, if you are bringing it along for a job interview, then you can custom design your portfolio to fit the position requirements. A third common use of a portfolio is for your personal growth and reflection. Consider your training journal to be an essential piece of your portfolio, even though you are unlikely to be sharing it with others. Your journal, however, is your personal forum for noting your reflections and observations regarding the experiences documented in your portfolio.

What are some possible items for your portfolio? Obvious choices include written samples of your work, such as assessment reports, diagnostic reports, intervention plans, term papers, handouts for presentations, published articles, and important correspondence. Of course, you need to take care to protect the confidentiality of the clients you describe in these work samples. You also may want to have a section of works in progress, such as your philosophy of intervention, your evolving counseling and therapy theory, and ongoing projects. It can be useful to include a list of conferences and workshops you have attended, class presentations you have given, professional service activities, and awards. It's also a great idea to add scrapbook items, such as photographs, newspaper clippings, and program announcements, concerning your professional activities. Include drawings and comments by clients, notes from colleagues, and performance assessments from professors and supervisors.

Dualistic Thinking

As a novice in the field of counseling and therapy, your thinking is more likely to be characterized by a dualistic, right-or-wrong attitude (Young, 2013). At this stage, you tend to approach your learning in a somewhat perfectionistic manner. You may find yourself trying to determine which of the theories of counseling you are learning is *the* correct one. You may, for example, be attracted to a person-centered approach or a cognitive-behavioral theory, and you feel you must choose one or the other. After all, they can't both be right . . . can they?

The One

Juanita's Story

As a beginning counselor, I went through a series of infatuations with various counseling fads. The process later reminded me of the series of boyfriends I had had in high school. At first, I was completely fascinated with a particular counseling approach, certain that I had finally found "The One." However, as reality began to set in and I began to notice the imperfections and limitations of the technique, I quickly became disenchanted, "dumped" it, and went on to another counseling approach.

It was only later in my training, when I began to look closely at myself and to value what I brought to the counseling relationship that I realized that I could set aside my desperate search for "The One."

Perfectionism

Besides embarking on a quest for the perfect theory, as a novice, you are more likely to be demanding perfection from yourself in your performance. You may come to your class in basic counseling skills believing that your performance must be impeccable; otherwise, you will be an absolute failure. With so much at stake, instead of really listening to the person who sits before you as your client, you may be focusing on what to say next. You may feel queasy as you attempt to make sense of what your client is saying. Nervous mannerisms, such as rhythmically kicking your foot or saying "um–hum," begin to pop up. You feel under pressure to come up with the answer to your client's problem, and if you don't, you believe that you have not been helpful at all, so you wind up saying something ineffectual and lame such as, "Have you tried talking to your roommate?"

As you reflect on your feelings of incompetence at the beginning of your program, you might secretly believe that you are a fraud and that sooner or later, you will be found out and excommunicated from the ranks. This impostor phenomenon (Sakulku & Alexander, 2011) is common among both women and men. Don't become too worried about it. Most trainees feel that way at the beginning of their programs. In fact, we will let you in on a little secret in the counseling and therapy training profession. We warn one another, "Be afraid, be very afraid!" about any beginning trainee who is supremely confident that he or she is already a genuine master of the art of counseling and therapy. People who think that they have already arrived see no point in going on a journey—and they make terrible travelers.

Keeping a Beginner's Mind

> When you forget the beginner's awe, you start decaying.
>
> —Nobuko Albery

As an undergraduate, you probably spent a great deal of time ingesting information to regurgitate later on a test. You may have memorized definitions, names, dates, formulas, or scientific principles without fully understanding them or being able to apply them. You became expert in how to beat the system and make grades, sometimes perhaps even at the expense of gaining meaningful knowledge. Now you are in a program in which you must go beyond mere information and begin to use concepts to guide your everyday behavior. The test now becomes whether you can actually walk the walk, not just talk the talk.

As you will read in Chapter 4, your present dilemma may be that you have spent so many years going through the motions of learning that you have forgotten how to truly learn by heart. You find yourself in a situation in which some of your former strategies will not apply. You are a rank beginner, and you are confused in this new environment. These circumstances certainly make you feel insecure, and you may attempt to cover your feelings of inadequacy by acting as though you know more than you actually do and by sticking to those areas of knowledge in which you are expert.

However, we are encouraging you to allow yourself to know nothing—to be a beginner. The Zen philosopher Suzuki (2006) once made the seemingly paradoxical statement, "In the beginner's mind there are many possibilities. In the expert's mind there are few" (p. 1). The Zen masters would teach students by confusing them, sometimes using a koan, such as asking them to answer the question, "What is the sound of one hand clapping?" The Zen method of the koan is the way the master would convince students that expertise is precisely what keeps them from understanding fully the truth of a situation. The koan would throw the student into ambiguity so that the problem at hand would then be approached naïvely.

An expert knows how to do things and how to think about things. Expert thinking often proceeds automatically as a convergent problem-solving process. On the other hand, someone who is not an expert must approach each circumstance as novel and must discover fresh ways of adapting to its demands. It is much harder work to stay fresh than to behave automatically. You have to burn a lot of calories dealing with something you have never encountered before. As you will learn in more detail in Chapter 8, the neuroscience research reveals that keeping a beginner's mind involves the process of focusing one's neocortex, the brain's topmost layers, in a top-down process that counteracts the brain's tendency to automatize routines (Goleman, 2013). Be careful about becoming an expert at helping, because every person you are helping and every situation in which you will find yourself *will* be novel.

At a fundamental level, being a novice is not a stage but an attitude of approaching life with openness and curiosity. In fact, the best therapists always behave as if they are naive beginners and never as if they are experts. There is a freshness and awe in their therapeutic stance with clients. It is a bit like a story we once heard about a woman who told a 4-year-old that her job was to teach college students how to draw. Perplexed, the young girl asked, "What happened? Did they forget?"

Being an Apprentice

We work to become, not to acquire.

—Elbert Hubbard

When you have completed your basic courses, you are no longer in the role of a novice. As you proceed to the next level of your training program, you begin to take on more responsibilities as you assume a new identity—that of an apprentice. As an apprentice, you are under close supervision, but you now have opportunities to practice your professional skills. For example, you may be assisting a professor on a research project, offering counseling services at a practicum site, presenting a guidance unit at a school, or cofacilitating a personal growth group with an intern.

Once you have demonstrated that you can succeed in a graduate training program, you can, for example, apply for membership in Chi Sigma Iota, the counseling professional honor society. This society recognizes excellence in counseling and helps create an atmosphere of professional commitment. You are invited to apply for membership each semester. Activities often include philanthropic projects, presentations, and social events.

Multiplistic Thinking

As you shift from a novice to an apprentice, you progress from a dualistic to a multiplistic way of thinking. At this point in your development, you begin to give up the idea that there is one correct answer or a single right way to work with people. Furthermore, you begin to see that your standard of right and wrong is not shared by all the people you meet and that their views have merit. You feel less threatened by ideas that once seemed strange—or just plain wrong—to you, and you become more accepting of other lifestyles. Instead of wanting to argue with people who see things differently, you become curious and intrigued with their way of experiencing the world. Now, you spend less of your energy attempting to figure out what your professors expect of you and begin to operate more on your inner sense of how to carry out a project.

Still, at this stage of your development, you may be overwhelmed by all the new possibilities that are presented to you and a bit suspicious of those who attempt to persuade you to go in new directions. You may find that you become frustrated and confused in your supervision during this phase of your training (Young, 2013).

A Deer Caught in the Headlights

Bill's Story

"You're the first counseling graduate student I've ever met who's atheoretical!"

After recovering from the initial shock of that statement from my practicum supervisor, I rather dumbly replied, "Oh, I guess I have a theory, I just don't know what it is yet."

"Maybe it's time you found out," he responded. "You are trying to counsel from your personality alone, just being a nice person. I think your clients may be looking for more than that from you," he concluded.

He was right. My secret was out. I was a deer caught in the headlights. I really didn't have a clue about integrating theory into practice. Oh, I had completed several theory and technique classes, even received great grades in them, but somehow the content of those classes had not yet become a reality for either my counseling work or for me. It was time to begin the quest for a theory I could claim as my own.

It was not an easy journey. I had to work more, read more, question more. Being "eclectic" seemed like a cop-out to me. I really wanted to discover a theory that made sense to me, that worked for me in helping relationships, and that allowed me to be me at the same time. After two practicum experiences and a yearlong internship, I landed on what I now call "holistic-integrative" counseling. It includes many aspects from well-known theories, such as those of Carl Rogers, Albert Ellis, Fritz Perls, Salvador Minuchin, and Virginia Satir, yet it also became uniquely mine—an integration of my personality, experiences, and worldview. The really neat part is that it is open-ended, allowing for constant adjustments based on new discoveries I make. In other words, I'm still growing, and so is my theory.

The "Sophomore Slump"

While perusing the news media, you may have heard the term *sophomore slump*. Sports commentators use it to refer to the disappointing follow-up performance of athletes after a promising rookie year. Film critics have borrowed the term to describe movie sequels that did not live up to the success of the original. And, of course, it is a common characterization of the lower grades of many sophomores following a successful first year. Similarly,

G. Neimeyer (personal communication, March 12, 2001) has observed that many graduate students experience a sense of disillusionment during their second year of training. During their novice year, students go through an intensive, challenging time, and generally they make fine progress. However, they may be disappointed in themselves that they do not keep up this promising momentum the following year.

Your high expectations for another extraordinary year of dramatic advances in your knowledge and skills, breakthroughs in your self-awareness, and spectacular personal growth may set you up for disappointment. To prevent a sophomore slump, you can first of all cut yourself some slack by pacing yourself, setting aside your nagging demands for perfectionism, letting go of your need to meet the high expectations of others, and practicing some of the mindfulness techniques we describe in Chapter 5.

Having an impossibly full appointment book and frantically attempting to run a marathon distance at a sprinter's pace can quickly make you feel overwhelmed, but it can also be a way to keep you from looking at yourself. A demanding educational environment requires time management on your part and a more refined vigilance to the cues of your professors. So go ahead—use all the newest apps to schedule your life, make your way through all your "to do" items on your list, and make sure that you are keeping up in all your courses. But remember, when you find yourself feeling like you are being hit from all sides by the expectations of others, don't just do something—*be* there. As you will read in the next chapter, there is much wisdom in that old cliché about stopping to smell the roses.

Learning From the Inside Out

Teresa's Story

At the end of my first year in the counseling program, I felt like I was walking around inside out. I was certain when I started that I wanted to become a counselor, but I didn't know that this would entail such microscopic self-examination. In my classes, outside my classes, in conversations with my fellow peers, I explored so many crevices, dark holes, and files that had been shoved away—even those that wanted to remain hidden. It was a relentless process, and many days I came home feeling a mix of exhaustion and exhilaration from uncovering layers of meaning and emotion.

One of the most important discoveries that I made is that I have a great need for people to be happy with me—so much so that I lose myself and my needs in striving to be ALL for everyone. Because of the intensive focus on MY thoughts, MY feelings, MY contributions, and MY beliefs, I embarked on a slow process of change—of wanting to become my authentic self and to shed the self that I THOUGHT others wanted me to be. This process is not easy, and it felt, and still feels, strange—like I had entered into the Land of Fog, and everything in my life became murky. Nothing was clear until I accepted the strangeness and the realization that ambiguity is a state that can be traveled through.

As I muddle through my second year, this is by no means a resolved challenge, but I have learned how to read my own map. And, at least now, I am aware of what I am doing and can forge ahead in hopes that the result of this journey will be to emerge as the self that I am genuinely happy and comfortable being.

Your Relationships With Faculty

As a novice, you not only demand a great deal from yourself, you also have high expectations of your faculty and supervisors. During your undergraduate days, you may not have worked closely with faculty members. Consequently, you may not have realized that the average university faculty member works well over 50 hours a week, with direct teaching duties accounting for only a small fraction of this time. Now that you are working more closely with the faculty members, you may notice that they are often heavily overcommitted, with work schedules that are like a middle-aged man's old blue jeans: dangerously tight.

Certainly, the members of your faculty want to collaborate with you as you progress through the training program. However, they also have to juggle the demands of a challenging teaching load, supervisory meetings, multiple scholarly projects, never-ending committee work, and service to the profession and community. There will be times during which they do not respond quickly to your frantic e-mail messages, seem distracted when you share a concern, or are unavailable when you have an important question. In short, your teachers will not always be there for you. However, take care not to assume that they are disengaged or unconcerned about your well-being. The more likely reason is that they are stretched too thin and overburdened—sound familiar?

Whatever you do, watch out that your minor frustrations and disappointments don't crystallize into a general sense of disenchantment and a specific resentment against the faculty. This is a common dynamic in counseling and psychotherapy groups. People are tempted to find a scapegoat to blame for their unfulfilled needs. If you find yourself regularly grousing and griping about the faculty with your fellow students, it is time to deal productively with the hostility before it gathers momentum. Recognize that your feelings are normal and that you can communicate your concerns in direct and respectful ways with your teachers, supervisors, and mentors.

Comprehensive Examination

Near the end of the apprenticeship period of your training, you complete a comprehensive examination. Its purpose is to document that you have integrated essential knowledge of counseling and psychological theories, research, and practice. The format of the comprehensive examination differs from program to program. One popular format is the Counselor Preparation Comprehensive Examination (CPCE). The CPCE is a knowledge-based multiple-choice examination that reflects the eight core curriculum areas approved by the Council for Accreditation of Counseling and Related Educational Programs (CACREP). Another common format for the comprehensive examination is a series of essay questions.

Some programs require a portfolio of documents that demonstrate the student's knowledge. In a few programs, students provide a sample of their counseling work, such as a video recording of a counseling session and other supporting documents, for the comprehensive examination. A number of programs also use some combination of written and oral examinations.

Whatever its format, a successful comprehensive examination involves more than merely passing. Your comprehensive examination serves as an important rite of passage for you. You can use this experience to help you pull together useful information and ideas from your earlier courses and therapeutic experiences. In meeting the challenge of the examination, you also discover a great deal about yourself, both personally and professionally. The comprehensive examination experience gives you a chance to demonstrate not only to faculty members but also to yourself that you are ready to become a professional. You can thrive during this rite of passage, emerging from this process with a greater sense of personal and professional confidence.

The following strategies can be helpful in preparing for the examination:

- *Train well from the start.* From the start, be actively involved in all facets of your training. The best way to prepare for a successful comprehensive examination is to be a successful trainee in the program.
- *Work long and hard.* There is no quick and easy way to be successful in your examination. It requires intense preparation involving hours of

study and review. Once you have laid the groundwork, however, you are more likely to come to the examination feeling equal to the task and confident.

- *Review previous course material.* You will find it helpful to look over all the information, concepts, and issues that you have addressed in your earlier classes.

- *Focus on yourself.* Use the examination preparation to reflect on your own theoretical perspectives, personal issues, competencies, and limitations as a beginning counselor or therapist. Take time to explore your own personal and professional development.

- *Link with an informal support group.* Sharing concerns and encouragement can be helpful. It is also reassuring to find out that you are not the only one to have doubts and worries about your performance.

- *Take care of yourself.* You can do this by taking time to relax and rest. On looking back after successfully completing the examination, most students report wishing that they had not worried so much.

- *Be confident.* The comprehensive examination is your opportunity to demonstrate what you have learned from your hard work and long preparation. Come to the examination looking forward to your chance to demonstrate your knowledge and readiness to be a professional.

Although you will only complete this examination once, we encourage you to do your part to make this a thriving experience for other students. You can help by supporting your fellow students as they embark on this rite of passage, encouraging them as they confront their own doubts, and congratulating them on their successes.

An Emerging Professional

> One's work may be finished someday, but one's education never.
>
> —Alexandre Dumas

For many of you, the final stage of your graduate training involves the completion of two important capstone experiences: your internship and your research project. *Capstone* refers to the finishing stone of a structure. In your training, your capstone experiences are the culmination of all your work and preparation. You began the program as a novice, progressed to become an apprentice, and have now developed into an emerging professional. Your internship, which we discuss in detail in Chapter 8, gives you an opportunity to practice an important dimension of your emerging professional role. Although you will continue to need supervision and advising, you have demonstrated your readiness to successfully complete your formal training and to graduate.

Relativistic Thinking

As an emerging professional who is nearing the successful completion of your program, your thinking continues to evolve, from multiplistic to relativistic. At this last stage of your training, you begin to tailor your responses to the circumstance at hand, realizing that there are "different strokes for different folks." During this period of development, you probably use one kind of intervention with people who present with specific phobias and another kind of approach with those who seem "existentially lost." As you learn more about the various theoretical approaches, you begin to see commonalities among them. You may begin to become more eclectic or trans-theoretical in your attitudes. Instead of viewing your clients as ignorant or misguided, you begin to understand the circumstances that have brought them to their current situation.

As you enhance your therapeutic skills, you also become more cognitively complex (Little, Packman, Smaby, & Maddux, 2005). You judge your own responses in sessions based on whether they seem to produce the desired effects in the client. You grow less preoccupied with your own performance and become much more focused on helping your client achieve his or her goals. In your classes, you begin to notice that you are no longer working for the grade as much as you are working for self-improvement. Your learning shifts from "outside in" to "inside out."

The benefit of taking a perspective that involves stages of development is that you can view your own challenges as normal (Young, 2013). Throughout your program, you are continually progressing. If you are recording your counseling work, you may want to save your first recording—provided that this is not a breach of confidentiality and that you have the permission of your client. Saving this recording can be helpful to you because your progress is often gradual and imperceptible. If you have a recording, you can look back and be amazed at how much you have improved over the course of your training.

As we have mentioned earlier, keeping a journal is helpful in tracking the metamorphosis you are experiencing. However, no matter how long your training program may be, you must remember that this journey is lifelong (Duncan, 2014). You may have expected that you would graduate and leave your training as a more or less finished product. Once you realize just how much more you have to learn, you may at first feel inadequate, disappointed in yourself, or disillusioned with your training. These reactions are simply more of those normal, typical, and common feelings that you'll experience in your professional development.

Keep in mind that in order to become a master counselor, you will need years of practice, intense supervision, and many varied experiences. It has been said that it takes as many as 10,000 hours of practice to achieve mastery in a field, whether it is playing the violin, computer programming, or playing a sport (Gladwell, 2008). However, according to Goleman (2013), that rule is too simple. Merely putting in the time is not enough. The secret of achieving mastery is not the amount of time that you invest but the quality of that time. For truly quality time, you need to practice smart by giving your full attention to enhancing your skills. In addition to your complete concentration, you also need to include a feedback loop to make your practice sessions successful. Under the guidance of a coach, mentor, or supervisor, you are much more likely to become aware of errors and to correct them. Practicing under the expert eye of a true master is essential.

Right now, your training journey to becoming a master counselor or therapist may seem both long and arduous, but if you are truly committed to becoming a helping professional, you *will* become one with many hours of focused practice and constructive feedback. The information in this book will help you keep your journey in perspective. There will be times, however, when you judge yourself harshly for not being good enough. Remember to trust in yourself and in the process. Wherever you are right now in your progress through these stages, just be there! Go with the flow. You'll get where you want to go.

Research Project

The purpose of the thesis or dissertation is to provide you with an opportunity to complete an intensive and comprehensive scholarly project that makes an original contribution to the profession (Cone & Foster, 2006). In most programs, you have a wide variety of possible topics that are acceptable for a thesis or dissertation, as long as you demonstrate relevance to the field. Your final report will include a review of the professional literature and a discussion of implications. It may take one of the following forms:

- *Research report.* The research report involves collecting and analyzing quantitative or qualitative data to answer a particular research question.
- *Program evaluation.* An applied study may involve assessing the needs of a population or evaluating the effectiveness of an intervention or program.

- *Technique or program development.* Your research project may involve developing an innovative therapeutic technique or program.
- *Critical review.* A critical review of the literature regarding an issue in counseling and therapy would be more than merely a summary of the literature. The critical review should offer new and creative ways of looking at an issue, develop a useful conceptual framework, or give a well-reasoned critique of the material.

You may have been using a journal to explore the emotional nuances of your training, but you can also use it in your research to jot down your hunches, speculate on possible topics, or sketch out your plans. You can get much more out of keeping a journal if you do more than merely summarize your experiences. For example, consider what is particularly interesting, meaningful, unusual, or even puzzling about the research you are doing. Date your entries and write regularly, at least two or three times a week. Use your journal to explore your thoughts, sort through your feelings, recollect memories, and develop ideas. You can use a variety of strategies: questioning, synthesizing, speculating, and brainstorming.

Selecting a Committee. You need to select a faculty committee for your thesis or dissertation. Typically, your committee consists of one chair and at least two members. You may be able to elect to have an additional reader if this person has expertise relevant to your research project.

As you work on your project, keep in mind that it is your responsibility to keep your chair and committee members informed of your progress. Typically, you will have at least two meetings with the entire committee— one at the beginning of the project and another at its completion. At the first meeting, the committee considers your proposal. The purpose of the second is to discuss your final report, recommend revisions, and make a final decision on whether to accept it.

Completing Your Final Draft. The format for the final report should follow the guidelines presented in your institution's handbook for theses and dissertations and in the *Publication Manual of the American Psychological Association* (American Psychological Association, 2010). The institutional guidelines impose stringent conditions on the format, such as quality of paper, size of margins, font type, and legibility requirements.

Evaluation Criteria. The chair and readers of your thesis or dissertation will be evaluating your performance based on several criteria. First, the report must be a thorough consideration of the topic that you have selected. No matter what type of research you perform, you must present a comprehensive review of pertinent professional literature. Another criterion is originality. You must offer a contribution to the professional literature that is based on your own ideas and work. Your report must be more than a summary of the thoughts and efforts of others; it must have the distinction of presenting your individual notions and views. Finally, the most fundamental criterion is the extent to which you are successful in accomplishing what you set out to do in your proposal. Whether it was to perform an empirical study, to develop an innovative program, or to write a critical review, your final report will be assessed in terms of your attainment of that goal.

Graduation and Commencement

The graduation and commencement exercise is a widespread and long-standing tradition. We invite you to personalize this final ritual by saying good-bye to one another as students and professors and greeting one another as professional colleagues. Savor the moment, and soon you will begin to see that the intuition that brought you to the training program in the first place is still valid. You really are a professional helper!

Summary

Your training journey is a metamorphosis from student to professional. This transformation involves much more than gaining knowledge and acquiring skills. You take on new roles, progress through developmental stages, and pass important milestones. Successfully completing this journey sets the stage for launching your career as a professional.

Resources

Several books are available that can help you with your training journey. We recommend Kerr's (2000) *Becoming a Therapist: A Workbook for Personal Exploration*. This workbook includes activities for helping you to experience therapy processes, such as empathy, change, and feelings. Other activities invite you to explore personal topics, such as enhancing your relationships, expressing your feelings, and taking care of yourself.

As its title states, Cone and Foster's (2006) second edition of *Dissertations and Theses From Start to Finish: Psychology and Related Fields* helps you plan and complete your research project from beginning to end. The authors offer useful suggestions on getting organized, finding a topic, developing a proposal, and selecting a chairperson.

Many websites offer information, advice, and access to resources. Following are a few of the best that we have discovered:

The Center for Credentialing & Education, Inc. (CCE)
http://www.cce-global.org
3 Terrace Way, Suite D
Greensboro, NC 27403–3660
336–547–0607 or fax, 336–547–0017

Council for Accreditation of Counseling and Related Educational Programs (CACREP)
www.cacrep.org
1001 North Fairfax Street, Suite 510
Alexandria, VA 22314
703–535–5990

References

American Psychological Association (2010). *Publication manual of the American Psychological Association* (6th ed.). Washington, DC: Author.

Becvar, D. S., & Becvar, R. J. (2013). *Family therapy: A systemic integration* (8th ed.). Boston, MA: Allyn & Bacon.

Cobia, D. C., Carney, J. S., Buckhalt, J. A., Middleton, R. A., Shannon, D. M., Trippany, R., & Kunkel, E. (2005). The doctoral portfolio: Centerpiece of a comprehensive system of evaluation. *Counselor Education and Supervision, 44,* 242–254.

Cone, J. D., & Foster, S. L. (2006). *Dissertations and theses from start to finish: Psychology and related fields* (2nd ed.). Washington, DC: American Psychological Association.

Duncan, B. L. (2014). *On becoming a better therapist: Evidence-based practice one client at a time* (2nd ed.). Washington, DC: American Psychological Association.

Giordano, P. J., Davis, S. F., & Licht, C. A. (Eds.). (2013). *Your graduate training in psychology: Effective strategies for success.* Thousand Oaks, CA: Sage.

Gladwell, M. (2008). *Outliers.* New York, NY: Little, Brown.

Goleman, D. (2013). *Focus: The hidden driver of excellence.* New York, NY: Harper.

Hibbard, H. (1974). *Michelangelo.* New York, NY: Harper & Row.

Kerr, D. R. (2000). *Becoming a therapist: A workbook for personal exploration.* Prospect Heights, IL: Waveland Press.

Kersting, K. (2005). First-year hurdles: Make the most of your initial year in graduate school. *gradPSYCH, 3,* 14–16.

Little, C., Packman, J., Smaby, M. H., & Maddux, C. D. (2005). The skilled counselor training model: Skill acquisition, self-assessment, and cognitive complexity. *Counselor Education and Supervision, 44,* 189–200.

McAuliffe, G., & Eriksen, K. (Eds.). (2011). *Handbook of counselor preparation: Constructivist, developmental, and experiential approaches.* Thousand Oaks, CA: Sage.

McKee, J. E., Smith, L. W., Hayes, B. G., Stewart, A., & Echterling, L. G. (1999). Rites and rituals in counselor education. *Journal of Humanistic Education, 38,* 3–12.

Norcross, J. C., & Sayette, M. A. (2014). *Insider's guide to graduate programs in clinical and counseling psychology* (Rev. ed.). New York, NY: Guilford.

Sakulku, J., & Alexander, J. (2011). The impostor phenomenon. *International Journal of Behavioral Science, 6*(1), 73–92.

Suzuki, S. (2006). *Zen mind, beginner's mind.* Boston, MA: Shambhala.

Young, M. E. (2013). *Learning the art of helping: Building blocks and techniques* (5th ed.). Upper Saddle River, NJ: Pearson.

3

Meeting Your Basic Needs

One of the oldest human needs is to have someone to wonder where you are when you don't come home at night.

—Margaret Mead

Dance like no one is watching, love like you'll never be hurt, sing like no one is listening, and live like it's heaven on earth.

—William Purkey

We receive love . . . not in proportion to our demands or sacrifices or needs, but roughly in proportion to our own capacity to love.

—Rollo May

Many cultures have addressed the question of what constitutes our basic needs. A Navajo legend (Zolbrod, 1984), for example, tells the story of the Spirit Being, who created People to share the beauty of the world with all other living things. The Spirit Being then spent a summer with the People to teach them what they needed to know to survive in the earth world. They were taught how to build shelters, hunt for game, and grow crops. However, according to the legend, the Spirit

Being's most important teachings were the songs and chants that would keep the People healthy and in harmony with their world. The lesson here for us is that our basic needs are not confined to food, clothing, and shelter. In fact, our needs for meaning, beauty, and balance are just as fundamental.

The Bread and Roses organization, founded in 1974 by Mimi Fariña, is a more recent expression of this lesson. The mission of Bread and Roses is to present free, live entertainment to institutionalized and isolated people. Well-known performers, who could demand big money for their talents, have given freely of themselves in hundreds of concerts. The organization is named after the poem written in 1911 by James Oppenheim, who was protesting the miserable conditions in the sweatshops of textile workers. It is a powerful statement about fundamental human needs to be nourished by both food and beauty.

Like those textile workers, you do not live by bread alone. Of course, you must find shelter, feed and clothe yourself, purchase books, and gather the various other accoutrements of academic life. But remember not to neglect your other needs, which will always be present. Be sure to nourish your heart during your time in graduate school. Stop to plant, nurture, give, receive, savor, and, of course, *smell* the roses.

In this chapter, we present suggestions and strategies to help you satisfy your basic needs while you are a graduate student. Contrary to the typical view, it is possible both to take care of yourself and to succeed in your training program. You do not have to sacrifice your health and well-being in order to become a counselor or therapist. In fact, dealing with your needs with flexibility, creativity, and sensitivity can actually help you to thrive as a graduate student and later in your professional career.

As you perceive them, your needs are, in part, a reflection of your own values. You have acquired these values through your parents and extended family, religious teachings, educational institutions, and the media—in short, your culture. When people move from one culture to another, they often experience culture shock. You are entering a graduate training program in which you may hear language unfamiliar to you, face situations that seem awkward, and encounter behaviors that were not typical in your own culture. You are likely to feel off balance, self-conscious, and perhaps defensive because you find this new environment slightly strange. You are entering the graduate school culture of counseling and therapy. As you become acculturated, not only will you begin to feel more comfortable with this new community, you will also carefully examine and change many of your values and assumptions about human needs.

Your Personal Hierarchy of Needs

The things that matter most must never be at the mercy of the things that matter least.

—Goethe

Any discussion of your basic needs would not be complete without referencing the classic work of Abraham Maslow. Maslow (1970) identified a hierarchy—usually depicted as a pyramid—of needs that motivate humans to strive toward self-actualization. His pyramid is one of the best-known concepts in the behavioral sciences. Beginning at the bottom of the hierarchy, people tend to satisfy the needs at each level before moving on to the next higher need area. Maslow named the following five levels of need that must be fulfilled for psychological well-being.

Physiological. These needs, which are basic for survival, include such necessities as drinking, eating, and sleeping.

Safety and security. This level of the hierarchy includes the need to be safe from physical harm and to have adequate shelter.

Love and belonging. These are the needs for affiliation with others and for both giving and receiving love.

Self-esteem. This level refers to the needs to have confidence in yourself, to feel worthy of regard, and to believe in your own value and capabilities.

Self-actualization. At the peak of the hierarchy are the self-actualization needs, which refer to the fulfillment and realization of your potential. Finding ways to express your creativity and feeling a sense of accomplishment are self-actualization needs.

More recently, researchers Taormina and Gao (2013) have developed tests to measure the needs in Maslow's hierarchy, and theorists Kenrick, Griskevicius, Neuberg, and Schaller (2010) have recommended minor renovations to the pyramid based on current evolutionary theory. Nevertheless, Maslow's hierarchy actually bears a striking resemblance to a model of the soul that Plato proposed more than 2,000 years earlier (Leahey, 2010). The lowest level is the "desiring soul" that resides in the belly and below. This level includes selfish desires for food, money, and sex. Today, you may recognize people at this level on many popular daytime talk shows or court programs.

The next level up is the "spirited soul," which resides in the chest. This level of soul is motivated by fame and glory, exemplified today by professional athletes, politicians, or movie stars. The highest form of soul is the "rational soul," centered in the head, which seeks the Good and True, even at the expense of lower desires. People who have achieved this highest level are our spiritual leaders, mentors, and sages.

Our reason for presenting Plato's model is not merely to put Maslow's theory in an historical context. Instead, we offer it because Plato emphasized a vital point that has been lost in most discussions of Maslow's hierarchy of needs. Although Plato's model was certainly inaccurate in its understanding of human physiology, he did hit the mark regarding our essential human capacity to *choose* what desires we fulfill, to arrange our own personal hierarchy that reflects our fundamental values. We are not condemned to remain at the lower levels merely because those needs are not currently being met. Instead, we can decide to strive for higher values—to forgo satisfying all our lower needs as we reach for the stars.

In this chapter, you will explore how you can meet your physiological and safety needs by finding and creating a home, investigating options for financial assistance, and maintaining your physical wellness (Myers, Mobley, & Booth, 2003). However, Plato's emphasis on choice can alert you to opportunities for thriving even in times of scarcity. Therefore, we discuss how you can fulfill your self-actualization needs in spite of other deprivations in your life. Let's begin by exploring ways in which you can not only fulfill your needs but also thrive in this unfamiliar culture.

A Constant Challenge

Ellen's Story

Meeting basic needs is a constant challenge! I find I do well for some time, but then I look up and realize I've neglected them again. I have trouble remembering to take time for myself. With a husband, kids, and a job, it is easy for me to feel like school is "my time." Even though it's rewarding, it is not the same as having time to myself for meditation, reflection, journaling, or just having fun! My goal is to create some time for ME every day— some days it will be ten minutes, other days an hour.

The other basic need that I often neglect is getting enough sleep. I run close to empty most days of the week. I have come to realize that I often

(Continued)

(Continued)

use my fatigue as an excuse—for yelling at my kids, for saying "No" to things, for not being intimate with my husband, and for having an extra glass of wine at night to unwind. I think I have become addicted to the cycle of being exhausted, getting one or two nights of good sleep, then feeling so good I stay up late and begin again.

I realize as I write this that so much of what counseling is about is getting our basic needs met: needs like intimacy and love. I know that having those needs met for me is difficult when I am sleep deprived and leaving no time for myself. When I am well rested and deeply connected with myself, I am in a good place to give and receive love and to create the kind of relationships I want in my life—relationships that I need to be a healthy, fulfilled person.

Shirley MacLaine (2000) wrote an account of walking the Santiago de Compostela Camino, a grueling 500-mile pilgrimage across northern Spain that people have undertaken for centuries. Like a true pilgrim, MacLaine traveled alone on her month-long journey and took only the necessities she could carry in her backpack. She discovered that she needed little more beyond water, good shoes, and a floppy hat. By discarding all the distracting unessentials that can clutter one's life and embarking on a demanding quest, she gained an important new perspective.

In graduate school, you are traveling on rough terrain, and as MacLaine's pilgrimage illustrates, you need to decide what is truly essential. You may find that some seemingly pressing needs will fade or even disappear. You may be a little confused and perhaps feel pressured—out of sheer force of habit—to respond to old needs. At the very least, you are likely to be uncomfortable at first, so consider reframing this situation as an invitation to explore your fundamental motivations and values in life. You see, we don't notice when our needs are met. It is only when we believe our needs are not satisfied that we are motivated to reflect, decide, and act.

Basic Needs and Self-Actualization

Life is easier to take than you think; all that is necessary is to accept the impossible, do without the indispensable, and bear the intolerable.

—Kathleen Norris

In Ellen's story, she engaged in two very important steps toward self-actualization: taking time to identify just what is important to her and then finding ways to address those basic needs. What needs are truly essential to her? How can she organize her day to satisfy them? Most students, faculty, and staff—in fact, most people—face similar challenges in trying to balance needs and demands in their daily lives (Licht, 2012). At first, juggling all your family commitments, personal needs, and graduate school requirements can seem utterly hopeless.

Remember the old riddle about a farmer who had to figure out how to safely transport a fox, a chicken, and a sack of grain to an island? The farmer could only take one of them at a time in a small boat. However, the fox couldn't be left alone with the chicken because the fox would eat it. By the same token, the chicken couldn't be left alone with the grain. The farmer solved the problem by deploying resources and manipulating the conditions in a creative way. How did the farmer resolve this dilemma? (One answer to the riddle appears at the end of the chapter.)

Like the farmer in the riddle, you face a similar conundrum of meeting basic needs, personal obligations, and training demands. Leading a reasonably fulfilling life while learning to be a counselor or therapist requires ingenuity, quick wits, and lots of energy. This balancing act is challenging enough, but the idea of reaching the self-actualizing needs at the highest rung seems like a catch-22. You entered into training to realize your potential, but the stresses and deprivations inherent in your life as an impoverished graduate student seem to make scaling the pyramid impossible.

A quick reading of Maslow may lead you to assume that focusing on self-actualization needs is achievable only when you are well-off financially and relatively stress free. Like caviar, self-actualization may seem to be a delicacy that only the fortunate and affluent can afford to experience. How in the world can graduate students—in debt up to their ears with student loans, living in austere accommodations, and trying to cut corners every which way they can—seek self-actualization? And what about people who are returning to school after rearing their children or after a financially successful career? Aren't they moving *down* several rungs?

Maslow (1962) himself criticized the simplistic interpretation that sees personal growth as merely "progression toward self-actualization in which the basic needs are completely gratified, one by one, before the next higher need emerges" (p. 24). As Plato pointed out, humans are not slaves to their desires. We can choose to seek self-actualization even though our pursuit may deprive us of basic comforts, take away our financial security, and threaten our personal safety.

EXERCISE 3.1 Take That Job And . . .

A Guided Fantasy Exercise

Imagine that instead of going to graduate school for the next few years, you accepted a job that would offer a huge salary, excellent benefits, a beautiful home, job security, a close-knit group of colleagues, and plenty of recognition for your accomplishments at work. In short, this job would satisfy every conceivable physiological, safety and security, belonging, and self-esteem need. The only catch is that you could not fulfill your personal potential for self-actualization.

As you consider this possibility, write about the needs you would be sacrificing.

_____

_____

_____

_____

_____

Now, write how you plan to ensure that you will address these self-actualization needs in your training.

_____

_____

_____

_____

_____

_____

Conducting a Needs Inventory

The hardest thing to learn in life is which bridge to cross and which to burn.

—David Russell

Below, Renee shares her story of leaving a successful career and enrolling in a training program in which she had to live away from her home and family several days a week. In her story, she conducts an informal needs inventory for herself.

Touch the Sun

Renee's Story

When tackling this portion of my training journey, I first had to identify what my basic needs were. I cheated a little and I borrowed my hierarchy of needs from Maslow, as he seemed to have the right idea. He may not be basic enough for this point in my life, though.

According to my mother and my kids, I am not doing a good job meeting physiological needs. Sleep would indeed be a wonderful thing, but I haven't figured out how to work that in as of yet.

A need for safety has become very important. My family home is in a nice residential area with regularly spaced signs proclaiming "Neighborhood Watch in Effect." While at school, I try to handle my fear of living alone by leaving lots of lights on.

Being part of a family fulfilled my belonging and love needs. However, right now it seems like distance doesn't make the heart grow fonder—it just makes communication harder. My husband and I are maintaining a long-distance relationship, and we're sure our love can stand the test of time, as the songs say. But I really miss him and my family.

I find I need a social circle here, too. Friendships are beginning to develop, as I tentatively move past the point of "socialized" hellos into the more meaningful depths of knowing someone.

I am working on feeling competent, independent, successful, respected, and worthwhile in order to claim good self-esteem. At the moment, though, I feel I have lost my sense of self, and because I am not successfully satisfying the preceding needs, I have to fall short somewhere. Can a "high-maintenance, emotionally needy" person even hope to reach this goal?

Without successfully attaining the needs for self-esteem, I won't even begin to comment on where I stand with self-actualization. Isn't that the thing we're all supposed to be striving for, anyway? I'd hate to touch the sun too soon.

As you read Renee's story, with what parts did you find yourself identifying? Did you notice that Renee was dealing with needs at several different levels? Assessing your needs and taking action to address them are both effective methods of coping. But what about thriving? Renee suggested that she cannot address self-actualization needs until she has met her self-esteem needs. What do you think? Would Renee be "touching the sun" too soon? How could Renee use her struggle to help her thrive in her training?

Dealing with the challenges of satisfying your personal needs in graduate school can actually enhance your training in two fundamental ways. First, your own strivings are far better than "book knowledge" in helping you to understand and appreciate the struggles that people face in their lives. So as you try to balance your needs, remain aware of your fatigue, yearnings, and sense of deprivation. These experiences can help you in building an empathic bridge to your clients, who may be seeking counseling to deal with different concerns but who are also struggling. Second, your own successful endeavors to live a full and balanced life can help remind you of the perseverance, creativity, and resilience that your clients have. Even though you have felt overwhelmed at times, you have discovered personal strengths and social resources that have helped you through these difficulties. With your assistance, your clients can also uncover their own hidden abilities and sources of support.

If you stay alert for learning opportunities, you are likely to gain surprising insights regarding your needs. For example, students conducting a parenting group often found that the session they had prepared for the group contained a valuable lesson for themselves, too. The following is one experiential exercise that routinely helped the counseling student group leaders as much as it did the parent members. One student who completed this exercise found, to her dismay, that decorating the sea star was the most fun she had had in a long time. She realized that she had been neglecting her mental need to engage in creative activities. By the way, you can vary this activity to use with a couple or family in counseling. For example, you can encourage them to first come up with a thriving list completely unrestricted by finances, time, family, or work constraints. After the list is generated, they can look over the options and circle ones they can help each other to do, given their current circumstances.

EXERCISE 3.2 The Sea Star

A Balancing Exercise

By watching the sea star, or starfish, you can learn a lesson on being responsive to your needs. The sea star has five distinct arms that work together gracefully. Even if an appendage breaks off, the sea star regenerates its lost arm to ensure that it can thrive in its environment. Your thriving needs, like the sea star's arms, can work together in harmony, but some of your "arms" may be better developed than others. In fact, most people are able to satisfy certain needs more successfully than other needs. This exercise reminds you of the different types of needs and how you can address each of them.

On a large sheet of newsprint, use markers or crayons to draw a sea star and label each of the five arms with one of the thriving needs: physical, mental, emotional, relational, and spiritual. Consider how well you are currently fulfilling these thriving needs. Draw a line somewhere on each arm to reflect your satisfaction with that particular need—the larger the area within that arm, the greater your fulfillment. Your sea star figure will now have a line at some point across each of its five arms.

Now, using the area that you have set aside in each arm, draw the ways that you are meeting that need. The more you are fulfilling a certain need, the more room you have to draw. Feel free to decorate each area however you would like. For example, you might draw certain people, activities, or symbols to portray how you thrive in that area.

You may be surprised at how successfully you are satisfying some needs and how little you are attending to others. What did you discover about the balance of your thriving needs?

Crafting a Balanced Life

> Happiness is not a state to arrive at, but a manner of traveling.
>
> —Margaret Lee Runbeck

A cow is a ruminative animal because it chews its cud but gains no nourishment from the process. When you ruminate, you may obsess or worry for hours on end but gain no benefit from this activity. Well, if you are a ruminator, then it is time to put aside the ways of the cow and bring balance to your life. Fully commit yourself to the task of the moment, but when you have completed it, then set it aside. Returning to reflect on your work, pondering its meaning, and sorting through it to find nuggets of success can certainly be nourishing. However, take care not to become so caught up in your work that you can never set it aside and just *be*.

In another ancient Navajo story (Duncan & Begay, 1996), when Spider Woman gave Weaving Woman her ability to weave, she also instructed her to walk the Middle Way by keeping her life in balance. Weaving Woman was able to maintain this harmony at first, but then she began to weave night and day until she collapsed, unable to move or speak. She had woven her spirit into her work and could not escape. Like Weaving Woman, you may be learning important skills but may also be having a very difficult time keeping your life in balance. Regularly pulling "all-nighters," ignoring relationships, and never taking any breaks from work means that you are losing yourself in the role of a student. Here is how Beth achieved a satisfying balance and avoided weaving herself into her work.

We Have Nothing to Fear But . . .

Beth's Story

Recently, I sat down and wrote about my greatest fear. I was afraid that as a student, mother, wife, teacher, daughter, and friend, I couldn't balance all my roles and responsibilities. I worried that my children would suffer. I was the one who stayed home from my part-time job when they were sick. My part-time job required enormous energy and frequent attendance at meetings. Would there be enough time? My marriage was shaky at best. How much would it suffer? How would I take care of everything? How would I take care of me? Finally, I told myself that if I couldn't keep a healthy balance, I could quit graduate school. Telling myself that it's okay to stop my training if it wasn't working calmed me.

Beth found that reminding herself that she had the power to bring balance to her life helped her gain a sense of peace. Feeling overwhelmed by unmet needs is a concern that you will hear from your clients, fellow students, and significant others. Why can it seem so challenging to create a balance, to satisfy all these needs? Using your list from the earlier sea star exercise may provide a different perspective.

EXERCISE 3.3 Your Needs in Context

A Systemic Exercise

On a regular sheet of paper, draw three small sea stars. One of the stars represents you, so quickly draw a simple, miniature version of your previous star by just adding the lines indicating how well you are satisfying the five thriving needs: physical, mental, emotional, relational, and spiritual.

Now select two people who have a deep emotional connection to you. You may choose a partner, family member, best friend, or roommate. Put their names at the top of the other stars and, using your best guesses, draw lines to reflect to what extent they are meeting their thriving needs.

Draw walls and a roof around the three stars to enclose them in a single house. If you like, you can add other details and decorations to make it more a home. This picture illustrates two important points. First, meeting your needs can sometimes feel overwhelming because you live under the same emotional roof with relatives, friends, and colleagues who have their own needs to address, too. In what ways do their unmet needs complicate your life? At the same time, your picture also portrays the second important point—these people are also excellent resources! You cannot achieve self-actualization by yourself. In fact, you can join with others synergistically to fulfill many of your thriving needs. How can these people help you?

Pathways to Balance

> Paint as you like and die happy.
>
> —Henry Miller

So what can you do? A helpful psychological construct to use in situations such as yours is termed *equifinality*. Equifinality means that there are multiple pathways to the same end. Beth's pathway was to deliberately acknowledge that attending graduate school was a choice to which, for the present, she was saying "Yes." At some time in the future, she may also choose to say "No."

Another pathway to achieving balance is described in the conclusion of the legend of Weaving Woman. According to the story, to free the spirit of Weaving Woman from her work, Spider Woman made the blanket she had woven less perfect. By pulling out a thread, Spider Woman created a pathway for Weaving Woman's spirit to leave the blanket and return to her. Weaving Woman thankfully said she had learned her lesson and began to teach others the importance of not trying to make their weavings perfect. She taught them how to make spirit trails in their weavings so their spirits would not be trapped in their work.

Weaving Woman learned to meaningfully engage in the work of creating beauty, but not at the risk of losing herself in the process. You may notice some similar themes between Weaving Woman's story and your own life. Do you try to make your work absolutely perfect? Who do you ask for help when you feel you may be getting trapped? Who lets you know when you are "weaving" too much?

As you continue to enter the culture of counseling and learn more about yourself, you can periodically conduct an inventory of your needs and, using all of who you are and what you know, create pathways to a more meaningful and satisfying life. In the next section, we discuss the base from which you will operate—your home.

Housing

> Home is where the heart is and hence is a moveable feast.
>
> —Angela Carter

Finding affordable and suitable housing can be a daunting task. You may be tempted to rush this process, but take time to reflect on all the needs you want to address by the seemingly straightforward task of obtaining housing. Are you concerned with safety, convenience to the university, proximity to good elementary schools, or availability of public transportation? Do you prefer to have a roommate? Do you want to keep a pet? What values and meanings are embedded in your selection of a home?

Much like producing a research paper, finding housing requires that you first frame your question and then collect data to answer it. In this case, the data collection includes finding listings from the local and university newspapers, the university housing office, other students, or real estate agents. You may find that taking this step is an opportunity to become acquainted with helpful resources in the university and larger community.

Most universities have an office designated to assist students in finding housing. The office typically provides rental information, housing guides, bus schedules, and student directories. Like a chamber of commerce, the office can assist you with other aspects of settling in the area, such as finding grocery stores and places for recreation. Find out if the office can help you with potential housing concerns, such as lease difficulties, landlord conflicts, parking limitations, and transportation problems. Many universities also have separate housing available to graduate students. Although living in graduate student housing offers some conveniences, you may want to explore other possibilities.

For example, using information from the off-campus housing office and the advertisements in the local newspaper, Jocelyn and Michael set out to find an apartment that was not "a stack of red bricks that looked like one big red brick." Unfortunately, they discovered that the community's view of students—at least the typical landlord's view—was very negative. They began to feel like second-class citizens. They found their predicament further compounded by their commitment to find a place that would accept them and their three cats. As Jocelyn said, "Evidently, adding a third cat puts you in the 'Crazy Cat Person' category." For Jocelyn and Michael, however, their pets helped them keep a sense of balance in their academic lives.

Other potential sources of housing information for you are your program adviser, peer mentor, and fellow students. They can help you become settled by answering your questions not only about housing but also about the university and the surrounding community in general. They can provide support, encouragement, and some very helpful tips about how to create your base of operations.

After you have collected enough data, you are off to the field to conduct the applied portion of your research project—finding the locations. Once again, equifinality can be a useful idea to keep in mind, because there are many paths to the same end. The following story illustrates a rather casual approach to finding a new home.

Adventures in Subsidized Housing Land

Chris's Story

Like most beginning grad students, I needed to visit my school's community well before classes started in order to secure someplace to live. This was not so easy in that I knew nothing of the town. I didn't know where the shortcuts to school were, where the grocery stores hid, where the fast-food joints nested, or where to get a Slurpee at 3:00 in the morning.

I had very specific requirements for the apartment itself. These included walls, floors, and if at all possible, a ceiling. In other words, I wasn't choosy. I figured I'd be spending a lot of time up at school, so my housing only needed to be comfortable enough for me. So it all came down to cash. I took the cheapest place.

Taking the cheapest place wasn't a bad idea—it's just that there were certain tradeoffs. One was the roommates I got—hundreds and probably thousands of little six-legged tenants. Now I have lived in some rundown places, and I'm okay with that, but marauding armies of roaches were a new experience for me.

(Continued)

(Continued)

Fortunately, the other apartment dwellers (the human ones) are wonderfully diverse—ethnically, racially, and linguistically. As a member of just about every privileged majority there is, I find myself in an interesting position. Here I am, pursuing an advanced degree, while living with marginalized folks who are struggling to get by.

By living where he did, Chris discovered the striking and vast inequalities in the everyday worlds of his neighbors—an essential lesson for a student of human strivings, challenges, and resilience.

As you make your own decisions about housing, consider what needs your home may help to satisfy. Attachment theory emphasizes the importance of having a secure base from which to explore the world and a safe haven to return to for comfort and support (Marvin, Cooper, Hoffman, & Powell, 2002). Such a deep and abiding relationship with someone who is emotionally available and responsive to your needs is an essential anchor in our lives. Although early attachment theory focused on the importance of the bond between infants and their caregivers, current proponents of attachment theory have extended the construct across the entire life span. The protective influence of having a secure base and safe haven is now considered a prominent factor, similar to the importance of Maslow's needs, for people of all ages.

A primary benefit of this relationship—your home base—is that it helps you successfully explore your surroundings. It is natural to feel both apprehensive and excited when you are in a new setting and living among unfamiliar people. You may typically cope with the anxiety by using some combination of defenses: withdrawing into isolation, retreating to your secure base, or "overexploring" the new environment. When you were a freshman in college, you probably observed students who resorted to these defenses. For example, they may have attended classes, but then they seemed to evaporate into thin air. Other students were homesick and scurried home whenever possible. And then there were the classmates who were always frantically zipping everywhere around campus.

These defensive strategies, however, are neither satisfying nor, in the long run, successful in fulfilling your needs for safety or belonging. Instead, you can make time to deliberately connect with the people who can provide you with your base for emotional security. By maintaining a firm foundation in those relationships, you will be better able to explore and keep your bearings as you investigate and build your new community.

Jocelyn and Michael helped incorporate their established secure base into their new surroundings in a number of ways. For example, they regularly e-mailed friends and relatives with news about their discoveries, mishaps, and adventures in adjusting to their new lives as graduate students. They also relied on generous doses of humor. As transplants from the East Coast to the Midwest, Jocelyn once commented to Michael about driving: "Today, I used my turn signal and someone actually made an opening in traffic so I could get over! Isn't that a sign of weakness where we come from?" They found a farmer's market and made a ritual of going there every Saturday morning and of always frequenting the same little coffee shop.

By taking similar steps to preserve your secure base and build your new community, you are more likely to create a comfortable place—both physically and psychologically—for yourself in graduate school. Give yourself some time to relish your new surroundings and reflect on the changes.

Giving Up City Life to Fit Into a Small Town

Dara's Story

My car's license plate is the only reminder of the city life that I left behind to do my doctoral training in a small community, where everyone's paths cross each other's every day. My faculty adviser's office is next door to mine. One of my student colleagues is seeing the same therapist that I am. People's lives overlap so much here that the thought keeps crossing my mind, "What ever happened to the idea of six degrees of separation?"

Growing up in L.A., it would have been a miracle to drive from one side of town to the other in less than 10 minutes, but it's an everyday experience here—and that's with what the locals call "traffic." It would have been extraordinary if all your L.A. friends knew what you did last night—before you even woke up in the morning. Yet it's commonplace for everything to be everybody's business in this town. And nobody in L.A. ever asked me with incredulity, "Why did you ever move to *this* place?" But I get that question all the time in my new community, where the elegant restaurant is Cracker Barrel and chipped beef is considered exotic food. My Jewish values feel so out of place—the bakery here sells only two challahs a week.

(Continued)

(Continued)

As a city transplant in a small town, I have discovered that it really helps to receive care packages of familiar foods. In my apartment, I have hung pictures of my favorite city scenes as comforting reminders. I even have a screen saver on my computer showing different sights in L.A. I stay connected to my friends back at home. Regularly, I make excursions several hours away from here for a dose of the big city life. And finally, I share my culture—my favorite dishes, music, and movies—with my new friends here.

EXERCISE 3.4 It Takes a Community

An Exercise in Imagination

You have heard the African proverb, "It takes a village to raise a child." Well, it also takes a community to support a thriving graduate student. Because your needs do not remain static during graduate school, it is helpful to spend some time periodically envisioning the ideal community setting for you to continue your development.

Build an imaginary community that would fulfill your needs. Where would you be living? In a house or an apartment? With or without a roommate? Who and what else would be in your neighborhood? What cultures would be represented? What family configurations would be present? Would there be a place of worship? A park, woods, or playground? A vegetarian restaurant? Is the setting urban or rural?

List these essential elements or draw a picture of this ideal community. What characteristics of your make-believe community exist already for you? If they do not exist wholly, are there parts you recognize? How can you build your community in reality? Who will you ask to help?

Financial Assistance

Spare no expense to save money on this one.

—Samuel Goldwyn

Lack of money is no obstacle. Lack of an idea is an obstacle.

—Ken Hakuta

Let's face it—graduate school is expensive. As you already know, tuition, fees, living expenses, and educational supplies present an enormous burden. No matter how much financial assistance you have been able to arrange so far, you are still likely leading a monastic lifestyle as a graduate student. As Hoskins (2000) urged, "Ask yourself, how much macaroni and cheese do I want to eat for the next three to five years?" (p. 32). It is important to realize that the ways in which you are addressing your financial needs can have an impact on your progress through the program. For example, are you working while you are attending graduate school? How is your job affecting your available study time or commitment to your training? Are you borrowing or using funds from family members? How do these arrangements affect your relationships?

The good news is that throughout your graduate education, it is likely that you will be encountering additional opportunities for financial assistance, such as grants, scholarships, fellowships, assistantships, and loans. Keep an eye out for announcements regarding these opportunities. Below we offer brief descriptions of these various sources of aid.

Grants, Scholarships, and Fellowships. These awards may be given on the basis of need, merit, or membership in a targeted group. They are the most preferred type of financial assistance because they do not have to be repaid. Grants may be sponsored by the government or private organizations and can often be used to cover not only tuition but also research, travel, or service project expenses. Scholarships, which may take the form of one-time or annual payments, are typically given in recognition of academic excellence or offered to meet financial needs or awarded as prizes in competitions involving the submission of essays or other projects. Fellowships for graduate students have become rare in recent years but can involve stipends for up to several years.

You can be resourceful by looking for these forms of financial support from professional organizations and service organizations, such as the Kiwanis. The American Counseling Association, for example, offers a scholarship award to a graduate student who wins its annual essay competition. Assistance is sometimes available if you plan to work in particular areas of specialization, such as autism or dementia.

Assistantships. Graduate assistantships usually include both coverage of your tuition and a stipend. You receive this financial assistance in exchange for working about 15 to 20 hours a week during the academic year. To be eligible for an assistantship, you are required to carry a specific number of credit hours and to be enrolled in a degree program. Assistantships are generally available in your department, as well as through grants, other academic programs, and services across the campus.

Assistantship responsibilities are quite varied and can range from collecting and coding research data, grading undergraduate papers, providing counseling services, and assisting with laboratory assignments to photocopying and filing. You may qualify for a teaching, research, or clinical assistantship if you meet specific qualifications. With a teaching assistantship, you may be responsible for teaching an undergraduate class or helping a faculty member with specific course responsibilities. With a research assistantship, you may be interviewing participants, gathering data, analyzing results, and carrying out countless clerical duties involved in a grant-funded study. With a clinical assistantship, you may be providing supervision, assessment, and counseling services at a university-based mental health center.

If you are seeking an assistantship, contact your university's financial aid office or the graduate office manager of your department. Most assistantships are 1-year appointments, so you will probably need to apply each year that you wish to obtain this form of financial assistance. If you did not receive an assistantship your first year, don't give up! You may be more qualified for one as an advanced student.

Competition for assistantships is often keen, so there are no guarantees that you will be offered one. Graduate school offices report that depending on funding, there may be three times as many graduate applicants as there are assistantships. These odds may seem tough, but there are some steps you can take to improve your chances:

- *Take care of the basics.* Just like the lottery, you have to play to win. The sooner you complete (and return!) the application form, the better your chances. Also, always make copies of the paperwork you submit, noting dates and to whom it was submitted. You will want to be able to construct a "paper trail" to ensure that your application has not been delayed anywhere.
- *Know how the system works.* Each university will have its own administrative network for conferring assistantships. Some universities have a single clearinghouse; others have more decentralized operations, in which programs operate as separate fiefdoms, with dramatically different application procedures for assistantships. Take care to learn the system and play by its rules.
- *Let people know.* Make certain that your program director, faculty adviser, and student mentor know of your interest in obtaining an assistantship. Ask for their advice and suggestions. While you're at it, give them your e-mail address so they can contact you easily if they hear of an opportunity.

- *Highlight your skills.* The application forms for assistantships typically ask you to list your skills. Keep in mind that computer, research, and people skills are in demand, especially for nonacademic departments.
- *Remember that neatness does count.* Yes, your elementary teachers were right, so be careful when filling out the application materials. People will assume that the care you show on these documents indicates the care that you would take with job assignments.
- *Be persistent.* Faculty and staff members are busy people, so it is important for you to be persistent and not be afraid to ask questions about graduate assistantships.

Student Loans. Financing graduate education with a student loan is the most commonly used pathway for students in the helping professions. If you are considering this option, there are many resources that can assist you in finding and evaluating potential loan sources (Leider & Leider, 2011). Again, your university's financial aid office is an excellent source of information about federal loans. A major source of financial assistance is the Federal Stafford Loan, both subsidized and unsubsidized. You begin the application process by completing and submitting a Free Application for Federal Student Aid (FAFSA) online at *www.fafsa.ed.gov/*

During this process, there are several time-saving strategies you can follow. First, before you begin to complete the online form, gather the documents you need, such as Social Security number, driver's license, income tax return, bank statements, and investment records. Second, print a hard copy of the FAFSA on the Web Worksheet. You then can write in your answers before transferring the information to FAFSA online. Third, speed up the process by using a PIN (personal identification number) to sign your application electronically. If you have a valid e-mail address, you can apply for a PIN. It takes up to three days to obtain a PIN electronically instead of the 10 days it could take a signature page to be processed through the mail. Fourth, check your eligibility for federal student aid. Read carefully the requirements and restrictions regarding assistance. Finally, apply as early as possible, beginning January 1 of each year.

After you have submitted your FAFSA electronically, the Department of Education will process your application and send you a Student Aid Report (SAR). Your school will also receive an electronic copy of your SAR. You should review this report, make any necessary corrections, and return it to the financial aid office as quickly as possible. The financial aid office staff reviews the SAR to determine your eligibility for aid and notifies you of its determination. Need is based on a hypothetical student budget, minus any family contribution, that the financial aid office calculates on a yearly basis.

If you qualify, you then receive the loan application form. You should complete the application and return it immediately.

If you are an incoming student or have taken a summer class at another school, you also can facilitate the process by arranging for your transcripts to be sent to the university's financial aid office rather than waiting for the office to request the records. You will help speed up the process if you meet the deadlines for each stage.

One routine interruption of the procedure is the need to verify tax records. Some applicants are chosen at random for verification, and the financial aid office is then required to look at all their tax forms for the past year. If you are chosen for verification, simply provide the information requested. Typically, you are asked to present a signed tax form. If your need is great enough, you may be offered a work-study job that you can choose to accept or decline. Other possible funding sources are graduate scholarships or fellowships.

One final point about financial assistance: Research has consistently identified the presence of a dedicated friend or determined advocate as a crucial contributor to an individual's resilience. Give yourself permission to rely on the help of others as you seek financial assistance, decipher directions on forms, and complete the process. Because financial assistance is an area that can change quickly, we urge you to use the Internet resources listed at the end of the chapter.

Wellness

> I'm not into working out. My philosophy: No pain, no pain.
>
> —Carol Leifer

> Leisure time is that five or six hours when you sleep at night.
>
> —George Allen

The dominant Western culture spends a great deal of time giving you messages about how to take better care of your body, how to eat healthier foods, and how to be more physically fit. Unfortunately, many of these messages are driven by the desire to promote corporate profits, not personal wellness. The emerging field of health psychology is reporting important findings about the relationship between your physical and mental well-being. Indeed, many of the results support a more traditionally Eastern concept of the wholeness of yourself.

Like most people, you probably know a lot more about healthy exercise and nutrition than you put into practice. Graduate students in counseling generally report high levels of wellness (Lambie, Smith, & Ieva, 2009), but when you take on more and more commitments in your training, you may find yourself tempted to abandon some habits that promote physical well-being. Eating poorly, sleeping fewer hours, and exercising little can quickly become your lifestyle as a graduate student. As one student commented, "Sure, I drink plenty of water every day—if Dr. Pepper, Mountain Dew, and coffee count. And, yes, I also eat a well-balanced diet from the basic food groups—donuts from the round group, tortilla chips from the triangle group, and candy bars from the rectangle group."

As you consider your nutritional and activity needs, reflect on the meaning that eating well and exercising have for you. Here are a few questions to get you started: What messages did you receive about food when you were growing up? In what ways was food part of family and community celebrations? Did you associate nurturance and comfort with food? Did you worry that there was not enough food for everyone? Was finishing your plate an expectation? Why? What is the relationship between stress and eating for you? Is feeding other people a demonstration of your love?

What does fitness and activity mean to you? What were the models in your family for eating and exercising? Were there gender-related messages about fitness? What messages do you believe about your self-esteem and your wellness? From your spiritual perspective, how do you view the human body? After you have reflected on these questions, you can come to a deeper appreciation of the regenerative power of eating well and the exhilaration of engaging in physical exertion.

Another useful perspective for looking at possible alterations in your lifestyle is that of the transtheoretical model of change (Prochaska, Norcross, & DiClemente, 2013). Counselors and therapists have focused on the change process that clients go through, but in this chapter, the focus in on *you*. The changes you will experience in your training and throughout your career will not be time-limited events, but ongoing processes involving five important stages. *Precontemplation* is the first stage of change and, at this point, you do not intend to take any action in this particular area of your life. Of course, the reason for this inertia may be due to lack of information, sense of futility, denial, or fear. As your consciousness is raised, you enter the second stage of *contemplation,* in which you begin to consider making a significant alteration. However, you also feel ambivalent about this new and threatening prospect. In fact, you may feel stuck as you constantly go over the pros and cons of this possible change, procrastinating and delaying any real or meaningful action. *Preparation* is the third change. At this point, you have made a significant shift in your thinking. You have overcome the barriers of resistance and now truly believe that change is possible. Fourth, you engage in *action* by performing the specific, detailed, and overt modifications in your day-to-day life-style. Finally, *maintenance* involves sustaining the new action and handling successfully the inevitable relapses that you encounter in any significant change. As you emerge from this change process, you have now entered into a new reality and have become a transformed self.

What does this model mean for you? Well, it's a great way for you to accelerate the momentum of the change process whenever you discover that your consciousness has been raised. For example, as you read and hear more about physical and psychological well-being, you may begin to contemplate a variety of changes in your lifestyle, such as better nutrition, more exercise, more fulfilling relationships, or more conscientious personal health care. Whatever alterations you consider, you can use this model to facilitate the change process. You can overcome your resistance by making plans, becoming energized, enlisting the help of others, and readying yourself for this transformation.

One counseling student, realizing that she was compromising her physical well-being, developed a plan. "I made an agreement with myself that I would get at least three hours of exercise a week to release stress, feel better about myself, and fit into my clothes again. My new schedule book would have that workout time in it" (Belcastro, 2000, p. 12). Another student, Martin, entered graduate school with many healthy practices already in place. He had attained a black belt in karate and was extremely careful to protect his practice time. After awhile, his classmates learned to refrain from complaining about being tired in front of him because they knew he would tell them, "You must not be exercising enough!" It was particularly irritating to hear his words because they knew he was right.

Kicking and Sleeping

Martin's Story

Even though I would like to have maintained a more consistent exercise regimen than I have since entering the training program, I regularly do a Tae Bo routine, a kind of kickboxing/dance-workout video. I make sure to do this whenever I feel stressed and have a need for physical activity. Also, in spite of my demanding schedule, I try to get at least eight hours of sleep a night. Getting a good amount of sleep replenishes my internal drive to tackle the demands and events of the upcoming day.

Finding and Creating Perspective

Compared to what we ought to be, we are only half awake.

—William James

Martin's observation above is consistently supported in the research literature. If you take good care of meeting your physiological needs, you have more energy to use for other pursuits. You may heartily agree but believe that you just can't find the time for exercise. Stephen Covey (1989) offered a wonderful example to illustrate the fallacy of not making the time to satisfy your wellness needs. Imagine that as you are taking a stroll in the woods, you encounter a person laboring frenetically to saw down a tree. The person, who's sweaty and haggard, is obviously worn out but has barely made a scratch in the tree after sawing for hours. Trying to be helpful, you suggest that if the person stopped and sharpened the saw, the work would go much quicker. But the person protests, "I don't have time to sharpen the saw. . . . I'm too busy sawing" (p. 287).

Covey's point is that we truly do not have the time to *not* eat well and exercise. Because we know these are very important activities, why do we often systematically neglect them? He believed it is because we fool ourselves into thinking that the consequences of not fulfilling wellness needs are neither immediate nor significant. We know enough to do the right thing, but we need some help, as the Nike commercials encourage us, to "just do it."

The Road From Orange Crackers to Rice

Anne's Story

I had limited success in eating healthy meals as a graduate student. Nearly every day at lunch, for the better part of three years, I ate frozen raspberry yogurt ("You mean ice cream," a nutritionist finally told me) and those peanut butter and bright orange cracker sandwiches. Fortunately, my body was in good enough health to somehow withstand this simultaneous neglect and assault. My weak defense was that the nearby little grill did not have vegetarian entrees.

What finally helped me was to link my nutritional and exercise needs to my need for belonging. I now enjoy lunch with friends and make sure I eat a healthy meal. I take regular walks with my neighbor. Actually, I *talk* with my neighbor and we move while we do it. The other meaningful context is related to my role as a mother. It is important to me that my children develop good health habits. I know my children will be influenced by what they see me do in these areas, for better or worse.

As you reflect on your needs and ponder their meaning for you, keep in mind that you are not alone. Linking with others to meet your needs can lead not only to good nutrition and exercise but also to good company. By addressing more than one area of need, you increase your thriving quotient (TQ) in ways that are both gratifying and enduring.

These "good habits" are similar to informal rituals observed in healthy families. Research informs us that having meaningful rituals in our lives provides a sense of cohesiveness and security (Imber-Black & Roberts, 2004). For example, a group of male graduate students decided to meet each Sunday to enjoy a meal together. First, the eating was paired with watching sports, a dominant interest for them in their pre-graduate school lives. Over time, they regularly added a study component to their shared meal. Later, their Sunday ritual evolved into an informal men's support group—with good food.

EXERCISE 3.5 I'll Have the Combo

Meeting Multiple Needs

Think over Maslow's hierarchy of needs and jot down some activities that you want to do that correspond with the types of needs. Look for activities that might naturally combine to meet several needs simultaneously.

For example, to address your safety and security needs, you may want to learn self-defense. You could enroll in a course that would teach you defensive skills, provide an excellent workout, and offer opportunities for developing new friendships. Looking at the need to belong, you might find a camping or hiking club or a gourmet cooking club that could simultaneously address wellness and friendship needs. In addressing self-esteem and self-actualization needs, you might pair yoga, tai chi, or dance instruction with your exercise routine.

_____

_____

_____

_____

_____

Sometimes you hear another perspective and it immediately rings a bell. One student related that the most centering and helpful advice from her adviser was to picture the span of her entire life and then make a ratio of how much time she would actually spend in graduate school—an intense but relatively small part. The reminder helped this student put the challenges of school in a better frame. Like dental work, graduate school does not last forever—and reminding yourself that an ordeal is temporary can make it endurable. You can then focus on how you can use this limited experience to forge a lifestyle of balance, beauty, and well-being.

Although you may focus more energy on satisfying safety and belonging needs at the start of graduate school, you'll find it helpful to regularly tend to these needs throughout your training. For example, you may focus on financial aid more at the beginning, but you may find that additional support is available later for specific activities, such as funding designated for research or presentations at professional conferences. In the same manner, as you become more familiar with your community and make new friends, you may decide your belonging or safety needs will be better met by changing your living arrangements.

Five hundred years ago, Ficino (cited in Moore, 1992) gave this good advice for staying well: "You should walk as often as possible among plants that have a wonderful aroma, spending a considerable amount of time every day among such things." Sounds good! Maybe you can even invite a friend to join you.

Summary

In this chapter, we presented suggestions and guidelines for finding safe and affordable housing, obtaining educational loans, applying for financial assistance, taking care of your nutritional needs, and maintaining an active and healthy lifestyle. Meeting your needs in graduate school is not easy, but the experience can contribute to your thriving as a trainee. Through your struggles, you build an empathic bridge with the people you counsel. And in your successes, you gain an appreciation for your clients' personal strengths and social resources.

Resources

The undisputed leader in guidance for finance is Leider and Leider's (2011) *Don't Miss Out*, now in its 35th edition. The authors describe the common myths about obtaining aid, steps in completing federal forms, role of the university, and company-sponsored education. It includes information of particular interest for women and persons of color. The book is comprehensive and has a terrific listing of suggestions and contacts.

About Graduate School

http://gradschool.about.com

About Graduate School is a website that provides practical advice for dealing with the many challenges that students confront in graduate school. The brief articles are well written and provide detailed information on a wide range of topics, including financial assistance and time management.

Free Application for Federal Student Aid (FAFSA)

http://www.fafsa.ed.gov/

The U.S. Department of Education publishes these electronic guides that provide comprehensive information about applying for federal financial aid. You can also request print versions by calling the Federal Student Aid Information Center at 1–800–433–3243.

Funding Education Beyond High School: The Guide to Federal Student Aid

https://studentaid.ed.gov/students/publications/student_guide/index.html

This U.S. Department of Education site is a comprehensive resource on student financial aid programs. Grants, loans, and work-study are the three major forms of aid available through the Department's Federal Student Aid office.

References

Belcastro, A. L. (2000, February). Finding balance in school and life. *Counseling Today, 43,* 12.

Covey, S. (1989). *Seven habits of highly effective people.* New York, NY: Simon & Schuster.

Duncan, L., & Begay, S. (1996). *The magic of spider woman.* New York, NY: Scholastic.

Hoskins, C. M. (2000, August). Get a life! Top 10 list for a first-year student. *Counseling Today, 43,* 32, 36.

Imber-Black, E., & Roberts, J. (2004). *Rituals for our times.* Lanham, MD: Rowman & Littlefield.

Kenrick, D. T., Griskevicius, V., Neuberg, S. L., & Schaller, M. (2010). Renovating the pyramid of needs: Contemporary extensions build upon ancient foundations.

Perspectives on Psychological Science, 5, 292–314. doi:10.1177/17456916 10369469

Lambie, G. W., Smith, H. L., & Ieva, K. P. (2009). Graduate counseling students' levels of ego development, wellness, and psychological disturbance: An exploratory investigation. *Adultspan Journal, 8,* 114–127. doi:10.1002/j.2161–0029.2009 .tb00064.x

Leahey, T. H. (2010). *A history of psychology: Main currents in psychological thought* (6th ed.). Upper Saddle River, NJ: Prentice Hall.

Leider, A., & Leider, R. (2011). *Don't miss out* (35th ed.). Alexandria, VA: Octameron Associates.

Licht, C. A. (2012). Self-care in graduate school: Finding your optimal balance. In P. J. Giordano, S. F. Davis, & C. A. Licht (Eds.), *Your graduate training in psychology: Effective strategies for success* (pp. 101–113). Thousand Oaks, CA: Sage.

MacLaine, S. (2000). *The Camino: A journey of the spirit.* New York, NY: Atria.

Marvin, R., Cooper, G., Hoffman, K., & Powell, B. (2002). The Circle of Security project: Attachment-based intervention with caregiver-pre-school child dyads. *Attachment and Human Development, 4,* 107–124.

Maslow, A. H. (1962). *Toward a psychology of being.* New York, NY: Van Nostrand.

Maslow, A. H. (1970). *Motivation and personality* (2nd ed.). New York, NY: Harper & Row.

Moore, T. (1992). *Care of the soul.* New York, NY: HarperCollins.

Myers, J. E., Mobley, A. K., & Booth, C. S. (2003). Wellness of counseling students: Practicing what we preach. *Counselor Education and Supervision, 42,* 264–274.

Prochaska, J. O., Norcross, J. C., & DiClemente, C. C. (2013). Applying the stages of change. In G. P. Koocher, J. C. Norcross, & B. A. Greene (Eds.), *Psychologists' desk reference* (3rd ed., pp. 176–181). New York, NY: Oxford University Press.

Taormina, R. J., & Gao, J. H. (2013). Maslow and the motivation hierarchy: Measuring satisfaction of the needs. *American Journal of Psychology, 126,* 155–177. doi:10.5406/ameripsyc.126.2.0155

Zolbrod, P. G. (1984). *Diné bahané: The Navajo creation story.* Albuquerque: University of New Mexico Press.

Answer to the Riddle: The farmer first takes the chicken to the island, leaving the fox with the grain. The farmer then returns, picks up the fox, and ferries it to the island. Instead of leaving the fox alone with the chicken, the farmer brings the chicken back on the return voyage, drops off the chicken, and transports the grain to the island. Leaving the fox with the grain on the island, the farmer returns for the chicken once again to make the final transport.

4

Enhancing Your Academic Skills

People get wisdom from thinking, not from learning.

—Laura Riding Jackson

Reason is, and ought only to be, the slave of the passions.

—David Hume

The Chinese character that represents the act of listening combines not only the symbols of ears but also those of eyes, heart, and mind (Adler, Rosenfield, & Towne, 1989). This wonderful fusion of symbols expresses the essence of successful counseling. As a counselor or therapist, you involve yourself totally—ears, eyes, heart, and mind—in a process of truly encountering your client in a helping relationship. Because counseling is a dynamic and complex process, you need to cultivate not only your observational competencies and emotional sensitivities but also your mental abilities. The purpose of your graduate curriculum is to prepare your mind, heart, eyes, and ears for the challenging work of counseling and therapy.

In this chapter, we discuss how you can use four basic academic skills—reading, researching, writing, and presenting—to make the most of your training. Reading is the original virtual reality; it allows you to broaden and enrich your limited experiences by tapping into the observations, ideas, and discoveries of others. Research skills enable you to think critically, observe carefully, collect information systematically, and draw appropriate conclusions. Writing skills help you give voice to your own experiences, make your thoughts visible, and clarify your vague hunches by putting them into words. Finally, presentation skills enable you to share your expertise with colleagues, clients, and the general public. Whether you are sitting in traditional classrooms, taking online courses, or engaging in hybrid classes involving some distance learning (Chamberlin, 2009), you will be relying constantly on these skills.

You may be wondering how simply improving your academic skills can help you become a better counselor or therapist. Just as these skills are essential during your training, they are no less indispensable throughout your professional career. Keeping current with developments in the field, staying curious, and approaching your work mindfully can help you to maintain your professional vitality and prevent burnout.

More Than I Had Bargained For

Bonnie's Story

I remember being the first person in the room for the first meeting of my first course in my training to become a counselor. That was a lot of "firsts"! There I sat, a 45-year-old woman, successful accountant, mother of two wonderful teenage girls, wife of nearly 20 years in a loving marriage, and now a brand-new counseling student. I had finally decided that if I really wanted to become a counselor, it was now or never. Generally, I'm a pretty confident person but not right before my first class! Every other student entered the room as if he or she belonged there, and I couldn't help noticing how young they were. Some of them looked like they were still in college, and I must have been the oldest student by at least 10 or 15 years. I was even older than my professor! What, I wondered, was I doing here?

Sure, I had been a good student in college. Over the years, I had continued to read voraciously and to write newsletters for a volunteer organization for the mentally ill. I even helped my daughter with her calculus! But my days as a student were a long time ago. Even though I felt a calling to become a counselor, I was worried that I couldn't handle the demands of reading textbooks, writing term papers, and taking tests.

Of course, throughout that first semester of my training, I had to do a personal crash course on using the newer research services. I was so out

(Continued)

(Continued)

of it that I thought Article Express must be a paper train, and WorldCat sounded like a new super hero. Now, I've become an old hand at using the PsycINFO database, and I've discovered I'm still a pretty good student.

My biggest surprise has been how emotionally charged and personally involving the training is. I've found that I cannot be a spectator, detached and disengaged, in my learning. Instead, I've watched my own life unfolding in the course on life span development. I've noticed all my own symptoms, as well as those of my relatives and friends, in the diagnostics class. And my counseling skills class has stirred up all sorts of personal issues for me.

Early that first semester, we were watching a scene from a documentary, "The Farmer's Wife," which is a powerful account of a woman's courage in enduring all the stresses of modern-day farming. I started crying because that could have been my mother up on that screen. When it was time for the class to discuss the scene, I decided to share the memories and emotions that the scene had evoked in me. One student later thanked me for "enriching" her understanding of these issues. You know, this is more learning than I had originally bargained for, but I'm truly grateful that I'm able to take advantage of the opportunity.

Hearts and Minds

> The heart has its reasons which reason knows not.
>
> —Blaise Pascal

In his autobiography, Carl Jung (1965) described his journey to the American Southwest, where he encountered Ochwiay Biano ("Mountain Lake"), a Native American who was chief of the Taos Pueblo Tribe. Ochwiay Biano shared with Jung that he considered the Whites to be crazy, explaining that they were under the delusion that they thought with their heads. Surprised, Jung asked Ochwiay Biano where he thought. "'We think here," he said, indicating his heart (p. 248).

This account is more than just a "Jung at heart" story. In fact, research on emotional intelligence (Goleman, 1995) indicates that we think with *both* our heads and our hearts. According to Antonio Damasio (1994), who is a neuroscientist, Descartes made a huge mistake when he left emotions out of the thinking process. Damasio's research has revealed that emotions are actually essential to good thinking.

Like many students who enter graduate programs in counseling, you may have been more of a "heart" person as an undergraduate student. When you first read a poem, you probably responded emotionally rather than thinking about it critically. You may have found yourself passionately involved in projects that captivated your attention. As you enter graduate school, you may view the academic courses in your training curriculum as merely ordeals that you must endure—the hoops you have to jump through—in order for you to qualify for the real learning experiences that take place in your clinical placements. If this brief sketch sounds like you, we invite you to examine carefully your academic skills. You can learn to study better, rather than harder, and make your academic work as personally rewarding and successful as the practice you will do in your clinical training.

On the other hand, you may be more of a "head" person in your learning style. You may have been a very competent undergraduate student, participating actively in your classes, carefully reading the assigned material, and completing assignments conscientiously. For you, emotions might seem to get in the way of thinking objectively. Consequently, you may be less personally engaged and more emotionally detached in your approach to learning. If this description sounds more like you, you may find it challenging to explore yourself, your clients, and the counseling process in your graduate training.

These references to your undergraduate education may feel like ancient history to you. You may be one of the increasing number of nontraditional students returning to an academic setting after years of pursuing another calling, such as engaging in a different career or raising a family. As a result, you may have only some vague memories about those distant days as a college student—and some very strong apprehensions right now about entering the academic life once again. Whether you were passive and disengaged or active and involved during your undergraduate years may be irrelevant. After all, you are at a different stage now in your life—more seasoned, mature, and thoughtful. These acquired qualities are going to be wonderful assets for you, but you probably have at least one major worry: that your academic skills may be too rusty.

In this chapter, we describe how you can develop critical reflection by enhancing the core academic skills of reading, research, writing, and presenting. "Isn't this stuff too basic for graduate training?" you may be wondering. "Aren't these just a variation of the three Rs—reading, 'riting, and 'rithmetic?" It is true that these are basic skills that you have been practicing for years. However, like many other tasks you will perform in your graduate training, they will be a little more complex and a lot more interesting. We share with you here some tricks of the trade, but more important, we challenge you to commit both your heart and your head to becoming a lifelong learner and successful practitioner. After all, counseling students and professionals with higher levels of emotional intelligence also demonstrate greater counseling self-efficacy (Martin, Easton, Wilson, Takemoto, & Sullivan, 2004).

Developing Critical Reflection Skills

> The function of education is to teach one to think intensively and to think critically. Intelligence plus character—that is the goal of true education.
>
> —Martin Luther King Jr.

Put simply, critical reflection is the process of carefully and systemically examining ideas (Meltzoff, 1998). When you think, read, and respond mindfully, you challenge yourself to use higher order thinking skills—to engage in critical reflection. Critical reflection is a requisite skill for you to become a successful helping professional because you must ultimately rely on your own knowledge and judgment. Of course, you should never work without regularly seeking supervision and consultation from others. However, when you are alone dealing with a troubled client in a session, responding on the telephone to a suicidal caller, or even presenting a difficult case in a staffing meeting, you must count on your own abilities. At these crucial times, you have to be able to gather data, analyze complex information, synthesize different factors, present your ideas coherently, and then act on them mindfully.

To begin developing your critical reflection skills as a practitioner, you have to gain a thorough knowledge of theories, develop a repertoire of counseling and therapy skills, achieve insight into your clients, recognize their cultural contexts, appreciate the intricacies of interpersonal dynamics, and become more aware of yourself. Mastering all this material is a daunting task, but it's still just the beginning. Once you have gained some familiarity with these components, you need to play with the pieces to see where they fit and then arrange these elements into a complete picture. Ideally, the resulting mosaic will then serve as a working model for successful counseling and therapy work.

One way you can facilitate the development of your own critical reflection ability is by striving to be mindful. Langer (1997) described mindful learning as being open to new information. Mindfulness is to thinking what flexibility is to athletics. Being mindful allows you to reach further, notice connections, and discover parallels that you might otherwise miss.

We encourage you to stay mindful and stretch your intellectual muscles as a graduate student. As someone once said, "My thoughts are like waffles—the first few don't look too good." If that's true for you, then keep cooking! Langer (1997) suggested that two ways to improve your mindfulness are to ask good questions and to look for novel distinctions. You can ask these questions of your peers, your professors, your texts, and yourself. As you do so, try to expand the ways in which you categorize the answers you receive. Rather than labeling a response as merely good or bad, for instance, search for a more nuanced evaluative description. At the same time, stay open to ideas or tasks that may at first seem unappealing or even boring. Approaching them mindfully by actively seeking novel aspects can actually increase your enjoyment of learning.

Learning by Heart

> There is only one quality worse than hardness of heart and that is softness of head.
>
> —Theodore Roosevelt

As we have mentioned earlier, the underlying assumption of most discussions about thinking has been that it is much better to use your head than to follow your heart. Emotions, according to this orthodox view, only contaminate good thinking. Therefore, the traditional goal of Western higher education has been to promote dispassionate thinking. However, the work of Goleman (2013) has demonstrated that emotions play a vital role in helping us to perform well in academic tasks, engage in effective problem solving, remain open to new ideas, and think creatively. In this section, we focus on three important ways in which you can use your emotions to strengthen your academic skills: riding the perturbation wave, finding "the zone," and using the Zeigarnik Effect.

Riding the Perturbation Wave

> The word "yes" may bring trouble; the word "no" leads nowhere.
>
> —Bantu proverb

In any significant learning experience, your mind is in a state of dialectical tension (Presbury, Echterling, & McKee, 2008). On the one hand, you are excited to discover new ways of thinking and to experiment with new ways of acting. On the other, you strive to have some sense of certainty and familiarity.

This tension between chaos and order is the essence of learning. If your thoughts have been thrown into chaos, you feel overwhelmed and confused. However, if you are not experiencing enough challenge, you feel bored and stagnant.

The secret to making the most of any learning opportunity is to ride the wave of perturbation. Just as in surfing, you seek out the situations that make waves and create turbulence. You will take a tumble now and then, but the adventure is well worth the risk. The learning tasks you encounter under these circumstances will be challenging and may even knock you off balance, but they are rarely overpowering. In contrast to our surfing analogy, the traditional ideal of disengaged, dispassionate thinking is like standing on the shore—you may never be in over your head, but neither do you experience the exhilaration of being carried away with an idea or totally caught up in performing a task.

Mihaly Csikszentmihalyi (1997) described this invigorating process, in which you find yourself completely immersed in an activity, as *flow*. You are more likely to experience flow when several conditions are met. The first condition is that the situation requires specific actions to achieve explicit goals. When, for example, you are weaving, running, playing chess, or studying for a test, you are more likely to "become" that activity and achieve flow. Another condition for flow is that you receive immediate feedback on your efforts. You can see the pattern emerging as you weave, the route you are completing as you run, the new positions of your chess pieces as you move them, and your understanding enhanced as you continue studying. The final, and most important, condition is a manageable challenge. You can achieve flow if successfully completing a task requires that you make the most of your emerging skills. When the weaving pattern is particularly complex, the running route especially demanding, the chess game intriguing, and the subject matter challenging, you have the opportunity to immerse yourself in the productive and satisfying experience of flow.

If you are a new student, you may not realize just how challenging your training experiences will be. Of course, like other graduate programs, the intellectual content of your curriculum will involve some difficulties, and the workload will be heavy. But graduate training in counseling and therapy may seem to you to be much more manageable than other programs. The textbooks, for example, appear much more readable than those in physics, medicine, or law. Your counseling professors may seem nice—after all, they are also counselors—so you may initially assume that they will not be so demanding. However, you will soon find that your counseling faculty, curriculum, readings, and learning experiences will all work together to consistently challenge you to deal with emotionally charged material, face your own personal issues, practice complex skills, and learn painful lessons. Your training is more than hard work; it is *heart* work. The ride may turn out to be much more turbulent than you thought!

One of the common sources of turbulence you will encounter as a counseling student is questioning your assumptions about yourself, other people, and life in general. These familiar assumptions that you have developed over the years are like an old pair of comfortable shoes—you are reluctant to give them up, even though there are holes in them. Particularly when you first begin to question your assumptions about cultures, gender, and values, you are likely to feel confused. As Milton Erickson (Erickson, Rossi, & Rossi, 1976) pointed out, people have a powerful need to resolve confusion. Because you cannot rely on automatic thinking anymore, you become attentive, focused, and mindful (Goleman, 2013). At these times, you will embark on an intense search for new ways to view yourself, others, and the world. Embrace your confusion! Out of this chaos you can create a deeper, richer sense of order and harmony.

Relying on automatic thinking can cause you to see other people as stereotypes instead of mindfully noting the unique qualities of those you encounter. Such reliance can also blind you to the often subtle forms of oppression that others must endure every day.

EXERCISE 4.1 The Birdcage

Encountering Oppression

Frye (1995) offered a powerful metaphor to perturb our thinking about oppression. Take a couple of minutes to read the following brief fantasy.

Imagine that you are seeing a birdcage for the first time. However, the birdcage is so close to your face that you can only focus on one of the wires. With the wire right before your eyes, you can see minute details—the gleam of light on its shiny surface, the texture of the paint, and its cylindrical shape—but not the other wires. If your conception of a birdcage was based only on this close examination, you could continue to examine it carefully and be incredulous to hear that a bird could not escape from it. Why couldn't a bird simply fly around this wire anytime it wanted? What's wrong with this bird? Lack of initiative? Some personal flaw? Or just plain laziness?

It's only when you have an opportunity to step back and gain a macroscopic view of the birdcage that you can begin to appreciate how this

(Continued)

(Continued)

systematic network of barriers works. Alone, each wire presents no obstacle to the bird's freedom, but together, these slender threads are just as effective as any prison made of solid stone.

Consider the meaning of this fantasy for you and write your reflections below.

_____

_____

_____

_____

_____

_____

Finding "The Zone"

Life loves to be taken by the lapel and told: "I'm with you kid. Let's go."

—Maya Angelou

Cozolino (2010) proposed that a moderately energized emotional state is essential for successful therapy. The classic Yerkes-Dodson Law shows how your state of emotional arousal affects your performance. You perform poorly when your emotions are at either extreme—disengaged or highly aroused (Martindale, 1981). At a moderate level of emotional arousal, you're at your best—adrenaline pumping, memory enhanced, neurons firing, and attention focused. When you're in "the zone," you can do your finest work.

One study discovered that new doctorate students in counseling were plagued by concerns about the unknown and doubts about their capabilities to succeed (Hughes & Kleist, 2005). However, what helped these students to enter the productive zone was to remind themselves of their personal strengths and previous successes. This emphatic belief in their capabilities, in spite of the uncertainties of these new challenges, was the essential catalyst for engaging fully in the process of discovery and learning.

Most guides on academic success emphasize the importance of managing your time, but more crucial is managing your emotional arousal. If you led with your head as an undergraduate student, encourage yourself to follow your heart more in your graduate training. Become a passionate scholar! Psyching yourself up can become part of your preparatory ritual before you open a book, attend class, or start an assignment. You may want to remind yourself of the goals you are working to achieve, to visualize yourself as a successful counselor, or to ask yourself important questions that your academic work can help you answer. Get personal with the material. Explore, for example, how you can use a particular concept to gain insight into yourself. How have you experienced enmeshment in your relationships? When have you used denial? How has modeling influenced you? Engaging with these concepts in such a personal way is like playing a sport—you are a participant in the process, not a spectator.

If you have followed your heart throughout most of your previous education, you may be more likely to hit the higher end of the Yerkes-Dodson curve when you are facing important tasks in a counseling graduate program. In that case, your routine for preparing for a challenging assignment or test may include practicing relaxation and focusing activities. When it comes to engaging your emotions in the learning process, you need to follow the "Goldilocks Principle"—not too hot and not too cold.

Using the Zeigarnik Effect

> The suspense is terrible. I hope it will last.
>
> —Oscar Wilde

Did you ever wind up binge watching an entire season of suspenseful episodes of a TV series? No matter what show you may have watched, it never seemed to fail that just as someone was disclosing a dramatic piece of news, the episode ended with this new plot twist left unresolved. When you were a child, you may have found yourself caught up in reading an adventure comic book that ended with the aggravating notice "to be continued" just when it looked like the hero was facing certain doom. Remember how badly you wanted to know how things were going to turn out? You may have replayed the events over and over in your mind, speculated about the possible consequences, and talked about the circumstances with friends. Until the program's next episode or the comic book's following issue, your curiosity continued to nag at you. At those times, you were experiencing the Zeigarnik Effect.

Hergenhahn and Henley (2014) described how Kurt Lewin, the famous Gestalt psychologist, hypothesized that a person who has not finished a task or achieved closure on a topic will remember the material better. Bluma Zeigarnik (1938), a student of Lewin, tested this hypothesis in an experiment in which participants were permitted to finish some tasks but not others. As predicted, she found that participants later remembered many more of the uncompleted tasks than the completed ones.

What the Zeigarnik Effect means for you is that if you want to "chew" on an idea rather than forget it immediately, you should not rush to make up your mind about it. Similarly, because no graduate class ever resolves all the issues you will face in your counseling career, there is always naturally "unfinished business" in your personal and professional development. If you allow yourself to leave a classroom holding on to at least one suspenseful note, you are more likely to keep reflecting on it as you seek a richer and deeper understanding of the subject matter. In fact, we have a multitude of unresolved issues that face us in the counseling profession, unanswered questions that confront us in our personal lives, and vast unexplored territories that beckon us in our own psyches. Invoking the Zeigarnik Effect could be a great daily ritual to stay open, curious, and engrossed.

As you read the following material about the basic academic skills, keep in mind that you can enhance your abilities in each of them by using your emotions to help you learn by heart.

The Core Academic Skills

Reading

> Reading is a means of thinking with another person's mind: it forces you to stretch your own.
>
> —Charles Scribner Jr.

> To read fast is as bad as to eat in a hurry.
>
> —Vilhelm Ekelund

Literacy is a fundamental skill for elementary school students, and the same is true for you in your graduate training. "Hey, reading is no big deal!" you may think. "I already read e-mails, newspapers, magazines, novels, and nonfiction books. I read all the time. What's so tough about the reading I'll do in a graduate training program?"

Well, the reading that you will do in graduate school will differ in significant ways from what you have done in the past. In addition to course textbooks, you will be expected to read seminal works in the field, manuscripts by your professors, drafts of collaborative papers by your fellow students, psychological assessment reports, client files, program evaluations, evidence-based practice protocols, and the most recently published professional literature. Some books and articles have become such standards in the field that they are often considered unofficial required readings for all counselors and therapists. You may want to ask your faculty advisor and instructors for their recommendations of favorite "Golden Oldies."

Although the material you read in graduate school will vary tremendously in its content, style, and purpose, it has several common characteristics. First and foremost, the sheer weight of the readings will seem intimidating. You may not be able to prevent eyestrain, but many graduate students do invest in backpacks that can manage heavy loads without straining their backs. Second, unlike a book you might take to pass the time on the beach, this reading is not fast food for the mind. The subject matter is likely to be challenging in several ways: It may be difficult, complex, provocative, demanding, or even emotionally painful to read. The content requires a commitment from you to give it your full and complete attention. Otherwise, you are likely to miss subtle nuances and crucial details. You also need to read the material critically—with an inquiring mind. And afterward, you need to reflect on what you have read. This material is not something you can swallow in one quick gulp. You need to take the time to digest it.

Successfully handling both the breadth and depth of the readings you will encounter in your graduate training is like baking a cake—you just have to combine a few basic ingredients.

The Place. First, take some time to determine what environment is best for helping you engage in productive, intensive, and extensive reading. Do you concentrate best in silence? With others around? With or without music?

Karen, a graduate student with two children, found that she did her best reading and reflection in a coffee shop near school. The smell of the coffee, the arrivals and departures of others, and the piped-in classical music were soothing to her. She could sit for hours, occasionally getting a refill of coffee or a biscotti, without being interrupted by family members. The others in the shop served as a welcome distraction when she needed to take a break, and she enjoyed getting to know the coffee shop employees, who occasionally inquired about her school work.

Rae, on the other hand, found that she was most able to read with depth and comprehension when she was at home, in total silence, sitting on a folding chair

at a plain card table tucked in a small monastic-like alcove of her apartment—
no coffee, no food, no distractions, and no visitors. You may want to experiment
to determine where and how you do your best reading. Once you have discovered what setting works for you, then find and claim it.

The Time. Second, you need to set aside plenty of time for reading. This sug-
gestion, like the first, will depend on you and your preferences. Many students find that when they begin graduate school they have enough
opportunities to handle the assigned texts and articles. As they become more
involved in their classes and other activities, however, they find that the extra
time has evaporated. They then struggle to keep pace, if not one step behind,
with their reading assignments. After you have found your ideal place to
read, figure out the best time to do it; then claim this time, like you did the
place, as yours. Kelly, for example, found that the only way he was able to
protect the time he had set aside was to schedule appointments for "R.T."—
"Reading Time."

Yourself. Of course, you have to put more than time into your reading, but
you have to put more of yourself into it, too. Read mindfully, asking questions of the material and of yourself. What does this information suggest to
you? If you had to explain the information to someone else, or perhaps
defend it to someone else, what would you say?

Whenever you read a text, consider yourself to be entering into a partnership with the author. Your role is to custom design a personalized book
based on the generic one that the author has provided. As a collaborator, you
will be jotting down comments in the page margins, outlining the material
in your own way, drawing visual representations of the ideas, critically
evaluating the book's arguments, and even engaging in a dialogue with the
author. In your own journal, you can also write at greater length about your
own epiphanies—"aha experiences"—as you read the book. You will find
that this collaborative approach to reading is much more engaging than
simply highlighting your text.

When the material is so challenging that you are having problems concentrating on it, you can use two strategies. First, remind yourself of the simi-
larities between reading and counseling. Both involve an encounter between
people through the medium of words. You certainly don't expect to completely understand any client in one session. You may have trouble at first
reading your client's emotional state, deciphering the meaning of comments,
or even comprehending important motives. In spite of these difficulties, you
can remain committed to working with your client because the payoff for a
successful counseling experience makes it all worthwhile. You will find that

you are much more successful in your reading when you bring this same level of commitment to understanding an author. When you read, you don't have to fully comprehend every intricacy of the author's theory or be able to articulate each nuance of an argument. Nevertheless, you can do your best to engage with the author by mindfully attending to the written word.

Another strategy you can pursue when you feel overwhelmed by your class readings is to remember that you are not alone in this endeavor. As one counseling student recommended, "Do not be afraid to ask for help or for what you need. No one gets through this on his or her own" (Hoskins, 2000, p. 36.). Ask a colleague to read or study with you. Together, you can support and encourage one another, helping each other read and reflect. When you are tackling particularly tough material, you can discuss it with your reading partner.

EXERCISE 4.2 What? So What? Now What?

We mentioned the three Rs earlier, but the three Ws can serve you well, too. Choose a chapter in a text and take notes while you are reading it. Pay particular attention at first to capturing the salient points of the content—the "What?" Then think about what you just read and figure out what it means—the "So What?" For example, you may want to jot down some of the implications of these ideas for counseling. Finally, now that you understand this material, consider what you are going to do with it—the "Now What?" How are you going to apply it? How are you going to connect it to material from other courses? Write about this experience in your journal. Keep using the "What? So What? Now What?" approach with all your reading until it becomes second nature to you.

I Learned how to Read all Over Again

Brian's Story

This weekend, I learned how to read all over again. Last week, I kept facing my textbook with my highlighter in my hand, trying to find the motivation to keep going. As I read, I realized that my book was starting to almost

(Continued)

(Continued)

glow with all the yellow marks in it, but I couldn't recall a word. There seemed to be too much information and I couldn't prioritize it, so I wasn't retaining anything. I'm new to this field, so I don't know enough yet to recognize the important concepts!

I finally asked my professor how to read this text. She told me to take my time. Pay attention to the organization of each chapter. Then figure out what points the authors were trying to make and pay particular attention to anything that didn't make sense to me. If I don't understand something, it's important that I take note of it and ask for clarification in class. I started taking notes when I read, and now I feel like I'm not only retaining more, but I'm starting to see the internal structure of the material. I'm starting to see how concepts relate to each other. Wow, I was really starting to feel worried for awhile that I couldn't do it.

Researching

Research is formalized curiosity. It is poking and prying with a purpose.

—Zora Neale Hurston

The Need for Research Skills. You may be wondering how research is relevant to becoming a competent helping professional. You came to a graduate training program to learn how to help people, not to crunch numbers—right? Well, there are several important reasons for integrating research into your training experience. First and foremost, if you are going to be an effective therapist, you also need to develop the fundamental skills of a scholar. You must be able to make careful observations, systematically collect relevant data, and organize this material into a coherent case conceptualization. Research is not limited to the laboratory. When you gather background information on a school or community agency, when you review recent studies on a particular problem, and when you read about a new theoretical perspective in therapy, you are doing important research. The knowledge you gain from these scholarly activities is essential to being a capable professional who stays current in the field.

Second, research experience itself will hone your critical thinking skills. You are entering a complex, challenging, and ambiguous line of work. When your clients come to you in deep anguish and searing pain, it may be tempting to latch onto highly touted but untested techniques. However, you need to maintain a healthy skepticism regarding fads, cure-alls, and biases in the field. Research experience reminds us softhearted helpers to be hard-nosed about the evidence we need to validate therapeutic effectiveness.

Third, throughout your training, you will be learning to plan, design, implement, and evaluate programs that meet the therapeutic needs of communities and schools. Once again, you will need to rely on your research skills in order to assess people's needs accurately and to evaluate programs carefully.

Another important reason for integrating research into your training is that it is one of the major ways that you can advance the profession. As an emerging professional in the field of counseling and therapy, you have an obligation to contribute to our growing knowledge base through your own scholarly activity.

Fifth and finally, an immediate and practical training benefit of research is that it provides excellent opportunities for you to collaborate with faculty members and other students on important and stimulating projects. As you become more comfortable engaging in scholarly activities now, you will be more likely to continue to reach out to others in collaborative research efforts later. After you have graduated, you are likely to find that practicing as a counselor can feel isolating at times. Unfortunately, it is likely that you will not have the benefit of a peer group that is always available to you. Working with others to explore areas of interest is a great way to build and maintain a community of supportive colleagues.

If you still are not sold on the importance of research, consider this scenario. You have graduated and have a position in a school, mental health center, community agency, or hospital. You begin to work with a client who has a problem that is complex and challenging. The situation may not necessarily demand that you refer the client to someone else, but you realize that if you are going to work effectively with this person, you will need to find out more. The process of finding out more is essentially research. The more skilled you are at researching now, the more resourceful you will be later when your client's well-being is on the line.

Learning Research Skills. So how do you become skilled at research? This question may be especially pressing if you are nervous about, or slightly afraid of, courses on research methods and statistics. Perhaps you are one of the many who read only the beginnings and ends of journal articles, casually skipping over the method, results, and analysis sections in the middle. Heppner and his colleagues (1999) stated that both the graduate school environment and the personality styles of the students themselves cause some trainees to struggle with research. The implication is that students who have investigative interests or statistics skills, or who are in research-oriented graduate programs, may have an advantage over other students.

However, certain activities in graduate school can increase your comfort with research and improve the chances that you will continue to engage in research efforts after graduation. Participating in research teams with other students can help you identify what aspects of research come more easily to you (yes, there will be some things you do quite well!) and which areas are more challenging for you. You and your colleagues can then pool your expertise and help each other. In the process, you become not only more comfortable with research but also more critically reflective.

You can gain valuable research experience by joining faculty members' research teams or volunteering to work individually with a faculty member who is investigating an area that is interesting to you. Consider asking if you can assist, even if your help would consist primarily of literature review or library searches. If you're able to watch the research process from beginning to end—problem identification to manuscript completion—you will likely increase your research self-efficacy.

You may find that a literature search, which typically occurs early on in the research process, is a daunting task. It may seem overwhelming to find so much information on so many facets of your topic available in so many places. You may feel like you are looking for clues in a hall of mirrors and doors. Which doors are real and offer you access to important information? Which doors only look real, but are actually reflections of others? The following tips may help you choose wisely.

- *Develop your online search skills.* Ideally, your undergraduate education provided you with training in online search skills that you can use at the library or at home. If you feel rusty or underprepared, sign up for a workshop or ask the reference librarian for help. Most libraries use common databases, such as ERIC or PsycINFO, but the manner of accessing those databases may vary. Do not hesitate to ask for help, and when you do, take notes! You may want to replicate a search later. Similarly, don't limit yourself to one database. If you are truly stretching your thoughts and thinking critically, you may find that interesting connections exist within fields such as social work, biology, sociology, philosophy, anthropology, literature, medicine, and theology.

- *Be organized.* Even if you are not methodical as a rule, take on some obsessive-compulsive traits when you work on your research. Keep your trusty old notepad or new portable electronic device with you at all times so that you can keep track of your searches. You will want to remember what keywords you used to initiate your searches and what databases you used. You may want to download, print out, or e-mail yourself your search histories so that you won't have to start from scratch the next time you go to the library or sit down at your computer.
- *Download your sources.* As you find materials that relate to your topic, read the abstracts available on the databases and identify which articles and books you would like to read. You can then download those sources that are available electronically and check out the most promising books. Because no library's collection is complete, you will also want to take advantage of interlibrary loan services.
- *Keep detailed notes.* Save yourself lots of headaches by making sure you have complete citation information for each reference you may use. Develop electronic documents of all your notes as you read through and digest the material. You can then assemble them into a rough draft of your research project. Store all your documents in a labeled physical binder or in a folder on your computer.

One advantage of doing scholarly work is that the process itself tends to use higher order critical thinking skills. As you practice and gain experience with research, you may find that you are more mindful in general. You will have a broader knowledge base from which to draw, and your ability to make thoughtful conclusions will improve.

Remember that your research should be related to topics that you find truly intriguing. If you focus on what is captivating to you, you will find that the process is not only easier but also genuinely exciting. Some students opt to choose one primary area of interest at the start of their program. They read about that area, investigate it, and focus in on it whenever possible in course assignments. Those students generally go on to write theses or dissertations that build on their initial investigations. Other students find that they have several areas that call to them. They may focus on play therapy when working with children in a practicum and then explore substance abuse issues when they take an addictions course. Advantages and disadvantages exist with both of these approaches, so don't worry that there's one right way to begin your research efforts. The key is just to begin!

EXERCISE 4.3 Doing a Little Detective Work

Think about the helping profession—what interests you right now? What would you like to know about counselors or therapists? Clients? Problems? Processes? If you were to formulate one question you want to explore, what would it be? Remember that notepad you keep handy to jot down ideas and questions while you are reading? Use it now to write down your question. Now think about ways in which you may go about answering it.

At this point, imagine that you are a detective, either a sophisticated British variety or a tough American private eye. Whichever you choose, what would you want to know about your question (your subject)? Whom would you ask? What would you ask? If you had to prove that there is a connection between two things, how would you do it?

Spend a little time thinking about this scenario. Don't worry right now about exact measurements, procedures, or instruments. Just try to expand your mind and become fully engaged and interested in your subject. After you know your question, go to the library and engage in a literature search.

EXERCISE 4.4 Critiquing

Use your critical reflection skills to analyze the articles, chapters, and books you gathered in the first exercise. Maybe you have assumed that if research is published, it must be of good quality. We hate to disillusion you, but as blues singers often point out, "It ain't necessarily so."

Check this out by looking at how the articles are written, from beginning to end. How are research questions phrased? What hypotheses are presented? What information is gathered, and by what method? How does this information relate back to the hypothesis? If particular instruments are used, are these instruments reliable and valid? How are participants chosen? Are sampling procedures adequately described? Do you see any inherent complications in the sample or procedures? How are data analyzed? Look at your statistics textbook and see if the researchers' data match the assumptions of their analysis.

Writing

> Writing is not what the writer does after the thinking is done; writing is thinking.
>
> —D. Murray

> Writing is like driving a car at night. You can only see as far as the headlights, but you make the whole trip that way.
>
> —E. L. Doctorow

The third core academic skill is writing. Perhaps more prosaic than Doctorow's elegant simile above, writing is also a little like eating raisins. People tend to love it, to dislike it intensely, or to enjoy it in small doses, as long as it is mixed into something good—like oatmeal cookies. If you belong to one of the latter groups, then the bad news is that you're going to have to write a great deal throughout your graduate training, and do it well. The good news is that you can both improve your writing and develop a taste for it—even if you don't care for raisins.

The Need for Writing Skills. At first, you may be tempted to assume that whatever writing skills have brought you this far in your academic career will be sufficient to carry you through your program and professional career. After all, how frequently are people actually called on to write during their everyday activities? Actually, if you become a counselor, you'll be writing more than you think, especially if you plan to contribute to the field by sharing your research and clinical experiences (Beins, 2012).

Even if you decide not to pursue a career in academia, you'll be writing case notes, treatment summaries, reports, and correspondence on a regular basis. Your case notes must be clear and accurate in describing what occurred in the session. Likewise, your treatment summaries and reports must be thorough and complete, ensuring that another professional will be able to understand your words and use them to design an appropriate intervention strategy. Similarly, correspondence is another important way you will be representing yourself as a professional.

Learning the Hard Way

Susan's Story

In my first internship as a school counselor, I had the chance to present a guidance unit for students in the third grade. I decided, with the approval of my supervisor, that I would send a letter home to the students' parents introducing myself and explaining the purpose of the guidance unit. Like many interns, I was always busy, so I frantically wrote the letter late one evening, quickly showed it to my supervisor, and then sent the letter out to parents.

Within 3 days, the school had received two telephone complaints about the misspellings and grammatical errors in my letter. In addition, one parent returned the letter with each of the three mistakes circled in red, along with a written note admonishing me to review basic grammar rules and improve my writing skills before sending another letter on school stationery.

I felt humiliated! My supervisor was embarrassed, the principal was angry, and the parents were concerned about the quality of their children's education. I realized that I had made several foolish and serious mistakes here. First, I didn't take seriously my responsibility as a writer. Instead, I assumed that people would understand my meaning and give me the benefit of the doubt because I cared so much about the students. My second mistake was relying on my computer spell-check program to catch all the misspelled words. Finally, I had imposed on somebody else to carefully proofread my writing for me. As a result of my carelessness, my professional reputation suffered.

Fortunately, my story didn't end there. My internship instructor urged me to take that parent's advice and referred me to the campus writing lab. At first, I felt ashamed about going to the lab, especially because I was near the end of my school counseling training. Now I'm glad that I went. If I am going to be a good counselor, I need to communicate effectively in writing, as well as in speaking.

P.S. One reason that I have written this story is to share with other students an important lesson that I learned the hard way. Another reason is to show you that I can write clearly and spell correctly!

As a trainee and professional, you will be expected to express yourself clearly and to write in a style appropriate for your audience. Those conventions may feel stifling or rigid, but they are the minimum requirements for professional writing. When you write a term paper, research report, thesis, or dissertation, you'll want to have handy a copy of the sixth edition of the *Publication Manual of the American Psychological Association* (APA; 2010).

Baird (2014) also has written an excellent resource for writing effective case notes and summary reports.

"Oh, how boring!" you might think. "Where's the opportunity for me to express myself as a creative person?" Don't despair. You will probably find that using the APA *Manual* will actually help you improve your ability to express yourself. Another helpful and much more entertaining guide is the fourth edition of *The Elements of Style* (Strunk & White, 2000). Writing well, in a manner that is engaging and comprehensible to the reader, does not require you to be boring—just clear.

Learning Writing Skills. Earlier, we said that writing is like eating raisins, so now we'll present you with another metaphor. (Metaphor, by the way, can be a great way for you to express yourself.) Writing is also like playing a musical instrument. When you're learning to play an instrument, you have to focus on the mechanics under the careful guidance of an instructor. Where do I put my fingers? How do I hold the instrument? How do I read music? The answers to those questions come with regular instruction and diligent practice.

The same answers apply to writing. If you have not mastered some of the basics of composition and grammar, seek instruction and begin practicing. As you practice, you will find that soon you no longer worry about the basics. A musician progresses from struggling to reach the high notes to striving to improve his or her tone and phrasing. As a writer, you move from attempting to write transition sentences to focusing on being more concise, vivid, and engaging. Along the way, you set higher expectations for yourself as a writer, and you probably find that writing becomes easier and more enjoyable.

If you haven't already done so, consider asking other students to join you in your writing exercises. Read each other's work and talk about it. As you read one another's writing, focus on what stands out for you as particularly vivid, clear, and organized. Take risks with your attempts to express yourself, stretching yourself to engage fully in the process, and reaching to pull out of the air the words to give voice to your experience.

You have probably guessed by now that this section on writing focuses primarily on practice. Of course, the practice can take a variety of forms. In Chapters 1 and 2, we recommended that you keep a journal to document your training journey. The habit of keeping a journal is not only a wonderful way for you to reflect on your experiences but also a great technique for practicing the craft of writing. As the process of capturing your thoughts and expressing your feelings becomes a daily ritual, you can then read back over your journal to hear the emergence of your own voice and to recognize when it's particularly authentic and clear. Those are the occasions that you will want to pay attention to and build on as you work on improving your writing strengths.

The journal has the added benefit, by the way, of allowing you to make discoveries for yourself in your own time and place. Many students report that writing a journal, especially during their practicum and internship experiences, helped them see not only important issues regarding their clients but also vital information about themselves as counselors. If Chapters 1 and 2 didn't convince you to keep a journal yet, we hope that this third time is the charm!

Writing Mindfully. Mindful writing—taking care to give voice to your experiences and ideas through the written word—is a skill that you can develop with practice and feedback. We think you will find that it is well worth the effort because the improvements will not be limited to your writing. You will find that you will also know yourself better, think more clearly, and trust your creative hunches more.

EXERCISE 4.5 Writing Twice-Told Stories

Take a few minutes to write down a story about yourself that you have often shared. For instance, you might have described how you met your significant other, the way your family spends its vacations, or how you acquired your nickname. A friend's favorite story is how he was lost for several days in the Everglades! No matter what your story is, write it down. Write it out completely, imagining a listener hearing the words as you write them, anticipating the questions a listener might ask you, and providing enough detail so that you capture the experience as vividly as possible (Metzger, 1992).

In a couple of days, make the time to write down another story. Then, a couple of days later, write down another. As you practice, you will find that writing comes more effortlessly. Expressing yourself through the written word, finding your own voice, and saying what you want to say will become second nature.

EXERCISE 4.6 Reading

A Writing Exercise

Read. Read literary novels: As we mentioned in Chapter 1, this also increases your empathy and interpersonal sensitivity. Read newspapers: This keeps you up to date on social issues that affect your clients. Read journals: This keeps you current in the field. Read the backs of cereal boxes: This keeps you happily occupied while you munch on your Cheerios. Read. Now go back and improve one of the "Twice-Told Tales" that you wrote.

Structuring. So far, the writing exercises we have offered have had the feel of narratives or stories that naturally take form as you are writing them. Now you are ready for a different type of skill. The next exercise is to put some structure into your writing.

When you have finished this exercise, applaud yourself. Organizing your material can be tough, but it is essential if you want others to be able to understand what you have written. Even when you write case notes, you may find that your supervisor asks you to follow a specific organizational structure. The ability to organize, along with your understanding of the writing conventions mentioned above, will help you to frame your writing and clarify your thinking.

EXERCISE 4.7 Structuring

A Writing Exercise

Remember the topic that you investigated in the section of this chapter on researching? Imagine that you will be writing a paper about it, and develop an outline. What are the most important areas to cover? How do those areas arrange themselves into headings and subheadings? Is there a natural or implied sequence in the headings and subheadings? Write down possible transition sentences you would use to connect the various components of the paper.

Presenting

> A speech is like an airplane engine. It may sound like hell but you've got to go on.
>
> —William Thomas Piper

The Need for Presentation Skills. The fourth core academic skill is presenting. "Presenting?" you may be saying. "What do you mean? I want to be a professional helper—somebody whose career is listening and responding to clients." Although it may be true that you will do most of your therapeutic work with individuals and small groups, sooner or later you will be asked to share your expertise with others, and that process will often take the form of a presentation.

Many graduate courses require that you gain some experience in presenting your ideas to other students. As a matter of fact, in one graduate program, the last two weeks of all courses were devoted to student presentations. Some cynical students claimed that the instructors were simply tired of teaching. There may be some truth to that interpretation, but it is more likely that the instructors recognized that assigning students the task of preparing and giving a presentation is a great pedagogical technique.

If you are wondering why counselors and therapists need presentation skills, keep the following in mind. School counselors regularly present guidance units for classes, educational programs for parents and community members, and training sessions for school personnel. Mental health clinicians often present educational talks to the public; psychoeducational programs to groups; and reports to boards, funding agencies, and local governments. In addition, many counselors and therapists find that presenting at state, regional, and national conferences enhances their own professional development while building a community of colleagues that can extend across the country. For private practitioners, offering mental health-oriented programs to the public is often an effective strategy for finding appropriate clients and referral sources.

It is likely that there have been many times when you have been practicing your presentation skills without even realizing it. When you participate in your classes, discuss issues with your colleagues, and meet with your mentors and teachers, you are practicing how to present your thoughts with clarity, simplicity, and power.

Class Participation. Let's begin by discussing the everyday presentation skills that you practice when you participate in your classes. Class participation (the two words that stir great dread in those students who are a little shy) does much more than enhance your grade—it offers a tremendous boost to the richness of your training experience. It improves your comprehension, keeps you focused, and helps you make connections. Furthermore, when you participate in class, you are more likely to have read assignments carefully and systematically and even prepared in advance what you might contribute to the class discussion. Participating fully also involves building on the contributions of other members of the class. It means that you can be counted on to offer honest reflections, insightful observations, and supportive comments that contribute significantly to a stimulating learning environment. Like an excellent group therapist, you can bring to class a sense of presence that stimulates productive group dynamics without dominating the process.

In spite of all these benefits, the idea of class participation may still be intimidating to you. Deborah, for instance, found that when she started to share an idea or respond to a professor's question in class, she would immediately flash back to the time she threw up in front of her fourth-grade class. Of course, she knew that she was unlikely to repeat that scene in graduate school, but even recalling her sense of profound embarrassment would make her recoil and flinch in her counseling and therapy classes. By the time Deborah regained some composure, the opportunity for participating had passed. Over time, she simply quit trying to contribute her comments. Similarly, in Chris's first graduate classes, he found that his heart would race and his face would feel hot whenever he spoke in class. He began to fear that he was blushing, and although he could not identify what would make him feel so self-conscious, he decided to stop speaking in class.

Unfortunately, both Deborah and Chris taught themselves *not* to participate. In doing so, they not only deprived themselves of opportunities to connect more deeply with the course material and with their colleagues, but they also created an additional stressor for themselves. Every class period became nerve racking because they dreaded that they would have to speak in class.

Certainly, some faculty members can be intimidating when they put on their game faces and challenge students in class. Keep in mind, however, that if you are having a problem with a particular faculty member, your first and best option is to make an appointment to discuss the issue directly with the person. If that doesn't help to address your concerns, then by all means contact your adviser, another faculty member, or the program director.

In many cases, though, students who are hesitant to be more fully involved in class are apprehensive regardless of the instructor. If you are one of those who are plagued by participation anxiety, keep in mind the fact that the class experience is yours—you are entitled to it. You can do with it what you please. If you walk out of class not understanding something because you didn't ask, you have made a choice to accept less than you deserve. You can also choose to become more involved in the learning process. For example, you can set a goal for your participation. Maybe this week you will ask one question; next week, you can make a comment. Another strategy is to ask your instructor for help. If you have an instructor with whom you feel relatively comfortable, ask her or him for some time to talk about enhancing your involvement in class. The two of you can identify some ways to ease you into greater participation.

Presentation Skills. Class participation typically is improvisational and in the moment. Giving formal presentations is undoubtedly essential for succeeding as a student and practitioner but demands a more comprehensive skill set that takes time to master (Yandell, 2012). The first obstacle you may need to overcome is the common fear of speaking in public. A more fundamental barrier is that you may not even consider yourself a potential public speaker. If you do not have a dramatic flair or enjoy being the center of attention, you may assume that you are not cut out for giving presentations. However, being a good therapist and a good presenter are not mutually exclusive. In fact, people who are successful in both roles have several important characteristics in common. First, they focus their complete attention on each endeavor, whether it is counseling an individual client or presenting to a large audience (Goleman, 2013). Second, they allow themselves to trust the process and stay immediate with both their audiences and their clients. Third, they are adept at tuning into the emotional states of others and resonating with them. Whether it is counseling or presenting, they read the reactions of their clients and audience members.

Improving Your Presentations. When preparing for your presentations, remember that you want to challenge yourself and your audience. You can help your audience reflect critically on your topic by deciding what points you want to make and identifying the most effective ways to do so. People enjoy being challenged if you provide sufficient support.

Keep in mind that you do not have to be a world-class orator to give a fine talk (Walker, 2010). Below are some simple and practical tips for dramatically improving your presentations both in classes and at professional conferences.

- *Organize the format.* Decide how you want to impart the information (for example, brief lecture, discussion, or group activity) and how much time you want to spend on the various points of your presentation. Some people follow the presentation rule: "Tell them what you're going to tell them. Tell them. Then tell them what you told them."
- *Know the audience.* Does your audience consist of other students whose knowledge of the topic is similar to yours? Or are they relative newcomers to the subject? You will design your talk to address the audience's needs. Similarly, if the audience is a class of third-grade students, your presentation style will differ dramatically from what you would employ with adults.
- *Practice.* Practice more than once. If you can't find an audience with whom to practice, practice in front of the mirror. Go through the entire presentation again and again so that you develop a sense for timing, clarity, and organization. Heppner and his colleagues (1999) found that practicing increased counseling students' self-efficacy and confidence. The researchers found that presentations not only were an effective way to learn public speaking but also promoted higher order thinking skills. As you can see, these findings provide vindication for those instructors who require student presentations.
- *Prepare for pitfalls.* You might expect 30 people to show up and find five in the room. Or 150! You might reserve the last 10 minutes of your

presentation for a question-and-answer period and find that not one person has a single question. You might plan to use PowerPoint and then realize there is no equipment in your room. What do you do in these situations? Try to anticipate what might throw a kink into your works and have a backup plan. Better yet, have several backup plans.

- *Know your subject matter.* We recently attended a presentation in which the speaker made frequent errors in summarizing the relevant research. The result was confusing and frustrating. Be sure you know your subject, including the details regarding any figures and graphs that you may use to supplement your talk. Anticipate the possible questions that audience members may ask.

- *Keep it lively.* Many appealing public speakers pepper their talks with stories, slides, and video clips to dramatize their material. Whenever they have the opportunity, they also include role plays, group activities, or panel presentations to keep the audience engaged. Thinking creatively about how you can best communicate your ideas will likely improve your presentation and keep audience members interested. One cautionary note—avoid being too cute. A YouTube clip of playful kittens may be precious, but it can be insensitive if your subject is a serious one. Also, you can stretch some metaphors only so far before the audience becomes bored, or even worse, groans.

- *Ask for feedback.* Receiving feedback on your presentation can be enormously valuable, but remember that you may be your own best evaluator. In class, as well as conference presentations, the speaker typically receives some type of evaluation. Occasionally, especially at conferences, the evaluations will provide unhelpful comments, such as "Temperature was too cold," "Room was too crowded," or "I thought this was something else." At times, though, an insightful participant will make a comment such as, "The section on unique characteristics was especially helpful. The part about the relationship could have been more thorough."

  Frequently, presenters will find that the evaluations are consistent with their own take on the presentation. They know, for instance, that they rushed the ending or lost their focus a little in the middle. The point is, then, to read the evaluations, but don't be crushed if some of your audience members are critical. Pay attention to the constructive criticism and set goals for yourself to continue enhancing your presentation skills.

- *Watch others present.* Attend talks whenever possible and critique them for your own benefit. What worked? What didn't? Learn from the successes (and mistakes) of others.

- *Use your emotional arousal.* Finally, and perhaps most important, use your emotional arousal by channeling that energy into productive work. Whenever you find yourself starting to tense up and worry, decide what particular task you can carry out to prepare for your presentation. Perhaps the task is to design your handout materials, develop your PowerPoint presentation, imagine yourself successfully articulating your major points, practice your delivery, or just enjoy a relaxing run. Whatever the specific task, you are transforming that worry and tension into positive and productive preparation—and the more prepared you are, the less anxiety you'll feel.

The tension related to public speaking can be unpleasant and distracting, but as you gain experience in using your arousal, you'll find that you're not just feeling more relaxed, you're also feeling more confident. One technique that we're certain will not work for you is avoidance. Unless you develop your presentation skills now, the anxiety will remain, lurking and waiting for the chance to emerge. Then, when you're called unexpectedly to present, you'll be less prepared to handle it.

Take time now to practice, and remember, many of your peers are just as nervous as you are. You can be great resources for each other, so make the most of this time together and support each other as you try your hand at presenting.

EXERCISE 4.8 Preparing and Practicing

Take the topic you have been investigating as you have read through this chapter. You now have an outline for a paper, so use it to formulate a 10-minute presentation. Ask your study group if you can present it to them for their feedback on your presentation style.

This approach worked for Adrian, who was very apprehensive about public speaking. She asked her statistics study group if they would listen to her presentation on human development and give her suggestions for improvement. The students not only listened and gave advice but also shared their own fears of public speaking. Soon, all the students in the group were sharing tips, encouraging each other, and providing general support. If you don't have a study group yet, ask your roommates or classmates to serve as an audience for you.

EXERCISE 4.9 Imagining Success

Prior to giving a presentation in class, take time to imagine yourself as successful. Find a quiet, private place and sit or lie comfortably. Close your eyes and imagine that you're in the classroom and that it's time for you to go to the front of the class. You have all your materials ready, your name is called, you pick up your materials and walk confidently to the front of the room. You feel just excited enough to be sharp and energetic. You know your material. You're confident in your ability to present it effectively. Continue to go through your presentation, anticipating questions and feedback, and see yourself as you plan to be. Don't stop the imagery until you have finished the presentation, received applause or acknowledgment, and returned (triumphantly!) to your seat.

EXERCISE 4.10 Breathing

Lie on your back with your hands on your stomach. Breathe in and out, paying attention to how your stomach rises and falls with each inhalation and exhalation of breath. Do this for several minutes until you have a sense for what this feels like. Now sit up and continue to breathe in the same manner. Breathing diaphragmatically will help ease your tension and slow you down. It will also improve your voice tone!

Summary

Being a successful counselor relies, at least to some degree, on your ability to think mindfully about the helping process, your clients, and yourself. Through reading, researching, writing, and presenting, you can savor the pleasures of pursuing knowledge, refining your skills, and gaining personal awareness. Academic skills do so much more than just help you earn good grades—they help you succeed as a counselor.

Resources

gradPSYCH

www.apa.org/gradpsych/index.aspx

An excellent resource is gradPSYCH, a magazine that the American Psychological Association of Graduate Students publishes with quarterly digital editions. Every issue includes articles providing tips on succeeding in graduate school, interesting profiles of students, and advice on specific challenges, such as coauthoring with faculty, writing the dissertation discussion section, and pursuing an internship.

Study Skills Self-Help Information

www.ucc.vt.edu/stdysk/stdyhlp.html

This site provides information that is basic, but if your academic skills are a little rusty, then reviewing these practical tips could be very useful. It covers such topics as scheduling time, setting priorities, and taking notes.

References

Adler, R., Rosenfield, L., & Towne, N. (1989). *Interplay: The process of interpersonal communication.* New York, NY: Holt, Rinehart & Winston.

American Psychological Association. (2010). *Publication manual of the American Psychological Association* (6th ed.). Washington, DC: Author.

Baird, B. N. (2014). *The internship, practicum, and field placement handbook* (7th ed.). Upper Saddle River, NJ: Prentice Hall.

Beins, B. C. (2012). Effective writing: Did you mean to say that? In P. J. Giordano, S. F. Davis, & C. A. Licht (Eds.), *Your graduate training in psychology: Effective strategies for success* (pp. 117–132). Thousand Oaks, CA: Sage.

Chamberlin, J. (2009, November). Are online classes for you? *gradPSYCH, 7*(4). Retrieved from http://www.apa.org/gradpsych/2009/11/e-learn.aspx

Cozolino, L. (2010). *The neuroscience of psychotherapy: Healing the social brain* (2nd ed.). New York, NY: Norton.

Csikszentmihalyi, M. (1997). *Finding flow: The psychology of engagement with everyday life.* New York, NY: Basic Books.

Damasio, A. (1994). *Descartes' error: Emotion, reason, and the human brain.* New York, NY: Putnam.

Erickson, M. H., Rossi, E. L., & Rossi, S. I. (1976). *Hypnotic realities.* Hoboken, NJ: Wiley.

Frye, M. (1995). Oppression. In M. L. Andersen & P. H. Collins (Eds.), *Race, class and gender: An anthology* (2nd ed., pp. 37–41). Belmont, CA: Wadsworth.

Goleman, D. (1995). *Emotional intelligence.* New York, NY: Bantam Books.

Goleman, D. (2013). *Focus: The hidden driver of excellence.* New York, NY: HarperCollins.

Heppner, P. P., Rooney, S. C., Flores, L. Y., Tarrant, J. M., Howard, J. K., Mulholland, A. M., . . . Lilly, R. L. (1999). Salient effects of practice poster sessions on counselor development: Implications for research training and professional identification. *Counselor Education and Supervision, 38*, 205–217.

Hergenhahn, B. R., & Henley, T. (2014). *An introduction to the history of psychology* (7th ed.). Belmont, CA: Wadsworth.

Hoskins, C. M. (2000, August). Get a life! Top 10 list for a first-year student. *Counseling Today, 43*, 32, 36.

Hughes, F. R., & Kleist, D. M. (2005). First-semester experiences of counselor education doctoral students. *Counselor Education and Supervision, 45*, 97–108.

Jung, C. G. (1965). *Memories, dreams, reflections.* New York, NY: Vintage Books.

Langer, E. (1997). *The power of mindful learning.* Reading, MA: Addison-Wesley.

Martin, W. E., Easton, C., Wilson, S., Takemoto, M., & Sullivan, S. (2004). Salience of emotional intelligence as a core characteristic of being a counselor. *Counselor Education and Supervision, 44*, 17–30.

Martindale, C. (1981). *Cognition and consciousness.* Homewood, IL: Dorsey.

Meltzoff, J. (1998). *Critical thinking about research: Psychology and related fields.* Washington, DC: American Psychological Association.

Metzger, D. (1992). *Writing for your life: A guide and companion to the inner worlds.* New York, NY: HarperCollins.

Presbury, J., Echterling, L. G., & McKee, J. E. (2008). *Beyond brief counseling: An integrative approach* (2nd ed.). New York, NY: Pearson.

Strunk, W., & White, E. B. (2000). *The elements of style* (4th ed.). New York, NY: Allyn & Bacon.

Walker, T. J. (2010). *How to give a pretty good presentation: A speaking survival guide for the rest of us.* Hoboken, NJ: Wiley.

Yandell, L. (2012). Developing your presentation skills. In P. J. Giordano, S. F. Davis, & C. A. Licht (Eds.), *Your graduate training in psychology: Effective strategies for success* (pp. 175–184). Thousand Oaks, CA: Sage.

Zeigarnik, B. (1938). On finished and unfinished tasks. In W. D. Ellis (Ed. & Trans.), *A source book of Gestalt psychology* (pp. 300–314). New York, NY: Harcourt Brace.

5

Mindfully Managing Stress

There were only two times when I felt stress in graduate school—night and day.

—A colleague

What man needs is not a tensionless state but the striving and struggling for something worth longing and groping for.

—Viktor Frankl

B y this stage of your life journey, you have probably heard a great deal about stress management. You may even think you already know all you need about stress and taking care of yourself. However, before you are tempted to skip this chapter with the assumption that you have heard it all before, please read on. Have you ever considered *embracing* your stress? Developing resilience under stress is an excellent way to thrive throughout both your training and career, and one very effective way to address stress and to promote well-being is to engage in mindfulness awareness. This level of awareness can actually help you learn to be intrigued by, and open to, your stress.

Although graduate school can be challenging and stressful, the way you view and handle the work involved in earning a graduate degree can be critical. Jon Kabat-Zinn (1994), who is credited with helping usher mindfulness practices into mainstream America via the medical profession, shared a profound thought about the way we work: "What is my job on the planet with a capital 'J'? You can start asking this question at any time, at any age" (p. 206).

Keep this quote in mind as we explore elements of stress and ways to mindfully manage it throughout this chapter. In all honesty, training is stressful. In fact, all forms of training—athletic, academic, or occupational—are designed to involve increasingly demanding and challenging tasks. Physical exercises, comprehensive examinations, and field placements are all different forms of stress. Of course, successful training also includes plenty of support and guidance as you gradually progress through achievable steps. Although stress can become *distressing* to individuals when there are negative ramifications, *eustress* is a form of stress that provides a healthy level of challenge or a sense of positive motivation for action. The trick is that stress can become either distress or eustress, depending on your perception of the stressors (Fevre, Kolt, & Matheny, 2006).

As a trainee in a helping profession, you will experience stress on a daily basis. You may often feel as if you are living by the law of supply and demand. You have limitations regarding your "supply"—resources such as time, energy, money, and information. But in the meantime, your training, as well as life in general, continues to place seemingly limitless "demands" on you—tests, reading assignments, work obligations, and family responsibilities. It's no wonder that you may feel overwhelmed and depleted. At especially stressful times, you may feel like you are flailing and thrashing around like one of those giant dancing windsocks outside of a used car dealership.

Because stress is an essential part of your training anyway, perhaps now is the time to learn how to welcome your stress. Just as you may relish a vigorous physical workout, you can be enthusiastic when you are engaging in the challenging experiences that help you to grow stronger as a counselor and therapist. In the first half of this chapter, we offer specific tips for successfully managing the stressors that you will face in your graduate and professional life. We also present important principles for dealing with stress. Balance, harmony, pacing, and a healthy perspective are important components of keeping your bearings along your journey (Rollins, 2005). Remember that although many of our recommendations may appear to be commonsense advice, if you—and indeed most people—fail to practice these steps regularly, then how common are they really? Isn't it ironic that as counselors and therapists, we want to help *others* deal with stress, but we're often reluctant, unwilling, or unable to address our own?

Once we have covered these practical approaches to managing stress—the "how" questions—we turn to the meaning of stress—the "why" questions. In the second half of this chapter, we encourage you to do much more than merely manage your stress as you follow your calling to become a helping professional. We invite you to make your stress meaningful. In his book *Psychotherapy and Existentialism,* Viktor Frankl (1967) asserted, "What man really needs is a sound amount of tension aroused by the challenge of a meaning he has to fulfill" (pp. 87–88).

What meaning do *you* have to fulfill by completing a challenging and rigorous training program? You are going to graduate school because you feel a calling to become a helping professional. You know it is not an easy journey, but how meaningful is it to you right now? Certainly, you realize that attending graduate school adds stress to your life. You have made a public commitment by embarking on this adventure, but you have no guarantee that you will succeed. How will you make that stress worthwhile? What point is there to the struggles and frustrations you must encounter in your training?

You might be wondering how your life experiences would change if you actually accepted—even embraced—the stress that is inevitably part of a productive training and professional career. We believe your outcome would be considerably different! Like an oyster that transforms an irritating grain of sand into a pearl, you have the chance to accept stress and eventually create something beautiful.

Stressed Out

Bill's Story

One particular year was a very stressful time in my life. I had just returned home after serving several months in the Middle East with the Air National Guard during the war. My mother died very suddenly of a massive stroke. My marriage of 11 years was crumbling. On top of all that, I had just started a graduate program in counselor education. The demands on my life were overwhelming!

By October of that year, I was completely stressed out. I began the painful journey of a separation and divorce, moved into an apartment, started visitation with my son every other weekend, and watched helplessly as my bank account dwindled into nothingness. I found myself feeling isolated, alienated from others, depressed, and lifeless.

How did I survive? Faith and hope helped tremendously. I believed that the stressful time would not last forever and that I would become stronger, wiser, and more compassionate from enduring the pain of those life events. A few very close friends and family members also enabled me to keep going because they accepted my situation, supported and encouraged me, and truly lightened my load as I made this difficult journey. I am very thankful for the people who allowed me to vent my anger, shed my tears, and express my fears. I am also grateful that I had the courage to seek professional therapy. The therapeutic relationship empowered and strengthened me to move on with my life.

I learned to take responsibility for my own life (and my thoughts, feelings, and actions) and became intentional about eating better, sleeping more, and exercising regularly to regain my energy and relieve some of the pressure in my life. The people who really cared about me never gave up on me, and as a result, I learned to never give up on myself.

Stress

We learn the rope of life by untying its knots.

—Jean Toomer

If you have ever watched nature programs on television, you have probably noticed that those shows typically feature some hapless insect, bird, or mammal being eaten by another animal. On a recent program, a narrator calmly explained how the world is divided into predators and prey. To illustrate the concept, a mink was shown dragging along a reluctant muskrat to dinner—presumably as the main course, rather than as a companion. While a cow was shown grazing, the narrator pointed out that some creatures are herbivores. The program went on to present a sampling of carnivores—a weasel enthusiastically chewing on a mouse—and omnivores—a raccoon eating a fish and, for dessert, a plant. The narrator concluded by asserting that at the top of nature's food chain are humans, the only species on the planet without a natural enemy.

So humans have *no* natural enemy? If that's the case, why are so many of us dying before our time every year? For Americans, the answer is a line from "Pogo," a comic strip from years ago: "We have met the enemy and he is us." Suicides are among our top killers (Violence Policy Center, 2012). Our own behaviors—smoking, poor nutrition, and lack of exercise—are also major contributors to our early deaths. One factor, however, is a common thread among all the major causes of death. That factor is stress. Many researchers now believe that stress is involved in more illnesses than any other single contributor known to science (Barlow, Rapee, & Perini, 2014).

Our problem as human beings is that even though we are at the top of the food chain, what seems to be eating us is stress.

In a very real sense, stress is a natural part of living. Stressors are any demands placed on you by life events and circumstances that require your attention, time, or energy. Not all stress is bad. In fact, you may feel bored, empty, and unfulfilled without enough stress in your life. As you will read in this chapter, a certain level of stress can enable you to perform at your best, but too much may deplete and overwhelm you. Would you ever study for a big test and put in all the necessary time for an important paper if you didn't feel some stress about your performance? Yet when examinations, papers, relationships, and work are clamoring for your attention all at once, you can quickly feel overwhelmed. At these times, you are in a state of distress. Your life demands are far exceeding your personal resources, and the results may feel anything but positive.

The Stress of Helping

> One cannot be deeply responsive to the world without being saddened very often.
>
> —Erich Fromm

Helping professions are very stressful occupations. The responsibility inherent in counseling and therapy, combined with the professional isolation that often occurs, can cause many practitioners to become so physically and emotionally distressed that they burn out. People with higher levels of coping resources, such as self-care activities, recreation, and social support, however, tend to report lower levels of occupational stress (McEwen, Gianaros, & Milliken, 2011). This research suggests that graduate school is an ideal time for you to improve your stress-related skills. Now is the time for you to take positive steps to handle stress and prevent burnout in your career.

Distress

> The process of living is the process of reacting to stress.
>
> —Stanley Sarnoff

When you begin to feel overwhelmed by particularly stressful events or circumstances, you may notice personal signs of distress. First, you may observe any of these physical symptoms: racing heartbeat, dry mouth, and increased sweating. You may also develop indigestion, feel nauseous, develop migraine headaches, and sense pain in your neck and shoulders. You may discover that you are sick more often with colds and viruses. Then you may observe, on an emotional level, that you feel more irritable, fatigued, sad, or apprehensive. You may discover that you laugh nervously or that you have the urge to cry, scream, hide, or argue more than usual. On a cognitive level, you may find that you have more difficulty concentrating and making decisions. Finally, on a behavioral level, you may notice that you act more impulsively, are more prone toward accidents, or feel tempted to smoke, drink, or medicate yourself. You may find it difficult to relax or sleep.

Prolonged symptoms of distress may also include increased blood pressure, increased secretion of stomach acids, and decreased immunity protection against other diseases. The more of these signs you notice in yourself, the more assertively you will need to respond with healthy stress management strategies.

Stressful Events

What you can do is learn to take better care of yourself, now and in the future. Life is filled with situations both large and small, joyful and tragic. Any of these can lead to stress or, when multiplied together, distress. An online adaptation of the classic *Social Readjustment Rating Scale* (Holmes & Rahe, 1967) measures some of these life events and their impact on us. Take a few moments to visit this website and take the inventory: http://www.acc.com/aboutacc/newsroom/pressreleases/upload/srrs.pdf.

As you consider the number of stressful life events you have encountered over the past year, ask yourself how you have handled all these events. These researchers noted that unresolved stress can accumulate over time, multiplying the pressure on your life. Please note that the higher your score, the more attention you will want to give to healthy stress approaches.

When It "Hurts Good"

Rachel's Story

When I entered my graduate counseling program, I anticipated a great deal of stress. However, in a smug sort of way, I thought that I was prepared for it. As a massage therapist, I was already in the business of dealing with

(Continued)

(Continued)

stress. I ate well, exercised every day, and practiced deep breathing and meditation. I wrote in my journal, sought solitude, prayed, listened to soft music, and all while the sweet fragrance of aromatherapy dispensed itself throughout my house.

These stress reducers worked very well for a while. What I did not foresee was the stress that was to come out of getting to know myself in a more in-depth and revealing way. That first semester, not only did I worry and stress out about the normal things—grades, finances, and relation-ships—but also my program required me to take a very close look at myself. "This is not what it's supposed to be about," I thought. "I'm here to help *other* people."

Later, a professor explained to me, "You can't expect clients to confide in you their flaws and imperfections if you are not willing to do the same work yourself." This made sense, but I thought, "I'm not sure that I'm pre-pared to deal with this AND worry about writing papers."

I stopped exercising because I felt that the time would be better spent studying. I started eating a lot of those little snacks from machines to quell my anxiety. Meditating was out because statistics problems kept popping into my "white space." The stress was beginning to consume me.

Fortunately, in my second semester, as I became more familiar and in tune with the therapeutic process of counseling others, I also benefited. I began to discover better ways of looking at things and more effective ways of expressing myself. I was also learning, through my experiences, all of the things that I would want to provide for my potential clients. Of course, there were growing pains, but they were like the soreness that is felt when I am getting a massage and the therapist is working directly on the painful spot. It is a hedonistic pain that hurts—but it "hurts good." I was gaining more from my counseling program than just a master's degree; I was gaining the ability to function more productively in the world.

All this is not to say that I have no more stressful days—for there are plenty. I have come to learn how to balance my schoolwork with exercise, meditation, and time for myself. However, it has been the personal growth through the trials and tribulations of my program that has helped me to become a stronger, healthier person.

Responding to Stress

> You can out-distance that which is running after you, but not what is running inside you.
>
> –Rwandan Proverb

The ability to effectively respond to stress, like many other skills, varies tremendously. Some people fall to pieces if they break a fingernail, but they are not likely to be admitted to graduate programs in the helping professions. It is a safe bet that you have been able to manage stress pretty well. In fact, you probably can face looming deadlines, car breakdowns, and financial woes without being overwhelmed. However, you cannot put your life on hold when you enter training, so the added pressures of graduate school can be a tremendous strain. Now is the time to consider specific steps you can take to better handle stress.

Cannon (1927) coined the popular phrase "fight or flight" to characterize two fundamental and alternative reactions to stress. Although you have heard it countless times in our popular culture and everyday conversations, the phrase actually would be more accurate if it were reversed. Flight is by far the much more common response to an alarm in virtually every species that has been studied (Schmidt, Richey, Zvolensky, & Maner, 2008). Recently, researchers have proposed expanding this model to include another key response: "freeze." To freeze (Barlow, 2002) is an option that is especially frequent in situations in which the threat is perceived as overpowering and overwhelming. As a result, many therapists currently use the phrase "fight, flight, or freeze" to characterize the three common reactions to trauma.

Much of the research on stress has focused on animals, and the model of three typical responses has been a generally accurate description of their reactions to stress. However, humans are much more complex. They are likely also to care for those around them and bring others into their social network during times of stress. Therefore, Taylor (2006) suggested adding "tend and befriend" to the stress response model. Her research found that humans are more likely to tend to the needs of the most vulnerable—the young, ill, and aged—and to befriend strangers by offering social and practical support.

These studies do not necessarily suggest that animals respond only to stress in certain ways and humans in others. In fact, some species of animals with high levels of oxytocin affiliate when threatened (Taylor, 2006). And some humans resort more frequently to violence when stressed. You may want to think about the ways in which you personally respond. If you have maximized your flight or fight responses, perhaps those perpetual butterflies in your stomach are a reminder of just how good you have become at this reaction. Maybe it is time to look at new ways to make the most of the energy that stress can provide you. Reaching out to others, drawing strength from relationships, and contributing to your community are also fine ways to transform your stress into connections and creativity. Of course, there are times when escaping for a while from stressors by finding refuge in nature, sunbathing on the beach, or reading a novel can be wonderful, relaxing, and refreshing breaks. And there are other times when fighting the good fight, advocating for the rights of your clients, and speaking forcefully about important issues are essential. The key for you is to recognize the possibilities and then take advantage of your own ingenuity to adaptively respond to stress.

Whether you decide to flee, fight, freeze, tend, or befriend when you encounter stressors, you can also develop a wide range of adaptive responses to manage your stress. Consider the following suggestions and recall the personal examples illustrated in the stories earlier in this chapter. As you read through this section, assess your own stress response strategies.

Resting

This may not be as easy as it seems, but find ways to relax and "let go" of each day's events so that you can get the rest you need. Many people under stress may say they are sleeping "like a baby," but what that really means is that they are waking up crying every couple of hours! Adult human beings need between seven and nine hours of sleep to function well. In many cultures, there is also a rest or "nap" time during the middle of each day. Recent research actually demonstrated that taking a nap enhanced learning (Debarnot, Castellani, Valenza, Sebastiani, & Guillot, 2011). So perhaps our parents, caretakers, and kindergarten teachers were on to something. You are, after all, human, and your body must rest to replenish your energy supply, yet you may be sleep deprived at the most critical times, when you need rest the most. Are you getting the rest you need?

Eating Well

In Chapter 3, we considered healthy eating as one of the essential ways to meet your basic needs. Good nutrition is also important because it provides your body with the fuel to deal with the daily hassles and struggles. Especially because you are leading the hectic life of a graduate student, you need to eat more fruits and vegetables to function well. When under stress, you may be tempted to grab quick foods on the run or to skip meals altogether, but eating nothing or foods with little nutritional value, such as Pop Tarts, potato chips, and pizza, will not provide you with critical energy when you need it most. Also, carefully monitor your consumption of drinks with caffeine and alcohol, which you may be using to become alert in the morning and to calm yourself at night. Moderation and balance are the key. How do your nutritional habits measure up?

Exercising

As we also discussed in Chapter 3, activities such as walking, jogging, biking, swimming, aerobic classes, and weight training are fun ways to improve your fitness level and sense of well-being. However, they also relieve stress and provide you with additional energy to persevere in your training. People who exercise regularly find that they usually rest better at night. Make it a part of your daily routine to exercise moderately for at least 30 minutes.

Have you ever noticed that when you are under stress you find it hard to remember things? Studies of the impact of prolonged stress show a marked degeneration of the hippocampus (Veenit, Riccio, & Sandi, 2014), which can lead to poor memory. The good news is that research has suggested that new cells can actually be generated in the hippocampus through physical exercise (Ferreira-Vieira, Bastos, Pereira, Moreira, & Massensini, 2014). Spending time in the gym can do much more than relieve stress and improve muscle tone. It may also improve your memory and help you "bulk up" your brain!

Of course, what you do for exercise is up to you, but make sure that you have some fun with it. A word of caution here: If you have not exercised for quite some time, getting a health screening is the best place to start. And take care! A few precautions, such as stretching your muscles and wearing safety gear, can help you avoid injuring yourself. Remember that your primary goal is to feel better, not tear yourself up. How would you assess your physical fitness at this time?

Using Humor

There is much truth to the sentiment that laughter is the best medicine. Laughter releases endorphins in your brain that help to relax and calm you (Weems, 2014). Humor can also be a powerful therapeutic tool for developing rapport with your clients and promoting their resilience (Gladding, 2006). Being able to laugh at yourself is probably the best single sign of a healthy self-concept.

Of course, you can add some humor to your life by renting a comedy movie, watching a situation comedy on television, reading the comics in the newspaper, or reading humorous literature. You can also make a point of being with people who add laughter to your life. Even more important than appreciating humor is expressing it. You are probably not a professional comedian, but you definitely have the potential to see the humor in the daily aggravations, nuisances, and hassles you encounter. By putting a funny spin on such annoyances, you can "thumb your nose" at them and laugh some of your stress away. As Langston Hughes said, "Humor is your unconscious therapy." How's your humor quotient?

Relaxing, Refreshing, Renewing, and Revitalizing

Do something just for *you*—a trip to the spa for a therapeutic massage can work wonders when you are under a lot of pressure. Yoga, prayer, meditation, mindfulness exercises, tai chi, and biofeedback classes are just a small sampling of the countless everyday strategies that promote relaxation responses. Even in the moment, you can mindfully take in a long, slow, deep breath, allow the tension to drain away, and give your soul some time to replenish itself.

Seeking Professional Help

Talking with someone you can trust, whether it is a counselor, therapist, nutritionist, or personal trainer, can provide you with some guidelines for leading a healthier lifestyle. If you are feeling so overwhelmed by stress that it is impairing your performance and sabotaging your well-being, contact the counseling or health center on your campus. Professional helpers can guide and support you through this difficult time. In Chapter 7, we also discuss the added benefit of seeking professional help for a student of counseling and therapy. You gain the invaluable experience of knowing exactly what it's like to be a client, which will enhance your empathic skills once you begin working with others. One final note about seeking professional help: If you have been suffering from prolonged stress, anxiety, or depression, do not postpone your decision a minute longer. Set this book aside and make an appointment right now!

Reflecting

Confucius once said, "The person who wants too much will always be in need." You may find that much of your stress comes from wanting too much.

Monitor carefully what you may merely want and what you really *need* in order to live well. For too many Americans, enough rarely seems to be enough. Watch what you are striving for and keep tabs on your thoughts and attitudes. Negative attitudes can drain you of valuable energy and add insult to injury when you are under duress. An anonymous writer once cautioned, "Watch your thoughts; they become your words. Watch your words; they become your actions. Watch your actions; they become your habits. Watch your habits; they become your character. Watch your character; it becomes your destiny."

Managing Your Time

Set realistic goals and prioritize your life events. Because you cannot do everything or please everyone in your life, you must learn how to say "No" to some things and make room to say "Yes" to your higher priorities (Covey, Merrill, & Merrill, 1994). You can practice ways of saying "No" and "Yes" in the exercise later in this chapter.

Mindful Management of Stress

Mindful Schools (Fernando, 2013) is an innovative program that offers training to teachers, school counselors, and school psychologists to educate elementary, middle, and secondary school students in the practice of mindfulness techniques. By learning the basics of mindful breathing, listening, and moving, students are able to sit with their stress, allowing the associated thoughts and feelings to pass through their awareness, acknowledging the stress, but not allowing it to impact them. These fundamental and practical techniques have been found not only to reduce stress but also to enhance learning.

Mindfulness teaches that experiencing negative emotions is not wrong; it is simply part of being human. In fact, these emotions are necessary at times, especially in cases of perceived danger. As you will read in Chapter 8, when the amygdala stimulates the sympathetic nervous system, you are more able to react quickly to a perceived threat. These responses can be very adaptive, but the stress hormones they create also stay in our bodies, causing us to feel "charged." Human beings take longer to discharge these physiological reactions than do animals. Therefore, the more time we spend in such heightened states, the more stressed our bodies feel, leading to maladaptive physiological and behavioral patterns. So what starts off as helpful can become harmful (i.e., decreased immune function, psychological distress) in the long run if we do not learn to mindfully manage our stress.

Fortunately, cultivating positive experiences through mindfulness practices, such as tapping into feelings of love and compassion, can help stimulate the parasympathetic (rest and digest) nervous system, which allows us to balance out the stress on our sympathetic nervous system. This cultivation of positive emotions can have a remarkable effect on our overall happiness and even counterbalance stress and increase recovery from stress-related illness (Fredrickson, 2002).

Mindfulness practice can take many forms. Simply engaging in quiet, mindful breathing for a few minutes a day can have calming effects. In fact, Mendelson and colleagues (2010) completed a 12-week study demonstrating the effectiveness of school-based mindfulness and yoga interventions. They found that students, teachers, and administrators were attracted to these techniques. More important, the interventions had significant positive outcomes, including reduced rumination, decreased intrusive thoughts, and lowered emotional arousal.

If you are a kinesthetic learner, you might prefer mindful movement through yoga, meditative walking, or exploring a labyrinth. Another mindfulness technique involves cultivating gratitude and loving-kindness (Kielty & Gilligan, 2013). For example, girls experiencing multiple life stressors participated in a loving-kindness mindfulness meditation that took place outside in the spring-green grass, underneath a majestic oak tree, beside the track outside of the school. The girls sat on the ground, touched various parts of the earth, such as a stick, a leaf, or the grass, and then closed their eyes. They spent five minutes engaged in mindful breathing and imagined being surrounded by kindness and love, in whatever form made sense for them. One girl imagined her grandmother, and another said that she encountered herself as a young woman. The girls then walked quietly outside for a few moments and came back to the circle.

After practicing the loving-kindness mindfulness exercise, the girls talked about why a sense of being loved seems to evade them and how they would like to learn to feel peaceful and grounded in spite of the fractured relationships and pain swirling around them. They also expressed gratitude for the small things in life and shared what brought happiness into their lives, such as the warmth of the sun or the smile of a friend. The girls then offered ideas about how they could use mindfulness practices for themselves in distressing situations. Several of them shared that they felt they could tap into this sense of peace and self-love they experienced during the mindfulness exercise.

Ironically, although it is rapidly gaining popularity in grades K–12, the mindful schools movement has not reached the same level of acceptance in undergraduate and graduate education. So this is your opportunity to be one of the pioneers who applies mindfulness techniques to enhance your own learning and to manage your stress. Practice some loving-kindness for yourself!

EXERCISE 5.1 Stress for Success

You cannot have made it as far as you have in your life without encountering a variety of stressors. Take a few minutes to reflect on how you have successfully dealt with stress by answering these questions.

1. What were the major stressors you faced during the past year?

_____

_____

_____

_____

2. What reactions did you notice yourself having to these stressors?

_____

_____

_____

_____

3. How did you manage to handle your stress?

_____

_____

_____

_____

4. What important lessons did you learn from these experiences?

_____

_____

_____

_____

Keep your stress successes in mind as you read the following suggestions on managing stress. Like Rachel in the preceding story, you may need to remind yourself of the strategies you have already successfully used.

EXERCISE 5.2 Ways of Saying "No" and "Yes!"

Saying "no" to others is probably difficult for you. After all, you want to become a professional *helper*. Here are some different variations on the theme of declining requests.

- *The polite no.* "I'm sorry, but I really have to pass on your request."
- *The postponement no.* "I might be able to do this in the future, but I can't right now."
- *The considerate no.* "It was very nice of you to think of me, and I'm honored you asked. However, I won't be able to help you with that right now."
- *The backpedaling no.* "I'm sorry, I made a mistake. I shouldn't have committed myself so soon. I must either reschedule or back out this time."
- *The forthright no.* "I'm sorry, but I have no desire, time, energy, or inclination to do anything like that."

Saying "no" can be disheartening if you don't also consider what priorities you are affirming when you turn down a request. Consider that each time you say "no" to an opportunity, you are saying "yes" to another, so be sure that every "no" counts for something important. Here are some ways to remind yourself of the positive values and goals you are pursuing when you say no to certain things.

- *The committed yes.* "I'm determined to do my best in my practicum class."
- *The dedicated yes.* "I want to be sure that I stay a vital contributor to my family's well-being."
- *The playful yes.* "I'm making time for some recreation in my busy schedule."
- *The spiritual yes.* "I'm preserving my time for meditation and reflection."
- *The compromise yes.* "Instead of what you're requesting, I can help out in a smaller way."

Think about the last time that somebody made a request that you wished you had declined. In the space below, write out a couple of answers you could have given by combining one type of "no" with one type of "yes."

_____

_____

_____

_____

_____

_____

_____

Beyond Stress

Life is at its best when it's shaken and stirred.

—F. Paul Facult

The idea of stress has inspired a great deal of productive thinking, fruitful research, and useful interventions in counseling and therapy. However, the concept does have its limitations. For one thing, its physiological emphasis fails to capture the complexities and depth of the human experience. When we must confront challenges or endure difficult conditions, we do have physiological reactions. But as human beings, we are also reaching out to others, creatively coping with threats, courageously sacrificing ourselves, or experiencing spiritual transcendence. Labeling these responses as merely reactions to stress is like using the concept of arousal to capture the essence of romantic passion. It is foolish to reduce our mysterious strivings and deeply powerful emotions to only physical functioning.

Another limitation to the concept of stress is that it does not take into account the creative, transformative powers that human beings can demonstrate under challenging and difficult circumstances. This mechanistic model suggests that humans may be able to reduce the negative impact of stress but can never actually gain positive transcendence through facing stressors with courage, hope, and perseverance. Think about the most important achievements you have accomplished, the greatest lessons about life that you have learned, and the times in your life that you went through the most dramatic positive changes. Our bet is that you did not reach these new heights without some stress.

We began this chapter by inviting you to embrace your stress. In the previous section on mindfulness, we encouraged you to allow stress to pass through your awareness. Now, once again, we urge you to face your stress and to learn from it. Taking this stance toward stress now, while you are in graduate school, will strengthen your ability to take good care of yourself later in your career. You will find that the personal exploration that you engage in during your training experience will remind you of your own resilience and strengths. Embracing your stress can lead to surprising discoveries and delightful rewards. After all, "stressed" spelled backward is "desserts"!

Resilience Under Stress

> Life does not happen to us, it happens from us.
>
> —Michael Wickett

You will read more about the concept of resilience (Echterling & Stewart, 2008) in Chapter 9, where we focus on crises, traumas, and disasters. We mention it now because resilience, which is the ability to bounce back from life's blows, is also an important quality for recovering from the more routine stressors you encounter day in and day out. These everyday hassles, pressures, and disappointments come with the territory. As we articulated earlier in this chapter, stress is an integral part of your training. These common setbacks and frustrations do not have the crushing impact of traumatic events, but they can wear you down over time. One way to maintain your day-to-day resilience and overall wellness is by strengthening your spiritual identity (Faull & Hills, 2006).

Many counselors and therapists now regularly address spirituality, which is distinct from particular religious affiliations and practices, in their work with clients. One model of spirituality conceptualizes it as having four important dimensions: inner resources, meaning and purpose in life, transcendence, and positive interconnectedness (Briggs & Shoffner, 2006). These four factors are vital pathways for promoting resilience to stress. In one study, Denz-Penhey and Murdoch (2008) discovered that a deep sense of experiential spirituality enabled patients with serious illnesses to transform their experiences into something meaningful. The important implication of these findings is that you are not merely the product of your environment—even if the environment is stressful, challenging, and deadly. You have the potential not only to survive hard times but also to actually thrive and prosper under stressful conditions.

Of course, when you are feeling overwhelmed by stressors, you are less in touch with your own personal strengths and not as aware of the resources available to you. These feelings can undermine your confidence, sap your motivation, and cloud the once-clear vision you had of your future. At these times, you need to make a special effort to consciously look for your strengths and resources—to search for those clues that point to a successful strategy of thriving.

Making Meaning of Stress

> Meaning, not raw facts, is what humanity seeks.
>
> —Alvin Kernan

What makes you resilient under fire? Why aren't you a passive victim of your environment? Fundamentally, you are the master of your own fate because you can choose how to make meaning of your circumstances. Even if you lose everything else, according to Frankl (1969), you still have "the last of human freedoms—the ability to choose one's attitude in a given set of circumstances" (p. 73). You may have noticed that mindfulness techniques we described earlier do much more than merely soothe your emotions. Practicing mindfulness also transforms your awareness to allow you to make positive meaning of your stress.

Telling Your Story

> You are the hero of your own story.
>
> —Mary McCarthy

What makes humans unique is our ability to create meaning by weaving the raw material of our lives into a fabric of stories (Atkinson, 1995). The stories that you spin to give coherence and meaning to your life also help form your own identity. They encourage you to take on certain roles, play out particular expectations, and choose some options over others. Yes, you have stories to tell, but your stories also tell you.

Recently, researchers have found that writing about the stressful events you have experienced can produce a wide range of benefits (Lepore & Smyth, 2002). People who wrote about some traumatic stress experience had significant improvements in their health, emotional well-being, and physiological functioning compared with control participants who wrote only about neutral events.

Once again, we find support for the tremendous value of keeping a journal of your training experiences. The process of telling your story helps you to find some meaning in the challenges you are enduring. One student, Steph, noticed that the length of her journal entries were an accurate barometer of the stress she felt. The more stressful her day, the longer her journal entry was. She also found herself returning to write about particularly stressful times.

The mindfulness you bring to your studies can be especially helpful in seeking understanding and insight into your own experiences. As you shift through the rubble of a setback or failure, be on the lookout for those golden nuggets of strengths and resources among the disappointments and mistakes. By looking carefully, you can find plenty of examples of your own resilience, determination, creativity, and courage. Remember, it's also okay to compliment yourself in your journal. When you're under stress, your self-esteem and confidence may suffer, so at these times you can benefit from some reminders of your strengths and abilities.

EXERCISE 5.3 The Embracing Attitudes

A Quick Check Exercise

Here are some quick tips for embracing stress successfully along your journey:

- Look for puzzles that intrigue you.
- Involve yourself in meaningful causes.
- Strive for progress—not perfection.
- Forgive yourself and others.
- Take the message contained in the Serenity Prayer to heart: "Grant me the serenity to accept the things I cannot change, the courage to change the things I can, and the wisdom to know the difference."
- Start a "feel good" file. Keep encouraging notes, cards, letters, and e-mails people send you. Even if you don't have immediate access to these important people in your life, you can find consolation in their words. When you're having a particularly difficult day, pull out your file and read the words these people have written about you. It will amaze you how uplifting a few of these can be on a stressful day!

Thriving Under Stress

> Power is the ability to achieve purpose.
>
> —Martin Luther King Jr.

Most approaches to managing stress begin by assessing your stressors. For example, years ago Sowa (1992) developed a process by which you carefully list all the stressors in your life, assess how much each is under your control, decide how important each stressor is, and then consider your options. But focusing on all your stressors at once can seem both daunting and disheartening—especially for counseling trainees, who feel demoralized too often already (Watkins, 1996).

Envisioning Your Goals

To truly thrive under stress, begin on a positive note by envisioning your goals. Remember, you are always a work in progress—extending, evolving, and expanding. Therefore, you want to regularly orient yourself to where you are heading, especially when you are going through stressful episodes. During these dark times, your goals can serve as beacons to light your way and keep you on track.

EXERCISE 5.4 Mission: Possible

An Exercise in Envisioning

What do you hope to accomplish as a result of completing your graduate program? Reflect on your training hopes and dreams. Once your vision of the future has come into focus, write down your training vision statement. Be sure to develop goals that are positive, specific, and achievable. Knowing why you are going through stressful times can enable you to thrive under stress.

My Training Vision

_____

_____

_____

_____

_____

_____

Using Your Strengths

You are going to be relying on your personal talents to succeed in your venture. Now is the time to bring your positive qualities to the foreground as you begin planning your strategies for thriving under stress. Earlier in this chapter, for example, you reflected on your success experiences in dealing with stressful events and circumstances.

EXERCISE 5.5 Panning for Gold

Uncovering Strengths and Resources

Recalling your accomplishments is a great way to recognize special talents that you may be taking for granted and to remember important people that you may be forgetting. Write an inventory of your strengths and resources.

_____

_____

_____

_____

_____

_____

_____

_____

_____

Connecting With Others

Remember, we all stumble, every one of us. That's why it's a comfort to go hand in hand.

—Emily Kimbrough

Over and over again, researchers have found that social support serves as an important buffer against stress (Berscheid, 2003). Having traveling companions, the third principle of thriving, is particularly valuable if you are feeling overwhelmed with stress.

A supportive network of friends, relatives, peers, and others can make a world of difference when you're going through an ordeal. In fact, one of the surest ways to thrive in tough times is to reach out to others and face the stressors together. Cultures throughout the world have developed rituals in which family members and friends congregate to deal with difficult events—everything in life from births to deaths.

Talking to a trusted friend or family member, sharing time together, or joining others for a meal can lead you to the truth of the proverb: "A sorrow shared is half the sorrow; a joy shared is twice the joy." Even if your stressful circumstances involve only you, by telling your story to others, your experience becomes an episode of your network's shared history—a piece added to the communal mosaic. Sharing your turmoil helps to reconnect you, during a time when you may feel all alone and alienated, to others who can offer support.

EXERCISE 5.6 The Sea Star II

A Revisiting Exercise

Using the image of a sea star, we invite you to look at how well you are thriving on each of these five dimensions: relational, spiritual, physical, emotional, and mental. Using a scale of from 1 to 10, with 1 representing the absence of any sense of thriving and 10 representing your highest level of thriving, rate your current level in each area.

Whatever rating you give to each dimension of thriving, take some time to consider carefully what you can do to move from your present score to the next higher number. Describe the specific steps you can take. As you imagine possible strategies, you may discover that you have more capabilities and resources than you realize. Share your ratings and plan with a friend.

RELATIONAL THRIVING

My current level is a ——————————————— . I can move higher by ...

_____

_____

_____

(Continued)

(Continued)

SPIRITUAL THRIVING

My current level is a ——————————— . I can move higher by ...

_____

_____

_____

PHYSICAL THRIVING

My current level is a ——————————— . I can move higher by ...

_____

_____

_____

EMOTIONAL THRIVING

My current level is a ——————————— . I can move higher by ...

_____

_____

_____

MENTAL THRIVING

My current level is a ——————————— . I can move higher by ...

_____

_____

_____

Stress and Character

Character cannot be developed in ease and quiet. Only through experience of trial and suffering can the soul be strengthened, vision cleared, ambition inspired, and success achieved.

—Helen Keller

Loosely paraphrasing Buddha, life is not for sissies. You get knocked around quite a bit by just trying to get on with living, much less striving to realize your cherished dreams. Though advertisements would have you believe otherwise, you cannot avoid all of life's bruises and stresses. Advertisers try to sell the idea that with the right car, the right body, the right *something*, you will magically be insulated from any stress, loss, disappointment, and discomfort. For example, in a once-popular luxury automobile advertisement, the caption under the car said simply, "Fire your therapist." For many people, particularly in Western society, the ideal of personal happiness implies that life must be free of any suffering and stress.

Because you are attracted to the helping professions, it is likely that you do not believe personal fulfillment can be found either in static, Eden-like bliss or in a double overhead cam V-8 engine with a turbocharger. It is also likely that your journey toward becoming a counselor or therapist began as you struggled to respond to difficulties and painful stumbling blocks in your own life. You are interested in what makes you tick and curious about how you are put together. Perhaps there is something that draws you to looking at your own life head on—even the stressful and unsettling experiences that you sometimes would just as soon forget.

Regardless of how well you may have been shielded by benevolent circumstances, you have faced stressors and endured pain in growing up. Each of us has experienced injuries that originated in important caregiving relationships, disappointments at school, stressful experiences with peers, and heartbreaking losses of loved ones. Sometimes, our injuries are not so discrete or identifiable but emerged from nearly constant exposure to chronically stressful environmental circumstances.

One of the themes that appears again and again in your counseling training is the idea that although you can never expect to be completely free of painful life events, you can choose how you will respond to them. It is not the particular stressor or injury that determines the person you become; rather, it is your response to these painful experiences that shapes your process of becoming. Even times of suffering can ultimately become rewarding lessons in life, for they are enabling you to mature and sensitizing you to the anguish of others.

Converting your sufferings into wisdom and character is the work of personal transformation. Booker T. Washington, an African American educator, author, and orator whose life was filled with accomplishments, urged us to measure our success not by the position we have achieved but by the obstacles we have overcome. Always hard won and never trivial, your personal transformation is like the design of the Taoist yin-yang symbol. The whole figure is a circle, with two curving, intertwined halves—one black and the other white—lying side by side and dependent on one another to form the whole sphere. A dot in the center of each side reflects how each part is also embedded in the other. Our own circle of life includes both sufferings and joys. As a counselor in training, you will find that these tear-shaped halves represent a two-ingredient recipe for creating your own personal sense of wholeness.

Of course, this transformation is a lifelong project. The work of fully integrating and understanding yourself is never finished, and you have sustained injuries and faced difficulties in life that are still alive for you now. These experiences are often well hidden, but sometimes they become open wounds that show up in your relations with others, in your particular sensitivities and needs, and in your unique ways of protecting yourself from new painful events.

Your graduate training will include many courses with a variety of academic and experiential exercises to give you a firm understanding of the counseling field. You may find, however, that your training evokes a parallel process of self-examination and exploration that more fully reveals your areas of sensitivity and defensiveness (Adams, 2006). These are the sore spots that seem to keep getting nudged as you move through your program, especially in work with clients and supervisors. If it's any consolation, you can be sure that you are not the only one whose old wounds are resurfacing during this intensive training. If you are able to skate through your program without the experience bringing up charged issues in your own life, then you haven't fully engaged in your training.

Stress Into Strength

> Life is a grindstone. Whether it grinds us down or polishes us up depends on us.
>
> —Thomas L. Holdcroft

The poet William Stafford once observed in a personal conversation that unless one had experienced difficulty and personal distress in life, it would be impossible to be a poet. The same can be said of becoming a counselor. The trick, he observed, was to suffer intelligently and then to share that suffering with others. By this, he meant that you can mine the experiences of your own life for those nuggets of self-discovery—the invaluable images, feelings, and responses that characterize you as uniquely human. You can then communicate with others about a shared human situation. In this sense, the particular stresses you have faced and through which you have suffered intelligently represent personal strengths. These are your true areas of expertise.

The idea that your personal struggles have the potential to be your areas of greatest strength is not some cozy notion that we offer to reassure you. The words "what does not kill you makes you stronger" express something of the experience of having to develop some new talent or strength in response to a particular life struggle. History is replete with examples of people whose genius and wounds were inextricably linked. Winston Churchill, whose oratorical skills galvanized the Allies against Hitler's aggression, stuttered as a child. Django Reinhardt, the first great jazz guitarist, known for his astonishingly unique phrasings, had only two working fingers on his left hand (Dregni, 2004). Maya Angelou, the lyrical writer of transcendent prose and poetry, was mute for nearly five years after she was raped as a child. She transformed her struggles into works of beauty, such as her first work of literature, *I Know Why the Caged Bird Sings* (1970), and became a marvelously powerful and inspirational speaker. Even Carl Rogers, whose work dramatically changed the practice of our profession by advocating for interpersonal authenticity, warmth, and empathy in counseling and therapy, acknowledged that his early years were characterized by alienation, dysfunctional relationships, and avoidance of any genuine emotional expression.

Think about your own life. In what ways have you transformed the "slings and arrows of outrageous fortune" into your personal character? Perhaps you have used your stress as a teacher. You may have learned valuable lessons about life as the result of these experiences. It may be that you have used your suffering as an empathic bridge to help you connect with the anguish of your clients. Or you may have applied the lessons you have learned in coping with stress to gain an appreciation for the creativity, resourcefulness, and resilience of humans. However you have drawn upon your experiences of stress, you have done so by embracing it, engaging in the mindful process of making it meaningful, and finally emerging from that encounter as a better person and counselor.

Summary

In this chapter, we discussed how stress is an essential part of any successful training program. We described a variety of strategies, such as mindfulness techniques, rest, and exercise, that you can use to manage stress. We also encouraged you to embrace stress as a means of thriving in your training. Connecting with others, making meaning of your stress, and envisioning your goals are ways in which you can transform stress into wisdom, empathy, and character. Finally, we end this chapter as we began, with a thought from Viktor Frankl (1967). You are "called upon to make the best use of any moment and the right choice at any time: it is assumed that [you know] what to do, or whom to love, or how to suffer" (p. 93).

Resources

Because we quoted him several times, it should come as no surprise that we recommend the writings of Victor Frankl as a wonderful resource for reflecting on the meaning of your stress and suffering. A survivor of Nazi concentration camps, Frankl (1984) described his harrowing experiences in *Man's Search for Meaning: An Introduction to Logotherapy*. In this painfully honest and unsentimental account, Frankl (who originally had intended to write it anonymously, using only his prison camp number) explored the psychology of suffering and our struggle to make meaning. His approach to therapy, which is an outgrowth of his concentration camp experiences, invites us to confront the essence of our existence and challenges us to create a meaningful life through faith and love.

Mindful Schools

mindfulschools.org

There is a proliferation of websites dealing with mindfulness techniques, but we highly recommend the Mindful Schools website because it explicitly addresses how students can use mindfulness not only to manage their stress but also to boost their academic performance.

ResilienceNet

www.resilnet.uiuc.edu

This site offers information on resilience, including guides and teaching materials, program descriptions, and evaluative reports. There is a virtual library with full-text publications of articles and reports. An on-site discussion group gives you an opportunity to interact with others interested in resilience.

References

Adams, D. (2006, May). How I lost my voice and found it again. *Counseling Today, 48,* 12–13.
Angelou, M. (1970). *I know why the caged bird sings.* New York: Random House.
Atkinson, R. (1995). *The gift of stories.* Westport, CT: Bergin & Garvey.
Barlow, D. H. (2002). *Anxiety and its disorders.* New York, NY: Guilford.

Barlow, D. H., Rapee, R. M., & Perini, S. (2014). *Ten steps to mastering stress.* Oxford, England: Oxford University Press.

Berscheid, E. (2003). The human's greatest strength: Other humans. In L. G. Aspinwall & U. M. Staudinger (Eds.), *A psychology of human strengths: Fundamental questions and future directions for a positive psychology* (pp. 37–47). Washington, DC: American Psychological Association.

Briggs, M. K., & Shoffner, M. F. (2006). Spiritual wellness and depression: Testing a theoretical model in older adolescents and midlife adults. *Counseling and Values, 51,* 5–23.

Cannon, W. B. (1927). The James-Lange theory of emotions: A critical examination and an alternative theory. *American Journal of Psychology, 39,* 106–124.

Covey, S., Merrill, A. S., Merrill, R. R. (1994). *First things first: To live, to love, to learn, to leave a legacy.* New York, NY: Simon & Schuster.

Debarnot, U., Castellani, E., Valenza, G., Sebastiani, L., & Guillot, A. (2011). Daytime naps improve motor imagery learning. *Cognitive, Affective, and Behavioral Neuroscience, 11,* 541–550. doi:10.3758/s13415–011–0052-z

Denz-Penhey, H., & Murdoch, J. C. (2008). Personal resiliency: Serious diagnosis and prognosis with unexpected quality outcomes. *Qualitative Health Research, 18,* 391–404.

Dregni, M. (2004). *Django: The life and music of a gypsy legend.* Oxford, England: Oxford University Press.

Echterling, L. G., & Stewart, A. L. (2008). Resilience. In S. F. Davis & W. Buskist (Eds.), *Twenty-first century psychology: A reference handbook* (Vol. 2, pp. 192–201). Thousand Oaks, CA: Sage.

Faull, K., & Hills, M. (2006). The role of the spiritual dimension of the self as the prime determinant of health. *Disability & Rehabilitation, 28,* 729–740.

Fernando, R. (2013). *Sustainability of a mindfulness-based in-class intervention.* Retrieved from http://www.mindfulschools.org/pdf/Mindful-Schools-Study-Highlights.pdf

Ferreira-Vieira, T. H., Bastos, C. P., Pereira, G. S., Moreira, F. A., & Massensini, A. R. (2014). A role for the endocannabinoid system in exercise-induced spatial memory enhancement in mice. *Hippocampus, 24,* 79–88. doi:10.1002/hipo.22206

Fevre, M. L., Kolt, G. S., & Matheny, J. (2006). Eustress, distress and their interpretation in primary and secondary occupational stress management interventions: Which way first? *Journal of Managerial Psychology, 21,* 547–565.

Frankl, V. E. (1967). *Psychotherapy and existentialism: Selected papers on logotherapy.* New York, NY: Pocket Books.

Frankl, V. E. (1969). *The will to meaning.* New York, NY: New American Library.

Frankl, V. E. (1984). *Man's search for meaning: An introduction to logotherapy.* New York, NY: Simon & Shuster.

Fredrickson, B. L. (2002). Positive emotions. In C. R. Snyder & S. J. Lopez (Eds.), *Handbook of positive psychology* (pp. 120–134). New York, NY: Oxford University Press.

Gladding, S. (2006). *Counseling as an art: The creative arts in counseling.* Alexandria, VA: American Counseling Association.

Holmes, T. H., & Rahe, R. H. (1967). The social readjustment rating scale. *Journal of Psychosomatic Research, 11,* 213–218.

Kabat-Zinn, J. (1994). *Wherever you go, there you are: Mindfulness meditation in everyday life.* New York, NY: Hyperion.

Kielty, M. L., & Gilligan, T. D. (2013, May). *Exploring points of entry for clinical applications of mindfulness with children and adolescents in primary and secondary education settings.* Paper presented at the First International Conference on Mindfulness, Rome, Italy.

Lepore, S. J., & Smyth, J. M. (2002). *The writing cure: How expressive writing promotes health and emotional well-being.* Washington, DC: American Psychological Association.

McEwen, B. S., Gianaros, H., & Milliken, M. (2011). Stress- and allostasis-induced brain plasticity. *Annual Review of Medicine, 62,* 431–445.

Mendelson, T., Greenberg, M. T., Daritois, J. K., Gould, L. F., Rhoades, B. L., & Leaf, P. J. (2010). Feasibility and preliminary outcomes of a school-based mindfulness intervention for urban youth. *Journal of Abnormal Child Psychology, 38,* 985–994.

Rollins, J. (2005, October). A campaign for counselor wellness. *Counseling Today, 47,* 22, 23, 42.

Schmidt, N. B., Richey, J. A., Zvolensky, M. J., & Maner, J. K. (2008). Exploring human freeze responses to a threat stressor. *Journal of Behavior Therapy and Experimental Psychiatry, 39,* 292–304. doi:10.1016/.jbtep.2007.08.002

Sowa, C. J. (1992). Understanding clients' perceptions of stress. *Journal of Counseling and Development, 71,* 179–183.

Taylor, S. E. (2006). Tend and befriend: Biobehavioral bases of affiliation under stress. *Current Directions in Psychological Science, 15,* 273–277. doi:10.1111/j.1467-8721.2006.00451.x

Veenit, V., Riccio, O., & Sandi, C. (2014). CRHR1 links peripuberty stress with deficits in social and stress-coping behaviors. *Journal of Psychiatric Research, 53,* 1–7. doi:10.1016/j.jpsychires.2014.02.015

Violence Policy Center. (2012). *American roulette: Murder-suicide in the United States* (4th ed.). Author: Washington, DC. Retrieved from http://www.vpc.org/studies/amroul2012.pdf

Watkins, C. E. (1996). On demoralization and awe in psychotherapy supervision. *Clinical Supervisor, 14,* 139–148.

Weems, S. (2014). *Ha! The science of when we laugh and why.* New York, NY: Basic Books.

6

Being With Others

All real living is meeting.

—Martin Buber

It takes one kind of mind to absorb facts, and another to absorb the presence of another human being.

—Abraham Maslow

As you begin your graduate training, you quickly become aware that you are entering a whole new educational culture, one much different from your undergraduate experiences. You are no longer thrown in with other students as a matter of chance; you share a dream with those around you of becoming a counselor or therapist. There is a different feeling as you join with others to pursue not only training goals and a degree but also a new concept of who you are. Together, you are reaching for something that is not entirely known but that you sense has wonderful possibilities for your own growth and your relationships with others. You are suddenly part of a new community.

This chapter is about being with others in the community formed by your peers, faculty members, support staff, mentors, and supervisors. It is also about how changes in you—as you evolve as a person and forge a new identity as a counselor—influence important others in your life. These important others may be relatives, friends, romantic partners, and fellow students. One thing is sure: You are taking a journey that will change you. Because you have such close-knit ties with others, your journey affects them all, and in some measure, they are taking the trip with you.

Changes in you are inevitable because you are entering into a new kind of interpersonal milieu, one you have never experienced before. You notice that in your new community, you are called on to respond in fresh ways, take risks, collaborate with others, and be open and flexible to a degree that might be unfamiliar to you. You are expected to be game for new ventures, such as role plays and experiential exercises. You become used to seeing yourself on video recordings when learning and practicing therapeutic skills. You also find that to really engage in a learning dialogue with others, you welcome the productive critique of supervisors and peers. Above all, being fully invested in forging your clinical and counseling skills requires you to be open, accessible, and collaborative with others, throwing your whole self into the experience (Carlson, 2012).

Don't worry; although you might feel that you don't know how to swim in these uncharted waters, you won't drown! Others are there to buoy you when you need it, and you can discover secret resources you never knew you had. At the same time, you find yourself learning new ways of relating to others that will serve you, not only with those who will one day seek your counseling but also with anyone whose life touches your own.

This chapter addresses the ways in which these new relational opportunities can test your ability to adapt, but also can provide memorable and joyful experiences. When you finally enter the fellowship of healing professionals as a full-fledged member, you may look back on your training and say, shaking your head, "What a long, strange trip it's been!" But you will be gratefully alive with a new capacity for relating to others that is at the core of what it means to become a counselor. The question to ask yourself now is, "Am I open to this experience?"

Being "Processed"

Rebecca's Story

I can still recall how strange it felt sitting in a circle with my classmates and thinking, "Who *are* these people?" It was my first experience in a "process" group. I wasn't sure what that meant, but whatever it was, I sure was leery of being "processed" by this bunch. They were so different from what I had expected. Looking back on it, I think I assumed that they would be more like me—you know, normal! Now, I can really appreciate the diversity in my classmates, but back then it felt like entering another world. I was disconcerted and a little scared. Later, I wondered how my earlier social world could have been so uniform. But at the beginning of that group, I felt a sense of being out of place.

Apparently, "process" meant that we were supposed to share our thoughts and feelings about stuff that we were experiencing as new graduate students. Some students seemed fine with this and openly talked about their excitement, as well as their frustrations. An older guy talked about being disoriented now that he's a student again. Somebody else talked about how her boyfriend felt threatened by her going on to graduate school. One African American woman described how it felt to be the only person of color in the class, especially because she was from a "Black" university. Her words about being in the minority stirred a guy to talk about his sexual orientation. Just when I was feeling like the most conventional person in the world, a young neohippy-looking guy, Robert, talked about "body-mind" stuff. He related how important yoga and meditation were to him. I thought to myself, "What a flake!"

I tend to be very private, so I felt like, "What am I doing here?" When it came to be my turn to share my experiences, I mentioned a few things that were not particularly deep, but nobody seemed to mind. It creeped me out that some people in the group talked so freely, especially about personal stuff. I gravitated to Alicia, who was quiet, like me, and who was also nervous about being processed. We stuck together like we had been cast adrift and were clinging to the same life preserver.

Over time, though, I started to feel a little left out of the group. I began to be interested in the experiences my classmates shared and felt like I wanted them to know me better, too. I started to open up a little, and it wasn't so bad! This kind of dragged Alicia along, too, and she began to loosen up around the others. By the time I was really feeling comfortable with everyone—well, almost everyone—we started our practicum.

This change set me back a little. It was hard because we had to show our work with clients and talk about our personal responses to client issues. I was afraid of being criticized and felt exposed again. Strangely enough, Alicia, who had complained about all this personal disclosure, seemed to really like the process group for our casework, and eventually I enjoyed it too because it helped me develop my counseling skills. It seems

(Continued)

(Continued)

like second nature now to discuss my personal responses to client issues or relate how a particular experience affects me. I now realize that appreciating diversity is not just about ethnicity or race.

Now I look back on how strange it felt to be thrown in with people who are so different from me, and I can't understand what I was nervous about. I am not as drawn to some of the people in the program, but I have been surprised that even they have something valuable to offer me. Sometimes it is the person who is most different from me that has helped me see things in a new way with my clients. Now the neohippy guy, Robert, is one of my closest friends, and I've almost got the inverted swan position in my yoga repertoire!

What's in Your Backpack?

Remember that thriving principle about packing for the journey? Well, your counseling journey is the most recent adventure in the larger journey of your life. You have things in your backpack already, and a lot of what is in there influences how you relate to others. You may be fully aware of some of what is in your pack, and you pull it out all the time in your relationships. But there is probably a lot in the backpack that you forgot—or never knew you had!

Like everyone else, you have a long history of interpersonal experiences that have helped to contribute to who you are and how you relate to others. It's nice when you discover in your backpack a quality or skill that helps you connect well with others. It's like when you were a child on the bus heading off to camp. Just as you were starting to get hungry, you found that peanut butter and jelly sandwich your mother or father packed for you. Now in your backpack, you may discover your ability to take risks and encounter people authentically in your new program. However, in addition to finding something nice in your sack, you may also discover that you have been carrying around a bunch of rocks—dead weight from old relationships that holds you back from engaging with others the way you long to. You wonder, "What is all this junk that I've been lugging around?"

Self and Relationship

It takes two to know one.

—Gregory Bateson

You are answering that question about lugging junk as you begin to participate in counseling, therapy, supervision, and other relationships that are essential for your development into a helping professional. Even if you are skilled at forging new relationships, the chances are that you will gain new perspectives as your counseling identity evolves. As you discover new insights, you will want to reevaluate your assumptions about how you interact with others.

In any profession, the practitioner has a set of tools. In the helping professions, the most valuable tool that you will have at your service is your ability to form a variety of interpersonal connections and relationships. Learning how your own experience manifests in your communications and becoming aware of the effect these communications have on others are the major challenges you face in becoming a helping professional (Edelstein, 2015).

During the early phase of your graduate training, your interpersonal awareness and skills are most relevant to developing relationships with your peers and professors. Later, awareness of how you structure your relations with others influences how you interact with your first clients. In your training, you learn new techniques, master new methods, and bring newfound knowledge to bear as you seek to help your clients. It is important to understand, however, that all of these are secondary to the interpersonal context in which you practice these skills (Matthews, 2005). For this reason, your professors and supervisors encourage you to become more aware of how you encounter them as you work together. These relationships, as well as those with your new peers, are the laboratories in which you can develop your greatest counseling tool—yourself.

Exploring Your Relational Worldview

We are here to hand one another on.

—Walker Percy

You have become who you are, in some part, because you developed in a unique psychological environment with people who are important to you. In that shared participation, especially with early caregivers, you forged a unique sense of self, as well as an awareness of how others behave in relation to you. It was in your early important relationships, for instance, that you learned to feel, regulate, and express emotion. The very structure of the way you experience your emotional life took shape in a relational system (Hoffman, Stewart, Warren, & Meek, 2015). During that time, you learned to make sense of people's behavior. You also discovered how your own actions, feelings, and expressions affected others. In these countless encounters that took place every single day of your young life, you developed a working model for structuring interpersonal relationships. More important, in the context of others, you became a self.

Building on this early formative matrix of relational experiences, you had to accommodate new interpersonal events as you grew and developed, sharing a psychological environment with friends, relatives, peers, and intimate partners. Emerging out of this participation, you developed an interpersonal style that reflects certain experiences, values, needs, traumas, motivations, and fears. All of these experiences are like features on a map showing where you have been in the past and where you are likely to go as you navigate new relationships.

Your unique map records all the relational terrain you traversed as you grew into a person. This map is an enormously complex collection of interpretive categories that take shape from your unique interpersonal history, which you bring to bear in each new relational event. These interpretive categories, with which you make sense of interpersonal encounters, are not often the focus of your conscious and deliberate examination (Stolorow & Atwood, 1992). Without even realizing it, you use these meaning-making templates all the time. You assume that they are accurate and reliable representations of some external reality because you have a fundamental need to make sense of your interpersonal life.

However, one reason for the success of your assumptions is that you develop relationships with people whose interpersonal assumptions are similar to your own. When you encounter someone with roughly similar sets of interpretive categories, you naturally feel that you understand the other person. You feel in familiar territory, and because you sense a connection, a relationship is more likely to grow out of the encounter.

Your new learning community, however, is not a freely selective social environment. Instead, you are thrown in with a wide assortment of people with whom you might not normally associate. Even though they may share a common commitment to a helping profession, your colleagues, professors, supervisors, and clients can have vastly different organizing frames of reference for interpersonal interaction. It is in this diverse and unfamiliar personality "salad bowl" that you are challenged to explore your own assumptions and expectations about others. In your class discussions, supervision meetings, and counseling sessions, you will be regularly stretching your capacity to accept alternate experiences of the same event. Like a prism that transforms a single ray of white light into a broad and beautiful rainbow, people can have a colorful range of reactions to a single, shared episode. In this psychological environment, you will come to truly appreciate that others' subjective experiences of interpersonal events are as real for *them* as your experience is for *you*. By accepting and valuing these alternate perceptions, you not only enrich and broaden your own perspective but also become a successful helping professional.

For example, facing the issues of racism and sexism can be very perturbing. White people, in particular, can be hesitant to bring up these concerns with others (Hayman, 2006). In your conversations, you may find yourself avoiding the topics of affirmative action, inequality, immigration, and race relations because you fear these will stir up strong emotions. One of the unfortunate results of this avoidance, however, is that you never become genuinely engaged in deep discussions about the pain of these social problems—and the ways of addressing them. Now, more than ever, is an excellent time for you to explore yourself as a gendered, ethnic individual.

A central goal of your training is to gain a thorough understanding of how you structure your interpersonal experiences in the unique way that you do. In other words, as you make explicit your organizing frames of reference for understanding relationships, you become a more effective helper (Adams, 2006). As part of this process, you also discover how you respond to relational events. In your learning community, you can be open to revising your map, exploring your own relational assumptions, and becoming more aware of the impact you have on your fellow traveling companions.

EXERCISE 6.1 Visitor From Another Planet

A Guided Fantasy

For the next few minutes, imagine that you are from another planet where people are androgynous. Your spaceship lands in the United States and several government officials greet you. After determining that you pose no threat, the officials decide to educate you regarding the U.S. culture. They suggest that you watch an evening of prime-time television and read national magazines and newspapers. Imagine what you see and read. What impression do you have about men and women? Women who are racial or cultural "minorities"? People who are Asian American, Latino/a, Native American, of African descent, or White? People who are gay, lesbian,

(Continued)

(Continued)

bisexual, or heterosexual? People with disabilities or special needs? Take a few minutes to write your impressions.

_____

_____

_____

_____

_____

   Now, imagine that these officials tell you that the United States is a meritocracy in which people inevitably achieve what they work for and deserve. Imagine that the officials tell you that the principles of the country's government state that all men are created equal. What are your opinions now?

_____

_____

_____

_____

_____

   To reflect on the meaning of this exercise for you, consider your opinions and assumptions that you have taken for granted. What do your findings imply about how different people may feel about their place in society? How might this information apply to your clients?

_____

_____

_____

_____

_____

Growing in Relation

When we are listened to, it creates us, makes us unfold and expand.

—Karl Menninger

Most students new to counseling programs are a little startled, and later excited, by how much their programs are structured around not only training but also personal growth, especially in relation to others. Alberta, for example, was having trouble with the emphasis placed on interpersonal self-awareness in her counseling program. Once she remarked with exasperation that her training felt "more like personal therapy." Alberta was striving to accommodate to how her interpersonal style, habits, and assumptions were challenged and made more explicit as she participated in forging new relationships with peers and supervisors. These relationships were centered on the cultivation of the person, as well as the skills, of the counselor.

Day after day, Alberta felt compelled to examine her interpersonal style and its effects on others much more closely than she would if she had chosen some other profession. However, at the end of her program, Alberta shared her feelings with her colleagues: "I thought that I could just come here and learn what to do, and not have to change myself. I guess I had this idea that I would only 'do something to' others rather than 'be someone with' others. Giving up that sense of control, and being open to change, and to all of you, was the hardest thing about the program."

One of the rocks that Alberta was carrying in her backpack was the desire to be in control all the time in order to feel safe with others. It was difficult for her to try new things or to be frank about her own thoughts and feelings because she reserved trust only for lifelong friends. Being open to helpful guidance, productive evaluation, collaboration, or mentoring was difficult because she felt threatened not being the one directing the show.

Quite different relational issues may be more troublesome to you. Clare had always been the "star" in her academic pursuits. She proudly declared that she had a "high need for achievement." As her relationships with supervisors and peers developed, however, Clare began to realize that she actually harbored a strong and unrealistic desire for perfection. At first, she had a hard time trying new skills because of her fear of making a mistake—and of not being the star. As others watched her videotaped sessions, Clare felt overly sensitive to criticism. Her unrealistic aspirations hit a brick wall when her competitive desire to outshine her peers and win accolades began to disrupt her supervision group. It was difficult for Clare to accept that her interpersonal style, rather than her external achievement, was fair game for discussion in this setting. However, as she began to understand how her interpersonal and counseling effectiveness were related, Clare's desire to become a good counselor eventually enabled her to be open and receptive and to accommodate the feedback that others gave her. She discovered how her competitive behavior reduced, rather than elevated, the esteem with which others regarded her. Clare was also able to explore these interpersonal dynamics in terms of the family system in which they had formed.

Like Alberta and Clare, you have a complex mixture of talents, fears, and interpersonal assumptions that serve as either peanut butter and jelly sandwiches or rocks in your backpack. Your expectations about relationships influence your defenses, fears, hopes, and aspirations. Some of your habits of relating and communicating can work well, but some get in the way of being open, honest, and fulfilled in your relationships. Unlike the latest diet fad, which can offer you no guarantees, we offer you two assurances about your training experience. First, whatever your interpersonal style, you can discover both its strengths and limitations as you continue on your journey. As you explore the baggage you bring to training, you can spread your backpack's contents on the ground so you can examine everything carefully before deciding what you want to keep carrying with you— and what you can discard. Our second guarantee is that as you successfully make your way through training with a lighter load, you will relate to others with a sense of grace, freedom, and fulfillment that you have never experienced before.

Mirrors

Your important relationships are like mirrors (Hoffman et al., 2015). You see yourself reflected back through the experience of those with whom you are in contact. Your professors, supervisors, peers, and clients form the relational laboratories in which you will forge your professional identity. Undoubtedly, there will be times when you see yourself reflected back in a way that seems familiar and confirming to you. But it is just as likely that there will be times when the reflection you see looks strange, unnerving, or disconcerting. As you ponder the many opportunities for growth that emerge out of these encounters, keep in mind that you are a work in progress and that the journey itself—not the destination—is most important.

The Childlike Feeling of Possibility

Antoinette's Story

It is a beautiful morning, so I decide to lie in the grassy arms of the campus quad. Sunlight speckles down on the noisy undergrads walking off the effects of last night's festivities. I am right next to the sidewalk. I wonder, "Is this somehow symbolic? In my life, do I dare not stray too far from safety?" I'm lying in a rare, unnatural pose of openness—bared arms, black skin shimmering in the fall sunshine, making me truly rainbow-like.

I feel the damp ground through my jeans. My black braids are long and soft. They comfort me as they sway in the breeze against the goose bumps on my skin. I sense the green, the wind, and the childlike feeling of possibility that I am often too scared to embrace.

I am almost 23 and I still fight the feeling of being alone. I can handle every day before I look in the mirror. No, I used to feel that way. But it still isn't a good idea to look for too long. Still, I see a life proposed again—one lived beyond mere survival. I am with these others, strangers and friends, different and the same. Now they are mirrors, too. I do not get the answers, but I ask the right questions, and I know there are options. I don't feel like I have to always question if I can live this life like somebody people know. And I don't feel like I am left alone with the world balanced between teeth and tongue. I can't help but wonder how long today will last inside of me. But today ... maybe today, I am strong and beautiful and confident enough to dare and say, "I belong."

The Counseling Qualities

> Our fate is shared.
>
> —Susan Griffin

Pondering what is in your interpersonal backpack is good preparation for having traveling companions on your journey. To really get the most from your program, you need to join with others to navigate your way through the variety of experiences designed to foster your growth as a helping professional. These important persons are your professors, mentors, supervisors, clients, and fellow students. Some of your student traveling companions will be farther along in the program and can guide you when you feel disoriented or lost. With your new companions, you can discuss new ideas, practice your emerging skills, observe one another, and give feedback as you seek to apply what you are learning. You can practice therapy skills by watching video recordings of one another's role plays and actual counseling sessions. You can become comfortable with giving and receiving constructive criticism and helpful observations. These activities can stretch your capacity for being "out there" and exposed to professors and fellow students in your learning process. If you open yourself to others, your companions can be there to encourage you when you need it—as well as challenge you to explore your potential to the fullest.

Two very important criteria must be present for these relationships to truly have a profound impact on your growth as a counselor or therapist. First, you have to cultivate these relationships in an interpersonal climate of honesty and understanding. You need to really know and appreciate your traveling companions for you to fully trust and respect them. The good news is that your advisors, supervisors, and learning companions are very likely to value openness. However, you also have to let others truly get to know you, too.

The second criterion for successfully creating dynamic and profound relationships is for you to be a vital and engaged participant. Go out of your way to offer your animated interest, sincere curiosity, and unique perspective to the people who form your new learning community. By sharing your ideas and experiences, expressing your doubts and confusion, and communicating forthrightly, you help promote an environment that encourages discoveries and facilitates growth for everyone.

Many of the qualities that are essential to becoming a helping professional are equally relevant to fostering your relations with your traveling companions. An attitude of respect and acceptance for persons different from yourself will enable you to reach outside your normal comfort zone and create connections with others whom you would not typically encounter.

For example, Hannah grew up in a close-knit community, all of whom shared her religious views. Until she learned to appreciate value systems different from her own, Hannah found it particularly difficult to create close and productive relationships with fellow students who were not religious. Her initial practicum experiences further challenged her to accept persons whose worldviews, values, sexual orientations, and religious beliefs were very different from her own. Hannah later acknowledged, "When I first started, I assumed that I would help people find answers to their problems. What I really assumed is that they would want *my* answers! It's still difficult for me sometimes to remember that my way of seeing things is not the only way."

Cultivating mutuality and interdependence means that you have to be open to give and take, to stand on an equal footing with others, and to be responsive to opportunities for engagement at a meaningful level. Many persons attracted to the helping professions enjoy the role of the "helper" but have a harder time with mutual relationships that require reciprocal self-disclosure and trust. Such reciprocity implies a willingness to be vulnerable at times and to take a chance that others will afford you the same acceptance that you are willing to show them.

For example, Deaken's peers celebrated him for his thoughtful and sensitive listening skills. Over time, however, his fellow students noticed that Deaken rarely revealed much when it was his turn to participate in counseling exercises and role plays. They also noticed, as friendships developed, that although he was supportive and caring to his fellow students in time of need, Deaken did not disclose his own struggles or feelings. When confronted about his one-sided relational style, Deaken acknowledged that he found it difficult to open up to others. His companions let him know that for mutual trust to develop, Deaken had to take the same risks that they did.

Mutuality implies that you are willing to be genuine with others, not merely pretending to show your real thoughts and feelings. For example, when his supervision group discussed his counseling recording, Elias remarked that everyone complimented him on his strengths and commented on only what he was doing successfully. How could he improve his skills if everyone was merely being polite? Elias's candor and lack of defensiveness showed his peers that he was trying to grow and that they could respond forthrightly to him without creating ill will. When the other members pointed out where he had missed some important client expressions, Elias began to trust the integrity of the group process and to feel he was getting his peers' real reactions. You must do your part in helping to create a community of learners by sharing yourself, supporting and respecting others, and by being invested and engaged with all those whose lives are joined with yours in becoming helping professionals.

Truth With a Capital T

Truth is always what a person believes privately and emotionally.

—Hergenhahn

Postmodernism suggests that multiple truths exist. Therefore, you can only truly encounter others when you realize that your "Truth" may not be someone else's "Truth." The bottom line is that in order to be both a successful and ethical professional helper, you have to be able to accept others who are different from you.

Certainly, you have values that are sacred to you, but it is likely that you also consider yourself pretty understanding about different beliefs and life-styles. However, it is also just as likely that there are times when you react to certain differences with a "hard belly." Nothing about that different perspective seems to penetrate—everything bounces right off. When you hear people talk about their life circumstances, it is as though you suddenly have "abs of steel." At that particular time, you are unable to absorb the experience. When do you have a hard-belly response? The best way to figure that out is to look at what purpose it serves.

Your hard belly is an example of distancing behaviors, those reactions and protests that may arise when you're faced with challenging ideas about diversity. Distancing behaviors include statements such as, "We don't have those kinds of problems around here," or "I don't see color," or "We've certainly come a long way in race relations/gender relations/accepting diversity." Although these statements may contain some element of truth, they are directly linked to the hard belly. These reactions protect you from feeling the intense emotions of others and genuinely connecting with their experiences. You may even recognize this pattern in yourself, but how do you move beyond that? Simple insight isn't enough.

The video *The Color of Fear* (Wah, 1994) showed several men of different races and ethnicities who spent the weekend together to discuss their experiences of themselves and others. One White man, David, consistently listened to the other men's stories with a hard-belly attitude. He rejected the legitimacy of the other men's experiences, tried to convince them that racism isn't as bad as they think, and actually attempted to teach them to be more like himself in order to get along. Finally, Wah, a Chinese man who facilitated the group, quietly asked David what stops him from genuinely hearing the other men's experiences. David's reaction was startling. He began to cry, saying that if he believed the other men's stories, then he would have to face the fact that not everyone has the privileges that he has had as a White man.

As a future professional helper, you can learn from David's decision. These hard-belly behaviors do indeed protect you—not only from painful emotions but also from change and growth. You can make the commitment to engaging with others authentically by being open to and respectful of the reality of their experiences. The next time you feel yourself becoming rigid when encountering another person's experience, ask yourself, "What do I fear? What am I protecting myself from? What am I preventing myself from learning and experiencing?" This exploration is a vital part of your ability to be with others. In fact, it is a vital part of being an ethical practitioner. You are expected to know yourself and your own prejudices well enough to be able to practice effectively and refer appropriately.

EXERCISE 6.2 Your Hard-Belly Response

A Quiz

The American Psychological Association has adopted guidelines for therapy with lesbian, gay, and bisexual clients. You are expected to recognize how your own attitudes and knowledge about lesbian, gay, and bisexual issues influence your ability to assess and work with your clients. Let's test out your hard-belly response regarding this issue. If you are heterosexual, take the following quiz:

1. What do you think caused your heterosexuality?

2. When and how did you first decide you were a heterosexual?

3. Isn't it possible your heterosexuality is just a phase?

4. How does it feel to hear that heterosexuality doesn't offend me?

5. If you should choose to nurture children, would you want them to be heterosexual, knowing the problems they would face? (e.g., sexism and inequality in intimate relationships; high rates of divorce).

6. Why must heterosexuals be so blatant, making a public spectacle of their heterosexuality?

7. Heterosexual marriage has total societal support, but why are there so few stable heterosexual marriages?

Did you feel the hard-belly response? If so, take time now to explore what you were protecting yourself from. What would you give up if you set aside this response?

Giving and Receiving Feedback

> If you don't risk anything, you risk even more.
>
> —Erika Jong

Let's explore this idea of giving feedback to others a little further. As you can see, your psychological health and personal well-being depend greatly on the manner in which you conduct your interactions with others

(Polkinghorne, 2015). The ability to create and maintain cooperative and interdependent relationships is also fundamental to your success as a helping professional. Engaging in intimate communication with others is a personally nourishing experience, and such relationships help you to become more self-aware. There are two ways in which you can become more self-aware. The first is to listen to yourself and be sensitive to how you are feeling. The second is to seek feedback from others about how you are affecting them.

You are in a training program with other people who are very special. Like you, they recognize the value of authenticity in relationships, and they are also seeking to understand themselves better. You can help each other toward greater self-awareness—and thus greater psychological health—by engaging in truly honest discussion together. In such encounters, you not only disclose yourself to other people but you also give and receive honest and authentic feedback.

When you think about it, this may be the first time in your life when you have the opportunity to be in such a special setting, with colleagues who are acting in good faith to be helpful to you. Before, you may have been blind to the impressions and opinions others had of you. It is very hard to understand how the person who says, "Thanks for shopping at Wal-Mart," or asks, "Do you want fries with that?" actually feels about you. Even worse, you have been in situations in which other people talked behind your back, withheld information from you, or deliberately tried to deceive you in order to serve their own ends. Even in some of your close relationships, there have sometimes been so many hidden agendas that you could not fully rely on what significant others said to you. They may not have wished to hurt your feelings, or they may have been afraid that you would stop loving them if they told you what they really thought.

So this is your chance. While you are with other people who understand the value of straight talk, take advantage of the opportunity to use them as honest feedback sources. It's a bit scary at first, but also quite exhilarating, to learn how other people see you.

Giving Helpful Feedback

Given the right conditions, people can learn to trust that what others say to them can be accepted as given with good intentions (Brew & Kottler, 2008). Here are some guidelines for establishing a trusting environment in which feedback is helpful to you and others:

- *Offer honest feedback about the person's actions,* not about his or her personality.

- *Be specific in describing the behavior* rather than labeling it with a pejorative term. For example, you could say, "You talked a lot in today's group" rather than, "You've got diarrhea of the mouth today." The person likely will be less defensive, and you will still get your point across.

- *Emphasize what you observe* rather than offer interpretations. Instead of something like, "Just now I noticed that you were angry," you might say, "When Jane said that, your face got red and your lips narrowed." Leave the explanation of the behavior to the person receiving the feedback.

- *Highlight the present* rather than distant history. If you say, "Last month when I said 'hello' to you, you blew me off," the person may not remember the incident or may not be able to recall the mood of the moment. Keep your feedback as close to the "here and now" as possible.

- *Share your perceptions* rather than judging or giving advice. Advice always comes across as if you are establishing a one-up–one-down relationship. "Shoulds," "oughts," and other admonitions communicate that the person is not doing it right. Advice also makes you come off as an expert on the other person's life.

- *Make sure the other person is open to your feedback*—don't force it. You might ask, "Would it be okay with you if I said something about that situation that has you upset?" Conversely, you don't have to take feedback from others if you are not ready for it at the moment. Just hold up your hand for them to stop if someone is giving you more that you can process.

- *Focus your feedback on something the person can change.* Calling attention to the fact that someone blushes easily or that each of his or her eyes is a different color may be interesting to you, but it is probably not helpful. On the other hand, if the person does or says something that is bothersome to you, then it may be something the person can change.

- *Make sure that the feedback you are giving is motivated by your desire to improve your relationship* with that person rather than to cut the person down or to be self-aggrandizing. Obviously, any feedback that is intentionally hurtful or vengeful is not in the proper spirit. Such feedback can destroy a trusting relationship.

- *Timing is always important.* When it is given at the appropriate time and in a respectful and caring manner, feedback can be powerfully effective in helping us to become more socially skillful, more self-aware, and more comfortable in the presence of others.

The Johari Window

The Johari Window, named after the originators, Joe Luft and Harry Ingham (Luft, 1969), is a way of looking at the four areas of the self. "Known to Everybody" represents the public self that is known by others and ourselves. This area would be expanded as we disclose things about ourselves to others. "Known to Others, Not to Self" is the so-called bad breath area that is unknown to us but is known by others. This area would be reduced as we encourage feedback from others, while the area of free activity in "Known to Everybody" would be increased. "Known Only to Self" is the avoided or hidden area that only we know because we have not shared it with others. This area would be reduced by self-disclosure, and "Known to Everybody" would be expanded. "Known to Nobody" is the area of undiscovered mystery because it consists of material that neither we nor others currently know.

EXERCISE 6.3 Giving and Receiving Feedback

Briefly list four things that you would be comfortable disclosing in a training session with a colleague. These disclosures do not have to be deep, dark secrets but things about you (accomplishments, ideas you have, things about your family) that you usually would not share with anyone but a friend.

_____

_____

_____

_____

List four things that you have noticed about your training partner or significant other that you would be comfortable sharing with him or her as feedback. Even though this area is called the "bad breath" area, for the purposes of this exercise, we would like to have you offer observations that would fall into the "good breath" area, too. Remember to follow the guidelines for giving good feedback that appear earlier in the chapter and in subsequent sections.

_____

_____

_____

_____

Allow five minutes for one partner to give the other feedback. When you are finished, receivers describe what it was like for them to receive feedback in such a manner. Switch roles and repeat the exercise. Join the larger group and discuss if applicable.

Authenticity

> You don't have to be right. All you have to do is be candid.
>
> —Allen Ginsberg

All of the qualities we have been discussing are embedded in a concept that you will fully explore in your counseling and therapy studies—authenticity. The personal quality of authenticity is essential, not only to your relations with peers and professors but also ultimately to your work with clients as a helping professional. You probably have an idea what authenticity means in everyday language, but as you delve deeper into your studies, you will discover that the word *authenticity* has a very specialized meaning in the helping professions.

Social Masks

To some degree, you wear a mask in your relations with others. You manage an impression of yourself that represents how you would like to be seen and that you hope others will find acceptable, likable, and appealing. Your social mask also helps you negotiate the complex demands of a variety of interpersonal encounters by making a "version" of yourself available to others. At the same time, you protect and preserve more intimate aspects of your own experience from others' view. Your social mask is very useful.

The problem with your social mask is that sometimes it ends up getting stuck to you. Your mask, designed to be removable when you wish to encounter another closely and intimately, becomes a hindrance to deeper and more sustaining interpersonal connections. When your mask is stuck, you fail to authentically show yourself as you really are to others. Carl Rogers (Polkinghorne, 2015) argued that to truly encounter another person means to demonstrate a sense of transparency. By transparency, he meant that you allow your outer presentation to be completely congruent with your inner world of thoughts and immediate feelings.

Being and Seeming

The philosopher Martin Buber (1923/1958) described these dimensions of interpersonal experience as the difference between being and seeming. When you connect to another from your true being, your relationship has all the qualities that we have been discussing. These qualities include immediacy, mutuality, acceptance, openness, and a willingness to access another person's inner world, while being anchored in one's own experience.

When people encounter one another authentically, they can participate with each other at the deepest levels of human experience. Buber described this interpersonal event as an "I-Thou" encounter and argued that something is created that is bigger than each of the people. That is to say, in such a meeting, the whole is bigger than the sum of the parts. Something new and vital emerges that does not reside in either person but that exists *between* them. Buber said that this ability to meet one another authentically is really what defines us as human. Without it somewhere in our lives, we would live in an impoverished and shrunken interpersonal world. "All real living is meeting," Buber (1923/1958, p. 93) said, as a testament to the importance of our "I-Thou" connections with others. Carl Rogers acknowledged his debt to Buber when he made a variation of this idea the cornerstone of his theoretical and therapeutic model.

In contrast to relationships grounded in being with others authentically, you may sometimes settle for the poor substitute of *seeming* to others as a counterfeit for real connection. To protect you from encroachment or injury, you may develop a layer of protective shielding around your inner life. At the same time, however, your defenses also work against you by keeping you from being nourished and sustained by others at deep levels of engagement.

Of course, the needs you have for such nourishment and affiliation do not diminish just because you are unable to meet them in relationships. You still wish to be approved of, accepted by, and cared for by others. Instead of being authentic, you may seek connection without real engagement by managing an impression, cultivating a seeming self that you present to others to gain favor and approval. Usually your "seeming" mask is successful, and you can elicit from others a response that looks accepting and approving. Unfortunately, even when you get the reaction that you are looking for, it fails to sustain or nourish you because it does not reach beyond the mask to touch your authentic self. "If Sara really knew me," you might say, "she wouldn't say such nice things about me." The self that needs that response was not the self that was shown to others. Therefore, the approval, acceptance, or praise fails to stick and merely bounces off the mask. Buber 1923/1958) called this false and self-conscious presentation the "I-It" way of relating to others because it is designed to objectify and deflect real encounter with others.

The greatest asset that you can bring to your studies in the helping professions is the ability to form interpersonal relationships and connections with others. To the degree that your relationships are characterized by the aforementioned qualities, you are likely to become a successful healer and helper. As you move through your program and become knowledgeable about different approaches to counseling, you will study these concepts in more depth. Do not simply learn them. Make them *come alive* for you. Examine your own assumptions, stretch your empathic abilities, celebrate diversity, and discover a new willingness to take some interpersonal risks. (What? Did you think it was just going to be multiple choice?)

Important People in Your Training

> No matter what accomplishments you make, somebody helps you.
>
> —Althea Gibson

Always keep in mind that when you successfully complete your graduate program and launch your professional career, your professors and supervisors, as well as your fellow students and clients, go with you. Throughout your training, you are internalizing the important and most significant others you encounter. You already have had experiences with others that have changed your life and have stayed with you through time. In fact, the constellations in your mythological sky are populated by the figures of those who have had the most profound influence on you—and you have a vivid sense of them hovering over you still. At this very moment, you can easily recall someone whose presence and interest in you made a difference in who you are today.

Mentors

Most myths involving journeys have the hero setting out on a quest that is a metaphor for self-discovery. The "hero cycle" goes something like this. The hero sets out with high hopes, full of confidence and courage. He or she has many adventures that test the hero's strength and determination. In the end, after many trials and tribulations, the hero prevails and discovers or achieves something of great value. Not content to selfishly possess the thing of great worth, the hero brings it back to share with the greater community (Campbell, 1973). But there is one important part to this hero cycle that we have not mentioned here. That part, paradoxically, seems to be the most important pivotal event. At some point between the idealistic setting out and the returning in wisdom and accomplishment, the hero becomes hopelessly lost.

At this point in the story, the hero's weapons are broken, the food is gone, the horse is dead, and the reason for setting out in the first place is no longer clear. The hero is lost in an impenetrable forest, waterless desert, endless night, or desolate shore. It seems as if the journey is a failure and the hero is a goner.

But then something happens. Out of the deepest part of the forest, a person appears unexpectedly. This mysterious person always seems to be expecting the arrival of the hero and possesses some knowledge or secret that he or she shares with the hero. Sometimes this guide helps the hero understand, in a new way, something the hero already knows. At other times, the guide gives the hero a new tool or weapon that the hero's courage and determination have made him or her worthy to receive. The hero, fortified with new knowledge, self-understanding, and resources, eventually prevails, completing a journey that is perhaps less glamorous, but much more profound, than the one on which the hero began with naïve hopes of easy success.

There are plenty of epic myths—both ancient and modern—that feature mentors rescuing and guiding the lost heroes. Theseus, for example, went into the depths of the labyrinth, slew the Minotaur, and followed Ariadne's silver thread back into the light of day. Arthur had Merlin's magic to help and protect him. Luke Skywalker had crashed into a swamp, his spaceship—the horse equivalent—was nonfunctional, and he was out of options. It was then that Yoda appeared to guide his Jedi training. And when Dorothy crash-landed in Oz, she had the Good Witch to direct her to "follow the yellow brick road."

Believe it or not, your graduate school experience has a lot in common with the hero cycle. Just as there are times of adventure, achievement, and clarity, there are also times when you feel confused, depleted, and unsure which way to turn. In these bleak valleys, you may even forget the reasons why you even began the journey. It's at those times that you especially need mentors and faculty members who can serve as guides for you. Of course, you can't just count on your mentors appearing, as in the myths; you must cultivate a relationship with them.

Seek out the help, guidance, and experience of a supervisor or professor whose values, personal qualities, research interests, or professional activities appeal to you. Working closely with such a mentor who possesses the skills and knowledge you wish to acquire gives added meaning and dimension to your journey. A mentor is someone who not only teaches you what you want to know but who is the embodiment of what you wish to become. These are lessons that you cannot learn from a book. Rather, by modeling yourself after persons who have gone before you on the adventure, you can discover the things of value that you wish to bring to your own community. When you near the end of your hero journey, you will have developed a professional identity and philosophical orientation that represents and structures your work in the helping professions. In your undergraduate experience, you probably found that if you attended class, studied hard, and took your exams, you did pretty well. There was likely not as much opportunity—or demand—for you to become involved more directly with your professors. Fortunately, in most graduate programs, you can find faculty members who take a special interest in you. They can guide you to the kinds of experiences that stay with you long after you may have forgotten exactly what the Zeigarnik Effect is (see Chapter 4).

If you are wondering how you might connect with a faculty member whom you would like to have as a mentor, we'll let you in on a little secret. Professors, supervisors, and advisors love to work with sincerely committed, fully engaged, and curious trainees. Even mentors have a need to feel that what they do is meaningful and important; they like it when students want what they have to offer. Trainers of helping professionals are more than willing to really get to know you, to understand your needs and interests, and to help you in your journey by mentoring you along—if you are responsive. It is enormously gratifying to professors and supervisors when they feel that their investment in, and devotion to, the helping professions is being passed on to students who are their future peers. Your strategy is simple: Let your passion show!

Typically, the faculty member you want to get to know is incredibly busy, seems preoccupied with a wide range of projects, or simply appears to be hard to approach. That's okay. Just show how intrigued and fascinated you are by what your potential mentor is teaching, researching, or sharing. It is likely that he or she will make time for you. Then you can make the most of this opportunity to form a productive learning partnership—and a meaningful, lasting relationship.

In your graduate program there is someone waiting, just as in the myth, for you to stumble into that person's forest. He or she will help you understand what it is you need to discover in yourself and to carry back with you as you continue your journey. Your mentor won't be wielding a light saber, like Obiwan Kenobi, or waving a magic wand, like the Good Witch. But your mentor, whoever he or she may be, will help you recognize and realize your unique potential.

Support Staff

We have been discussing your relationships with peers and professors. It is worth noting, however, that your program's support staff members are essential to having a successful training experience. They are often the first people you speak to when you are in the application phase, and they help you with all the practical details of getting oriented. These staff members are typically underpaid and overworked but truly devoted to making your experience a good one.

You would be wise to cultivate the goodwill of the program support staff. The kindness that you show them will be returned to you in many ways. Every seasoned graduate student knows that in a practical sense, it is really the administrative assistants and clerical staff members who most often know what is going on. They have the power to facilitate your progress—and to prevent it from becoming a living hell! These support persons can assist you in negotiating the various technical and bureaucratic hurdles that are an inevitable part of any training program.

As you progress through your training, regularly drop in on the program's clerical staff and offer them your gratitude for their help and support. They are vital members of your learning community.

Significant Others

No one enters a graduate program alone. You have significant others in your life who are, in some small or large way, partners in your new undertaking. You may have been away from school for some time and have an established family or another career. If you are entering your graduate training with the support of someone important to you, the chances are that you have had many discussions about what this commitment means to your relationship. Perhaps you have to move to a new city, give up a good job, strain the family finances, or renegotiate family responsibilities. Perhaps your partner is concerned that you will not have enough time to spend taking care of your relationship or nurturing other family members. Whatever your unique circumstances, you have had to take into account the needs, views, and feelings of important others in your life.

Graduate school often places new and unique stresses on intimate relationships. The amount of time and energy that you pour into your studies may reduce the personal resources you have to give to others in your life. How will your significant others feel about you being frequently absorbed and preoccupied with your projects? In the economy of your relationship, what redistribution of time, energy, and attention will need to occur for your intimate connections to be preserved undamaged? Will you spend less time at the gym, with friends, or with the kids? How will you carve out a space in your life that is reserved exclusively for you and your partner to renew and nourish your love? Discuss these issues with your partner as you launch into your program. Throughout your training, keep your "relationship antennae" up to stay sensitive to the shifts and changes in your partnership. Devise ways in which you can communicate to each other when things are getting too far out of whack.

Your intimate partner may not have realized the degree to which he or she is now called on to adjust and to accommodate to your graduate school commitments. In very real ways, your significant other takes the journey with you but may, for some time, receive less gratification from the experience than you do. After all, graduate school was probably your idea. If you are embarking on the hero's journey, your partner may be the unsung hero, the one standing in the background holding the reins of the horse while you take on the world—the Sancho Panza to your Don Quixote. Just remember—as you are tilting at windmills, you will need your significant other to be there to celebrate your victory when it comes. And don't forget to discuss with your partner in advance some of the challenges you are likely to struggle with as you move into even more demanding and time-consuming phases of your training.

Graduate school, especially in the helping professions, also introduces a more subtle challenge to your intimate relationships. There is no doubt that if you truly throw yourself into the adventure of becoming a healer and a helper to others, you also gain new insights into yourself and your relationships with others. These insights and experiences can dramatically change you. You have a new lens with which to view yourself and others. You look at your life differently and begin to question your values, assumptions, and motivations. As you gain understanding of individual development and family systems, you may reevaluate your own history in the light of a new perspective. As you come to understand relational dynamics, you may find yourself realizing how certain themes play out in your own intimate relationships. You may begin to question the status quo and to ask your partner to take into account your new perspective and feelings. You will be excited to share and apply what you are discovering with others in your life.

Of course, your partner does not automatically share your newfound perspective and is not looking through the new lens on relationships that you have discovered. The changes you are experiencing may not be entirely welcome to your significant others because they upset the homeostatic balance of your relationship. Your newly discovered insights may be disorienting or even threatening to your partner's sense of connection with you. The context that you take for granted in the culture of your program and that makes certain kinds of interpersonal engagement possible may be unfamiliar to your family and friends. In your eagerness to share your new perspective on interpersonal dynamics, you may find yourself approaching intimate others in the same way that you communicate with your graduate school companions. One minute, for example, your partner is quietly eating corn flakes and reading the paper. The next moment, your significant other is being asked to consider the passive-aggressive implications of hiding behind a newspaper every morning!

You want to make real what you are learning by applying new insights to your life and relationships, but this can be disruptive. People grow and change, and relationships must accommodate to this change if they are to be vital and dynamic. Keep in mind, however, that one facet of empathy is to be sensitive to the degree to which others can adapt to new experiences. Your partner probably expected that you would go to graduate school, learn many new things, and later get a rewarding job. But like it or not, he or she signed on with you to a program that influences you deeply and profoundly and has implications for your growth together.

We offer one last consideration for you to ponder regarding how your graduate school journey affects your intimate connections. Remember that you are gaining a new community in which you make new friends, share very personal aspects of yourself, and create a new identity as a helping professional. You engage with your mentors, supervisors, and fellow students on a level that may have been reserved only for your most significant others. You are even fostering a sense of family with those special people in your program and forming bonds that last a lifetime. Your partner, although you may include him or her in social activities outside of school, may have a sense of being excluded from an area of your life that has become vital to you. Your partner may have mixed feelings about your forming close bonds with others who are not in your normal circle of friends. Because your partner may not be involved in the helping professions, it may seem as if you are learning a foreign language and talking with others in a manner unfamiliar to your normal way of being with others. Remember that change is good, but it is also destabilizing. It is likely that you will need to take care that you and your significant other find a new balance as your relationship seeks to keep up with the changes you make as you become a helping professional.

Summary

Have you ever fondly recalled an event and realized that your original experience of it was entirely different from the feelings you now have? Our lives and the most pivotal experiences in them involve multiple layers of meaning that are not revealed all at once. A sailor and fellow crewmembers may battle through a storm, frantic and filled with dread while they are caught up in the deadly throes of the tempest. However, later they may describe that episode with a deep sense of relief, gratitude, awe, and even humor. The sailors were never more fully alive, all senses keen, than when the challenge was the greatest.

Graduate school is a lot like surviving a storm at sea. It calls on you to bring to bear all your talents and abilities. At times, you feel overwhelmed and challenged to the utmost. Perhaps you even wish that you had never left the safety of the harbor. Later, when you have reached calm water, you will recall things differently. People and events that were, at the time, simply part of the changing scene stand out as important. What you are most likely to remember are those times when you felt totally engaged, striving, connected, and open to the experience itself. At the center of this memory will be all of the traveling companions—your fellow crewmembers—you had along the way. The most enduring, life-changing events always involve your encounters with others—those who share some part of your life journey.

Resources

COUNSGRADS: Counseling Student Listserv

The Ohio State University and American Counseling Association have formed a listserv to meet the needs of counseling graduate students. COUNSGRADS is an active listserv that enables graduate students from across the country to communicate with one another. You can talk about classes, internships, papers, and ideas about the profession. Darcy Haag Granello, a counselor educator at The Ohio State University, is the list owner. Questions regarding the listserv can be sent to her at *granello.1@osu.edu.* To sign up for the listserv, send an e-mail to *listserver@lists.acs.ohio-state.edu* with the following in the body of the message:

subscribe COUNSGRADS (your first name) (your last name)

PSYCGRAD: Psychology Graduate Student Listserv

The American Psychological Association of Graduate Students sponsors a general discussion list for graduate students involved in any of the specialty areas of psychology. To subscribe to the listserv, send an e-mail to *listserv@ lists.apa.org* with the following in the body of the message (leave the subject line blank):

subscribe PSYCGRAD (your first name) (your last name)

References

Adams, D. (2006, May). How I lost my voice and found it again. *Counseling Today, 48,* 12–13.

Brew, L., & Kottler, J. A. (2008). *Applied helping skills: Transforming lives.* Thousand Oaks, CA: Sage.

Buber, M. (1958). *I and thou* (R. G. Smith, Trans.). New York, NY: Scribner. (Original work published 1923)

Campbell, J. (1973). *The hero with a thousand faces.* Princeton, NJ: Princeton University Press.

Carlson, R. G. (2012). Developing your clinical and counseling skills. In P. J. Giordano, S. F. Davis, & C. A. Licht (Eds.), *Your graduate training in psychology: Effective strategies for success* (pp. 147–158). Thousand Oaks, CA: Sage.

Edelstein, B. (2015). Frames, attitudes, and skills of an existential-humanistic psychotherapist. In K. J. Schneider, J. F. Pierson, & J. F. T. Bugental (Eds.), *The handbook of humanistic psychology* (2nd ed., pp. 435–449). Thousand Oaks, CA: Sage.

Hayman, J. W. (2006, April). Evolving from a racist worldview: A White woman's perspective. *Counseling Today, 48,* 41, 45.

Hoffman, L., Stewart, S., Warren, D. M., & Meek, L. (2015). Toward a sustainable myth of self: An existential response to the postmodern condition. In K. J. Schneider, J. F. Pierson, & J. F. T. Bugental (Eds.), *The handbook of humanistic psychology* (2nd ed., pp. 105–133). Thousand Oaks, CA: Sage.

Luft, J. (1969). *Of human interaction.* Palo Alto, CA: National Press Books.

Matthews, M. (2005, December). Counselor know thyself: Education about intimate abuse. *Counseling Today, 47,* 7, 35.

Polkinghorne, D. E. (2015). The self and humanistic psychology. In K. J. Schneider, J. F. Pierson, & J. F. T. Bugental (Eds.), *The handbook of humanistic psychology* (2nd ed., pp. 87–104). Thousand Oaks, CA: Sage.

Stolorow, R. D., & Atwood, G. (1992). *Contexts of being: The intersubjective foundations of psychological life.* Hillsdale, NJ: Analytic Press.

Wah, L. M. (Producer). (1994). *The color of fear* [Videotape]. Berkeley, CA: Stir-Fry Productions.

7

Exploring Yourself

One of the most profound ways in which I can change myself is to change the story I tell myself about myself.

—Jerome Levin

Your vision will become clear only when you look into your heart.

—Carl Jung

Make Personal Growth Your Goal

A shop sometimes has a "Help Wanted" sign posted in its window with the instruction "Inquire Within." Those two words capture one of your fundamental tasks in becoming a helping professional: You must always inquire within yourself. As you make your training journey, you need time alone to check your bearings, process your experiences, and reflect on the discoveries you are making. Like someone taking a "selfie," you want to be sure to check the image you are capturing of yourself in the moment. And like an author writing a novel, you want to develop your character into the protagonist you hope to become. The "who I am," "where I stand," and "what I stand for" make up the person you have so far come to know as yourself. However, your self-concept, identity, and personal beliefs about the world and other people are constantly unfolding, emerging, and evolving (Polkinghorne, 2015).

Your training experiences also will challenge many of your ideas about yourself. Your first reaction might be to hunker down and defend your self-image and assumptions. Instead, we invite you to remain open to new possibilities and ideas. The one certainty about your journey is that you *will* be changed by it. In fact, achieving a personal transformation in your training is essential to becoming a successful professional helper.

In this chapter, we offer some guidelines for coping with the dramatic growth that you will experience during your training. Even when you are making positive changes, you will find that they can feel uncomfortable, unfamiliar, and strange. At some level, you may even fear that you are turning into a stranger whom you will not recognize. At these times, remind yourself that it is possible to become a new person while also preserving one's basic integrity. Although you may be altering your beliefs, trying out new ways of acting, and challenging your experience of yourself, you can trust that this change process is part of your personal and professional identity (Gibson, Dollarhide, & Moss, 2010).

Your essential being is always "becoming." Making personal growth your goal is the best way to stay vital both in your training and in your career (Dearing, Maddux, & Tangney, 2005). As one chapter of your life story, the narrative of your graduate training will involve enormous change—like the "growth spurt" you may have had as a child. You may discover that you are rewriting your life script as fast as you can. You are in training to make yourself into a helping professional, and you will find it an exciting process. At your center, you already have the basic ingredients to become who you wish to be, but you need to go through a metamorphosis to fulfill this potential. Consider your graduate program to be your chrysalis, the cocoon protecting you during this period of transformation. Such dramatic change is always stressful, but you have chosen to undergo this process. Welcome the change as you develop your wings. Enjoy the new heights you will achieve!

Thanksgiving Leftovers

Edna's Story

Thanksgiving, I recently discovered, can involve other kinds of leftovers besides the turkey, dressing, and pumpkin pie. This year, I was really looking forward to Thanksgiving because it was my first visit home since entering a program to become a therapist. I desperately needed a break and was excited about going home again. It was weird, though—it didn't seem like home anymore. I felt like a stranger in a familiar place. As an undergrad, I had gone to a nearby college and was home nearly every weekend—you know, so Mom could do my laundry and I could talk my parents out of a little more money for the upcoming week. So you might say that I was really never away from home before.

Now I find that playing the role of my parent's little daughter is getting harder for me to carry off like I used to be able to do. I'm just not that girl anymore. As we sat at the table on Thanksgiving, I was hassled to "eat up," my uncle was getting drunk, and my father told a racist joke. When I refused to laugh, he accused me of being "politically correct," and later, when I tried to tell people about what I was learning in school, they dismissed it as "psychobabble."

My mother scurried around like a servant and was up and down from the table so many times, filling people's glasses and offering second helpings, that she hardly ate a bite. She claimed not to be hungry because she had sampled so much while she was cooking the meal.

My cousins talked incessantly to each other as we ate and seemed to ignore me. We had been so close when we were younger, but now we didn't seem to have much in common. Then there was my best friend Jeannie, who's going to Tech and studying computer science. She kept talking about how much money she's going to make when she graduates. Dad said, "You see, Edna? You could be making the big bucks if you changed programs. You'll never get rich as a therapist."

I sat there watching these people with whom I had always been so close, and after awhile all I could hear was "blah, blah, blah." "Who are these people?" I asked myself. When I was a small child, I thought that when I finally got to sit at the big table on Thanksgiving, I would officially be a successful grownup. But somehow, I felt like I was still at the kids' table. Then it hit me, "I don't know who *I* am! I've been changing so much, I seem to have lost *me* in the process." I realized that I have a lot of leftovers here!

Your Sense of Self

Why is it that understanding and keeping track of yourself is one of the most difficult tasks you have to do? Perhaps it's because a "self" is not an object that you can observe and contemplate. Your sense of self is so close and yet so far. As Levin (1992) put it, "The self to which we think we are so close eludes definition and indeed becomes more elusive as we attempt to grasp it" (p. 1).

Because the self is not a material substance but rather an experience that is constantly with you, it may seem like an illusion. Part of yourself is pure emotion or sensation. When you are "on top of the world," this feeling is vivid, but when you are ill or sleepy, the feeling is vague. Another facet of yourself is your concept of who you are—your identity. In large part, this self-concept is an active determiner of your behavior and your feelings (Hoffman, Stewart, Warren, & Meek, 2015). In addition, who you consider yourself to be is shaped by cultural influences. Your family, your gender, your race, and even your location on the planet have all contributed to your conception of self. You have entered a training program for helping professionals in which you are asked to be authentic—to be the self you really are. At the same time, however, you are being asked to change. It can all be pretty confusing.

Concepts that can help you gain some insight into this paradox come from Linehan's dialectical behavior therapy (Linehan & Dexter-Mazza, 2008). Although her work has focused on clients with borderline personality disorder, the dialectical issue of self-acceptance and change applies to all humans. How do we resolve our need, on the one hand, to accept ourselves as we are now and our fundamental impulse, on the other hand, to constantly change and grow?

Your willingness to embark on a personal transformation may be sabotaged by worries about possible abandonment. At some deep level, you may wonder if your friends and family will accept and love the new you. Nevertheless, you can learn to be comfortable with—and even welcome— change in yourself, others, and the world around you. One strategy that Linehan (Linehan & Dexter-Mazza, 2008) recommended is the Zen practice of mindfulness. In Chapter 5, you learned how mindfulness can help you manage stress, but it is also an excellent way to deal with the sense of engulfment that you may experience during especially troubled and distressing times, when emotions seem to overwhelm you. When you practice mindful acceptance and validation of your emotional turmoil, you discover that you can transform and transcend those negative feelings.

Your identity is really the story you tell yourself about yourself. You update your identity as new experiences alter your beliefs, your values, and your worldview (Sadler-Gerhardt, 2005). Usually, this process is slow and difficult to notice. But now, with your entry into graduate school, you have been thrown into chaos, and you are developing your new identity more rapidly than ever before. It is your goal to become the best counselor or therapist you can become. Goals such as this become a part of your self-concept and then act like powerful magnetic forces that invisibly draw you toward your future, helping you to focus your energies and organize your day-to-day activities (Goleman, 2013). However, your current self is different from the self you hope to become as a helping professional. This disparity is probably causing you some distress because you are feeling as if you are a page or two behind in your story.

EXERCISE 7.1 "I Am ..." versus "A Counselor Is ..."

On a piece of paper, write "I AM ..." at the top. Then take a little time to consider the qualities and characteristics that define who you are, what you believe, and what you can do. Finish the statement by writing the twelve words or phrases that best describe yourself.

Then, on a separate sheet, write "A COUNSELOR IS ..." at the top. Reflect on the traits and qualities that characterize a successful counselor. Write a dozen words or phrases that describe the person you are training to become.

Finally, do the following task. On a scale from 1 to 10, with 1 indicating that you currently possess none of the attributes of a successful counselor and 10 meaning that you already possess all the traits of a successful counselor, rate where you are now.

Obviously, you would not give yourself a 1. If you had thought you possessed none of the characteristics of a counselor, you would not have entered a training program. You already have many of the attributes you will need to be successful as a helping professional. On the other hand, neither are you a 10. If you thought you had already arrived, you would not have embarked on this training journey.

Whatever number you assigned yourself to show where you currently are, ask yourself this question: "What changes will I notice in myself that will let me know I am on the way to the next higher number?" Instead of immediately trying to get to 10, you'll be taking this process one step at a time. So what do you need to do to get to that next higher number? As soon as you answer that question, you have begun your journey.

Ontological Security

You really have to spend time with yourself to know who you are.

—Bernice Johnson Reagon

R. D. Laing, in his 1969 classic *The Divided Self,* created a vivid picture of what it means to have a secure base in life by contrasting this security with an uncertain experience of the world. According to Laing, "an *ontologically* secure person will encounter all the hazards of life . . . from a centrally firm sense of [one's] own and other people's reality" (p. 39). If someone does not achieve this secure base, the person grows up ontologically insecure, and everyday life seems threatening.

You may believe that in order to be a successful helping professional, you must first attain complete ontological security. But most of us have achieved an ontological security that is only good enough, and we usually can recognize a small glimmer of our insecurity in the dark corners and recesses of ourselves. Furthermore, when we are in circumstances in which our self-esteem is on the line, we feel this insecurity more intensely. Your training program will require you to practice your skills in clinical sessions while being recorded or observed through a one-way mirror. At these times, you are likely to feel at least a little insecure. You may find yourself so focused on what you are going to say next that you hardly hear what your client is saying.

Of course, making mistakes is inevitable in such training situations. At first, you are likely to be both self-conscious and self-critical. However, as you begin to truly listen to what the other person is saying, you will enter into the sense of *flow* that we described in Chapter 4. In flow, you lose yourself and become absorbed in what is happening. The paradox here is that when you get to the point at which you really listen to your client rather than merely wait for your turn to talk, not only will you lose your self-consciousness, you will also be more ontologically secure.

"I" and "Me"

Your self-system is inherently divided between the core of yourself (the "I" awareness) and the contents of yourself (the "me" and those experiences that seem to happen to "me"). William James (1890) has been credited with making this distinction between the "I" and the "me." Deikman (1996) proposed that the "I" is what gives you your subjective sense of existence. The "I" is the center of your existence, whereas the "me" is the object of your perception— the part of yourself you can observe. We do not begin to form an identity until we are about 18 months of age, and we do not consolidate our identity until we are in our 20s. If you are recently out of undergraduate school, then you may still be in the process of putting the jigsaw pieces of yourself together. On the other hand, if you are a nontraditional learner—someone who has returned to school after years of establishing your identity—you will be opening up your old self to make room for the emerging new you. In either case, there will be times when your sense of yourself will be less vivid and you will be experiencing ontological insecurity. At other times, you will be discovering surprising aspects of yourself that you will want to incorporate into your identity. You will find that these experiences of self-uncertainty are way stations on your journey. They mean that you are on course to stabilizing your "I" and consolidating your "me."

The Need for Personal Growth

The battles that count aren't the ones for gold medals. The struggles within yourself—the invisible, inevitable battles inside all of us—that's where it's at.

—Jesse Owens

Being a Do-Gooder

You are in a training program to become a helping professional because you wish to relieve the suffering of others. Because you are obviously altruistic, some of your more cynical acquaintances may sometimes tease you for being such a touchy-feely type, a bleeding heart, or a do-gooder. By these terms, they mean that you are too softhearted for your own good. In a cynical age in which it seems that self-interest and competition are essential to survival, someone with altruistic feelings for others may appear to be unnatural or naïve.

Actually, altruism appears to be the norm among humans and countless other species. Christopher Boehm (2012), an evolutionary anthropologist, investigated why animals and humans are so altruistic and concluded that it is not only natural but absolutely essential to the survival of a species that its individual members act unselfishly for the good of others. Animals do it to the point of self-sacrifice. For example, birds often sound alarms when predators are near. This behavior alerts the other members of the flock but also calls attention to the bird giving the warning, placing that individual in danger. Squirrels often give warning while risking their own safety. Bees, termites, and ants have developed societies in which certain members sacrifice themselves to save the rest of the group from attack. Higher order species, such as monkeys and apes, engage in similar behaviors for the benefit of the troop. One adult member of a wolf pack forgoes mating and its own territory in order to help the alpha male and female raise their brood. So you see, there is nothing unnatural or rare about doing good.

Of course, we can never be absolutely certain about the meaning of such behavior among animals. However, you certainly have witnessed many instances of self-sacrifice among your fellow human beings. What is even more remarkable about the altruism of humans is that they consciously choose to perform these acts and obviously display tremendous empathy for the plight of others. Charles Darwin considered empathy to be not only natural but also the very basis for an ethical society.

If you had chosen to be, say, an engineer, a physicist, or an accountant, you would expect your training to be centered largely on content and skills. You would be surprised if you were asked to work on who you are. But you have chosen to be a counselor, and the fact is that your success in this field will center largely on your personhood and the way you use who you are. In a comprehensive review of the research, Norcross (2011) found that the person of the therapist was the primary predictor of successful therapeutic outcome. Like members of the clergy who follow their vocation, successful helping professionals have somehow been called to their life's work and are ready to fully give themselves to it. The more willing you are to make such a commitment, the more likely you will be to experience joy and success in your work as a do-gooder.

Having Empathy for Others. The journey that has brought you to this training program has taken many years. Moreover, it is likely that the negative experiences you have had in your own life have sensitized you to the misfortune of others and stimulated in you the desire to be helpful. Sussman (2007) found that as children, many therapists had struggled with illness, loneliness, or bereavement. Counselors were more likely to have endured traumatic events, and their families of origin were often in turmoil. Such findings have given empirical support to the idea of the wounded healer (Zerubavel & Wright, 2012). The wounded healer, which originated in Greek mythology and shamanistic practices, has been portrayed in art, rituals, and cultures throughout the world. Its implications for the helping professions of today is that counselors and therapists are able to draw upon their own experiences of suffering to better heal the traumas of others. Of course, having been wounded does not automatically confer on someone this power of healing. Rather, survivors can achieve this potential only through their own recovery and posttraumatic growth (Calhoun & Tedeschi, 2006). These lessons learned can bring empathy for the pain, recognition of the resilience, and hope for the healing of their clients (Gelso & Hayes, 2007).

Firsthand experiences of loss and suffering are certainly helpful in understanding what life might be like for your clients. A counselor educator of our acquaintance often says, "I wouldn't give you a nickel for a counselor who hasn't suffered." Such painful events in the counselor's life are, however, a two-edged sword. Although they may aid in the establishment of empathy, they could also result in a countertransference in which the counselor overidentifies with the client's pain. At these times, you will need to check within yourself to see how strong your rescue fantasy might be. A rescue fantasy is the urgent need to fix your client's situation and then to be appreciated for your extraordinary intervention.

Handling Difficult Topics. You also need to explore your value system in order to become more aware of what pushes your buttons and what makes you uncomfortable. For example, you may have strong opinions regarding abortion, incest, infidelity, physical abuse, or alcohol and drug use. It's okay for you to have these opinions, but it is important that you work on respecting and accepting clients, even when their opinions or behaviors are dramatically different from your own.

Often, your discomforts and prejudices may lie beyond your awareness. In such cases, you may communicate to your client, without even realizing it, that talking about such subjects is out-of-bounds in the counseling relationship. For example, when he was a graduate student, Jack once had a meeting with an admired professor. In a horribly tragic turn of events, the professor committed suicide later that day. Although he retained feelings of guilt at having been the last person to see this man alive, Jack subsequently graduated and entered practice. Two years later, while discussing a particularly vexing case with a supervisor, Jack was asked if the client had talked of suicide. At that moment, Jack realized that none of his clients had ever spoken of suicide. Somehow, he had subliminally communicated to all his clients, "Don't talk about suicide—it makes me too uncomfortable." After that epiphany, Jack's clients often spoke of suicide.

Like Jack, you may unconsciously hope that your clients do not bring up certain topics in counseling because they might make you feel threatened or helpless. Do you know what those topics are?

EXERCISE 7.2 Things I Hope My Clients Never Say

An Aversion Exercise

Listed below are some of the things clients have said to us. As you read them, imagine that the client is speaking directly to you. Try to identify the

(Continued)

(Continued)

feelings you have as you read these quotes. Write your immediate reaction in the space below each quote; then think about what you could say that would be useful to the client:

1. "You look awfully young. I'm not sure you could understand a problem as deep and complicated as mine."

   _____

   _____

2. "I was raped last night."

   _____

   _____

3. "…and goddammit! I'm so fucking pissed off at her that I just can't think about anything else!"

   _____

   _____

4. "…I don't know, they just told me I had to be here. I don't have a problem."

   _____

   _____

5. "I come in here week after week and spill my guts, and all you do is listen. I don't think this is helping."

   _____

   _____

6. "I've been to lots of counselors, but they were the pits! They had no idea how to help me. But I get the feeling that you are the one who can solve my problem."

   _____

   _____

7. "How about meeting me this evening at that bar down the street? I'd like to get to know you better."

_____

_____

8. "I've tried everything to get past this problem. I'm pretty discouraged. If you can't help me, I guess it's all over."

_____

_____

9. "You don't really care about me, you're just paid to listen—but you don't really care."

_____

_____

10. "There is something I have been wanting to tell you, but I am not sure you would understand ....I'm gay."

_____

_____

11. "You remind me of someone I knew in college that I really hated."

_____

_____

12. "I was sexually abused as a child."

_____

_____

As you read some quotes, you may have found yourself hoping that your clients will never say something like that to you. To which statements did you have greater confidence responding? How did you develop this self-assurance? Which quotes were most threatening to you? How will you go about developing the confidence to respond to these statements?

Consider Counseling for Yourself

> The key to understanding others is to understand oneself.
>
> —Helen Williams

In Chapter 5, we recommended that you consider engaging in your own personal counseling to help you manage your stress. Here, we also urge you to become a counseling client to enhance your self-awareness and develop your therapeutic skills. Although none of us will ever be problem free, it is our responsibility as counselors to always work to maintain personal soundness. Not surprisingly, therapists were likely to have been clients themselves even before beginning their graduate education (Orlinsky, Schofield, Schroder, & Kazantzis, 2011). However, if you continue to have serious unresolved issues during your training and practice, your ability to be effective as a counselor will be compromised. For this reason, many counseling programs advocate personal counseling for their trainees.

In one study, graduate students who were currently enrolled in counselor education programs reported that receiving counseling services for themselves significantly reduced their overall personal problems, including their levels of anxiety and depression (Prosek, Holm, & Daly, 2013). Besides these benefits, participating in counseling for yourself can illuminate for you the dynamics of therapy with an incandescent clarity. Experiencing counseling as a client is a profound lesson in seeing the process from the client's point of view; you can emerge from it with a deeper appreciation for the courage every client demonstrates when entering a therapeutic relationship.

Of course, you don't have to be a paragon of mental health in order to be a successful counselor. All of us have our ups and downs, and counseling is useful for everyone. It helps you clear the circuits and stay in touch with yourself when the trials of everyday life make you begin to feel as though you have been nibbled to death by ducks. Working with troubled clients costs you a great deal of psychic energy and can result in a residual confusion and burnout unless you continually process your experiences. Remember, you don't have to be sick to get better!

It Feels Weird for a Counselor to Be a Client

Robert's Story

I enter the counseling center and take a seat in one of the empty chairs in the waiting room. People are coming and going, counselors are greeting their clients and then disappearing with them down the hall. The only sound following them is the squeak of the hinge as the door closes.

I know this feeling that is permeating my insides. I have had this reaction before but not for some time. Because I am in my third year of counselor training, I thought I should be past this feeling by now. As I sit in the waiting room, the realization hits me that I have absolutely no doubt that this is what I needed to do and where I needed to be. This is a wonderful feeling! I am proud of myself for taking this step because it contradicts some very unconscious stereotypical masculine notions. By making the phone call and following through with my appointment, I was able to feel good about this decision and not let my internal "critic" voice itself in derogatory ways about my manhood.

Each of us has a personal story to tell, and somehow I had lost or forgotten part of my story—what being a client was like. Books can convey a wealth of information and insight about counseling, but actual experience can be the door to true understanding. As my counselor appears in the waiting room, I realize that I have been so focused on learning how to be a counselor that I forgot how much was involved in being a client.

As soon as I sit down in the counselor's office, I am uncertain of my role. All at once, I feel entangled in a psychological web—confused as to whether I am a client or a counselor. I am immediately struck by my focus on the man sitting across from me. I am exploring every facial expression, scrutinizing each of his words, and making mental notes of his every move. I cannot help but compare and make judgments about what my counselor is doing and saying. "How dare you write down what I am saying? Where is the rapport building? I was taught to be present with the client, and taking notes was not encouraged. Where are the head nods, the empathic reflections, and the eye contact? I have taken risks to be here, and you are scribbling old historical stuff about me on a notepad. What's going on?"

I have learned to deal with a fair amount of ambiguity in my training program and have been challenged to think outside of my traditional gender and cultural mind-set, but how to be a client again? I guess that if I expect my clients to make an honest self-assessment, I must be committed to this same quest for self-awareness. I think I am ready to do this.

Allow Yourself to Mess Up

Life is very interesting if you make mistakes.

—Georges Carpentier

As a new counselor, you may tend to obsess over the mistakes you are making with clients. You may even consider these slipups to be the undeniable evidence that proves you were hopelessly wrong to think you could ever be a successful helping professional. This is your crisis of faith. Be assured that such crises come with the territory. In fact, counselors and therapists always make mistakes.

You are probably more sensitive to your errors because you really want to be good at this work and you somehow have had the idea that good counselors can do it perfectly. In the book *On Being a Therapist,* Kottler (2010) pointed out that it is not failures that cause us problems. Rather, it is our attempts to avoid acknowledging mistakes that undermine our confidence and sabotage our effectiveness. In fact, our therapeutic failures can lead to positive results because they can teach us to be humble, encourage us to reflect on our work, stir us to change, and promote our own professional development.

Maybe you have watched video recordings in which master counselors and therapists are modeling their approaches. You were probably in awe of some of them. You may also have felt overwhelmed, doubting that you could ever practice counseling with the poise, assurance, and finesse that they displayed so effortlessly. Please remember that these people have been at this work for a long time. Besides, do you think you would ever see the videos in which they really screwed up? No chance!

Explore Your Assets

When you decided that you had what it takes to be a therapist and applied to graduate school, you intuitively felt that aspects of your personality seemed to fit the role. Perhaps over the years people regularly came to you with their problems, and you wanted to learn how to be more helpful. Hold that thought. You have obviously been able to establish warm and empathic relationships, and studies have shown that the desire to be helpful to others is perhaps the most indispensable aspect of a counselor's personality. You were correct to think that you had the right stuff.

However, if being a good listener were all there was to successful counseling and therapy, you would already be an accomplished helper. Besides learning the theories and practicing techniques, you have to liberate your authentic self to use in the therapeutic relationship. As Parrott (1997) put it, "A counselor cannot fake authenticity; it is not something you do, but something you are" (p. 28). Being authentic is not easy. We have all been taught to be less than forthright in our social relationships, often to the point of feeling as though we have lost our way. The good news, however, is that under our social veneer we are all authentic. Underneath is who we really are. During your training program, you will need to find your way back to that person. Socrates admonished each of us to "know thyself." In order to achieve this level of self-understanding, you need to uncover experiences that you have sealed over or set outside of your awareness. Socrates also said that the unexamined life is not worth living. Make a commitment to examine your own life to find the real you. Although it is often exhausting work, you also will find the process to be an exhilarating one. And it certainly will make you a better counselor.

Avoid the Groucho Paradox

The term "Groucho paradox" (Swann, 1996) comes from a statement made by the famous comedian Groucho Marx, who explained his reason for withdrawing his membership from the Hollywood chapter of the Friars Club by saying, "I just don't want to belong to any club that would have me as a member" (p. 18). The point of this paradox for you as a graduate student is that when you are in the throes of an emotional slump and the target of your own slings and arrows of outrageous self-criticism, you probably find it hard to accept any praise or compliments from your teachers, supervisors, and cohorts.

Of course, as you make this journey through your training program, you occasionally will find yourself plagued with self-doubt (Hughes & Kleist, 2005). Because you have such high standards for yourself, you will sometimes feel vulnerable and incompetent, discouraged and confused (Egan, 2010). Your trainers expect this to happen, and they know that because you are being asked to change in ways that no educational experience has previously demanded of you, there will be times when you need to escape. At times like these, you can consult Chapter 5 to remind yourself of practical ways to manage mindfully your stress and to keep your balance.

There is the story of a woman, blind from the age of six, who had her sight miraculously restored by a new medical procedure. Prior to this surgery, the woman had done well in school, obtaining a doctoral degree. She married, had two teenage daughters, and held a responsible position in a rehabilitation clinic. With her sight newly regained, she first felt ecstatic, then ambivalent, then depressed. Her whole life, once happy in spite of her disability, began to deteriorate. She alienated friends and family, and her job performance suffered. On the face of it, something wonderful had happened, but the results were feelings of confusion and emptiness. She had undergone a profound change, and she just did not know how to act sighted. All aspects of her behavior had to be relearned, and she felt as if she had lost something terribly important in her life (Swann, 1996).

One would think that a positive change, such as suddenly being able to see, could yield nothing but good feelings. But think about your own situation. You were accepted into a graduate program of your choice. The day you got the letter was probably a major milestone in your life. You initially felt great. You entered your professional training with positive expectations and a little nervousness. Then, because you were expected to change in so many ways, you began to have your crisis of faith: "Maybe I can't do this," "Maybe I was deluding myself to think I had what it takes," "Maybe they made a mistake when they accepted me," or "Maybe I don't want to belong to a program that would have me as a member!" As you can see from the flow of these thoughts, the Groucho paradox is a variation on the theme of the impostor phenomenon we described in Chapter 2. You begin to believe that you put something over on the admissions committee members who decided you were a good candidate for this work.

It is important for you to know that you can expect, from time to time, to have major misgivings about becoming a helping professional. It is part of your developmental process. Despite the fact that you are finally preparing for the profession that has felt like your life's calling and that you are at last able to focus all your course work on this goal, the resultant feelings will not always be positive. You will question your decision to become a member of the helping professions, and you will probably have times when you are really down in the dumps as a result of the changes you are going through. No matter how much you may desire to become the "new you," there will be times when you long for the "old you," grieving for what has been lost. Gloria Steinem (quoted in Swann, 1996) once said, "Change, no matter how much for the better, still feels cold and lonely at first . . . because it doesn't feel like home" (p. 147).

Assimilation and Accommodation

Piaget (1970) stated that there are two major processes by which we develop our knowledge schemas: assimilation and accommodation. You're involved in *assimilation* when you route new information into knowledge structures that you already have in place. The process involved in this type of learning is a mere addition of information or elaboration of previous knowledge. In order to assimilate any new information that does not fit precisely within your existing schemas, you may be tempted to distort it. If you can't hammer the new data into some form that fits your knowledge structures, then you can either reject the information or accommodate it. You engage in *accommodation* when you actually change your own schemas and create new knowledge structures to take in and process new information.

Someone who assimilates but refuses to accommodate tends to become rigid and narrow in dealing with information. Chances are you know people like this. They claim to be experts on everything, but they seem to you to be merely prejudiced and set in their opinions. They suffer from hardening of the categories. Believe it or not, there are counselors who are like this! You can avoid becoming an expert by remaining open to new information and willing to accommodate—to change the way you see the world—as you encounter new experiences.

Clearly, you must be flexible to accommodate. If, however, you believe yourself to be the expert with regard to any new experience, you are likely to deem accommodation to be unnecessary. As children grow older and develop what they consider to be a sufficient set of categories or cognitive schemas, they sometimes become refractory or resistant to much of the new information that challenges them to accommodate. After all, accommodation can feel uncomfortable. Everyone knows how insufferable adolescent experts can be and how at this stage parents suddenly lose at least 30 IQ points in their teenager's eyes. Probably the motivation for the adolescent striving for expertise is the feeling of security that comes with the firm belief that one has everything under control and that no new disquieting mysteries are on the horizon. Adolescents become rigid in their beliefs as a defense against their rapidly changing world. Unfortunately, it is a transparent and feeble sort of expertise.

Accommodating Information About Yourself

Certainly, you have enjoyed the "aha!" exhilaration of discovering an accommodation that offers new and exciting breakthroughs in your ways of thinking. This is not always the case, however, when it comes to accommodating new information about yourself. Sometimes being open to learning about yourself results in jarring and confusing results. According to some reports, when the astronomer Galileo asked the College of Cardinals to look through his telescope, which was pointed toward the heavens, they refused because they were afraid they might see something contrary to their beliefs. All of us are reluctant to look at ourselves too deeply because we fear that we will find aspects, beliefs, or values that we didn't know were there and that we didn't want to be part of us. Like the adolescent, we may like to think we know everything about ourselves that there is to know. We can then have the sense of false security that we are completely in control of our behaviors and attitudes.

In the training program in which you find yourself, you have the opportunity to indeed discover who you are. You will realize that the ambiguity of the koan (see page 41) is rampant in all your life experiences. Many of your discoveries about yourself will make you uncomfortable, but that happens only because you are human. Humans are not perfect. Karen Horney (1970) said that if we erect for ourselves an "ideal self" and attempt to maintain it, the result will be neuroticism. The pathway to a true sense of well-being begins with accepting, valuing, and even cherishing yourself as you are; then approach the challenge of knowing yourself as a beginner, not as an expert.

Hold to Your Center

Graduate school is, to say the least, a demanding venture, and you can easily feel overwhelmed by all you have to do. You certainly need to keep a calendar of your appointments and a daily "to do" list to help you set your life in order. Dealing conscientiously with each of the tasks you have scheduled is a fine idea, but take care to hold to your center through all the distractions of your days. It is easy to pay so much attention to the demands of your world and to focus so much on the expectations of others that you begin to disappear. You then become, like Lewis Carroll's Alice, unreal. In *Through the Looking-Glass* (Carroll, 1896/1991), Tweedledee confronted Alice and triumphantly claimed that she was merely a character in the dream of the Red King, who was sleeping nearby. When Alice protested, Tweedledee gleefully retorted that if the Red King stopped dreaming her, her existence would be snuffed out like a candle.

Carroll's message to all of us is that we should take care not to let ourselves be defined by others or allow our self-esteem to be so dependent on the approval of others. In these situations that involve imposing on us conditions of worth (Rogers, 1961), we become acceptable to other people only when we measure up to their standards. If we try too hard to be what others want us to be, we become existentially ill. Ironically, when we feel that we are losing ourselves and becoming ontologically insecure, we may try even harder to validate who we are by seeking the approval of others. We may also distract ourselves by plunging into relentless motion so that we will not notice that we don't feel well. When we become so immersed in our activities that we lose contact with our center—our true self—we fear that the Red King may be waking and we will disappear.

Honor, but Modify, Your Style

Here's a news flash for you: No one has had a perfect childhood. Even when parents have tried to do right by us, we all came into adulthood with unmet needs. To the extent that our needs were not satisfied, we developed compensating strategies or styles in order to avoid the anxiety that arose out of our unique situation (Teyber & McClure, 2011). Karen Horney (1970) identified three prominent coping styles that people adopt. She called them the "moving toward," the "moving against," and the "moving away" strategies. These coping styles served to reduce anxiety when our needs were not met as children, but they can prove to be a liability in adulthood because we tend to enact them over and over, even though modifying them would be much more productive.

The *moving-toward* style manifests as the need to please people. Someone with this strategy is compliant and wishes to be seen as unfailingly nice and good. This style results in the need to be approved of by others and in the attempt to meet their needs in an almost servile way. Those with the moving-toward style have burdened themselves with the impossible tasks of being the perfect son, daughter, student, lover, and friend in their encounters with others.

People with a prominent *moving-against* compensatory style display a defiant or rebellious attitude toward any form of authority and react to any feelings of vulnerability by attempting to control themselves and others. Such people are strongly assertive, sometimes to the point of aggression, and they demand of themselves that they should quickly overcome all obstacles and difficulties. They try to control their feelings and to overcome their "bad moods" quickly by an act of will.

The person with a *moving-away* style compensates in situations that produce anxiety by physically withdrawing, avoiding, and attempting to become totally self-sufficient. Such an individual often works ceaselessly and doggedly in a misguided attempt to be self-reliant. In employing the moving-away strategy, the person avoids intimacy because becoming close to another person means to become vulnerable.

EXERCISE 7.3 Toward, Against, or Away?

A Moving Exercise

Obviously, the three coping styles are not mutually exclusive. You are likely to employ each of them at different times and under varying circumstances. All of them serve to ward off your feelings of anxiety. Because of this, you should be respectful of your need to use these compensatory strategies in your life.

(Continued)

(Continued)

STEP 1.

Draw and label circles representing the three styles and think about which one you employ most often. Put the number "1" in that circle. Then put a number "2" in the circle that represents your second most favored style, and a number "3" in the remaining circle.

The first thing to think about, after you have completed this ranking, is what purpose your dominant style serves in your life. How is it *helpful* to you? Reflect on recent stressful experiences in which your dominant style successfully dealt with the circumstances. Self-acceptance is a fundamental part of your personal growth. Just as you must honor resistance in your future clients, you must also honor it in yourself.

STEP 2.

There is, however, an annoying paradox involved in these defense styles. They help you to cope with anxiety-producing situations, but they also sometimes get in your way. The paradox is that although you have adopted these styles in order to compensate for unmet needs of childhood, they sometimes deprive you of getting your needs met as an adult. So the next step in this self-exploration exercise is to think about how this style *interferes* in your life, how it compels you to act in certain ways, and how your style may sometimes be off-putting to others.

STEP 3.

The next time you are in a stressful situation, you have the opportunity to complete the final step of this exercise. Use that opportunity to deliberately refrain from using your favored style. For example, if moving toward is your dominant style, instead of immediately considering how to impress and please others, focus on your own needs and desires in this situation. Practicing a new style will seem strange and uncomfortable, but it will allow you to become more flexible in how you respond to challenges.

Countertransference

It's déjà vu all over again.

—Yogi Berra

Inevitably, you have sensitive areas of emotional injury that are unexplored, hidden, and sequestered by protective layers of emotional shielding. Sometimes these unresolved injuries become activated in your present relations with others. Someone touches a nerve by bringing up a sensitive issue that provokes in you a reactive response that is out of proportion to the current situation with that person. Or perhaps you may find yourself responding very negatively toward someone, but you are unable to identify why you experience that person as so obnoxious. In other words, the ways in which you have been injured, frustrated, or disappointed in your past relations with others can affect how you perceive and respond to new relationships in the present.

This is particularly true if you have not yet fully explored and understood how past injuries or interpersonal problems with others have influenced you. Part of your journey of self-exploration will include becoming more aware of these areas of unresolved conflict. The less you are motivated by protective and defensive efforts designed to shield you from emotional pain, the more you will be able to engage others with full awareness of your authentic thoughts and feelings.

Playing out unresolved personal issues in your current encounters with other people is a human tendency that Freud (1924) called transference. In the therapeutic relationship, Freud observed that a client often acted as if the therapist were a sort of stand-in for another important person in the client's life. The client may express emotions toward and assign motivations to the therapist, but these feelings rightly belong to the client's experience of someone else. Gaining insight into the origins and meaning of the transference constitutes one of the main goals of psychoanalytic therapy.

Although you are not in training to become a classic psychoanalyst, you will encounter transference in your clients. What's more, you will find that clients will evoke in you certain feelings and reactions that touch on your own personal conflicts and unresolved issues. Freud called the therapist's reaction in this situation "countertransference." He cautioned that it has the potential to derail a productive therapeutic relationship because the counselor's own unresolved feelings and conflicts get in the way of the client's self-expression. In other words, the therapist distorts the client's behavior to conform to the counselor's own expectations or biases.

Freud's concept is not a relic that is irrelevant to either therapy or interpersonal relationships in general. Most modern forms of counseling include some variant of the concepts of transference and countertransference. You can probably think of times that stand out as examples of a strong transference reaction to someone. Of course, you will introduce your biases, distortions, and interpretive schemes in your subjective and unique fashion. The important point to remember is that self-awareness about how your past injuries become expressed in your interpersonal behavior is critically important to both your personal relationships with fellow students and teachers and to your counseling work with clients.

It is difficult to lift up bandages to look at old wounds and even more difficult to go poking around when they are not fully healed. But as you can see, those wounds that are still alive will invisibly influence your behavior toward others. Shoving painful life events down into a cellar of forgetting just makes you afraid to go down to that dark place in which your deepest, richest emotions may abide. It is a natural human tendency to want to move on from painful life events. How you choose to do so will decide whether you become an integrated and fully alive person or whether you surround yourself in a shroud of insulating forgetfulness. As Freud observed, it is what we forget that we repeat.

Getting Clear

> When one is a stranger to oneself, then one is estranged from others too. If one is out of touch with oneself, then one cannot touch others.
>
> —Anne Morrow Lindbergh

As should be obvious to you by now, becoming a successful therapist is not merely a matter of veneering a set of techniques and theories onto yourself. A counselor is someone whose very personhood is therapeutic, and authenticity is the counselor's most powerful asset (Edelstein, 2015). But in order for you to be honest with your clients, you must first be honest with yourself.

Most people, in everyday social situations, cannot trust that they are receiving feedback from others that is not veiled in some way. As a result, most of us are uncertain about how others truly see us. This is why honesty is one of the things that differentiates a counseling session from typical social situations. One of the most refreshing and therapeutic aspects of the therapeutic relationship for clients is that they can rely on the counselor to give them straight talk. As you read in Chapter 6, following certain guidelines will help you to offer effective feedback to your clients. But the most relevant rule in our discussion of countertransference is that your sole motive for offering the feedback must be to benefit your client and not to play out your own unresolved issues. Staying clear on your motives and values is a constant struggle that does not end with your training.

Trying to gain a clear impression of your client's personal dynamics is like taking a photo of that person. If your lens is clean and clear, then the image you have of your client will be reasonably accurate. However, if you have somehow stained the lens through which you view the world, you will not have a truly honest portrait. Striving to stay as clear as possible in your perceptions of others is a lifelong effort, and it requires that you commit to continually work on yourself. As Norcross (2011) affirmed, the actual techniques you use as a therapist are not as important as your unique personhood. The clearer you stay about yourself, the more room the client has to get clear on his or her concerns.

Finding Your Roots

Those of us who attempt to act and do things for others or for the world without deepening our own self-understanding, freedom, integrity, and capacity to love, will not have anything to give others.

—Thomas Merton

Exploring or knowing yourself goes deeper than trying to *understand* who you are. While this statement may, on first consideration, seem confusing, there are really two parts to knowing yourself. Complete self-exploration also means that you must come to understand how other people may regard you.

Look into the mirror. What do you see? That person in the mirror may not be the same person to whom others are responding. How do you appear to others? They see your ethnicity, gender, age, mannerisms, and many manifestations of your upbringing and values that are so much a part of you that you may not have even noticed them as being important. However, who you are to others creates an image that must also become part of your total self-understanding. Each time you encounter your clients, they will be responding to an image of you that may or may not be in alignment with how you see yourself. Moment to moment you must try to view yourself through their eyes and deal with their misgivings about whether you can be trusted, whether you can care, and if they will be safe in your company.

I Need to Pay Attention to Who I Am

Michelle's Story

Prior to my first practicum experience, I thought I knew myself pretty well. I had spent a good deal of time during my classes exploring my values and getting in touch with my beliefs. In one class we completed an exercise in which we imagined how it might be to counsel a pedophile, a substance abuser, or a wife batterer. I convinced myself that I would be able to transcend the "differences" of my clients and, as long as I treated each person with respect, my work as a counselor would be relevant and effective. Then I sat down with my first actual client. The client seemed nervous, which helped me overcome my own anxiety and assume what I believed to be a true helper role. I did my best to help the client feel at ease. After a few minutes of small talk and tentative "starts and stops," the client looked at me with a kind smile. "You know, I don't want to hurt your feelings, but I have to tell you I'm a little uncomfortable."

"No problem!" I thought.

I started to internally formulate a soothing reflective statement when my client continued. "I have a feeling you're probably Christian, and I really don't think I'll feel comfortable talking to a Christian counselor."

I can't begin to accurately express my reaction. All I can remember is a sinking feeling while I chanted to myself, "What do I do now? What do I do now?" I'll admit that in addition to feeling shocked, I was a little hurt that anyone would not want to talk to a Christian. "What's wrong with Christians?" I wanted to protest.

Later, after discussing this session with my supervisor and peers and experiencing a range of emotions, I discovered a few things about myself. During all my thinking about differences and what I can "tolerate" about other people, I never realized that the "different" one in the counseling room might be me. I also started to see that prior to that session I had never consciously explored my own ethnicity, religion, or socioeconomic status. As a person who sits squarely and comfortably in mainstream society (White, Anglo-Saxon, Protestant, middle class), I've never had to think about these things. Unlike my peers who are Latina or African American, for instance, I've taken my identity and its implications for granted. Thanks to my sensitive client, I've begun an exploration of myself and my identity as White, female, Christian, and middle class. All of those identities mean something to me, and they obviously mean something to my clients. I need to pay attention to who I am.

Michelle had a variety of options available in response to the client's expressed concerns. She could have acknowledged the client's concerns, addressed the religious differences, offered a referral, and so forth. In your training you will be developing skills in handling situations such as these, but our emphasis here is on your own self-understanding. As you can see, Michelle used this situation as a catalyst for her own growth experience and she came away from the session with a much greater sense of who she was. Such awareness is much more useful to her than learning a new counseling technique.

Find the "I AM" Experience

Rollo May (1983) wrote of a client who had rediscovered what he called the "I AM" experience. When asked what this experience was like, the client said, "[I]t feels like receiving the deed to my house. . . . It is my saying to Descartes, "*I Am, therefore* I think, I feel, I do" (p. 99, emphasis in original).

As you continue through your training program and discover the new you, you will find that it is also the old you that is discovered. Somehow, your "I" and your "me" become united. Your confidence in yourself increases, and your trust in who you are becomes solid and confident. This does not mean that you will never again feel insecure about who you are. We all experience times when we lose touch with ourselves. But once you get hold of that "I AM" feeling, you always have the deed to your house, and, contrary to what you have heard from Thomas Wolfe, you can go home again.

Summary

In this chapter, we have hammered home the point that in order to be an effective counselor, you must first be committed to your own personal soundness. Being personally sound does not mean that you are free of all wounds and troubles. In fact, the very training that you are going through will create new troubles for you and expose some of your old wounds, too. The main choice you must make is to remain open to the changes that are happening in you. The Greek philosopher Heraclitus said that a person cannot step in the same river twice. But because the person cannot remain constant either, Heraclitus might have gone on to state that the *same* person cannot step in the same river twice. You are always changing. You are different today than you were yesterday. As you make your journey through your training program, be sure to keep up with yourself!

Resources

We mentioned a number of classic books in this chapter, but we think that two of them especially merit a thorough reading. In particular, these two lively books will be helpful to you as you explore yourself and navigate your own process of change. Many of our students have reported that these books spoke to them and were personally reassuring during their "dark night of the soul."

The first is Rollo May's *The Discovery of Being* (1983). In it, you will discover radiant perspectives into our existential condition. We especially recommend the chapter titled, "To Be and Not to Be."

The second recommended book is the most recent edition of *Interpersonal Process in Psychotherapy* (2011) by Edward Teyber and Faith McClure. It contains many useful suggestions for enhancing your counseling skills. The chapters that may be most helpful to you as you attempt to make sense of your own formative experiences in life are Chapter 6, "Familial and Developmental Factors," and Chapter 7, "Inflexible Interpersonal Coping Strategies."

Each of these books can also serve as a very good source as you develop your own counseling theory. They are very evenhanded and nondogmatic texts, and you can incorporate the ideas within each book into your own approach to counseling.

Below are two websites that you also may find useful in your self-exploration process.

Authentic Happiness

https://www.authentichappiness.sas.upenn.edu

The Positive Psychology Center at the University of Pennsylvania developed this website under the direction of Martin Seligman. The purpose of this website is to provide free resources for understanding and promoting well-being.

PsychNet-UK

www.psychnet-uk.com

An interesting site containing links to articles, jobs, conferences, and humor related to mental health, counseling, and psychotherapy. You may find it interesting to see how the United Kingdom treats issues of personal growth and well-being. There is a special section on this site for students in the mental health professions.

References

Boehm, C. (2012). *Moral origins: The evolution of virtue, altruism, and shame.* New York, NY: Basic Books.

Calhoun, L. G., & Tedeschi, R. G. (2006). The foundations of posttraumatic growth: An expanded framework. In L. G. Calhoun & R. G. Tedeschi (Eds.), *Handbook of posttraumatic growth: Research and practice* (pp. 1–23). Mahwah, NJ: Erlbaum.

Carroll, L. (1991). *The complete illustrated Lewis Carroll.* New York, NY: Gallery Books. (Original work published in 1896)

Dearing, R. L., Maddux, J. E., & Tangney, J. P. (2005). Predictors of psychological help seeking in clinical and counseling psychology graduate students. *Professional Psychology: Research and Practice, 36,* 323–329.

Deikman, A. J. (1996). "I" = awareness. *Journal of Consciousness Studies: Controversies in Science and the Humanities, 3,* 350–356.

Edelstein, B. (2015). Frames, attitudes, and skills of an existential-humanistic psychotherapist. In K. J. Schneider, J. F. Pierson, & J. F. T. Bugental (Eds.), *The handbook of humanistic psychology* (2nd ed., pp. 435–449). Thousand Oaks, CA: Sage.

Egan, G. (2010). *The skilled helper: A problem management and opportunity development approach to effective helping* (9th ed.). Belmont, CA: Brooks/Cole.

Freud, S. (1924). *A general introduction to psychoanalysis.* New York, NY: Washington Square Press.

Gelso, C. J., & Hayes, J. A. (2007). *Countertransference and the therapist's inner experience: Perils and possibilities.* Mahwah, NJ: Erlbaum.

Gibson, D. M., Dollarhide, C. T., & Moss, J. M. (2010). Professional identity development: A grounded theory of transformational tasks of new counselors. *Counseling Education and Supervision, 50,* 21–37.

Goleman, D. (2013). *Focus: The hidden driver of excellence.* New York, NY: Harper.

Hoffman, L., Stewart, S., Warren, D. M., & Meek, L. (2015). Toward a sustainable myth of self: An existential response to the postmodern condition. In K. J. Schneider, J. F. Pierson, & J. F. T. Bugental (Eds.), *The handbook of humanistic psychology* (2nd ed., pp. 105–133). Thousand Oaks, CA: Sage.

Horney, K. (1970). *Neurosis and human growth.* New York, NY: Norton.

Hughes, F. R., & Kleist, D. M. (2005). First-semester experiences of counselor education doctoral students. *Counselor Education and Supervision, 45,* 97–108.

James, W. (1890). *Principles of psychology.* New York, NY: Holt, Rinehart & Winston.

Kottler, J. A. (2010). *On being a therapist* (4th ed.). San Francisco, CA: Jossey-Bass.

Laing, R. D. (1969). *The divided self.* New York, NY: Pantheon Books.

Levin, J. D. (1992). *Theories of the self.* Washington, DC: Hemisphere.

Linehan, M. M., & Dexter-Mazza, E. T. (2008). Dialectical behavior therapy for borderline personality disorder. In D. H. Barlow (Ed.), *Clinical handbook of psychological disorders: A step-by-step treatment manual* (4th ed., pp. 365–420). New York, NY: Guilford.

May, R. (1983). *The discovery of being: Writings in existential psychology.* New York, NY: Norton.

Norcross, J. C. (Ed.). (2011). *Psychotherapy relationships that work* (2nd ed.). New York, NY: Oxford University Press.

Orlinsky, D. E., Schofield, M. J., Schroder, T., & Kazantzis, N. (2011). Utilization of personal therapy by psychotherapists: A practice-friendly review and a new study. *Journal of Clinical Psychology: In Session, 67,* 1–15.

Parrott, L., III (1997). *Counseling and psychotherapy.* New York, NY: McGraw-Hill.

Piaget, J. (1970). Piaget's theory. In P. H. Mussen (Ed.), *Carmichael's manual of child psychology* (Vol. 1, 702–732). New York, NY: Wiley.

Polkinghorne, D. E. (2015). The self and humanistic psychology. In K. J. Schneider, J. F. Pierson, & J. F. T. Bugental (Eds.), *The handbook of humanistic psychology* (2nd ed., pp. 87–104). Thousand Oaks, CA: Sage.

Prosek, E. A., Holm, J. M., & Daly, C. M. (2013). Benefits of required counseling for counseling students. *Counselor Education and Supervision, 52,* 242–254. doi:10.1002/j.1556–6978.2013.00040.x

Rogers, C. R. (1961). *On becoming a person.* Boston, MA: Houghton Mifflin.

Sadler-Gerhardt, C. (2005, October). *Counseling Today, 47,* 7, 37.

Sussman, M. B. (2007). *A curious calling: Unconscious motivations for practicing psychotherapy.* Lanham, MD: Rowman & Littlefield.

Swann, W. B. (1996). *Self-traps: The elusive quest for higher self-esteem.* New York, NY: Freeman.

Teyber, E., & McClure, F. H. (2011). *Interpersonal process in psychotherapy: An integrative model* (6th ed.). Pacific Grove, CA: Brooks/Cole.

Zerubavel, N., & Wright, M. O. (2012). The dilemma of the wounded healer. *Psychotherapy, 49*(4), 482–491. doi:10.1037/a0027824

8

Becoming Neuro-Minded

Biology gives you a brain. Life turns it into a mind.

—Jeffrey Eugenides

The communication between the brain and the heart is a two-way dialogue.

—Mindie Kniss

W hen reassuring a new employee that a job is a simple one to master, a supervisor may say, "Hey, don't worry! It's not brain surgery." In this chapter, we argue that when you succeed in your counseling and therapy work, you actually are performing a procedure that changes neural pathways. So, in fact, your job is brain surgery!

For decades, critics have pejoratively referred to counseling and therapy as warm-fuzzy, touchy-feely treatments that unlike psychopharmacology and other biological interventions, lacked any scientific support for having any real impact on brain functioning. However, in recent years, neuroscience research has been uncovering clues that are solving some of the mysteries of the brain and discovering some of the mechanisms that make us tick. Now, based on the work of Cozolino (2014) and other neuroscientists, we have evidence that successful counseling actually promotes the development of new neural pathways.

The purpose of this chapter is to offer a sampling of the intriguing basic information that every counselor should know about the brain, such as the orbitofrontal cortex, amygdala, hippocampus, neural pathways, mirror neurons, oxytocin, and neural plasticity. As an emerging counselor, you can expect that you will become more "neuro-minded" (Montes, 2013, p. 35) in the future. Just remember that learning about the physiological underpinnings of the human mind does not violate your basic belief in the power of the relationships you establish with your clients. You still view them as whole, unique persons, and not just brains. Nevertheless, a fundamental understanding of neuroscience is now crucial for you to be an effective counselor (Ivey, Ivey, & Zalaquett, 2010), so this chapter is designed to be a brief introduction, or more likely a refresher, for you on how we humans are wired. With some neuroscience knowledge, you can appreciate how the amygdala may have hijacked a traumatized client's brain to the point that the frontal lobe's reasoning ability is overpowered. You can better understand the devastating and pervasive impact of brain chemistry on a client struggling with clinical depression. And you can even appreciate that your own brain is not in isolation from those of others you encounter (Mikulincer & Shaver, 2014). In fact, when you are empathically attuned with your client, definite areas in your client's brain become more active— and correspondingly, those same parts are active in your own brain, too (Posner, 2004).

In earlier chapters, we spoke of humans as social beings whose sense of self emerges from the countless interactions in which they engage with others through their development. In this chapter, we explore how humans are also embodied beings whose sense of self also emerges from the interactions of billions of neurons with trillions of synapses, forming amazingly complex neural networks. We encourage you not to be overwhelmed by the numbers. Instead, we invite you to feel a sense of awe for the beauty and majesty of it all—and to recognize the power of relationships in changing our brain functioning (Cozolino, 2010).

Neuroscience of Magic and Counseling

Let's begin with an example that is markedly different from counseling and therapy: professional magic. Stage magicians perform mystifying acts that seem to defy physics and to suggest that they possess mysterious powers. Interestingly, in addition to studying the work of therapists, neuroscientists have discovered that magicians create many of their illusions by exploiting cognition and perception principles, while also playing on the audience's mirror neurons and oxytocin levels. In other words, magicians are just as much practitioners of sleight of mind (Macknik & Martinez-Conde, 2010) as they are of sleight of hand. Magicians deceive audience members by redirecting attention away from their surreptitious methods and subtly guiding the members' awareness to focus on the "magic." They artfully manage attention and exploit the shortcomings of human awareness.

In contrast to magicians, who take advantage of neurological processes to trick their audiences, counselors use the same processes, such as managing attention and framing, to enhance neuroplasticity, expand awareness, and promote change (Echterling, Presbury, & Cowan, 2012). Consequently, a magic performance can leave a spectator mystified, but your counseling session can leave a client transformed. Now that's real magic! The point here is that a basic understanding of neuroscience can add to your therapeutic bag of tricks.

Therapists, Minds, and Brains

Ancient people noticed that when a person died, the body was still there, but some vitally important "something" was missing. This "something" seemed not to be made of the same material substance as bodies and brains. It could not be seen or touched. Five hundred years before the birth of Christ, the Greek philosopher Empedocles called this substance *soul*, which was the Greek word for *mind* (Jeeves & Brown, 2009). Much later, the philosopher Rene Descartes (1596–1650) formalized these dual aspects of our being. Descartes stated that the body/brain was a physical thing possessing a palpable existence, while the mind/soul was ethereal and without tangible substance. This viewpoint continues to be discussed by philosophers today under the heading "substance dualism." Gilbert Ryle called this notion "the ghost in the machine" (as cited in Leahey, 2013). This important immaterial substance, which seems to animate the body, has also been known as spirit or psyche, the root word of psychology.

The unfortunate result of this dual substance belief has long been the idea that if you are a counselor or therapist, your domain is the immaterial substance—the mind—and that notions about the physical brain/body domain should be left to physicians. Behaviorists declared that instead of worrying about the mind, therapists should focus only on altering observable behaviors. However, there is currently a powerful movement in our profession that calls for the unification of mind, brain, behavior, and spirit by stressing the importance of understanding neuroscience.

The Decade of the Brain

A Congressional resolution signed by President George H. W. Bush in 1991 declared the last decade of the millennium "The Decade of the Brain." As a result, brain research increased dramatically and with the assistance of new technology, such as functional magnetic resonance imaging, knowledge of how the human brain works is bringing together mind and brain processes. We now know that everything that happens to us, and our resulting thoughts, actions and emotions, alter the structure of our brains (Ivey & Zalaquett, 2011). The takeaway message from this discovery is that when you are counseling someone, you are also counseling a brain.

Not as Hard as You Thought

As you begin this chapter, you may be somewhat reluctant. Perhaps you are thinking, "The brain . . . that's too hard to learn." However, the growing recognition within the helping professions regarding the importance of such knowledge makes it imperative that you have at least a minimal grasp of how brain processes affect emotions, cognitions, and behaviors—and how these, in turn, alter the structure and processes of the brain. Besides, learning about the brain is not as hard as you might have thought.

Let's start with brain development. At an early stage of fetal development, the neurons of the baby's brain start to migrate to their assigned locations in the brain structure and take up their designated tasks. When the child is born, the brain is completely intact, though many of its areas are not yet fully functioning. Until recent years, it was thought that the structure of the brain was fixed at about age 10, and that no further alteration was possible. However, we now know that the frontal lobe, which considers the consequences of our actions, is not completely developed until the mid-20s, and the neural pathways of the brain are constantly changing throughout life (Draganski et al., 2004). That fact alone may help you gain a greater appreciation for the challenges that adolescents face!

The Material Brain

The human brain weighs about 3 pounds and has the consistency of tapioca pudding (Moffett, 2006). It has been the source of mystery for millennia. During the 4th century BCE, Aristotle thought that while the heart was the seat of intelligence, the brain was a cooling mechanism for the blood. As stated above, the 17th-century philosopher Descartes considered mind and brain to be of different realities. Although the brain was something material, the mind, he thought, was an ethereal substance. In many Western traditions, the mind/soul is thought to inhabit the body/brain at conception or sometime thereafter. Descartes wondered how the mind comes to reside in the brain. His solution to the problem was that the mind sits in the pineal gland of the brain as sort of a driver. He chose this location because it appears to be the only area of the brain that is not redundant, replicated from one hemisphere to the other.

Today, many people tend to think of the brain as a computing machine with a series of wires (neurons) that altogether somehow create a mind. Mind, in this metaphor, is the software that runs on the hardware of the machine. Furthermore, having heard the myth that we only use 10% or 20% of our brain, many think of it as having vast areas of vacant and unemployed potential. Our brain certainly has enormous potential, but it is not achieved by filling up some putative empty spaces. In reality, we use all of our brain all of the time. Furthermore, the brain is much more than a complex collection of wires. In fact, these so-called wires don't actually connect to each other.

The brain is wired with neurons that are separated by spaces called synapses. When a neuron is stimulated beyond a certain threshold, it fires, sending an electrical signal from the stimulated end along its shaft, the axon, to the other end, which contains chemical neurotransmitters. You have heard of some of these neurotransmitters, such as serotonin, dopamine, and norepinephrine. Depending on the location of the neuron, its particular neurotransmitters are released into the synaptic gap and they float across to the next neuron like little boats seeking a mooring. If the next neuron has the proper moorings, the "boats" dock and stimulate the neuron, which electrically fires a charge along its shaft until it reaches the end, and so on. Having completed their mission, the boats are drawn back to their original neuron in a process called "reuptake."

At this point, you also may be thinking, "Why do I care about what happens at the synapse?" One answer is that you will often have clients who are clinically depressed. The current theory is that in the serotonin circuit, not enough of this neurochemical is being received by the next neurons or is being reuptaken too soon by the original neuron. Too few of serotonin's "little boats" are reaching their moorings. In such a case, your client may be prescribed an SSRI (selective serotonin reuptake inhibitor) antidepressant medication. If the neurotransmitter norepinephrine is thought to be involved, the medication might be an SSNRI.

Conversely, the chemical dopamine could be too available at certain synapses, creating a thought disorder such as schizophrenia. The jury seems to still be out on the exact mechanisms involved, but suffice it to say that your client's moods and thoughts are highly dependent on what is happening at the synapse. As you can see, the chemicals that transmit information from one neuron to the next are crucial to the functioning of the brain/mind/emotions. In fact, neuroscience is more accurately described as the neurochemical science.

There have been many studies to support the evidence that combining counseling and antidepressant medication is the most promising treatment of clinical depression (Jones-Smith, 2012). If clients can be helped to examine their thought processes and alter their negative assumptions, they can find relief from nagging disparaging beliefs and catastrophic fantasies. The kind of work we do as counselors helps clients change the way their brains operate. So by changing the mind, we are probably changing the efficiency of the synaptic transmission. Descartes was wrong. The action is not taking place in the "mind *or* brain" but in *both* at the same time.

The Brain and Emotions

Deep within the interior of the temporal lobes, in the area many refer to as the limbic system, reside the amygdalae (one on each hemisphere). The amygdala is a relatively small part of the brain that takes its name from an almond, which describes its shape. In this case, size does not matter; the tiny amygdala is crucial to nearly all of our actions and is the grand central station for our emotions. This very old part of the brain stirs us to respond immediately to threats in a dangerous world (Heller & LaPierre, 2012). The amygdala "is poised, like an alarm, to activate the body's flight-or-fight hormones. This quick-response emergency route bypasses the executive cortex, sacrificing accuracy and discrimination for speed" (p. 105).

This rapid process is sometimes called "bottom-up," meaning the amygdala from below has sent a distress signal that focuses one's entire attentional spotlight on a threat. Consequently, we do not have to deliberate or engage the cognitive processes of our orbitofrontal cortex in order to respond to an emergency. Imagine that you are camping in Yellowstone National Park and are suddenly confronted by a hostile grizzly bear. At that very moment, you are primed for certain goals and actions, while others are inhibited. You aren't thinking about organizing your CD collection or flossing your teeth. You are not preparing to solve a crossword puzzle or take out the garbage: You are riveted on the bear and focused on checking for escape routes. You can do this with the aid of your primary emotions that are stimulated in the amygdala (Goleman, 2006).

But now imagine that you see that someone has chained that Yellowstone bear so that it cannot attack you. As you realize this, you notice that you are feeling calmer and you can observe the bear with wonder rather than fear. What has happened is that by a "top-down" process, your orbitofrontal cortex has signaled your amygdala below that there is nothing to fear. There are strong neural connections between your amygdala and that orbitofrontal part of your cortex. As your later-developing frontal cortex tames the initial fear reaction, you can regulate your emotions in a more reasonable manner. Ironically, the amygdala is already fully mature before you are even born, but your orbitofrontal cortex takes much longer to fully develop, so your ability to control the amygdala's alarm reaction is greatly hampered until your brain has matured (Cozolino, 2010).

Encountering a bear excites our bottom-up primary emotion. This emotion would be fear, a reaction to a truly threatening stimulus. In addition, there are top-down secondary emotions that are based on learned associations to events. For example, we are sometimes plagued by dread, which is when one anticipates something fearful when no threat is actually present. If this unnecessary stimulation of the amygdala causes so much distress that one is impaired in work and social relations, then it is likely that the person has an anxiety disorder.

Other secondary emotions may reveal themselves as revulsion or loathing. In such cases, our amygdala has learned to encode certain cultural biases. Philosopher Daniel Dennett (1991) is someone who seems to take delight in stimulating such emotions. Consider that when our automobiles breathe their last and they are beyond repair, we send them off to a wrecking yard to be put into one of those compactors where they are scrunched into a small cube and sent for recycling. But what about when people breathe *their* last?

Dennett (1991), in his typically outrageous way of using what he calls intuition pumps, perturbed us with a bizarre scenario: When someone dies, he wrote, most people with spiritual beliefs consider the soul to have left the body. The person who once existed is no longer residing in the corpse. In spite of this belief, most of us would be outraged if someone suggested that we could save thousands of dollars in funeral and burial expenses by merely bagging up the departed loved one and leaving the corpse out on the curb for the trash collector. Dennett, feigning a reasonable position, wrote, "A corpse can no more suffer an indignity than a log can. And yet, the idea is shocking, repulsive. Why?" (p. 452).

As you read this passage just now, were you aware of having any emotion? Did you feel anything? If you did, then Dennett's (1991) intuition pump performed its work. The emotion you felt would have been a secondary one. Secondary emotional processes begin with images that you conjure up, such as a dead person in a trash bag. Meanwhile, at a nonconscious level, networks in your brain react to these images, stimulating emotions that have been acquired by associations and beliefs. Simply put, your reaction to garbage bag corpses is probably learned rather than innate. After all, people in some cultures have traditionally either abandoned their dead or have eaten them. Reverence for corpses must be secondarily acquired.

This human brain's design has served our species well. When a bear confronts you, it is better to let your emotional processing system react to the situation and immediately goad you into moving. Allowing your analytical cortex to ponder the situation may be the last pondering you ever do! This efficient, reactive system comes at a cost, however, because we often develop fears that we don't really require for survival. "We have more fears than we need, and it seems that our utterly efficient fear conditioning system, combined with an extremely powerful ability to think about our fears and an inability to control them, is probably at fault" (LeDoux, 1996, p. 266). The result is that many need counseling or therapy to address this problem with our dysfunctional alarm system.

Whether your amygdala is stimulated by an actual feared event, by free-floating anxiety in the absence of a fearful circumstance, or by a learned set of cultural beliefs, this emotional brain process has been designed to protect you from harm. The benefit of a fight-or-flight reaction as the primary emotion in the presence of a bear is obvious. However, sometimes there is a continual, leftover stimulation after the feared event has passed, as in cases of PTSD (posttraumatic stress disorder). In addition, anticipatory anxiety and worry about the possibility of harm is, in many cases, not only unnecessary but also sabotaging our sense of well-being. Only if, as you worry about an upcoming event, your orbitofrontal cortex helps you plan for handling this situation will this brain interaction be useful. Finally, if your amygdala lights up with anxiety or revulsion at the thought of having to deal with someone of another race, religion, sexual preference, or social status, this negative reaction can certainly be limiting.

There's No Place Like Home

Kiara's Story

I remember watching an old movie on TV when I was a child in the hospital. I was seven years old and recovering from a terrifying car accident. The movie was about a girl who found herself trapped in a strange land. It was full of creepy flying monkeys, witches, and lots of other weird creatures. At the end of the movie, the girl discovered that she could have gone home any time that she had wanted. She only had to click her heels together and repeat three times, "There's no place like home."

As soon as the movie ended, I looked around the hospital room to make sure that I was alone, shut my eyes tightly, clicked my bare feet together under the covers, clinched my teeth from the pain of my cervical fracture, and recited the magic words with all the determination that I could muster.

Twenty years later, I'm now a graduate student in a counselor education program, and I look back on that little girl with a sense of protective tenderness for her magical thinking. Of course, the magic didn't work. I remained in the hospital for a couple more weeks before I was discharged to return home.

But even though I was home, I didn't feel at home. I was constantly anxious whenever I rode in the car, cried easily, was startled by any unexpected sound, and was plagued by nightmares. Seeing my little brother play with his toy cars would sometimes cause what I later learned were "flashbacks," one of the classic symptoms of PTSD. My parents were quick to seek help for me, and in addition to my physical therapy sessions, I found myself meeting with a play therapist for a few months.

I don't remember much about my therapy, except that I felt safe with her in the playroom. Eventually, after weeks of drawing and playing out my traumatic experience, I began to feel more secure and less apprehensive. I started to enjoy life again. I could ride in the car without being scared. I wasn't bothered by nightmares and I wasn't so clingy. My parents believed that the therapy brought them back the little girl that they had lost, but I disagree. During that time, I had grown and changed. I became more thoughtful and sensitive to the feelings of others. And of course, I think that I found my calling from my own therapy experience.

Promoting Neuroplasticity

The play therapist in the above account was not a magician, but she certainly facilitated the appearance of a new, transformed Kiara. Although a specialized intervention, play therapy shares the four fundamental therapeutic conditions that characterize any form of successful counseling that promotes neuroplasticity (Cozolino, 2010). The first, and most fundamental, condition for plasticity is a safe haven of empathic attunement. This resonating relationship with your client provides the ideal chemical environment for creating new neural pathways. Second, although excessive levels of stress inhibit cortical processing, a certain level of emotional arousal is ideal for consolidation and integration. At this optimal midpoint, the different brain structures work together most effectively. The integration of affect and cognition is the third counseling factor that promotes neuroplasticity. Neurons that fire together, wire together. New, complex, and elegant neural patterns can emerge when people engage in practices that are both expressive and mindful (Siegel, 2007). Finally, effective counseling involves co-constructing narratives of self-awareness and transformation that create new neural networks. These four factors not only stimulate neuroplasticity, they also allow you to use the same neurological processes that magicians rely on to perform tricks. However, in the case of counseling and therapy, you rely on these processes to deepen consciousness and promote personal change.

In the following sections, we explore these four factors of counseling and therapy that enhance neural plasticity: attunement, optimal emotional arousal, integration of affect and cognition, and co-construction of transformative narratives.

Attunement

Back before the invention of digital tuners, people listening to the radio had to carefully turn a dial in order to locate the frequency of a desired station, gently moving back and forth to find the greatest signal strength. Once the station had been tuned in, often it would inexplicably seem to drift, so that the listener would be required to retune in order to restore the highest fidelity. This process is an apt metaphor for your work as a finely tuned counselor who is attempting to gain an accurate empathic understanding of your client's world. The resonant frequencies of both you and your client must become carefully attuned to each other to achieve the highest fidelity in the relationship.

When this connection is lost, you must again carefully dial-in your understanding of the client's experience. A resonance circuitry in your brain accomplishes this sensitive attunement that is essential for understanding both yourself and others (Siegel, 2007). The mirror neuron system, the insula (an area located deep within the two hemispheres connected to the temporal and frontal areas), and the middle prefrontal cortex all work together to create this attunement, making empathy possible. You tune in to the inner life that constitutes an interpersonal connection between you and your client. When you listen carefully to your clients, you experience certain bodily shifts that inform you of your client's experience and intentions.

When your clients feel felt by you, they begin to experience more of their inner life. Your empathic response triggers emotional contagion in which, having been seen by you, your clients begin to see themselves with greater clarity. Siegel (2007) used the word interoception to describe this inner experience. He likened it to a sixth sense that can keep you attuned to yourself.

However, like the predigital radio, you sometimes drift away from a high-fidelity sense of both yourself and others. You then must first become more mindful of your own inner experience—tuning in to yourself. As a counselor, it is crucial that you stay mindful of your inner life. This fundamental fact is often overlooked. You cannot fully empathize with your clients if you are disconnected from your own experience. You must, as a counselor, constantly empathize with yourself.

Counseling actually changes brain patterns because it offers an enriching atmosphere for clients to enhance their ways of thinking, manage their emotions, and learn new ways of coping (Cozolino, 2014). In fact, your support, empathy, and encouragement support neural plasticity by increasing your client's levels of dopamine, serotonin, and other endorphins. In addition, during productive work, clients must be experiencing a moderately stressful safe emergency so that their brains are perturbed. The brain is a complex adaptive system that must be nudged into mild bifurcation and chaos, which can result in a new organization.

As clients experience the counseling relationship, their brains are rewiring themselves. This activity can be monitored with EEGs or functional MRIs. Such dramatic changes reflect the neuroplasticity of the brain, which can develop new neural connections throughout the life span and can respond to new situations or experiences (Draganski et al., 2004). Experience changes brains. Obviously, the brain's neuroplasticity has profound implications for the power and impact of counseling.

According to Ivey and colleagues (2010), new discoveries in brain research have been supporting what we already knew about counseling and the change process. Perhaps most important is the finding that a warm, supportive, and attuned relationship that focuses on the client's positive assets can significantly alter brain processes because the neuroplasticity of the brain allows new growth and learning at any age. If your client speaks only of painful events and difficult interactions with others, the networks that stimulate negative emotions remain activated. Part of your job as the counselor is to guide the conversation toward the hopeful and help give the neural circuits that support hope and resolve a chance to be stimulated. Neuroscience is vindicating our approach to helping people toward more neurologically integrated lives.

A Valentine Gift of Attunement

Gene's Story

Valentine's Day is a holiday that celebrates sharing heartfelt emotions. For me, it is now also a reminder of life's fragility and the immense power of attunement with others. On a February 14 several years ago, my brother Dennis, who lived across the country from me, gave me a call. He had recently returned from a trip to Thailand and wanted to share his adventures with me. I immediately tuned in to his stories about his travels, discoveries, and experiences. I was caught up in his descriptions of the beautiful temples that he had visited, the warm people he had met, and the fun he had parasailing for the first time. After nearly an hour, we ended our conversation. We wished each other a happy Valentine's Day and, as we had done in closing our telephone calls over the past several years, told one another "I love you."

Five days later, Dennis was killed in a mountain-climbing accident. The sudden and tragic loss of my brother was shocking. He left behind a young widow, two children, and many grief-stricken relatives and friends. In my heartache and anguish, I found that I took some small comfort in the fact that our final words were affirmations of our love to one another.

As each anniversary of my brother's death approaches, I feel even more strongly that Valentine's Day is a reminder to cherish and celebrate all forms of love. The fundamental challenge we face in life is not so much in finding true love with one special person as it is in tuning in to the true love that is all around us. The deep and heartfelt emotional attachments that tie us together take on many wonderful forms: a parent's rapt gaze into an infant's eyes, a mentor's patient presence in a student's life, a stranger's random act of kindness, or a lifelong friend's playful bantering. Whatever the form, attunement is the core of our humanity, the fabric of our shared sense of community, and the measure of our meaning in life.

I now feel a sense of urgency to make every day—not just Valentine's Day—a labor of love. I also have learned to treat every encounter as possibly the last I will ever have with someone. In that never-to-be-repeated moment, I have the existential choice to attune with a fellow human being by listening with empathy, speaking from the heart, acting with compassion, and showing unconditional acceptance.

I was lucky that my last conversation with my brother ended with our affirming how we felt for one another. But you and I cannot leave such a vitally important message to chance. If we are truly dedicated to personal growth and thriving relationships, then we must treat every day as if it were Valentine's Day. We need to exercise our hearts with daily workouts of attunement.

What We Learned From a Monkey

It was the 1990s in Parma, Italy, and a monkey sat in a special laboratory chair waiting for researchers to return from lunch. Wires had been implanted in the region of its brain involved in planning and carrying out movements. Each time the monkey had grasped an object, such as a peanut, the neurons in that region of its brain would fire and a monitor would register a sound (Blakeslee, 2006). In an event that is now legendary, a researcher came into the room holding an ice cream cone. When the researcher raised the cone to his lips, the monitor connected to the monkey sounded, even though the monkey had not moved. In subsequent experiments, the researchers noted that the monitor would sound whether the monkey was reaching for a peanut or only watching an experimenter do the same action.

It turned out that the monkey brain contains a special class of cells called mirror neurons that fire when the animal sees or hears an action and when the animal carries out the same action on its own. Furthermore, it later became known that the human brain contains this same mirror neuron system that specializes in not just mirroring the actions of others but in understanding their intentions and the social meaning of their behaviors and emotions. We have the ability to grasp the minds of others by direct stimulation rather than conceptual reasoning. We understand others, not by thinking but by feeling. And because these others also have mirror neurons, they feel felt by us when this happens.

Scientists now believe that mirror neurons are responsible for the evolution of culture and the pleasure we derive from viewing art, sports, and even erotica (Ramachandran, 2011). Mirror neurons have been cited as the reason for your ability to intuitively understand and empathize with clients. Studies have shown that those who rank high on measures of this type of empathy have particularly active mirror neurons. Your mirror neurons give you an almost telepathic ability to read a person's intentions. Our ability to do this simulation is very old. Even newborn babies arrive with the ability to mimic others. Stick out your tongue, and the infant will often imitate you. Amazingly, even though the baby is unable to see its own tongue, the infant matches the appearance of your tongue with the felt position of its own. Ramachandran (2011) proposed that mirror neurons are responsible for generating your embodied sense of self, as well as your ability to empathize with others. This makes sense because in order for you to have an accurate feel for someone else's experience, you must be able to sense it in yourself and accurately know what it is.

Moreover, your ability to experience pain is due, in part, to the functions of the anterior cingulate, the area that seems to be both limbic and cortical. This area of the brain appears to be an intimately connected aspect of the mirror neuron system. It has been shown that when someone sees another person being poked with a needle, the observer's pain centers respond vigorously—as if the observer had also been stuck with the needle. And think of how you feel when you see a small child fall and come up crying. You can hardly suppress your response, "Awwww!" This is the essence of empathy.

The discovery of the mirror neuron system has validated much of what Carl Rogers taught us many decades ago. But he had misgivings about the training of counselors in the use of empathic responses. Rogers eventually became dissatisfied with the idea that a therapist should learn to reflect feelings as a display of accurate empathy. Rogers (1987) said, "I even wince at the phrase reflection of feeling. It does not describe what I am trying to do when I work with a client" (p. 39). His concern was that reflection was being taught to counselors in training as an intellectual technique. He believed that this behavior might eventually become a sterile exercise and fall far short of the complex and rich interpersonal experience he had in mind when he first wrote of reflection as a technique. It is possible to reflect a client's feelings based on the counselor's cognitive grasp of the meaning of the words without a full empathic appreciation for what it means to be the client who is expressing these feelings (Presbury, McKee, & Echterling, 2007). At that point, the client may believe that the counselor's words are merely a gimmick rather than an authentic expression of empathic attunement.

Empathy is not a deliberate intellectual event. In fact, you are capable of experiencing another person's emotions without any conscious thought. You simply must remain open to the other's subjective experiences as well as your own. It is not a complicated process. You simply follow Fritz Perls' admonition (in Prochaska & Norcross, 2014) to lose your mind and come to your senses. Your mirror neurons will inform you as to the client's emotional state by stimulating a similar feeling in you.

What Is Empathy?

Perhaps no one did more to legitimize the place of empathy in the counseling process than Carl Rogers. The concept of empathy comes from the Greek empatheia, which means to perceive the subjective experience of another. This accurate empathic understanding takes place when the counselor senses clients' feelings as if they were his or her own. Rogers (1961) stated that this necessary condition for successful therapy was the ability to "enter into the client's phenomenal world, to experience the client's world as if it were your own without ever losing the 'as if' quality" (p. 284). When the counselor then communicates this awareness, the client feels felt and prized. By moving freely in the world as experienced by clients, you can grasp and communicate to them a deeper understanding of their experiences, of which they themselves may be only dimly aware.

The capacity to communicate this empathy is an important skill. Gladding (2004) stated that the term "primary empathy" refers to the counselor's ability to convey through verbal and nonverbal ways an understanding of the client's major themes and concerns. As Young (2005) put it, "An accurate reflection of feelings has the almost magical power to deepen the relationship between client and counselor" (p. 137).

Such a profound level of empathy is different from a more cognitive understanding of the client's position. Some counselors and therapists, especially those who rely primarily on behavioral techniques, refer to validation rather than empathy in order to suggest recognition that the client's responses make sense, given the circumstances (Prochaska & Norcross, 2014). Certainly, this level of understanding is important. It communicates that these behaviors are reasonable and that the client's attempts to deal with a situation have legitimacy. However, we wish to focus here on a deeper level of understanding in which the counselor actually experiences what the client experiences.

At this point in the reading, you may be wondering, "Is this really possible?" Our answer to this is that you were born with this ability. Even though your client is another person with a private subjective experience, it is still possible for you to "get" your client's experience in terms of both emotional experience and intentions. Perhaps, back in the day when Rogers (1961) stated that this level of empathy was not only desirable but necessary, it seemed he was only dabbling in the metaphysical. However, recent neuroscience studies support his assertions.

Such an empathic attunement is an "I-Thou" encounter, which we discussed in Chapter 6. It is impossible to achieve this level of authentic resonance if a counselor is merely attending to the client. Attention can be divided, but attunement is a complete connection. When you sit with a client and are thinking about what to say next or are considering various symptoms to arrive at a diagnosis, you are not attuned. Yes, empathy is a natural, wired-in phenomenon, but you must nurture this talent and be committed to attunement in the here and now with your client. You must clear away all distractions and completely "be with" your client. When you do this, empathy is automatic.

Optimal Emotional Arousal

The second factor for promoting neural plasticity is creating optimal emotional arousal in your counseling sessions. Often, therapists in training see their task as creating a situation in which the client can feel completely comfortable. However, in the interaction between the amygdala and the orbitofrontal cortex, there is an optimal balance to be struck. Excessive firing of the amygdala makes life a constant emotional crisis, but too little stimulation by the amygdala leads to stagnation. Excessive control by the orbitofrontal cortex can stifle emotional expression, but inadequate control leads to impulsivity and irrational behavior. In a counseling session, an optimal level of emotional excitement is a signal for movement; it motivates the client for action and change. Excessive calm, on the other hand, leads to inertia and passivity. Your job as the neuro-minded counselor is to create an ideal intensity of emotional arousal that energizes the client to strive for therapeutic growth.

Emotional processing goes on at a level beneath our awareness. It is only when emotions become conscious that they become feelings we can address. Sometimes stress can help in the formation of explicit memories, making them stronger. Memory and conscious control are likely to be enhanced under conditions of mild stress due to the facilitative effects of adrenaline, but too much adrenaline will block memory formation. In addition, mild stress will increase attention. Too much stress tends to shut down our cognitive processes. How can stress both help and hinder our cognitive functioning?

This paradox is sometimes called the Yerkes-Dodson Law. There exists a curvilinear (inverted-U) relationship between the level of emotional arousal and efficiency of performance (Martindale, 1981). The Yerkes-Dodson Law (Yerkes & Dodson, 1908) reflects this phenomenon. Simply put, the quality of performance on any task—physical or mental—is a function of the level of emotional arousal. A very low level of arousal leads to inferior performance, while an excessively high level also sabotages effective functioning. Optimal performance occurs when emotional arousal is sufficient to motivate but not so high as to undermine behavior. Our counseling students have dubbed this ideal area "the zone."

According to the Yerkes-Dodson Law, a client who has absolutely no emotional arousal at all would appear nearly comatose, while someone at an acute level of arousal would be on the verge of a crack-up. At a less extreme low point on the continuum, people may merely talk about feelings or describe seemingly emotional situations in a flat narrative style. These clients have numbed their reactions and are not sufficiently aroused to do productive work with their concerns. Because such people have defensively withdrawn from any emotional awareness in their narratives, the therapeutic progress they may make likely will be sterile, superficial, and temporary. On the other hand, when people are so overwhelmed as to not be able to think straight, they are in a state of extreme crisis. If this level of emotional arousal remains unchanged, then any counseling intervention is not likely to be successful because their amygdala has hijacked their emotions.

In the case of a client who is vividly in touch with feelings associated with a crisis event and reacting with high anxiety, you would obviously want to attempt to soothe rather than to arouse the emotional reaction. You will read about many more crisis counseling strategies in Chapter 9, but suffice it to say for now that your immediate goal in this situation is to reduce your client's debilitating distress. Conversely, if your client comfortably engages in only an intellectual discussion during the counseling session, you will want to increase arousal. At the optimal midpoint of the Yerkes-Dodson curve, the different brain structures are working together successfully. Remember that emotions are motivating; having emotions means that a person is poised to act. Assessing your client's state of emotional arousal is, of course, more art than science. But there is good science to indicate that when you are helping to manage the emotional arousal of your client, you actually are changing brain functioning (Cozolino, 2014).

Necessary Self-Care

In order for you to continue to realize the richness and satisfaction of your work as a helping professional, you will need to maintain a healthy balance between your own amygdala and orbitofrontal cortex. As you read in Chapter 5, the emotional contagion of your client's stresses can lead to burnout. As a counselor, because you must constantly be confronted with the intensity of your clients' concerns, you will experience psychological stress more often than the average person. What happens in situations of chronic stress is that we tend to accommodate to the stress and carry on. But we can ignore our bodies only for so long. Eventually, a threshold is reached where the saturation of our bodies and brains by stress chemicals causes a breakdown of our immune system, and either we become ill or we decline psychologically.

If you find yourself experiencing fatigue, confusion, and withdrawal, you will have been living at the upper end of the Yerkes-Dodson curve for too long. Sometimes, in reaction to constant stressors counselors will develop a jaded attitude, tending to see all clients as "disorders" or "syndromes" rather than as unique individuals with specific life concerns. When this happens, these counselors are subject to what has been called "rust out."

It is vital that you take good care of yourself during your professional career. After all, you are the only instrument you have, and this instrument must be kept well tuned. Just remember that you, like your clients, will function best at the center of the Yerkes-Dodson curve, meaning that your amygdala and orbitofrontal cortex will remain well balanced.

Integration of Affect and Cognition

In earlier sections, we discussed the first two conditions for enhancing neuroplasticity: attunement and optimal emotional arousal. The third factor involves the integration of affect and cognition. We begin our exploration of this important condition by providing some background regarding the hippocampus and its vital role in emotional expression and meaning making.

The Hippocampus and Memory

Among the classic cases in the history of brain science is that of Henry Mnemonic (H. M.—not his real name). In 1953, H. M. underwent a surgical procedure to control an intractable seizure disorder. Since it was assumed at the time that all memory functions were distributed throughout the brain, the surgeon thought nothing of removing large sections of H. M.'s interior temporal lobes, especially the hippocampus. As a result, H. M. lost his ability to form explicit and conscious long-term memories (LeDoux, 1996). He could, for example, read the morning paper and then, a few hours later, read it again as though it were brand-new information. In fact, his memory was so impaired that he could hold on to information for only a few seconds. The surgeon who performed the procedure later said, "I intended to cut out the epilepsy, but took the memory instead" (Szasz, 1996, p. 54).

H. M. became the most famous neurological patient in the world. He still remembered how to read, write, speak, and who he was. His I.Q. was unchanged; it was 10 to 15 points above average. He could recite the Gettysburg Address and could state the year that Lincoln was elected. However, if H. M. were to walk from the living room to the bathroom, he could not find his way back. He became dependent on others to help him know how to plan and to navigate his world. So don't leave home without your hippocampus!

Another important function that the hippocampus is in charge of is that of new learning. Much of the information that comes into the brain has to go through the hippocampus to become consolidated. It resonates there for a couple of weeks, and if it stays in long enough and it's important enough, the memory is sent on to long-term memory, which is then distributed throughout the cortex and the rest of the brain.

Since the time of H. M.'s surgery, the roles of both the hippocampus and the amygdala in memory formation have become clearer. While memories do seem to be stored all over the brain, these are two areas within the interior of the temporal lobes that are responsible for memory formation. The hippocampus appears to encode "explicit memories," while the amygdala creates "implicit emotional memory" (LeDoux, 1996, p. 202). In a stressful situation, the amygdala primes us for action and registers an emotional memory of the event, while the hippocampus lays down a conscious memory of the situation. These two areas respond simultaneously to the stressor, developing for us an emotionally tinged memory, which captures our experiential reactions, along with a memory of the circumstances or context, which creates our conscious recollections.

The *implicit* memory system develops earlier and is functioning well at birth. It appears to be closely associated with the right hemisphere and subcortical areas, especially the amygdala. The *explicit* system develops later and is associated more with the cortical and hippocampal areas of the brain. Explicit memories are declarative (can usually be talked about), organized in language, and are about life episodes and narratives of experience. People can usually retrieve these memories because they are generally conscious and about events. Implicit memories, on the other hand, do not lend themselves to language and tend to have emotional associations. They are more felt than thought, and as such, they make themselves known nonverbally. If you recall that Freud (1924) suggested that much of our knowing is unconscious, like the part of an iceberg that is submerged, you will appreciate how much of the implicit memory system is unavailable to normal conversation.

As the brain develops, there are sensitive periods of exuberant growth that are genetically and environmentally triggered and which bring a new set of skills (Cozolino, 2014). For example, the right hemisphere of the brain undergoes a major growth spurt during the first 18 to 36 months of life. During this period, the infant is learning how to regulate emotions and how to connect with important caregivers. The learning that takes place during these early months is, for the most part, unconscious and lays the emotional foundation for all our encounters with the world and other people before our conscious awareness develops (Cozolino, 2014). Therefore, the preverbal attachment and bonding experiences are imprinted on our social brains and powerfully affect our adult relationships.

Amygdala and Hippocampus Collaboration

If the amygdala and hippocampus are working together, it makes sense that situations that stimulate feelings of danger should be remembered so they can be avoided next time. While memories are not actually stored in these two areas of the brain, damage to either will result in a long-term memory impairment.

Damage to the amygdala can result in someone not knowing how to feel about intense events (Damasio, 1994). Damage can also occur to the hippocampus because of the corrosive effects due to stress (LeDoux, 1996). When people are exposed to stressful situations, many hormones are released into the blood stream. These are known as stress hormones. They flow to the amygdala, the hippocampus, and other areas of the brain. The hippocampus tends to help produce a calming effect because it sends signals to slow down the secretion of stress hormones.

When someone is in a chronic state of emotional arousal, the amygdala and the hippocampus are at war with each other. The amygdala is stimulating the production of stress hormones throughout the body and brain, while the hippocampus is attempting to slow down this production. Engaged in such a conflict, the hippocampus may be unable to carry out its usual functions that support memory. In fact, the continued flooding of the hippocampus with stress hormones, such as cortisol, eventually kills neurons in the hippocampus! Studies of people who have suffered prolonged stress show a marked degeneration of the hippocampus.

Although optimal amounts of stress can enhance memory and performance, intense levels of chronic stress and traumatic events cause abnormal functioning of the hippocampus, as demonstrated by the poor memory of individuals with clinical depression and the reexperiencing of traumatic memories that characterizes those with PTSD (Davidson & Begley, 2012). For example, we once knew a person who had served as an army medic. This heroic individual had risked his own life on the battlefield to save wounded warriors who were often horrifically maimed and wounded. Years later, as soon as he would walk into a grocery store in his small American community, he would immediately notice the odor emanating from the meat department. He would then momentarily flash back to his war memories with such vividness that he felt as if he were there again, reexperiencing all the emotions of horror and fear. His amygdala stimulated the emotional memory, and his hippocampus was no longer effective at separating the context of war from the context of Kroger's.

For most of us, if we perceive that a current situation is safe, we are able to set aside any troubling memories of past events that took place under similar circumstances. However, people with PTSD have difficulty with such separation and often fail to take in the present cues that signal safety. They are *tuned out*, lacking sensitivity to context which is caused by inadequate hippocampal functioning. On the other hand, some clients are *tuned in* so completely to any current context that they lose a grounded sense of their true self and smother their own spontaneity. Spurred on by hyperactivity in the hippocampus, these clients are like chameleons, their personality changing dramatically to fit in with whatever their circumstances (Davidson & Begley, 2012). This camouflage may help them in conforming to social cues, but such inhibited people are in danger of losing their individuality in the process.

You regularly will encounter clients near either extreme of the continuum— either clueless and tuned out or highly cued and tuned in. Clueless people are not reading the situation appropriately, while highly cued people are seemingly held prisoner by the situation as they attempt to comply with unspoken rules. It is almost as though they cannot remember how things are supposed to go in certain situations, so each new event is, indeed, new.

Clients who have had highly emotional and chaotic childhoods may be prone to be clueless at times. Those who were required to conform as children or risk punishment and humiliation may turn out to be highly cued adults. Either way—diminished hippocampus or hyperactive hippocampus—these emotional styles have left the person in agony. As your clients experience the counseling process, their brains are rewiring themselves. When you are work-ing with client memory systems, you are facilitating the regulation of the hippocampus and helping the client respond more appropriately to the con-texts they encounter with an ongoing sense of self-awareness.

The Right-Brain to Right-Brain Connection

The brain also is divided into left and right hemispheres. You often have heard the simplistic generalizations that left-brained people are the logical ones and right-brained individuals are the creative ones. However, recent research has demonstrated that the degree of separate, lateralized functions of the two hemispheres has been exaggerated (Nielsen, Zielinski, Ferguson, Lainhart, & Anderson, 2013). Nevertheless, some functions seem to domi-nate one hemisphere, while other functions are more likely to be involved in the other side. For example, the right hemisphere is more likely to be involved with emotional expression and perception of nonverbal communi-cation, while the left hemisphere tends to be dominant in language functions (Alfano & Cimino, 2008).

One of the challenges in counseling that is a consequence of the lateraliza-tion of hemispheres is that your clients cannot recall or articulate their early, preverbal experiences before the later development of the left hemisphere. Nevertheless, these events gave shape to the fundamental worldview, sense of self, and attachments of your clients. Consequently, accessing these implicit, powerful memories is important for counselors and therapists to promote changes in neural pathways.

So if this remembering cannot be expressed explicitly, how is it expressed? Because both you and your client come to the counseling relationship equipped with social brains, you are able to establish a brain-to-brain connection. This process may sound like Spock's telepathic Vulcan brain meld that was portrayed in "Star Trek." However, such a brain-to-brain connection in the therapeutic relationship has been documented in neuroscience studies. In particular, by resonating with your client in a right-brain to right-brain encounter, you gain a deeply empathic understanding of his or her implicit memories (Schore, 2012).

As you immerse yourself in the experience of conducting counseling, you will be acquiring a tremendous amount of information. In addition, you will be expanding your awareness, accumulating implicit knowledge, trusting your gut more, and refining your clinical intuition—all of which strengthens your growing ability to perform right-brain processing with your clients. According to Schore (2012), "This implicit relational knowledge is nonverbally communicated in right-brain to right-brain affective transactions that lie beneath the words within the therapeutic alliance" (p. xiii). This right-brain connection between the counselor and the client is implicit, outside awareness, cannot be fully characterized in words, and exists in the form of unexpressed emotion. Maroda (2005) asserted that the essential clinical question you face as a counselor is, "How do you relate empathically to an unexpressed emotion?" (p. 136).

Counseling and psychotherapy are in the midst of an emotional revolution, recognizing that cognitive approaches alone are inadequate interventions (Ryan, 2007). Since the core of who we are in relation to others has been laid down by our right hemisphere/limbic systems before we are even 12 months old, then this unconscious pattern must be somehow stimulated in the counseling session. Therefore, you must give voice to these emotions and needs as your client evokes them in you, enacts them in the counseling session, and literally embodies them. As you read the nonverbal language of your client's presentation of self through facial expressions, tone and rhythm of voice, breathing, gestures, and body posture, you begin to empathically understand. Your intuition is based mostly on your own mirror neuron system, which allows you to feel the client's feelings. This means that you must remain sensitive to your own experience while also bearing witness to your client. If not, you will lose valuable implicit information regarding the client's moment-to-moment emotions.

Co-Construction of Transformative Narratives

The fourth factor of effective counseling and therapy that enhances neural plasticity is the co-construction of transformative narratives (Cozolino, 2014). When people become more emotionally aroused, the reticular activating system at the brain's stem lights up and sends stimulation to the rest of the brain, and selective attention, or focus, stimulates areas in the thalamus, which acts as a spotlight. When you are counseling, you are focusing the client's attention on certain aspects of the story and ignoring others. You are also managing the client's emotional arousal so that it is in a range that is best for productive thinking.

When your clients are speaking of their concerns, they are retrieving situations from memory, and your work is to help them reconstruct their memories in such a way as to make them less hurtful, more meaningful, and ultimately more hopeful. Even though we do not know the exact location of memories, we do know that they are maintained in neural networks and are open to change. Successful counseling offers support to Tom Robbins's (1990) assertion that "It's never too late to have a happy childhood" (p. 288). You cannot change history, but you can help your client to transform old, stagnating narratives of the past into rejuvenating accounts that highlight his or her personal strengths, resourcefulness, and resilience. Now that they are entering a new chapter of their lives with the help of counseling, your clients can savor the joys of life that were once impossible when they were young. Their transformed neural pathways enable them to experience a childlike sense of wonder, to appreciate the enchantment of everyday life, and to embrace the exuberance that life now offers. Now that's a happy childhood!

When you are attending to one of your client's narratives, you must be careful to allow him or her to take the lead, while you adopt an "I'm not from around here," nonexpert attitude. This is important because the client is drawing on memory, and various studies over many years have demonstrated that memory is constructed (Loftus, 1997). Recent research in "false memory" suggests that if the counselor leads the discussion, the client may produce memories of events that never happened. Brain scans have shown that different areas of the brain are activated when people produce false memories than when they are retrieving memories of events they actually experienced. Probing questions can influence the client's thinking in unintended and unproductive ways (Ivey et al., 2010).

We counselors do wish to help clients retrieve memories that will counter their stories of despair, and we even want to insert the possibility of remembered events that have not been stored in useful ways for the client—those exceptions to negative memories and overlooked incidents of success. We need to be careful not to probe for painful material because by doing so we may be putting even more negative ideas and emotions into the conversation. Clients will produce negative material on their own, so you don't need to dig for it. While we attend to and acknowledge the client's story of pain, we want to take care not to exacerbate the agony. Instead, we must show the clients that we can hold their pain and that it will not overwhelm us.

As you listen to your client's story, your face and body are resonating to the moment-to-moment emotions of your client, while you are also offering a faint smile. Smiling is a primary way of communicating warmth and acceptance (Restak, 2003). However, since smiles can communicate many messages you do not wish your clients to receive (e.g., mocking or sardonic smiles), you may want to focus on your facial expressions when you review your video recordings and ask your supervisor to give you feedback on your nonverbal communication with your client.

Positive feelings stimulate areas of the frontal cortex of the brain and serve to calm turbulent aspects of the emotional limbic system, such as fear and anger, that are encoded by the amygdala. For example, when clients are angry or depressed, their left frontal cortex activity decreases, and when they are happy, activity in the same area increases. More complex emotions also seem to be organized in the frontal cortex (Kolb & Wishaw, 2009). We intuitively know that our feelings can exist in layers, and these layers can contradict each other. Ivey and colleagues (2010) offered the scenario of receiving a gift from someone you care about. Say, for example, that you don't really like the gift. Perhaps it is your birthday, and your partner has given you a new vacuum cleaner. At one level, you may feel irritated at this gift giver for not recognizing that something more personal would have been appropriate. At another level, you appreciate the fact that your partner remembered your birthday at all, and you also feel guilty for not accepting that it is the thought that counts. At still another level, you worry that your lack of enthusiasm on receipt of the gift will betray your disappointment and make your partner feel foolish and ashamed. Finally, all these conflicted levels of emotion may then result in an outburst of anger and you blow a fuse. Obviously, many different areas of the brain will have been stimulated during this hypothetical event. It is important for you to remember that emotions and brain activity do not come in only one flavor. This is why we discourage our counselors in training from asking clients, "How did that make you feel?" Feelings are much more complicated than the simple answer your client is likely to offer in response to that question.

Oxytocin

The neuropeptide oxytocin, which has been found to increase interpersonal trust (Bartz, Zaki, Bolger, & Ochsner, 2011), is an essential ingredient of any successful counseling relationship. Recent studies have demonstrated that oxytocin levels quickly rise when individuals laugh together, show affection, demonstrate empathy, and participate in trust-building activities (Feldman, 2012). In one study of couples (Lux, 2010), husbands who had more positive marital relationships were significantly more effective in soothing their wives, who had been placed in a magnetic resonance tomography scanner and confronted with fear-provoking stimuli. The better the relationship, the more oxytocin was available in the brains of those married couples.

Similarly, in a counseling relationship characterized by unconditional positive regard, both counselor and client will have an increase in oxytocin and will feel more trusting of one another. In order for this to take place, the counselor must be congruent: Caring cannot be faked (Norcross, 2002). Nevertheless, in spite of the unconditional positive regard you may be showing your clients, they may not trust you enough to be their truly authentic selves. That's where you need to refine your crap-detecting skills.

Crap Detecting

We read each other through our eyes, and anatomically they are an extension of our brains. When we catch someone's eye, we look into a mind.

—Siri Hustvedt

When you see a dear friend and you smile, your specialized smile circuit has activated the basal ganglia in your brain. These are clusters of brain cells found between the higher cortex and the lower, older thalamic area (Ramachandran, 1998). In a fraction of a second, the emotional center of your limbic system has received the message that this is your friend and in turn has informed your basal ganglia, producing a natural smile. But if your friend should whip out a camera and ask you to smile for a photograph, the best you can do at that moment may be one of those pained "say cheese" smiles. This is because the higher cortex, where thinking and planning take place, is now orchestrating that grimace you are offering in place of a genuine smile. Obviously, some behaviors produced by the brain are better done the old-fashioned way.

A 19th-century anatomist with the somewhat ponderous name of Guillaume Benjamin Armand Duchenne de Boulogne is credited with being the first to write that when someone exhibits a smile of true happiness, the eye muscles, along with the mouth and cheek muscles, move (Davidson & Begley, 2012). However, if there is no "crinkling" around the corners of the eyes, you are viewing a social smile. The fake, or social, smile has come to be known as the "Say Cheese Smile." It is sometimes called the "Duchenne Smile."

As counselors, we need to possess what some have called a "crap detector" which alerts us to when our clients may not be telling us the truth. In order to successfully support a lie, one must arrange the face in a deliberatively composed, and seemingly congruent, configuration. Davidson (Davidson & Begley, 2012) pointed out that while "both hemispheres can generate spontaneous facial expressions, only the dominant left hemisphere can generate voluntary facial expressions" (p. 291). While this may seem a trivial difference, it shows that there is neural dissimilarity between a spontaneous genuine smile and a fake smile. Scientists have discovered that these two types of smiles are actually controlled by two completely different parts of our brain.

One of the fundamental challenges in counseling is that clients often do not reveal their true selves with complete and total honesty. They may feel ashamed or they may not trust you enough to risk sharing some vulnerable part of their secret selves. Whatever the motive, you may notice that there are minor discrepancies or distortions in their stories. More commonly, you will observe an incongruity between their words and their nonverbal accompaniment. Perhaps they are attempting to shift blame to someone else or are otherwise trying to look good to us. This is sometimes referred to as impression management. As a matter of fact, we all do this at times. In a job interview, for example, we try to compose our face in a way that looks socially acceptable in that context. We try to manage our impression so that we will be viewed in the way we hope.

When you detect an uneasiness in yourself with how your client is speaking of his or her experience, you may be responding to your crap detector, the aspect of your mirror neuron system that suggests a lack of authenticity. Your client's dominant hemisphere is controlling how he or she is attempting to be seen instead of the brain being deeply connected with areas that produce more spontaneous expression. This is important information. While you might not know the motivation for your client's incongruence, still you can suspect that something is wrong with the way the story is being told.

Counselors who are good at crap detecting can usually sense when an emotional expression is actually voluntary and intended to create an impression. But what is the metaphorical message contained in a client's attempt to manage the way in which he or she is viewed? An untrained person would simply dismiss this impression management attempt as deception. All of us lead with our façades in social situations with which we are unfamiliar, but if a client persists in this form of self-monitoring, the message may be that he or she believes that the real self, with its true emotions, is unacceptable and must be masked by a social self.

Carl Rogers characterized this attitude as one in which the person has been raised under conditions of worth (Presbury et al., 2007). During his or her developmental years, the message the person has received from others is, "I will love you if—and only if—you become the person who is acceptable to me." The problem that arises from conditions of worth is that if we attempt to live as others wish, we may be "persuaded by our own appearances: we become the persons we appear to be" (Snyder, 2003, p. 135).

High self-monitors are people who are particularly good at deliberate emotional expression that is designed to impress others (Snyder, 2003). Those who excel at this ability are good at picking up cues and quickly learning which behavior is appropriate in social situations, and they exercise good control over the way in which they are perceived. Extremely high self-monitors are usually considered phony if they are transparent and Machiavellian if they are not. On the other hand, very low self-monitors may be seen as without guile, or even crude, in their interactions with others.

Freud (1912/1958) observed that although people can deceive us with their words, the truth can be seen in the drumming of their fingers. Everyone can sometimes paste on a fake smile, put on a happy face, and deceive others about their true emotions. Snyder (2003) pointed out that while high self-monitors may present an impression that they have designed, they are usually "less skilled at controlling their body's expressive movements. Accordingly, the body may be a more revealing source of information than the face" (p. 134).

Sherwood and Cohen (1994) cautioned us not to confuse being nice with being truly empathic. Your task as a therapist is not to be tirelessly sympathetic, ceaselessly pleasant, and relentlessly cordial with your client. You need to recognize that your expression of empathy may cause a client to feel exposed, even uncomfortable, in the bright and revealing light of authenticity. While you will often use your empathic ability to understand your client's pain, at other times you will need to reveal what is beneath your client's mask. At such times, you will need to carefully and compassionately confront this duplicity because it may not be completely clear to the client that he or she is not being truly real. You do not confront such behavior in order to "catch them at it" but rather to help your clients toward a more congruent and authentic life.

Summary

New data in brain research have been supporting what we already knew about counseling and the change process. Perhaps most important is the finding that a warm, supportive relationship that focuses on the client's positive assets can significantly alter brain processes because the neuroplasticity of the brain allows new growth and learning at any age. In this chapter, we presented a sampling of the basic information regarding the neuroscience of counseling and therapy. Although this overview has been a simplistic and all too brief one, we hope that you have gained a greater appreciation for the complexity of the brain, the graceful beauty of its architecture, and its interdependent connections with the brains of our fellow human beings. You will want to stay current in this rapidly developing field that not only is offering supportive evidence for the impact of counseling and therapy but also is providing exciting discoveries of techniques that can enhance the power of your interventions. You are more effective in your therapeutic work when you are neuro-minded. The four factors that promote neuroplasticity are an excellent conceptual framework for reflecting on your work with clients. To what extent have you achieved a deeply empathic attunement? Do you regularly achieve an optimal level of emotional arousal in your sessions? To what degree have you facilitated your client's integration of thoughts and feelings? Have you co-constructed transformative narratives with your client? If so, then your client will terminate counseling having grown both personally and neurologically.

Resources

The Secret Life of the Brain

http://www.pbs.org/wnet/brain/index.html

As a companion to the excellent PBS series of the same name, this website has many fascinating features, including a three-dimensional tour of the brain and a dizzying variety of mind illusions.

Society for Neuroscience

http://www.sfn.org

The Society for Neuroscience website provides educational resources for both students and the general public. It provides detailed information on the latest scientific discoveries and their implications for treatment.

References

Alfano, K. M., & Cimino, C. R. (2008). Alteration of expected hemispheric asymmetries: Valence and arousal effects in neuropsychological models of emotion. *Brain and Cognition, 66*, 213–220.

Bartz, J. A., Zaki, J., Bolger, N., & Ochsner, K. N. (2011). Social effects of oxytocin in humans: Context and person matter. *Trends in Cognitive Science, 15*, 301–309.

Blakeslee, S. (2006, January 10). Cells that read minds. *New York Times*. Retrieved from http://www.nytimes.com/2006/01/10/science/10mirr.html

Cozolino, L. (2010). *The neuroscience of psychotherapy: Healing the social brain* (2nd ed.). New York, NY: Norton.

Cozolino, L. (2014). *The neuroscience of human relationships: Attachment and the developing social brain* (2nd ed.). New York, NY: Norton.

Damasio, A. (1994). *Descartes' error: Emotion, reason and the human brain*. New York, NY: Putnam

Davidson, R. J., & Begley, S. (2012). *The emotional life of your brain: How its unique patterns affect the way you think, feel, and live—and how you can change them*. New York, NY: Hudson Street.

Dennett, D. C. (1991). *Consciousness explained*. Boston, MA: Little, Brown.

Draganski, B., Gaser, C., Busch, V., Schuierer, G., Bogdahn, U., & May, A. (2004). Neuroplasticity: Changes in grey matter induced by training. *Nature, 427*, 311–312.

Echterling, L. G., Presbury, J., & Cowan, E. (2012). Neuroscience, magic, and counseling. *Journal of Creativity in Mental Health, 7*, 330–342. doi:10.1080/15401383 .2012.739947

Feldman, R. (2012). Oxytocin and social affiliation in humans. *Hormones and Behavior, 61*, 380–391.

Freud, S. (1958). Recommendations to physicians practicing psycho-analysis. In J. Strachey (Ed. & Trans.), *The standard edition of the complete psychological works of Sigmund Freud* (Vol. 12, pp. 109–120). London, England: Hogarth Press. (Original work published 1912)

Freud, S. (1924). *A general introduction to psychoanalysis*. New York, NY: Washington Square Press.

Gladding, S. T. (2004). *Counseling: A comprehensive profession* (5th ed.). Upper Saddle River, NJ: Merrill/Prentice Hall.

Goleman, D. (2006). *Social intelligence: The new science of human relationships*. New York, NY: Bantam Books.

Heller, L., & LaPierre, A. (2012). *Healing developmental trauma: How early trauma affects self-regulation, self-image, and the capacity for relationship*. Berkeley, CA: North Atlantic Books.

Ivey, A. E., Ivey, M. B., & Zalaquett, C. P. (2010). *Intentional interviewing and counseling: Facilitating client development in a multicultural society* (7th ed.). Belmont, CA: Brooks/Cole.

Ivey, A. E., & Zalaquett, C. P. (2011). Neuroscience and counseling: Central issue for justice leaders. *Journal for Social Action in Counseling and Psychology, 3*(1), 103–116.

Jeeves, M., & Brown, W. S. (2009). *Neuroscience, psychology, and religion: Illusions, delusions, and realities about human nature*. West Conshohocken, PA: Templeton Press.

Jones-Smith, E. (2012). *Theories of counseling and psychotherapy: An integrative approach*. Thousand Oaks, CA: Sage.

Kolb, B., & Wishaw, I. (2009). *Fundamentals of neuropsychology* (6th ed.). New York, NY: Worth.

Leahey, T. H. (2013). *A history of psychology: From antiquity to modernity* (7th ed.). Boston, MA: Pearson.

LeDoux, J. (1996). *The emotional brain: The mysterious underpinnings of emotional life*. New York, NY: Simon & Schuster.

Loftus E. (1997, September). Creating false memories. *Scientific American, 51–55.*

Lux, M. (2010). The magic of encounter: The person-centered approach and the neurosciences. *Person Centered & Experiential Psychotherapies, 9,* 274–289.

Macknik, S. L., & Martinez-Conde, S. (2010). *Sleights of mind: What the neuroscience of magic reveals about our everyday deceptions*. New York, NY: Picador.

Maroda, K. J. (2005). Show some emotion: Completing the cycle of affective communication. In L. Aron & A. Harris (Eds.), *Relational psychoanalysis: Vol. 2. Innovation and expansion* (pp. 121–142). New York, NY: Analytic Press.

Martindale, C. (1981). *Cognition and consciousness*. Homewood, IL: Dorsey.

Mikulincer, M., & Shaver, P. R. (Eds.). (2014). *Mechanisms of social connection: From brain to group*. Washington, DC: American Psychological Association.

Moffett, S. (2006). *The three-pound enigma: The human brain and the quest to unlock its mysteries*. Chapel Hill, NC: Algonquin.

Montes, S. (2013, December). The birth of the neuro-counselor? *Counseling Today, 56,* 32–40.

Nielsen, J. A., Zielinski, B. A., Ferguson, M. A., Lainhart, J. E., & Anderson, J. S. (2013). An evaluation of the left-brain vs. right-brain hypothesis with resting state functional connectivity magnetic resonance imaging. *PLoS ONE, 8*(8), e71275. doi:10.1371/journal.pone.0071275

Norcross, J. C. (Ed.). (2002). *Psychotherapy relationships that work: Therapist contributions and responsiveness to patient needs*. New York, NY: Oxford University Press.

Posner, M. (2004). *Cognitive neuropsychology of attention*. New York, NY: Guilford.

Presbury, J. H., McKee, J. E., & Echterling, L. G. (2007). Person-centered approaches. In H. T. Prout & D. T. Brown (Eds.), *Counseling and psychotherapy with children and adolescents: Theory and practice for school and clinical settings* (4th ed., pp. 180–240). New York, NY: Wiley.

Prochaska, J. O., & Norcross, J. C. (2014). *Systems of psychotherapy: A transtheoretical approach* (8th ed.). Stamford, CT: Cengage.

Ramachandran, V. S. (1998). *Phantoms in the brain: Probing the mysteries of the human mind*. New York, NY: Morrow.

Ramachandran, V. S. (2011). *The tell-tale brain: A neuroscientist's quest for what makes us human*. New York, NY: Norton.

Restak, R. (2003). *The new brain*. New York, NY: Rodale.

Robbins, T. (1990). *Still life with woodpecker*. New York, NY: Random House.

Rogers, C. R. (1961). *On becoming a person: A therapist's view of psychotherapy.* Boston, MA: Houghton Mifflin.

Rogers, C. R. (1987). Comments on the issue of equality in psychotherapy. *Journal of Humanistic Psychology, 27,* 38–40.

Ryan, R. (2007). Motivation and emotion: A new look and approach for two reemerging fields. *Motivation & Emotion, 31,* 1–3.

Schore, A. N. (2012). *The science of the art of psychotherapy.* New York, NY: Norton.

Sherwood, V. R., & Cohen, C. P. (1994). *Psychotherapy of the quiet borderline patient: The as-if personality revisited.* Northvale, NJ: Aronson.

Siegel, D. J. (2007). *The mindful brain: Reflection and attunement in the cultivation of well-being.* New York, NY: Norton.

Snyder, M. (2003). The many me's of the self-monitor. In W. A. Lesko (Ed.), *Readings in social psychology* (5th ed., pp. 130–137). Boston, MA: Allyn & Bacon.

Szasz, T. (1996). *The meaning of mind: Language, morality and neuroscience.* Westport, CT: Praeger.

Yerkes, R. M., & Dodson, J. D. (1908). The relation of strength of stimulus to rapidity of habit-formation. *Journal of Comparative and Neurological Psychology, 18,* 459–482.

Young, M. E. (2005). *Learning the art of helping: Building blocks and techniques* (3rd ed.). Upper Saddle River, NJ: Merrill/Prentice Hall.

9

Intervening in Crises, Traumas, and Disasters

The most authentic thing about us is our capacity to create, to overcome, to endure, to transform, to love and to be greater than our suffering.

—Ben Okri

We must embrace pain and burn it as fuel for our journey.

—Kenji Miyazawa

Like many other students in the helping professions, your most overwhelming concern, strongest doubt, and deepest apprehension may be that you are unprepared, both personally and professionally, to deal effectively with serious crises (Morris & Minton, 2012). However, no matter what area of specialization you may focus on in your practice, we can guarantee that you will be working regularly in such extreme circumstances. In this chapter, we introduce you to crisis intervention, suicide prevention, and disaster response. Of course, you will receive much more training in these techniques throughout your program, so the material here serves only as a brief primer to familiarize you with the basic principles and strategies. We also will offer you some helpful tips for managing your own emotional turmoil in these difficult situations.

In recent years, counselors and therapists have become increasingly active in serving vital roles as crisis interveners, providers of psychiatric emergency services, and members of disaster response teams. Accrediting bodies also have been requiring training programs to prepare students to perform these important functions (Minton & Pease-Carter, 2011). As a result, the most emotionally challenging experiences that you will face in your program, and perhaps the most important lessons you will learn, are likely to be those in which you are dealing with crises, traumas, and disasters. When you encounter an emergency situation, you may feel like someone who is trying to watch a breaking news account on CNN. You scan the scenes of devastation that flash before your eyes, hear the reporter's narrative in the background, and frantically read the "crawl" of text flowing at the bottom of the screen. It's just too much to take in! So in this chapter, we offer some guidelines that can help you focus your attention on the crucial elements in the midst of the chaos. We also provide a crisis intervention protocol to follow for promoting the resilience of survivors. The stakes are high, but the potential benefits of providing immediate and intensive services in such troubled times are enormous.

Fundamental Concepts

Trauma and Crisis

Let's begin by making an important distinction between the concepts of trauma and crisis. Trauma, which comes from the Greek word for *wound*, refers to a serious psychological injury that results from a threatening, terrifying, or horrifying experience. Metaphorically, a psychological trauma can "bleed" like a physical wound, but in this case it may spread throughout all the crevices of one's being (Solnit, 2013), profoundly impacting a person's cognitive abilities, emotional reactivity, behavior, and even neural functioning (Gaskill & Perry, 2012). Consequently, a significant number of trauma survivors can develop posttraumatic stress disorder (PTSD) and other disorders, so trauma-informed treatment may be the treatment of choice (Steele & Malchiodi, 2012). The good news is that studies also have found that resilience is much more common than was once believed (Echterling & Stewart, 2008). In fact, many people report posttraumatic growth (PTG), reflecting profound and positive changes that they had undergone as a result of successfully coping with their suffering and anguish (Calhoun & Tedeschi, 2006). These benefits include more self-confidence, enhanced relationships, deeper compassion, and greater maturity.

The concept of crisis provides a useful complement to that of trauma. Crisis comes from the Greek word for decision, and its Chinese symbol combines the figures for danger and crucial moment. A crisis is a pivotal turning point that involves both peril and promise. Not everyone in crisis is automatically dealing with trauma, but anyone who is traumatized is also in crisis. And in contrast to the treatment of disorders precipitated by traumas, the purpose of crisis intervention is not to achieve a cure. Instead, it is to meet the survivor's immediate needs by providing comfort, making meaning, regulating emotions, and promoting successful coping. Because you intervene at such a crucial point in a person's life, a seemingly small intervention during this time can make a profound difference for years to come.

Resilience

We live in a time of highly publicized crises and catastrophes during which the news media bombard the public with countless stories portraying survivors as pitiable victims. Occasionally, a broadcast may spotlight one or two individuals who are depicted as inspiring heroes who overcame extraordinary obstacles. However, in contrast to these misleading accounts you may see on television or in the newspapers, the vast majority of survivors are neither helpless nor superhuman. Instead, the research has documented that they are typical human beings doing their best to adapt to abnormal circumstances and to embark on the long, hard mission of rebuilding their lives—in other words, most are resilient (Prince-Embury & Saklofske, 2013).

In physics, resilience refers to the extent that a material can endure strain and return to its original shape. Counselors and therapists have found resilience to be a valuable perspective when considering people in crisis (Cohrs, Christie, White, & Das, 2013). Instead of concentrating on only ameliorating the negative consequences of crises, you can also focus on the positive goal of promoting resilience. So your fundamental task as a crisis intervener is to recognize that people are survivors, not pathetic and passive victims. In the midst of their emotional turmoil, they have undiscovered strengths, overlooked talents, and unnoticed resources.

Hundreds of studies on the process of resilience have consistently identified four general factors that promote successful resolution of crises and traumas (Masten & Reed, 2002). These four pathways to resilience are social support, making meaning, managing emotions, and successful coping strategies. As survivors begin to experience their own sense of empowerment, recognize their untapped capabilities, and reconnect to sources of sustenance and nurturance, they build the psychological scaffolding for resilience and growth. Fundamentally, resilience is the process of victims' becoming survivors who can then go on to thrive in their lives.

Intervention Principles

Before describing specific intervention techniques, we want to mention some basic principles you need to follow when you work with people in crisis. First, always offer LUV by listening, understanding, and validating. These are the essential ingredients of any therapeutic encounter (Echterling, Presbury, & McKee, 2005). By LUVing, you are actively *listening* to the person's verbal and nonverbal messages, communicating your deeply empathic *understanding* of the individual's thoughts and feelings, and *validating* unconditionally his or her innate worth as a person. Unless the individual in crisis experiences your LUV, then your interventions, however elegant, can seem more like manipulative ploys or gimmicks. In contrast, your LUVing presence creates a safe haven, a psychological refuge, and a nurturing environment that is so vital in troubled times.

LUV the Survivor

Of course, you are being trained already in the fundamentals of counseling, such as engaging in active listening skills and communicating empathy, but we are addressing these elemental qualities here to emphasize just how essential they are with someone in crisis. So always intervene with LUV; your work will seem heartless without it. At first glance, you may think that providing LUV is woefully inadequate and feeble compared to the intensity and severity of a crisis, trauma, or disaster. But keep in mind that you are not the rescuer. Instead, by offering your supportive and attuned presence, you supply the ideal environment in which healing and posttraumatic growth can take place. With LUV, you tune in to your client's words, gestures, tone of voice, posture, and facial expressions throughout your encounter. You perform the dance of attunement when you keep in step with the survivor, responding to the nuances and rhythms of the person's moment-to-moment experience of a profoundly life-altering event.

Listen. As you learned in Chapter 8, listening takes place when you concentrate your awareness on what you hear through the process of top-down attention. It requires tuning out all irrelevant sensory input as you focus your attentional spotlight entirely on the survivor. You can communicate to your clients that you are indeed truly listening to them (Egan, 2010) by conscientiously performing the following tasks:

- *Face the survivor* with an engaged, inviting manner. You are giving your undivided attention by setting aside any other tasks and focusing entirely on the individual. Facing the survivor enables you to listen with both your eyes and your ears, observing what the person's facial expressions, gestures, and body posture are communicating while also hearing the words that the survivor is saying to you.
- *Assume an open, nonthreatening posture.* Your physical manner reinforces the idea that you welcome whatever the person has to say, no matter how painful, embarrassing, or horrific it may seem. Your bearing suggests nonverbally that this relationship is a safe haven in times of turmoil.
- *Lean toward the survivor* with an expression of concern. Showing a sense of compassionate regard reflects that you are attuned to the distress signals that the person is likely sending. With this nonverbal communication, you are also taking care to honor and observe any cultural expectations (Smith, Domenech Rodriguez, & Bernal, 2011) regarding appropriate interpersonal distance and touch.
- *Make good eye contact.* When people are sharing their crisis stories, they are often defocusing their eyes or gazing away from you as they delve into these deeply disturbing experiences. In other words, their own accounts take them back into the "there and then" and away from the "here and now." So it is especially important that you continue to look to their eyes because survivors will regularly glance to check that you are still connecting with them.
- *Keep a sense of poise.* In addition to showing your compassion, you also want to keep your composure. Such a balance demonstrates that you are committed to bearing witness to the survivor's emotional turmoil while also serving as an interpersonal anchor. You should adopt a "therapeutic distance" between being too close, and thus overwhelmed, and being too distant and not being affected at all by the story.

Understand. The techniques above can show that you are listening, but how does the survivor know that you truly understand? Your deep, empathic encounter with a person in crisis is like a border crossing from the relatively safe, predictable, and secure land of your own everyday life into that uncharted and dangerous territory of unexpected threats, torments, and sufferings. Empathic understanding enables you to travel from here to there—a leap of faith that places you within the heart of another person's narrative (Solnit, 2013). To serve as an empathic witness to another's raw suffering requires an act of courage on your part to span that gulf and join the survivor. The term *schadenfreude* refers to the malicious pleasure that some people take in seeing the misfortunes of others. They are like the rubbernecking drivers who slow down to gawk as they pass the scene of an accident—but never stop to offer assistance. As someone called to be a helping professional, your natural empathy prods you to reach out to a fellow traveler left stranded by a crisis. Whenever you reach out to someone in need, there are several practical strategies that you can use to communicate your empathic understanding.

- *Repeat or paraphrase* what the survivor is saying. Often, a powerful technique is to repeat the single, most emotionally charged word that vividly captures the essence of the survivor's statement. When it comes to what you say to a survivor, sometimes less is more. By communicating your understanding with such clarity and power, you can dramatically express your sense of attunement and encourage the survivor to explore this uncharted emotional terrain.
- *Check your understanding* by stating what you think the survivor means and by asking for a confirmation. You are inviting the person to verify, correct, or refine your comprehension of the message.
- *Nonverbally resonate to the survivor's mood,* talking in a way that echoes his or her pace, rhythm, and manner of speaking. Your understanding is much more than merely cerebral; it is also heartfelt. Of course, your gestures, facial expressions, and speech will not have the same emotional intensity as the person in crisis. After all, you are responding with empathic understanding—not *reacting* with emotional contagion—to the survivor.
- *Tune in to both positive and negative emotions.* In your training, you may have practiced reflecting feelings with the formulaic statement, "It sounds like you're feeling . . ." Our guess is that the emotions you were taught to reflect were negative ones. Although survivors generally focus on their anguish and distress when they are in crisis, they also may express the entire gamut of emotions, including those of hope, compassion, relief, gratitude, and courage (Larsen, Hemenover, Norris, & Cacioppo, 2003). Your job is to communicate your empathic understanding of *all* the complex feelings the survivor expresses.

  Another example of the expression of a positive emotion is laughter. Over the years, many therapists have dismissed humor as merely a defense mechanism. They have portrayed it as a cheap attempt to find some comic relief from the pain of trauma. However, humor is a positive emotion that embraces the enigma, paradoxes, and mysteries of adversity (Milo, 2001). Laughing along with the survivor during those rare moments can be a powerful expression of empathic attunement.

- *Use words, phrases, and expressions that are similar to those of the survivor.* Be particularly alert for the metaphors that the person uses to describe the crisis. You can often build on these to create metaphors for resilience.

- *Scan for subtle cues of emotional arousal.* As we mentioned earlier, survivors express a wide range of emotions. You need to be vigilant to preludes of heightened emotionality because they are signals that survivors are treading near significant issues. Their rate of breathing may become more rapid and shallow. They may find themselves blinking more as their eyes begin to glisten. Their voice pitch may start to rise, their throat may catch, and they may have difficulty speaking. They may grow quiet, but the tense silence is nothing like a hushed, contemplative pause. These cues may be so subtle that the survivor may not even be aware of them. It is at this point that you may decide to offer an immediacy in which you share what you are observing in the here and now.

  Of course, the implicit and emerging emotion that you observe may be a positive one. You may notice the hint of a smile appearing on the survivor's face, or the person may be speaking with greater energy, or beaming with pride over taking a significant step forward. Whatever the encouraging hints or hopeful cues that the survivor is displaying, you want to be bearing witness to them.

Validate. Finally, once you have demonstrated that you are both listening and understanding, how can you convey that you value unconditionally the person's innate worth? By validating, you are indicating, in every way possible, that you not only believe what the survivor is saying but that you also *believe in* the person's abilities, strengths, and potential. There are a number of simple behaviors you can use to communicate that you support and accept the survivor.

- *Nod affirmatively* and slowly as the person speaks to you. This small gesture offers an ongoing and recurring refrain of affirmation. Even a slight nod of your head can be a wordless sign of acknowledgement, regard, and acceptance.

- *Smile warmly and with compassion.* As we discussed in Chapter 8, a broad smile in which you flash your teeth is not appropriate with someone in crisis, who is typically coming to you in emotional turmoil. As we mentioned above, by showing some concern, you are communicating that you are acknowledging the distress. However, you want to balance your dismay for the crisis with a warm expression of acceptance for the survivor.

- *Offer minimal encouragers* and interrupt rarely. These encouragers can take several forms, but they all have the advantage of not intruding into the flow of the survivor's narrative. For example, you can offer a few well-placed words, such as "I see," or "Yes." You may also find yourself regularly giving a well-timed paralinguistic utterance, such as "hmmm" or "ahhh."

- *You can even communicate nonverbally* to encourage the survivor to continue along a productive path. For example, when the person pauses, you can lean slightly forward with a sense of anticipation. Or at a particularly crucial point, you can tilt your head a few degrees to one side. Using this "Lassie Twist," you communicate that you are intrigued and absorbed in the person's exploration. Your hushed attentiveness can be powerfully validating.

- *Communicate your faith in the survivor* by expressing neither skepticism nor the desire to debate. When people are in crisis, they often doubt themselves, question their perceptions, and even wonder about their own sanity. Your quiet and accepting manner can promote a sense of validation that the person will appreciate in this time of turmoil and confusion.

- *Convey your confidence in the survivor* by not dispensing glib advice. Advice giving carries with it the message that you do not trust someone to know the best course of action. You may be tempted to protect your own vulnerabilities by offering empty platitudes to reassure and comfort. However, such misguided attempts merely serve to invalidate the survivor's emotions. Instead, by offering your supportive presence, you communicate your respect for the person's inner resources. Showing your belief in someone's capacities sends a forceful message of validation.

Crisis Intervention Techniques

You may have noticed that in the previous sections of this chapter, we have not employed the term *client*. Instead, we typically used *survivor* to refer to the person in crisis. Although you may be offering formal counseling and therapy to clients in crisis, you may also be providing crisis intervention services in situations in which no intake has been performed, no file has been opened, and no specific records are being kept. Nevertheless, whether you are talking with an anonymous hotline caller for 10 minutes, comforting a survivor for several hours at the site of a catastrophic accident, or treating an outpatient client who has just experienced a trauma, the process of crisis intervention has fundamentally the same dynamics. As we mentioned earlier, crisis survivors are more likely to be resilient when they reach out to others for support, make meaning of the experience, take heart by regulating their emotions, and move on by creatively coping with these challenges. Therefore, the techniques of crisis intervention we describe below parallel these four essential processes that promote resilience and facilitate successful resolution (Echterling et al., 2005).

Linking

Resilient survivors are not islands unto themselves. Research on crises has shown that relationships offer many vitally important resources, such as affection, advice, affirmation, and practical assistance (Berscheid, 2003). Therefore, your first intervention in any crisis is to link with the person by offering support, comfort, and sanctuary as the survivor prepares to embark on the journey toward resolution. To successfully link involves relying heavily on LUV and takes only a few seconds to initiate, but do not underestimate its value as the foundation for a successful intervention.

- *Connect rapidly.* The very act of rapidly connecting with someone in crisis is, in and of itself, a powerful form of intervention. Your presence as a concerned and caring person is reassuring to a survivor who may feel frightened, affirming to a person who may feel all alone, and supportive to someone who may feel helpless in the moment.
- *Introduce yourself and identify your role.* Because you may be offering crisis intervention to a stranger, you can bond quickly by making eye contact, giving your name, offering your hand (whenever appropriate), and describing your role. In a disaster assistance center or with an outreach operation, you may find it useful to wear an identifying tag with your name and position.
- *Offer asylum.* Of course, your caring presence is helpful, but you should also arrange, whenever possible, to meet with the person in a location that provides physical security and psychological refuge. Because survivors may remain vigilant to potential threats and become

easily distracted, they are especially appreciative of a safe and quiet setting. A haven can give the survivor an opportunity to focus on resolution instead of self-protection.

- *Convene others.* Crises can bring people together. In fact, cultures throughout the world have developed rituals in which family members and friends congregate to deal with developmental crises, such as births and deaths. An important role that you may play is helping convene relatives and friends who can offer emotional support and practical resources to address this crisis.

- *Offer encouragement.* Near the end of your encounter, you want to take a minute or two to mention the survivor's strengths that you have observed. While you have been listening, you have been alert to the instances of resilience, ingenuity, and perseverance. You've made a mental note of them so that you can then offer them as part of your encouraging comments.

Making Meaning

When people are in crisis, they are also experiencing a crisis of meaning (Silver & Updegraff, 2013). Telling their stories is one of the ways that survivors begin the process of crisis resolution. Once you have linked with someone in crisis, you can expect the person to have a desperate need to tell the story—and to have someone bear witness to it. Therefore, your second basic crisis intervention strategy is to help survivors in the task of making meaning. By sharing their crisis narratives, survivors give form to raw experience, gain some sense of cognitive mastery over the crisis, and make important discoveries about possible resolutions. Children may give expression to their crisis experiences in a variety of other ways—playing, drawing, sculpting, singing, and writing—but whatever form their stories take, the process helps children create meaning from the destructive event that has taken place (Federal Emergency Management Agency, 2012).

The themes that emerge from these narratives eventually shape the storytellers' sense of personal identity. In other words, the accounts that survivors create do more than organize their life experiences. They affirm their fundamental beliefs, guide important decisions, and offer consolation and solace in times of tragedy (Neimeyer, 2000). In crisis intervention, your ultimate goal is to help transform a crisis narrative into a survival story. Using the following techniques can facilitate that process.

- *Enter the crisis story.* When you invite people to tell their stories, avoid asking, "What happened to you?" Although this question is a general open-ended one that encourages someone to talk, it also suggests that the survivor is only a passive victim of circumstances. You are better off asking something like, "What have you been dealing with so far?" The question is open-ended and also suggests that the person has been actively involved in surviving the crisis.

- *Ask "getting through" questions.* In addition to acknowledging the crisis, you also will be looking for resilience. If you are conscientious and observant, you will find countless nuggets of strengths and resourcefulness. It can be tempting to find out details about the crisis, but your job is to ask questions that support resilience. So you empathize with the crisis experience, but you are curious about the surviving. For example, you may want to ask, "How did you manage to escape?" Or you may wonder out loud, "How in the world were you able to handle that?" Asking exploratory questions about ingenuity, such as, "Where did you get the idea to try that?" is also an effective way to draw out the survivor embedded in the crisis story.

Whenever you find examples of resilience, determination, creativity, and courage, be sure to acknowledge them. Remember: A person in crisis is one whose self-esteem and confidence have been damaged, so this is someone who can use frequent reminders of strengths and abilities. So for example, you might say, "It sounds like you were really determined to get through this."

Regulating Emotions

As a crisis intervener your third task is to help survivors regulate their emotions by reducing distress and enhancing feelings of resolve (Echterling et al., 2005). The purpose of the following interventions is to help survivors to take heart and manage their emotions productively.

A crisis is invariably a time of intense emotions, but a common assumption is that survivors are experiencing only negative feelings, such as fear, shock, and grief. People in crisis actually experience not only painful reactions but also feelings of resolve (Echterling & Stewart, 2014). These feelings of resolve include courage, compassion, hope, peace, and joy. Acknowledging and giving expression to the gamut of emotions, both negative and positive, can promote a successful crisis resolution.

- *Lower emotions of distress.* Catharsis itself is not a necessary component of the resolution process. Instead of encouraging people in crisis to have an emotional abreaction, you can help them focus on how they have been managing their distress. As they discuss their distress, you are looking for occasions in which they effectively used the distress and managed their emotions to cope with the challenges confronting them.

You want to take care in how you invite the person to talk about emotions. "How did that make you feel?" is another one of those counseling clichés that you should avoid. Every counselor and therapist in the movies uses that line, so instead of sounding like you're reciting some overused phrase, challenge yourself to genuinely encounter this person in crisis. Your words may not sound as polished and slick, but they're not from a script; they're from the heart. You may want to ask something like, "How have you been dealing with all the feelings you've been having?" Such an open-ended question not only offers people a valuable opportunity to add emotional themes to their survival stories but also suggests that they have continued to be resilient, in spite of their distress.

- *Enhance feelings of resolve.* During this phase of crisis intervention, you are helping people to identify the strategies that they have found successful—however briefly or slightly—in regulating their emotions. At times during this crisis, they have been able to redirect their attention, use their distress to mobilize themselves, or reframe the events. You are sifting through their narratives to find the times that they managed their distress. You can then explore these occasions in detail to uncover more concrete examples of resilience. At this point, you can respond, for example, "It sounds like you acted quickly on that fear to save yourself from getting killed."

As we mentioned earlier, in times of crisis, people sometimes wonder if their intense reactions may suggest that they are abnormal or even crazy. Many crisis interveners have been trained to play the expert role in this situation by asserting reassuringly, "You're having a normal reaction to an abnormal situation." As crisis workers, we know this statement is probably true, but to say it to the person in crisis is not useful! We would discourage you from taking on this one-up position over the survivor.

Moving On

As a crisis intervener, your concluding strategy is to help survivors envision new possibilities by inviting them to create positive goals. Once articulated, goals serve as beacons that light the way for resilience. In this section, we describe interventions that can help survivors begin the process of rebuilding their lives. Once they begin to see a future, survivors gain a sense of direction and hope, become more motivated, and increase their momentum toward resolution.

Keep in mind that even though someone may not have completely resolved a crisis, somehow the person has survived the initial onslaught. You can invite survivors to explore the achievements that they have already accomplished. By drawing attention to these instances of taking flight, dealing with challenges, and finding refuge, you can assist survivors in discovering unknown strengths, appreciating unrecognized resources, and achieving a sense of hope. These strengths and resources form the foundation for a successful resolution.

Immediately after the point of impact, victims are already becoming survivors. They are creatively evading hazards, courageously coping with dangers, and making the most of their few opportunities to protect themselves and others. However, because their focus may have been on the crisis events, survivors are usually not aware of their own resilience. Your goal in this phase of the crisis intervention is to help people in crisis to recognize their own strengths and appreciate their resourcefulness.

- *Ask "moving on" and "what if" questions.* Although the actual crisis events may now be in the past, the survival story is still a work in progress—unfinished and unfolding. Therefore, you want to invite the survivor to envision changes and future possibilities by asking, "What do you want to be doing next when we finish our conversation?" Or you may encourage someone to explore options by asking, "Where do you want to go from here?"

  At first, the person may not accept your invitation to envision the future and, instead, may begin to talk about the crisis experience again. If so, you can return to LUV. Keep in mind that retelling a crisis story is both common and important for resolution. After this retelling, you can extend another invitation to turn someone's attention to the future.

- *Offer suggestions and make a referral.* Because people in crisis usually need to connect with a variety of community resources, making a good referral is an essential part of crisis intervention (Miller, 2012). A good referral is much more than passing along a name and telephone number. Sometimes, taking just a few extra minutes can make a big difference. You can make the best referral when you have successfully linked, heard the person's story, helped to regulate emotions, and facilitated coping. After engaging in that process, both you and the survivor now have a better sense of the person's situation, strengths, resources, and goals.

Preventing Suicide

Since the anguish in times of crises may seem unbearable, some people may consider suicide as one possible resolution. If this issue arises in your intervention with someone, you may be tempted to try to talk the person out of this possibility. However, such an attempt on your part would be counterproductive and would only sabotage the working alliance you are developing (DeJong & Berg, 2002). Instead, we recommend that you return to LUV, continuing to look for strengths and resources buried in the crisis story that the person is sharing with you.

You may have the mistaken notion that bringing this issue out in the open could prompt someone to consider suicide as an option. However, addressing the topic in a concerned but open manner can be a relief to those who are struggling by themselves with this life-or-death decision. If they are not thinking about suicide, they will simply disavow you of that notion and then quickly return to the issues that truly concern them. So always ask if you sense that suicide is a possibility. It's a tough question to ask, but ignoring your suspicions and avoiding the issue can lead to a regrettable tragedy. If you do ask, it's helpful to remind yourself that the risk of suicide is on a continuum from very low to extremely high (Flemons & Gralnik, 2013). Suicide is rarely inevitable; the very fact that the person is talking to you is evidence of some ambivalence.

When someone is considering suicide, you also want to keep in mind that suicide is not the crisis; it is only an attempt to resolve a devastating crisis. Therefore, your ultimate goals of crisis intervention remain the same: to help the person survive the crisis and resolve it positively. By facilitating a positive resolution to the crisis, you have also prevented a suicide. In one study, clients who successfully overcame their suicidal thoughts and behaviors reported that the most important contribution from counseling was the relationship itself (Paulson & Worth, 2002). They especially appreciated how their counselor stood by them through their ordeal. Interestingly, the participants in the study reported that the most powerful suicide prevention techniques were offering empathy, compassionate support, and a listening ear.

Asking about and addressing the issue of suicide is crucial. However, in addition to assessing the risk, you also want to maintain your therapeutic alliance and explore the person's capacity for survival. By following the dual strategy of checking for risk and exploring for strengths, you can reduce the danger of suicide and enhance the potential for a positive resolution. And by preserving your authentic and caring relationship, your questions about risk express a counselor's concern for the welfare of a client. Too often, when assessing risk, the counselor's manner seems more like that of a detective interrogating a suspect.

In fact, whenever the question of suicide risk emerges, instead of abandoning your relationship, you want to enhance it by genuinely sharing your here-and-now experience of your encounter with the person. For example, you might say, "I really appreciate you sharing that you've been thinking more and more about suicide lately. That trust means a lot to me, and I also think it'd be helpful for us to talk more about this issue."

Below, we use the acronym BASICS (behavioral, affective, somatic, interpersonal, cognitive, and spiritual) to describe the factors that relate to suicide risk and to resilience (Echterling et al., 2005). We invite you to use this pneumonic device both to assess risk and explore strengths. As you read over the sample risk questions and strengths questions, you may notice that they differ in both content and form. For example, you presume that someone has coped to some degree with past crises, so your resilience questions take the form of "How have you gotten through tough situations in the past?" On the other hand, when you are assessing risk, you do *not* presume a past history of suicidal behavior. Therefore, you might say, "I'm wondering *if* you had ever tried to kill yourself before." Your basic approach to crisis intervention is to presume resilience, but when the issue of suicide comes up, you need to check on risk without making any assumptions.

You may also notice that the form of the risk questions is often closed-ended and specific. For example, you might ask someone, "Do you have a plan in mind for killing yourself?" As you can see, such questions focus narrowly on suicide. However, when you explore resilience, you are typically relying on open-ended and broad questions. You might ask, "Where did you find the courage to talk about this issue with me?" Your approach to exploring resilience is to cast a wide net.

- *Behavioral.* How is the person behaving that poses a suicide risk or suggests resilience? Whether someone is openly threatening suicide or only implying the possibility, you must address this serious matter immediately. For example, you need to find out if the person is making preparations to die by suicide, such as purchasing a firearm. Simple and direct questions, such as, "Are you doing anything right now to prepare for killing yourself?" are the most effective. While you gather information regarding any preparations, you also want to explore the person's current coping activities that indicate some amount of resilience. After all, the survivor is still alive and has contacted you for crisis intervention.

In addition to discussing current behaviors, you need to determine how the person has acted in the past. People who have made previous suicide attempts pose a greater risk of committing suicide. Again, you should be direct by simply asking, "You said earlier that you are thinking about suicide. Right now, I'm feeling concerned about your safety and want to ask you some questions about this issue. Have you ever tried to kill yourself in the past?"

Once you have information about any past attempts, you can then explore the many exceptions when the person opted for choosing life in spite of a crisis. You might ask, "How were you able to manage back then without following through on your thought of killing yourself?"

- *Affective.* Someone who is considering suicide is likely feeling overwhelmed by feelings of deep depression, unforgiving guilt, and a profound sense of hopelessness. If the person is expressing such intense feelings, you should check for the risk of suicide. In addition to openly exploring the negative emotions, you want to be alert to feelings of resolve that the person may also be evidencing—hints of hope, gratitude, and compassion, for example. Whenever you notice such life-affirming emotions, you want to explore for more details with the person. Another effective strategy is simply saying, "Tell me about what you'd like to see happen in your life."

- *Somatic.* The somatic facet of BASICS refers to the physical well-being of the person. If the crisis event is a life-threatening illness or profoundly disabling condition, you need to be alert to any signs that the person may be considering the possibility of taking his or her own life. Of course, you want to be sure to explore the person's resilience in addition to checking for any risk. For example, you might say, "When you pointed out that this cancer is threatening to end your life in the near future, how did you find the powerful determination to make this time meaningful?"

Another somatic factor is intoxication, which impairs judgment and lowers impulse control, so it's not surprising that in times of crisis it presents a significant somatic risk factor for suicide, particularly among young people. In fact, over one third of all individuals who died by suicide were legally intoxicated at the time of their deaths (Conner et al., 2014). You can check your impressions with the person by saying, in a nonjudgmental tone of voice, "Your words seem to be slurred, and I'm having trouble understanding you. Have you been drinking or taking anything?"

- *Interpersonal.* Individuals who die by suicide lack a sense of belongingness, feel a profound sense of disconnection from others, or believe that they are a burden on others (Joiner, 2009). If a person is in serious conflict with significant others or has experienced the tragic loss of a loved one, there is a greater risk. On the other hand, those who are fortunate to have a cohesive and supportive network are more resilient, even in times of crisis. You can assess this factor by asking, "Who are the people who are close to you?" Or you may inquire, "How are the important people in your life involved in this situation that you're facing?"
- *Cognitive.* People who pose a high risk of suicide seem to be wearing cognitive blinders that permit them to see suicide as the only means to resolve the crisis. If you are concerned about the possibility of suicidal thinking, often the best strategy for assessing risk is a direct one by simply asking, "Are you thinking of killing yourself?" A rare and fleeting instance of suicidal ideation is not unusual during a time of crisis. Nevertheless, it is essential that you assess the risk whenever someone mentions thinking, even momentarily, about suicide.

  If someone acknowledges having thoughts about suicide, then you want to determine if the person has a suicide plan by asking, "You said that you might kill yourself. Do you have an idea how you would do it?" If there is a definite plan of how, when, and where to die by suicide, along with access to a highly lethal method, the risk for suicide is dramatically higher.

  In addition to determining if the person has a suicide plan, you should also explore for a survival plan. If you hear the person mention a possible option or two for coping with the crisis, you might say something like, "It sounds like you've got some ideas about what you might do. Tell me more about those possibilities."
- *Spiritual.* Someone who is feeling a profound sense of spiritual alienation may see suicide as the only salvation. If you notice this theme emerging in the person's narrative, you assess for risk. During this assessment, you can also explore the potential for resilience by reflecting, "After everything that's been happening lately, it sounds like you're wondering right now if there's any point to life. What would need to be happening for you to begin feeling better about going on?"

Throughout this entire process of addressing these life-and-death issues, keep in mind that assessment is not an interrogation. Instead, it is a collaborative process that can deepen the therapeutic alliance and actually promote resilience. Engaging in an honest and penetrating exploration can spark new insights and kindle a growing sense of hope for the future.

Developing a safety plan. One popular suicide prevention technique has been the use of a "no-suicide" contract, but there is no evidence to support its effectiveness (Puskar & Urda, 2011), and such a strategy actually has the potential to cause harm (Edwards & Sachmann, 2010). Instead of relying on a contract that suggests a document that is legally binding (McMyler & Pryjmachuk, 2008), you can offer to help someone develop a client-generated safety plan (Flemons & Gralnik, 2013). This positive approach is focused on promoting resilience and involves several important tasks. Working together, you first identify helpful attachments—significant others who are personally committed to this person's well-being. Second, you need to counsel the person on eliminating easy access to highly lethal means of suicide. A third strategy that you can implement is to explore positive coping alternatives to suicide. Finally, whenever you encounter someone who poses some degree of risk for suicide, you must work to connect the person with services, particularly mental health treatment, to address the precipitating concerns. A referral is essential.

In spite of your interventions, if you find that someone continues to threaten suicide, you need to carry out emergency procedures for voluntary hospitalization. If the person presents an imminent danger to self and refuses to be hospitalized, you should seek, as a last resort, involuntary commitment.

Disaster Intervention

Given climate change and heightened international tensions, it is predicted that by the year 2050 natural disasters and wars will directly affect at least two billion people around the world (Ronan & Johnston, 2005). Such catastrophic events not only impact societies, economies, and environments, they also can have profound psychological consequences (Gulliver, Zimering, Carpenter, Giardina, & Farrar, 2014). In recent years, counselors and therapists have gained the well-earned acceptance and respect as integral members of crisis and disaster response teams. Their professional training and experiences make them uniquely qualified to be resources for all survivors, including children and families (Jordan, Perryman, & Anderson, 2013).

Disaster interventions include a wide range of services, including assessment, consultation, training, supervision, psychological first aid, and program evaluation, in addition to any rapid, brief, and direct assistance to survivors (Echterling et. al., 2005). Disaster work is strenuous and stressful, but it also has its unique rewards. As you can see in the following story, a major challenge of responding to a disaster is that the work does not provide the tidy containment of the traditional settings for counseling and therapy. Nevertheless, the experience of providing outreach services in a disaster setting can be both rewarding and transformative.

Out of an Emergency, Something New Emerges

Lennie's Story

Before a horrific disaster struck my community, my private practice work in counseling was a traditional one—50-minute sessions, appointed times, and a professional office setting where I displayed diplomas, certificates, and books that spoke to my legitimacy. But in the midst of the chaos and devastation that a local flood had left in its wake, I decided to organize a disaster response team. My encounters with survivors took place in shattered neighborhoods and primitive shelters instead of an office. Without appointments, I had to intervene on the fly. Without diplomas on the walls, I had to rely on my actions to demonstrate how I could be of help in this ground-zero environment.

I also learned a fundamental lesson: When I reached out to survivors, I discovered that virtually everyone welcomed me into their homes and temporary shelters. As my hosts, they often offered me coffee, invited me to sit on one of their salvaged chairs, showed me photographs of their disaster experiences, and most importantly, shared their survival stories. I was on their turf—not in my safe and secure office—and I learned that my initial intervention was to be a grateful guest who accepted their hospitality and bore witness to their resilience.

Although I am now a full-time professor of counselor education, I continue to be involved in crises, traumas, and disasters as a volunteer, trainer, and consultant. The work has been gut-wrenching, painful, and even heartbreaking at times, but I also have never found as much professional fulfillment and personal inspiration as I have in my encounters with fellow human beings whose courage, compassion, and hope continue to amaze me.

That lesson also has continued to serve me well in my more traditional counseling work. I became more comfortable with encountering my clients, not as the expert on their lived experience but as a guest who was being invited into their inner worlds. I found myself thanking my clients for their gracious and welcoming hospitality as they allowed me into their lives.

In an emergency, something new emerges. When I responded to the distress calls of a disaster, I discovered my own professional calling.

Although the appearance of your usual counseling and therapy practice may contrast dramatically with those you face in crises and disasters, there is one common element connecting these situations—you. In every encounter, whether taking place in your familiar office or a debris field, your most important and reliable therapeutic tool is *you* (Echterling & Stewart, 2014). So before you explore deployment possibilities as a member of a disaster response team, you must carefully reflect on your readiness to embark on such a challenging mission at this time. You must be emotionally prepared for the discomfort, ambiguity, distractions, and confusion of disaster intervention work. In addition, you may find yourself immersed in a different country in which not only the climate but also the dominant culture is radically unlike your own. It can be disorienting to be a stranger in a strange land, particularly in the wake of a disaster. Taking time to learn from survivors about their hopes, dreams, needs, and values is essential for the success of your disaster intervention efforts.

If you decide that you are adequately trained and emotionally prepared to work under the ground-zero conditions of a disaster, then you must deploy under the auspices of an appropriate sponsoring organization. Lone wolves who self-deploy and appear unannounced at a disaster scene to volunteer their services often do more harm than good. They undermine the coordinated efforts of disaster response teams. So, long before disaster strikes, participate in the training to qualify as a mental health disaster responder. Collaborating with a team enables you to make an enormous contribution to the resilience of survivors who have endured catastrophic events.

Providing Psychological First Aid

One important volunteer service that you can provide in the wake of a disaster is to offer *psychological first aid* (National Child Traumatic Stress Network, 2013). Once you have been trained in this evidence-informed intervention, you can be a vital resource to disaster survivors. The principles of psychological first aid are similar to those of medical first aid; the intervention is not treatment, and it does not require a licensed practitioner to provide it. Therefore, any concerned person can qualify for the training. You may find this training to be a great complement to your advanced course work in crisis and disaster intervention. The essential techniques of psychological first aid involve comforting survivors by meeting their basic needs, reaching out to them with a sense of compassion, offering social support, and creating a nurturing environment. At this early point in the recovery process, you are primarily concerned with ensuring the safety and security of the survivors, providing physical and emotional comfort, offering a calm and caring presence, engaging in reassuring conversation, and limiting their exposure to distressing stimuli. These interventions are crucial in creating a foundation for resilience in the chaotic aftermath of a disaster.

Mindfully Caring for Yourself

As we discussed in earlier chapters, your self-care is central to your success as a student and professional. However, one of the greatest challenges you face in performing any form of crisis intervention, trauma counseling, and disaster work ironically involves your greatest strength—your deep empathy with survivors. Your empathy provides a necessary spark for any healing, but it also can precipitate, by emotional contagion, a free fall into your own raw, unsettling emotional turmoil. Having an experienced and supportive supervisor is valuable anytime in your training and career, but it is absolutely essential when you are providing crisis services (Dupre, Echterling, Meixner, Anderson, & Kielty, 2014). Moreover, it is certainly possible that you will also face a personal or family crisis at some point during your training. You may be learning to help others, but how mindful are you that you must provide for yourself the same nurturance that you wish for other survivors?

Your commitment to mindful self-care is vital because you are subject to the same barrage of life's tragedies as everyone else. Moreover, compared to other professionals, you have a unique challenge because you function as the very instrument through which you perform your work. An accountant or mechanic may continue to be more or less effective in spite of what is going on in his or her personal life. On the other hand, your inner world of thoughts, emotions, and interpersonal sensitivity are the very tools you must use in counseling and therapy. Learning to stay balanced and well is absolutely essential for your success in graduate school and throughout your career.

When you are working with people in crisis, you build up a kind of psychic charge from being so deeply involved in their emotional turmoil. If you are not mindfully caring for yourself, you wind up discharging this buildup in some unexpected way—and then wondering why you are yelling at the dog. And when your personal life is in turmoil, you are in danger of importing your unmet emotional needs into your formal counseling and therapy work with your clients. This countertransference can hinder your client's ability to use you as a resource for achieving therapeutic growth. More insidiously, your clients, who can be keenly attuned to your emotional moods, might reenact old, self-sabotaging interpersonal dynamics by prioritizing the needs they perceive in you over their own.

When You Suffer a Loss

You need to learn to live alongside loss because it is an inherent part of a rich, loving, and fully engaged life. In your crisis intervention and disaster work, you will be dealing with survivors who have suffered enormous losses. Some losses, such as the death of a loved one in war or the destruction of a house in a disaster, are obvious, while others, such as the loss of a sense of safety or the loss of meaning in life, are not as immediately apparent. Nevertheless, in addition to reeling from the shock of their traumas, all survivors are also grieving for their losses. In order for you to be able to bear witness to their grief, you must have accepted, honored, given voice to, and ultimately incorporated your own profound losses into the person you are today. Ultimately, we are all survivors who have suffered losses.

When grief and loss come to your own life, it challenges you to seek a heightened level of awareness and achieve a deeper sense of self-acceptance. The process may take up more space in your thoughts and feelings than you would like, especially because you may imagine that you always have to "keep it together" and be a model of perfect mental health. The paradox is that by failing to fully honor a personal loss, your grief may not move and transform, and transformation from a loss of something "outer" to something that you are able to hold within is essential for your own well-being.

Our discussion of your own grief relates to the concept of the wounded healer that we described in Chapter 7. As we emphasized back then, the suffering that you have endured in your life can contribute to your overall effectiveness as a counselor. It may surprise you to know that nearly three out of four practitioners have reported that they have cried in their role as therapists (Blume-Marcovici, Stolberg, & Khademi, 2013). In fact, experienced clinicians acknowledged crying more in therapy than novice therapists, suggesting that they were more comfortable with these emotions in the therapeutic relationship. The crying often seemed to be the catalyst for positive therapeutic change. The point here is that honoring your own grief provides an empathic bridge with your client.

However, when you carry unresolved grief from old losses or when you are still in deep mourning for a recent loss, you may be unable to provide an adequate holding environment for your client's emotions. Perhaps you are not fully present with your client in the here and now because you are distracted by upwelling emotions that are completely unrelated to the counseling process. At that point, it is a disservice to your client to try to tough it out, and you've got to do something to attend to yourself.

We recognize that it is sometimes tough to go through life always cultivating your self-reflective awareness. Radio personality and author

Garrison Keillor once remarked, "Sometimes you just have to stand up to reality and deny it." However, as appealing as this advice sometimes sounds, this is not really an option for someone who has committed to the counseling profession. If you are coping well with your grief, it is perhaps because you have realized at some level that each developmental stage, every experience of personal growth, and every transformation involves a kind of death to your old self. Life is ever changing, and with that constant change comes the necessity of mourning the passing of the old, even while we may be celebrating the new. If we frantically try to keep our old selves immortal in a misguided attempt to avoid grief, we sacrifice our potential for joy.

In an effort to create rapport with your client who is experiencing a profound loss, it is tempting to reference your own losses and grief experiences, especially if yours are similar to those of your client. You may want to communicate to the client, "You can get through this as I have," or "I have been there so you can relate to me." The danger is that this sharing takes up emotional space that rightly belongs to your client. The client is temporarily obligated to understand your profound experience of loss. Your client may begin to wonder if his or her own expression of loss might distress you. In the worst-case scenario, your client may find that his or her loss cannot compete with yours or feels an overpowering need to make you feel better.

You do use your past experiences to help your clients get through their grief but not ordinarily by relating to the client the specific incidences or *content* of your experiences. Rather, your experiences of loss can enrich the *process* of the counseling and deepen your therapeutic alliance.

When you have experienced a great loss, you may recall how you, at least for a while, turned your attention away from trivialities and focused your awareness entirely on what was truly profound and important in life. If the loss was especially tragic, as the death of a loved one by accident or suicide, then the initial impact was shattering. You may have felt possessed by the heartbreaking tragedy and consumed by the unrelenting anguish. However, the experience may have eventually awakened you to the enhanced and deeper awareness that characterizes posttraumatic growth (Calhoun & Tedeschi, 2006); then you became more fully present to your life and its purpose, even though—or perhaps because—you could see how fragile it is. The loss may have spurred you to connect more deeply and authentically with others. Or perhaps you experienced what Buddhists refer to as *impermanence,* inviting you to enter the flow of your existence by letting go. This is the process of saying, "Yes!" to life, open armed, even in the face of great pain or loss. This is what crisis survivors and counseling clients are struggling to regain, and if you have fully embraced life with all its joys and sorrows, then you can help others to do it as well.

Summary

We end this chapter by reminding you once again of our guarantee: In your work as a counselor or therapist, you *will regularly* encounter people in emergency situations. This chapter has provided a brief overview and quick introduction to some of the knowledge and skills you will need to be effective in intervening in a crisis, preventing suicide, and responding to a disaster. Throughout your graduate education, you will cover this material in much greater depth in your courses, practicum, and internship. Just keep in mind that your training will necessarily be intense and emotionally demanding. Take to heart our suggestions for managing your own emotional turmoil at these times. These high-stakes situations present a risk for burning out if you are not taking care of yourself. Remember that the profession needs you for the long haul!

Resources

American Foundation for Suicide Prevention

www.afsp.org

This site provides up-to-date information about prevention programs and research projects. It includes a directory of support groups throughout the United States and Canada.

Federal Emergency Management Agency (FEMA)

www.fema.gov

The FEMA website contains training materials and modules for emergency personnel, teachers, clergy, and parents. See also FEMA for Kids at *www.fema.gov/kids*. This is an engaging and interactive site for children to learn about disaster preparedness and response through stories, games, and activities.

National Child Traumatic Stress Network

www.nctsnet.org/nccts

The mission of the National Child Traumatic Stress Network is to raise the standard of care and improve access to services for traumatized children and their families and communities throughout the United States. The website offers a wide variety of resources for caregivers, teachers, and mental health providers, such as *Psychological First Aid* and the recently developed *Skills for Psychological Recovery,* an evidence-informed, skills-building intervention for survivors and responders.

References

Berscheid, E. (2003). The human's greatest strength: Other humans. In L. G. Aspinwall & U. M. Staudinger (Eds.), *A psychology of human strengths: Fundamental questions and future directions for a positive psychology* (pp. 37–47). Washington, DC: American Psychological Association.

Blume-Marcovici, A. C., Stolberg, R. A., & Khademi, M. (2013). Do therapists cry in therapy? The role of experience and other factors in therapists' tears. *Psychotherapy, 50,* 224–234. doi:10.1037/a0031384

Calhoun, L. G., & Tedeschi, R. G. (Eds.). (2006). *Handbook for posttraumatic growth research and practice.* Mahwah, NJ: Erlbaum.

Cohrs, J. C., Christie, D. J., White, M. P., & Das, C. (2013). Contributions of positive psychology: Toward global well-being and resilience. *American Psychologist, 68,* 590–600. doi:10.1037/a0032089

Conner, K. R., Huguet, N., Caetano, R., Giesbrecht, N., McFarland, B. H., Nolte, K. B., & Kaplan, M. S. (2014). Acute use of alcohol and methods of suicide in a U.S. national sample. *American Journal of Public Health, 104,* 171–178. doi:10.2105/AJPH.2013.301352

DeJong, P., & Berg, I. K. (2002). *Interviewing for solutions* (2nd ed.). Pacific Grove, CA: Brooks/Cole.

Dupre, M., Echterling, L. G., Meixner, C., Anderson, R., & Kielty, M. (2014). Supervision experiences of professional counselors providing crisis counseling. *Counselor Education and Supervision, 53,* 82–96. doi:10.1002/j.1556–6978.2014.00050.x

Echterling, L. G., Presbury, J., & McKee, J. E. (2005). *Crisis intervention: Promoting resilience and resolution in troubled times.* Upper Saddle River, NJ: Merrill/Prentice Hall.

Echterling, L. G., & Stewart, A. L. (2008). Resilience. In S. F. Davis & W. Buskist (Eds.), *Twenty-first century psychology: A reference handbook* (Vol. 2, pp. 192–201). Thousand Oaks, CA: Sage.

Echterling, L. G., & Stewart, A. L. (2014). Creative crisis intervention techniques with children and families. In C. Malchiodi (Ed.), *Creative interventions with traumatized children* (2nd ed.). New York, NY: Guilford.

Edwards, S. J., & Sachmann, M. D. (2010). No-suicide contracts, no-suicide agreements, and no-suicide assurances: A study of their nature, utilization, perceived effectiveness, and potential to cause harm. *Crisis, 31*, 290–302.

Egan, G. (2010). *The skilled helper: A problem-management and opportunity-development approach to helping* (9th ed.). Belmont, CA: Brooks/Cole.

Federal Emergency Management Agency. (2012). Helping kids cope with disaster. Retrieved from http://www.fema.gov/coping-disaster#4

Flemons, D., & Gralnik, L. M. (2013). *Relational suicide assessment: Risks, resources, and possibilities for safety.* New York, NY: Norton.

Gaskill, R. L., & Perry, B. D. (2012). Child sexual abuse, traumatic experiences, and their impact on the developing brain. In P. Goodyear-Brown (Ed.), *Handbook of child sexual abuse: Identification, assessment, and treatment* (pp. 29–47). Hoboken, NJ: Wiley.

Gulliver, S. B, Zimering, R., Carpenter, G. S., Giardina, A., & Farrar, J. (2014). The psychological consequences of disaster. In P. Ouimette & J. P. Read (Eds.), *Trauma and substance abuse: Causes, consequences, and treatment of comorbid disorders* (2nd ed., pp. 125–141). Washington, DC: American Psychological Association.

Joiner, T. E. (2009). *Why people die by suicide.* Cambridge, MA: Harvard University Press.

Jordan, B., Perryman, K., & Anderson, L. (2013). A case for child-centered play therapy with natural disaster and catastrophic event survivors. *International Journal of Play Therapy, 22*, 219–230. doi:10.1037/a0034637

Larsen, J. T., Hemenover, S. H., Norris, C. J., & Cacioppo, J. T. (2003). Turning adversity to advantage: On the virtues of the coactivation of positive and negative emotions. In L. G. Aspinwall & U. M. Staudinger (Eds.), *A psychology of human strengths: Fundamental questions and future directions for a positive psychology* (pp. 211–225). Washington, DC: American Psychological Association.

Masten, A. S., & Reed, M. J. (2002). Resilience in development. In C. R. Snyder & S. J. Lopez (Eds.), *Handbook of positive psychology* (pp. 74–88). New York, NY: Oxford University Press.

McMyler, C., & Pryjmachuk, S. (2008). Do "no-suicide" contracts work? *Journal of Psychiatric and Mental Health Nursing, 15*, 512–522.

Miller, G. (2012). *Fundamentals of crisis counseling.* Hoboken, NJ: Wiley.

Milo, E. M. (2001). The death of a child with a developmental disability. In R. A. Neimeyer (Ed.), *Meaning reconstruction and the experience of loss* (pp. 113–134). Washington, DC: American Psychological Association.

Minton, C. A. B., & Pease-Carter, C. (2011). The status of crisis preparation in counselor education: A national study and content analysis. *Journal of Professional Counseling: Practice, Theory, and Research, 38*(2), 5–17.

Morris, C. A. W., & Minton, C. A. B. (2012). Crisis in the curriculum? New counselors' crisis preparation, experiences, and self-efficacy. *Counselor Education and Supervision, 51*, 256–269. doi:10.1002/j.1556–6978.2012.00019.x

National Child Traumatic Stress Network. (2013). *Psychological first aid: Field operations guide* (2nd ed.). Retrieved from http://www.nctsn.org/content/psychological-first-aid

Neimeyer, R. A. (2000). Searching for the meaning of meaning: Grief therapy and the process of reconstruction. *Death Studies, 24,* 541–558.

Paulson, B. L., & Worth, M. (2002). Counseling for suicide: Client perspectives. *Journal of Counseling and Development, 80,* 86–93.

Prince-Embury, S., & Saklofske, D. H. (Eds.). (2013). *Resilience in children, adolescents, and adults: Translating research into practice.* New York, NY: Springer. doi:10.1007/978-1-4614-4939-3

Puskar, K., & Urda, B. (2011). Examining the efficacy of no-suicide contracts in inpatient psychiatric settings: Implications for psychiatric nursing. *Issues in Mental Health Nursing, 32,* 785–788. doi:10.3109/01612840.2011.599476

Ronan, K. R., & Johnston, D. M. (2005). *Promoting community resilience in disasters: The role for schools, youth, and families.* New York, NY: Springer.

Silver, R. C., & Updegraff, J. A. (2013). Searching for and finding meaning following personal and collective traumas. In K. D. Markman, T. Proulx, & M. J. Lindberg (Eds.), *The psychology of meaning* (pp. 237–255). Washington, DC: American Psychological Association.

Smith, T., Domenech Rodriguez, M., & Bernal, G. (2011). Culture. In J. C. Norcross (Ed.), *Psychotherapy relationships that work: Evidence-based responsiveness* (pp. 316–335). New York, NY: Oxford University Press.

Solnit, R. (2013). *The faraway nearby.* New York, NY: Viking.

Steele, W., & Malchiodi, C. (Eds.). (2012). *Trauma-informed practices with children and adolescents.* New York, NY: Routledge.

10

Thriving in Your Practicum and Internship

Until you are willing to be confused about what you already know, what you know will never grow bigger, better, or more useful.

—Milton Erickson

As any traveler knows, preparing for a trip and actually taking it are two very different experiences. Your course work in counseling and therapy has prepared you well, and now you have the opportunity to put your skills into action with real clients. Your practicum and internship represent the next step of your journey to become a full-fledged helping professional.

As you embark on these experiences, you may want to look into your training backpack again—just to double check that you have all you need. At first, you may not see anything that appears useful. You may have overpacked with a lot of "just in case" items that now do not seem very helpful. Or you may feel as though you have left behind some important utensils and valuable supplies. In either case, you will want to take time to reflect on your preparedness, review the knowledge and skills you bring to this experience, and take stock of your readiness. You likely have more resources at your disposal than you realize.

When you are poised to begin counseling with actual clients, the responsibilities and complexities of clinical practice can seem overwhelming (Chin & Lewis, 2012). In this chapter, we offer practical information and concrete suggestions for completing a practicum or internship. We also invite you to thrive in these settings by creating a secure base from which to venture out, take risks, and grow.

You Are Ready, Although You May Have Doubts

> We are the hurdles we leap.
>
> —Michael McClure

During your practicum, you will face predicaments that challenge your sense of readiness. These dilemmas will continue to confront you later in your internship. In fact, most counselors who have been practicing for years will share that they still continue to face surprising situations. Facing these challenges is the point. Training experiences are demanding because you must be prepared to enter the challenging profession of counseling and therapy. Of course, there are other purposes to your practicum and internship. At these training sites, you will have plenty of opportunities to try out intervention approaches to see what fits your personal style and professional aspirations. A student recently shared that a dear mentor of hers told her, "Practicum is the absolute perfect opportunity to try all the things you'd like to try! And your supervisor will help you figure out what works best for you and your client."

While experimenting with different perspectives and techniques, however, you may be faced with issues of fitting in as a professional. And even though it is likely that you will be successful, you may sometimes feel as though you are playing a part or acting rather than actually being yourself. Remember reading about the impostor phenomenon in Chapter 2? We mentioned it then because it is especially common when students begin a training program. However, when you enter practicum, this phenomenon can reemerge with a vengeance. Now that you are working with real clients, you may agonize once again that you do not know everything that you need to know. You may fear that finally someone is going to find out and expose you for being, in this case, not a real counselor. Sound familiar?

Along the way, it's also likely that you will encounter people—besides yourself, of course!—who will question your abilities and decisions. For example, if you are a practicum student in school counseling, a parent may confront you with questions such as, "What do you know about children?"

and "Are you a parent?" If you are a young intern, some client will be sure to ask, "How old are you?" If you are an intern at a substance abuse treatment center, clients may want to know if you're in recovery. While no one looks forward to being questioned and confronted, you can quickly realize how exciting it can be to be able to think on your feet and make some discoveries about yourself in the process.

You may be assuming that because you are dealing with real world clients you should possess more skills and knowledge than you do. Give yourself a break! You have not been at this for a very long time. You are, after all, here to learn.

Someone has said that counselors and therapists—no matter how many years of experience they may have—are always feeling some guilt that they are not good enough. This adage is even true for your professors and supervisors. We must be willing to work constantly at improving ourselves and yet also to forgive ourselves for not being further along than we are. Keep your expectations of yourself reasonable, and when someone implies that you should be older, wiser, or more skilled, don't feel as if you have been "found out."

How Old Are You?

Jerra's Story

The first client I ever saw during my master's program was a woman in her mid-30s. I can still remember how nervous and excited I was to be actually working with a real live client! Although I felt relatively prepared for this first encounter, her first question for me threw me for a loop. After reciting my well-rehearsed informed consent speech, I asked her if she had any questions before we started. Without hesitation, she asked, "How old are you?"

It was a simple question. It had a simple answer if I were anywhere but in my first counseling session with my first, real live client. I was flustered. I felt as though she saw right through me and wanted to expose my lack of experience. I tried to gain my composure and decided to fall back on the classic evasive maneuver that counselors resort to in a pinch.

I asked, "I find it interesting that you want to know how old I am. How is that important to you?" I hoped that would suffice! Surely this redirection would prove my professional competence. I was wrong. She was neither impressed nor satisfied with the reply and responded, "You just look so young!"

(Continued)

> (Continued)
>
> I somehow managed not to answer the question and steered her off the topic. Much to my surprise, the following week's session started off in an equally unsettling way. Though I hoped that she didn't have any more "bombs" to throw at me, when I asked her where she would like to begin, she said, "Since you never answered my question last week, I'll ask it again. How old are you?"
>
> Off balance, without another counseling cliché, I meekly confessed, "Twenty-two." I felt like I was raising a white flag in defeat.
>
> After a pregnant pause—which I'm sure was not as long as I felt—she replied with an offhanded, "Oh." She did not get up and leave. She did not laugh. She did not have a look of horror on her face. All along, I feared that she needed qualities that I did not possess. Much to my surprise, all she really wanted was honesty.

How would you have responded to the question posed by Jerra's client? Did you find yourself immediately wanting to answer the question, or were you inclined to wonder about her motivations? As Jerra's example shows, there is no "perfect" way to handle complicated questions posed by clients. Sometimes, the best way forward is to trust your instincts while remaining open to the possibility that you may be wrong. Like Jerra, you will find yourself making valuable discoveries about clients, the helping process, and yourself. You will be developing a conceptual framework that makes sense to you, works for you in helping relationships, and allows you to be natural. Your practicum and internship experiences are special times in your training when you can consolidate everything you learned in your classes—and everything you've learned about your own personhood. A theory is only as good as the person practicing it. Explore how you can bring your theory alive by making it your own.

Preparing for Practicum: Who Are You?

This is your first step toward developing your identity as a professional. Give some thought to your previous work experiences and the expectations within those environments. This is a time when many students begin thinking about how to look the part. Engaging in discussions with your professors, adviser, or site supervisor on how to best present yourself through dress, timeliness, comfort, and relationship building are helpful prepracticum discussions.

Another emerging and important aspect of exploring your identity as a professional is taking a close look at your virtual presence. More and more professional organizations, such as the American Counseling Association, are factoring the role of social media into their professional guidelines and ethical codes. Some suggest that students begin by doing a Google search for themselves. What do you find? Potential employers may be looking at your virtual presence, so be sure you do, too.

Boudoir

Gabrielle's Story

A mature and gifted counseling student was in the process of securing a site for her practicum. Her interview at a local middle school seemed to go really well, and she felt a solid and personable connection with her potential supervisor. She was shocked to later receive an e-mail stating that they had opted to pass on offering her an invitation to complete her practicum at their school.

The site supervisor later called her and said they had concerns that students or parents might look her up online and discover her prior affiliation with an erotic photography business. What??? The student was horrified. When she Googled herself later that day, she realized that a small photography business that she had for several years did, in fact, appear in her search. Even though it was not in any way "erotic" photography, one of the paragraphs used the term "boudoir style" photographs. She realized it was time to talk to her adviser about the role of her virtual presence.

In addition to searching yourself, visit your security settings on your social media sites. For example, sites such as Facebook allow users to limit who can see their profile and what is available to the general public if they were to search for you. Make sure that the image you are putting forth is congruent with the professional identity you would like your site and your clients to see. People will, out of simple curiosity and even an effort to know you better, peek at your social media presence. Be mindful of what is available and consider it an extension of who you are.

Your Practicum

> The great end of life is not knowledge but action.
>
> —T. H. Huxley

The practicum is your first hands-on learning opportunity to work with actual clients. The services you may be providing include assessing, individual and group counseling, crisis intervening, consulting, educating, and promoting growth. Although the number of hours required for practicum varies across training programs, you will be expected to provide counseling and therapy services to both individuals and groups.

Your practicum is the first bridge for connecting the knowledge you've acquired in courses to the practical realities of working with clients. At times, this bridge may seem long, high, and precarious. To cross, you might avoid looking down, take a deep breath, and keep your eyes fixed straight ahead. You may even occasionally fear that if you venture a look to the left or to the right you'll feel dizzy or off balance. In other words, you may fear trying new things or making mistakes. At these times, you can remind yourself that you're not alone. You have an instructor, supervisor, colleagues, and staff to guide, support, and help you along. Just remember, not only does this bridge help you reach your destination it also provides a terrific view!

There are a couple of points you need to keep in mind as you begin your practicum. First, most sites have the dual mission of serving clients and providing a training ground for those entering the helping professions. Therefore, you may need to make significant accommodations, especially in the early phases, as you become oriented to the schedule and demands of the site. Clients, for example, may need to be seen at times that do not fit conveniently into your lifestyle. In these circumstances, it is best to remain flexible. Part of meeting clients where they are involves meeting them at the times that work for them.

It is also important to try and fit into the practicum site culture. As a representative of your program, you will want to present yourself in a professionally appropriate manner. For instance, in your classes, you may have found that students, as well as faculty members, dress very casually. Your practicum site, on the other hand, is a different culture. You'll want to fit in and meet the site's expectations of how a professional should look and act. It's not that difficult to figure out. Ask questions, observe, and don't forget the old saying, "When in Rome, do as the Romans do."

Patience

Your practicum will challenge you in unexpected ways. At times, you may feel aggravated, insecure, and uncertain. Occasionally, you will have the thought that you have no idea what you are doing. It is important to remember that you are just starting out and that having patience with yourself is just as important as having patience for your clients. Entering the subjective world of your clients and participating with them at this deep level of engagement will expose you to troubling events and disturbing circumstances. You may find it painful to deal with clients who are impoverished, drug addicted, or sexually abused. These encounters will provoke you emotionally and perhaps even disorient you at times. You will inevitably run into clients who are struggling with issues that are intensely personal to you or as they say, hit a little too close to home. It will happen, so realize that is a normal experience and that your supervisor is there to help you work through it and serve your client.

Clients are not the only ones who will be stirring up your emotions. The staff members at this site may intimidate you because they seem so competent and knowledgeable. You may doubt that you'll ever reach their level of professionalism. You may even begin to compare your own skills to those of your fellow practicum students. Even if you did not feel competitive in the classroom, it can be easy to wonder if you are measuring up to others. Insecurity is probably the rule rather than the exception, but your supervisors are there to help support you through this process. Every clinician was a beginner at some point, so as much as you can, embrace your own experience and be willing to ask for help when you need it.

Practicum students might struggle to make sense of the practical realities of working in an agency or a clinic. At times, the staff may also appear to you as less than caring in how they deal with clients. And no matter how supportive your supervisor may be, your sessions with this person will bring up issues that will be challenging and perturbing. Many of these encounters with clients, colleagues, and supervisors have the potential to leave you reeling and confused.

At some time during your practicum or internship, you may even wonder if you're cut out to do this line of work. When you have these doubts, use your journal to explore your concerns and take time to reflect on their meaning. Talk to your supervisor and friends. The trick is not to ignore your doubts but to use them to seek deeper answers. After all, you will face a "crisis of faith" regularly throughout your career. You'll be surprised how you can emerge from such an experience as a stronger and more resilient counseling professional.

Taking Pictures Along the Way

Many programs use video recordings of your counseling and therapy sessions to help you refine your skills. If you are like most people, you may feel self-conscious and embarrassed reviewing your video recordings when you are by yourself. However, watching these sessions with your supervisor, professor, or fellow students can produce real terror! Of course, you're not alone in feeling this way. Over time, you will discover how valuable it can be to revisit your sessions both by yourself and with others.

Your recordings are wonderful resources for exploring, discovering, and refining your skills. Since practicum is so busy and hectic, you may be tempted to move along to the next session before mining a recording for all its treasures. Baird (2014) recommends that you return to your recordings several times to view them from different perspectives. Each time you review the session, you can notice elements that were not apparent to you while you were participating in it. You can focus on the subtle nuances of phrases, emotional shadings, and minute gestures that offer a more textured and vivid understanding of the dynamics and themes of your therapeutic relationship. With each encounter, ask yourself, "What do I experience now as I focus on this element of the interaction?" Also ask yourself, "If I could do this session over again, what would I do differently?" This question will help you think about how to conduct the next session with your client and increase your general knowledge of how to make all future counseling sessions more productive.

Involving yourself fully in the process can help you get the most from your experience. Remember, you are not in this alone. If you have peers who are also at your practicum site, ask them to view tapes with you. Even if your supervisor does not specifically ask to see your tapes, have tape segments selected for supervision. Be sure to choose not only those sessions you consider to be good but also those that present questions and concerns for you. There is no shame in not being perfect. It's all part of the process, so just embrace the full range of your work.

Internship

> First to know, then to act, then to really know.
>
> —Bishr al Hafifi

As we described in Chapter 2, during the final stage of your academic training, you participate in an internship that serves as a capstone of your training. It is during this time that you undergo a major transformation. Your internship experience involves a change in your self-concept: You enter as a trainee and you leave as an emerging professional.

One of our counseling colleagues, John, remembers a moment during his internship when his concept of self was suddenly reframed. After a particularly stressful day in the clinic where he was doing his internship, John went to a local restaurant for dinner. He struck up a conversation with a server who asked him, "What do you do?"

Without thinking, John replied, "I'm a counselor." Immediately, he felt a rush of pride and thought to himself, "I really *am* a counselor!"

John recalled how wonderful it was to consider himself in this new way—as a counselor. Almost imperceptibly, he had metamorphosed into a new person! As a result of your internship experience, you also will find yourself developing a new identity. You really will be a helping professional!

Choosing a Site

Internship sites include community mental health centers; counseling agencies; programs for survivors of sexual assault; university student counseling centers; and elementary, middle, and high schools. The counseling services you may be offering within these settings include assessment, individual counseling, group counseling, family or couple counseling, emergency or crisis services, outreach services, consultation and education programs, prevention programs, and health promotion activities.

Training programs use a variety of methods for making decisions regarding internship placements. In your program, you may be responsible for contacting sites and obtaining a possible placement. In other cases, faculty members take responsibility for placing you while considering your interests, goals, and skills. In most situations, you have input into the placement decision.

When you explore your internship site options, you'll want to consider the services offered at the site, client population, reputation, location, and most importantly, the quality of supervision offered. According to Kiser (2011), the heart of your internship is the supervision you receive. Ask yourself this fundamental question about a possible supervisor: "Is this someone I think I can work with and who would be interested in helping me learn?" (p. 5). Since selecting a field placement is to be one of the more important training choices you must make, it is important not to take the decision lightly.

> **EXERCISE 10.1 Refreshing Your Memory and Plotting Your Course**
>
> *A Decision-Making Exercise*
>
> Gather all the handouts, textbooks, notes, counseling video recordings, journals, and papers you have written for all the classes you have taken so far. Mariners have navigated their courses by the stars since ancient times, so as you revisit each class, put a star by an activity you really liked, a written passage you found particularly meaningful or a microcounseling segment in which you excelled. Be careful not to let any preconceived notions get in your way. Pretend you are lost and are searching for directions. Even if you think you have a pretty good idea of where you are headed, completing the activity will be a good test of your reckoning.
>
> Now go back through everything; see how your stars line up and converge on one or two clusters of common themes. You can use these clusters to chart your internship course.

Writing an Internship Agreement

Once you have located an internship site and have spoken with a helping professional who has agreed to be your supervisor, you are now ready to formalize your relationship. Your training program develops an agreement about what the internship will include. Two types of agreements should be created before you begin an internship. First, there should be a written agreement between your academic institution and the internship site. Next, together with your instructor and supervisor, you should formulate an agreement that describes the specific details of your individual internship experience. These are important documents as they clarify the roles and expectations of all the parties involved. Occasionally, students may encounter a site supervisor who is too busy for the agreed-upon frequency of supervision, or a site may have a student who is having difficulty arriving in a timely manner and completing their requirements. While we certainly hope these are the exception, the internship agreement helps all parties involved attend to the situation and work things out in a manner best for everyone. Establishing such agreements in writing at the outset will help avoid any misunderstanding or confusion about what the internship site and supervisor expect of you and what you expect of them.

Professional Liability Insurance

Being a student does not exempt you from being sued. You need protection from the financial devastation that you would face in a lawsuit. Even if your program does not require it, we strongly advise you to obtain your own professional liability insurance. Both the American Psychological Association and the American Counseling Association have professional liability insurance programs for graduate students. You will need to be a student member of the organization, but the application process is simple, and the insurance rates are economical. In this chapter's Resources section, you will find information on how to contact these insurance trusts. Remember, while you are gaining valuable experience in practicum and supervision, your university, your faculty supervisor, and your site supervisor are also agreeing to be responsible for the work you do. Given the multiple layers of responsibility, professional liability insurance is a must to protect you, your clients, and everyone who is making it possible for you to have this experience.

Competence

The first and most important principle of most ethics codes is to operate within one's level of competence. Pope and Brown (1996) pointed out that the work you will be doing requires both *intellectual* and *emotional* competence. You may remember our mentioning that you think with both your head and your heart. Intellectual competence refers to knowledge and skill, but emotional competence refers to your ability to manage the emotional challenges of working with clients.

No counselor is competent to work with every client or issue. You may find that there are certain clients who push your buttons or overwhelm you. Don't try to fake it. Consult your supervisor and talk about these feelings. You will not be expected to work effectively with everyone. Furthermore, burnout, stress, family problems, and personal issues can impair your performance, regardless of your intellectual or technical skill. You can't take care of your clients unless you can take care of yourself.

Questions of competence always arise. For example, how can a person develop competence without experience? How do you know when it is okay to work with a client in order to gain experience and develop competence or when it is best to refer that client to someone else? Don't worry. Your supervisors understand this dilemma and will work closely with you to determine what is best for you and for the client. Just be sure that you are open with your supervisors and honest with yourself.

Informed Consent

Another important ethical principle is informed consent. Clients have a right to be informed about the treatment, assessment, or other services they will receive before they agree to participate in those activities. In order to ensure informed consent, you must give certain information in a manner and language that clients can understand. At a minimum, inform your clients about each of the following subjects (Baird, 2014):

- *Qualifications.* Clients should know that you are an intern and will be supervised. You should also explain your educational and training background.
- *Supervision.* Clients should have the name and qualifications of your supervisor, have an opportunity to meet with your supervisor if they desire to do so, and know how they can contact your supervisor if they have any questions or concerns in the future. Your clients should understand the nature of your supervision, including the frequency of supervision and the activities it will entail (e.g., reviewing case notes, listening to tapes of sessions).
- *Services.* Your clients should be apprised of the nature of the counseling or assessment to be provided, including a brief description of the approach to treatment or the purpose of an assessment and the instruments that will be used. The frequency and duration of treatment sessions, as well as a reasonable estimate of the typical number of sessions involved to treat a given concern, should also be discussed.
- *Client Responsibilities.* The client is expected to attend scheduled appointments, notify you in advance to cancel or change an appointment, and follow through with any therapeutic assignments.
- *Fees.* Information should include the costs for services and whether or not there are charges for missed sessions. You client should understand how and when payments are to be made, as well as the procedures that will be followed if payment is not made. Your discussion should also cover how insurance provider contacts will be managed and how this relationship impacts confidentiality. If a client's insurance policy limits the number of sessions the insurance company will pay for, an agreement must be reached about how to proceed if more sessions are needed and the client is unable to pay without the assistance of the insurance.
- *Confidentiality.* The nature and limitations of confidentiality, including what is said in treatment, as well as what is contained in the client's records, should be included.

- *Questions.* You should encourage your client to ask questions at any time.

Confidentiality

The essence of confidentiality is the principle that clients have the right to determine who will have access to information about them and their treatment. In clinical settings, clients need to feel that the information they share will stay with you and not be released without their permission. Without this assurance, your clients are less likely to explore and express their thoughts and feelings freely. This is likely to restrain the client's willingness to share certain information and may distort the treatment process (Nowell & Spruill, 1993). It is important to keep in mind that there are five instances in which absolute confidentiality does not hold and in which information must be shared. These exceptions include dangerousness to self, intent to harm others, legal proceedings, court orders, and insurance company inquiries. Be sure to let your clients know the limits of confidentiality before they share personal information with you.

Putting It All Together

Most agencies and schools probably have photocopies of an informed consent document that they give to their clients as soon as they walk in the door. Clients are supposed to read, sign, and date the document as if they have completely understood everything they just read. Right!

When most of us are given a legal document that begins, "Whereas the party of the first part, heretofore known as the ...," our eyes glaze over as we search the page for some clue as to the meaning of what we are about to sign. Nevertheless, before they can enter into a therapeutic relationship, clients have to understand their rights and responsibilities. In most cases, the job of informing a client falls to the counselor.

Before every flight, all airplane pilots are required to perform a preflight check. A detailed list of "must do" procedures is performed and checked off before the aircraft ever enters the runway. Just like a pilot, you need to be sure that your client understands the essentials before the session ever begins. Let's tune in as Eduardo, a counseling intern, is beginning the first session with his client.

(Continued)

(Continued)

Counselor: "Before we get started, there are a few things I'd like to discuss with you. You've probably heard the term 'informed consent' before, right?"

Client: "Yes, I think so"

Counselor: "You have heard of it, good. As you know, 'informed consent' means you have a right to know everything about the services you will receive here at the counseling center. We go through this procedure with everyone who comes to the center. It is the policy of the counseling center and our ethical responsibility as service providers. Speaking of responsibilities, you and I also have responsibilities in our work together. I'll go over mine first, then yours, and then we can discuss anything you may have questions about. How does that sound?"

Client: "All right, I guess."

Counselor: "There are quite a few things we have to cover, so I'll be using this checklist to make sure I don't leave anything out. First off, as you know, my name is Eduardo and I'm a graduate student in the School of Psychology at the university. I have been working as a counseling intern since September, and I'll continue working here until summer. Since I'm still in training, I am being supervised by two licensed professional counselors. One is on the staff here at the counseling center, and the other is my professor at the university. I meet with them both at least once a week and I confer with them about my clients. Sometimes I show a video of a counseling session. Both of my supervisors' phone numbers are on this sheet I'll give you so you can talk to them any time you want about any concerns you have about our work together. OK so far?"

Client: "OK, I guess."

Counselor: "Good. In addition to my two supervisors, two other graduate students will view the tapes and . . ."

Client: "Oh, great, that's all I need. Now everybody in town will think I'm a weirdo."

Counselor: "Don't worry. They are mostly focusing on my counseling and giving me feedback about my skills rather than sitting around analyzing every word you say. Plus, you are protected by confidentiality. I know you have heard that term also, but let's talk about it again, just to make sure. Essentially, what confidentiality means is that you have a right to say anything you want to say in our sessions without having to worry about it being repeated. What is said in this room stays in this room except for a couple of exceptions.

We have already discussed my supervisors and my classmates at the university watching video recordings of sessions. In addition, if someone I'm counseling tells me that he or she plans to hurt himself or herself or someone else, I have to report that to my supervisors and to the proper authorities. Also, if I am subpoenaed by the courts or a client's insurance company, the confidentiality of our counseling relationship may no longer apply."

Client: "So as long as I don't threaten to hurt myself or someone else, get in trouble with the law or with the insurance company, everything will be OK?"

Counselor: "Yes, that's right. We were told that it is standard practice pretty much all across the country."

Client: "What else?"

We aren't going to go through everything that needs to be covered in dialogue form, but we encourage you to develop your own "preflight checklist" for your site. Feel free to use what we've presented as a guideline. It is good professional practice to spend time reviewing in detail the informed consent documents of your site and having a conversation with your supervisor about the various aspects contained in the document. Becoming deeply familiar with this process allows you to have a more seamless and natural conversation with your clients about this very important aspect of the counseling relationship. You will also soon realize that occasionally revisiting this with your clients is helpful and reminds them of the mechanisms that are in place to protect them. The more comfortable you are with this, the more comfortable your clients will be.

Taking the High Road

In matters of style, swim with the current; in matters of principle, stand like a rock.

—Thomas Jefferson

As we discussed back in Chapter 1, the sixth principle of thriving in your training is to always take the high road. To succeed as an intern, you need to practice the highest values every single day. Ethical conduct requires more than having good intentions and merely following the rules. You will need to have a thorough understanding of the ethical standards that serve as the guiding principles for professional conduct (American Counseling Association [ACA], 2014; American Psychological Association [APA], 2010). The website locations of both the ACA and APA codes are included in the References section at the end of this chapter. Accepted ethical standards help you to structure the counseling relationship, place boundaries on its activities, and define aspects of its character that help you to promote client welfare. These rules are standards and are not in place to limit your work. In fact, they have been developed to create clarity, safety, and certainty for clients and for counselors with regard to the relationship they are forming. And within those clear boundaries, creativity, meaning, and effectiveness flourish.

Understanding your own values becomes especially important to your conduct as a professional when you confront ethical problems that require you to interpret or apply ethical principles in an ambiguous situation. Being ethical involves learning to make moral decisions based on criteria that emerge out of the goals and context of the helping relationship. As you read through the ACA and APA ethical guidelines, you will notice that they constitute a body of regulations and rules that you are expected to apply in your work with clients, but they do not apply to all situations. You must become an ethical person who can make judgments that will benefit your clients and remain within the general ethical guidelines for counselors.

Dual Roles

Another important ethical consideration is avoiding a dual role with clients. This means that you should not provide professional services for someone with whom you have another, nontherapeutic relationship which might interfere with your ability to function effectively. For example, according to the guidelines, it is unethical for you to provide counseling services to someone whom you employ. This employee may be your tax accountant or secretary with whom you have an ongoing relationship based on provision of goods or services. In relation to this person, you would assume a dual role because you interact with him or her in a specific context unrelated to the goals of your professional "helping" role. It is easy to see how this outside relationship involving the exchange of money, the expectation of quality labor, the clear structure of power, and the difference in function of each of the persons involved can undermine the intent of a separate helping relationship.

Consider, however, a slightly different scenario that is not so clear cut. Suppose you are one of only three mental health professionals living in a small town. Your son's seventh-grade history teacher seeks your help in addressing her problems with depression. You have expertise in this area, and she says she would feel comfortable with you as her therapist. In making a decision as to whether to accept this client, you must evaluate the situation in light of the ethical guidelines on dual relationships but also take into account other relevant information in making a moral decision. For instance, is there someone else to whom you can refer her who has similar expertise, or will she go without services? How acute is her need for intervention? How much contact are you likely to have with the teacher regarding your son? How might unforeseen events, such as after-hours emergencies or a hospitalization, influence whether the relationship is contained in the counseling sessions? What effect might these potential complications have on the teacher-parent relationship?

These are the kinds of questions that you need to consider when the ethical issue falls in the gray area of decision making. Therapists in very small towns face these sorts of ethical dilemmas frequently. They quickly understand that ethical questions are often complicated and usually involve more than a cut-and-dried application of rules. As an aside, the good news about avoiding dual relationships is that when your family and friends seek counseling from you because of your professional training, you can tell them that your ethics prevent you from being their counselor—and you are off the hook!

In addition to "live" dual relationships, ethical practitioners need to be mindful of dual relationships that may exist virtually. Social media has made connections the norm rather than the exception. A counselor recently described a situation in which her client came to session and angrily confronted her. The client had seen a friend's photograph on Facebook. The photo included a large group of people at a public fundraiser, and the counselor had been "tagged" in the photo. Also tagged in the photograph was the ex-boyfriend of the client, a topic of much of their work in therapy. The client felt angry, betrayed, and distrustful of the counselor. The counselor immediately pulled up the photograph and suddenly realized that she didn't even know half the people in the photo and definitely did not know the young man about whom the client was speaking. In fact, she did not even realize she had been tagged. As mentioned earlier, be sure to give consideration to your relationship with social media and the connections that are formed. Choose settings that mediate unintentional connections and unwanted access.

The application of ethics requires you to examine your own value construction. It is a vital part of knowing yourself as a person and professional and understanding the process by which you interpret information in making moral decisions. A developed sense of moral reasoning, especially in response to an ambiguous situation, is essential in becoming a truly ethical professional.

Ethical theory has long been of interest to philosophers and thinkers who are interested in understanding how persons may distinguish between what is morally right and what is wrong. According to Aristotle (Cohen & Cohen, 1999), the ancient Greek philosopher, moral virtues are character states that pertain to rational control and direction of emotions. However, recent discoveries in neuroscience have suggested that good social judgment depends as much on emotion as on reason (Cozolino, 2010). Sometimes, you have to rely on your gut feelings in situations that pose ethical dilemmas. Ethics are dependent on both head and heart. Examine the situation carefully, explore your motives, and be aware of your emotions. Taking time to reflect on your choices and staying committed to developing your personal character can also help you form an ethical worldview.

Because of your desire to help others, you are way ahead of the game! Our greatest reference points are the principles that form the basis of the therapeutic relationship itself. When you choose actions that best honor and actualize the goals of the counseling relationship, you remain faithful to an important set of organizing concepts that defines ethical values. Thus, your choices are based on values that reflect using your skills to foster growth and to communicate respect and acceptance of the person. Authenticity of expression, responsibility in actions, and courage to change become guiding principles when making ethical decisions. Fostering well-being and advancing the best interests of clients become touchstones for structuring your interventions and making your decisions. While your goals may be clear, their application in practice is often complex.

HIV

Eric's Story

While a practicum student, I counseled a man seeking help for depression. In the course of treatment, the man revealed that though he was married with two children, he promiscuously engaged in unprotected heterosexual and homosexual activities with many partners. This client learned that one of his frequent homosexual partners had recently tested positive for the HIV virus. The client had not informed his wife of his secret life nor of his own HIV status. He continued to have unprotected sex with his wife. When

I encouraged him to get tested for HIV, he declined, saying he did not want to know, though he felt guilty about his wife's potential exposure. When asked whether he was willing to discuss these issues with his wife, he protested, saying that she would leave him, take his children away, and ruin him financially.

Clearly, the ethical dilemma in this case is between maintaining the trust of client confidentiality or invoking the principle that when a client is a serious threat to self or others confidentiality may be breached. To not break client confidentiality may result in significant harm to a third party. At the time, the legal precedents relevant to such cases did not encourage informing a third party if a sexually transmitted disease were the only identifiable indicator of harm. This case illustrates that sometimes what is law and what is viewed as ethical may be in opposition. Provisions by the American Counseling Association (2014) include a "Contagious, Life-Threatening Disease" clause that allows disclosure in some cases if there is a known, demonstrable high risk of a third party's contracting a disease. This is undoubtedly a situation in which consultation and supervision is a must.

In this case, if the counselor had instantly broken confidentiality, the client would have left therapy feeling betrayed, and the therapist's ability to influence the situation would have been lost. The client would continue to have unprotected sex with other partners who would also be at risk. On the other hand, even though the HIV status of the client was undetermined, the counselor felt compelled to protect a third party from potential harm out of an ethical duty that transcended his relationship with the client.

Drawing on the principles discussed earlier, the counselor resolved to change the course of the therapy to address this central issue. First, the counselor secured an agreement from the client to cease sexual relations with his wife until the issue could be explored in therapy or until the client was tested. The client agreed to this provisional arrangement. The counselor concentrated on helping the client take responsibility for his choices, to be honest and authentic in his communications both inside and outside of the consulting room, and to rigorously examine the issues that led to such passive-aggressive behavior toward his wife and others. The frequency of sessions was increased, and within weeks of the initial discussion, with the strong support of the therapist, the client invited his wife to one of the sessions and disclosed to her the truth. He tested positive for HIV (his wife tested negative), and the couple divorced. The client continued to pursue therapy and to examine his sexual choices in regard to his HIV status, choosing to take more responsibility for protecting others. The client's wife was assisted in finding a counselor for herself as she sought to put her life back together.

Your personal morals and values will inevitably play a role in your work with clients. Although navigating ethical dilemmas, particularly those that trigger your own morals and values, may seem incredibly daunting, your supervisors will work to guide you through the process, so trust them. In addition, professional organizations such as the ACA include provisions within standards of professional practice and within ethical codes on ethical decision making. In fact, the 2014 ACA Code of Ethics for the first time provides a clear Ethical Decision Making Model so that all professionals have clarity on how to define the issue; seek consultation; consult relevant ethical codes, laws, and system policies; and document and determine the best course of action. Decision-making models are critical in order to maximize the best interest and safety of the client and the counselor and to protect the integrity of the relationship. Embrace the process! Here is a closer look at what it entails:

- *Seek consultation* about the potential ethical issue and work together to clearly identify the problem.
- In consultation, *give consideration of relevant ethical standards, principles, and laws that apply to the situation* as well as the organizational or systemic expectations. Document all the relevant ethical standards, laws, policies, and expectations clearly.
- Work together to *generate potential courses of action* that are compliant with the laws, ethics codes, and other expectations and are congruent with the values inherent in the counseling relationship.
- Engage in *deliberation of the risks and benefits* associated with each of the options. This should also be done in consultation and will need to be clearly documented.
- Finally, *agree on the selection of an objective decision* based on the circumstances and welfare of all involved. Document this process clearly, and document the course of action and the results.

The importance of consultation and documentation cannot be stressed enough. Remind yourself: *Consult, consult, consult. Document, document, document.*

Ethical conduct involves many other issues that are delineated in the codes. These principles include practicing within your scope of expertise, sensitivity to cultural differences, informed consent, and the nonsexual nature of the counselor-client relationship. The codes also address more practical matters, such as advertising, fees, bartering, and record keeping. Learn these ethical guidelines well. But remember: In consultation with your supervisor, you must seek to implement these guidelines wisely, keeping in mind the welfare of those that have sought your help and counsel.

Making Rest Stops Along the Way

In addition to performing your duties at your internship site, you will participate in weekly supervision sessions and may meet regularly with other interns. The internship class provides opportunities to share your internship experiences, explore the many opportunities for your professional development, look at your counseling work, learn from one another, clarify your professional goals, and help everyone to achieve those goals. It is also the time to exchange support and encouragement with your peers. It is a designated time for you to "fill up your tank" so you can continue on the journey. Upon reflecting on the internship experience, students have commented that they "didn't feel so isolated and alone after talking with other interns." Others described the experience as a "support system that cheered" them on throughout the semester.

These Poor People

Nathaniel's Story

I was seeing my first family in my practicum experience. In they trooped: father, mother, and daughter. Then another woman came in who was introduced as an aunt. "What's she doing here?" I thought. "Is this okay?" I was thinking about confidentiality and consent and trying to figure out what kind of family this was! Pretty soon, I found out. The mother was on house arrest. She wore an ankle monitor and was allowed to leave her house only for work and counseling. The aunt was with us in the session because she had assumed primary caretaking responsibilities while the family was adjusting to Mom's situation. The father seemed stunned. He reported that he and his wife had been fighting frequently. The daughter was bright and hopeful, but I was uncomfortable with the banter and teasing that went on between her and her mother.

"These poor people," I thought with sympathy. "They have no money, and this is their lifestyle. They probably don't know any better." As I listened

(Continued)

(Continued)

to their stories, I judged every one of them. I remember vividly how I left the session shaking my head and telling my supervisor there was little potential for progress with this "family."

My supervisor seemed confused. What was the evidence for my gloomy prognosis? The entire family had come in—all had expressed dissatisfaction with their current situation. Everyone present claimed a desire to work. What obstacles did I see to their progress and growth in counseling? I fumbled for words.

"Well, you know, they're ... well, it seems limited."

My supervisor looked at me inquisitively, patiently, and silently. Those were the longest few minutes of my life. It seemed as though my supervisor could see and hear every stereotype and prejudice that I had ever had. Furthermore, I started to suspect that I had been equally transparent to my clients.

My face began to feel as if it were on fire, and believe it or not, I started to get teary eyed. I was so unprepared to face the ugly stuff that lies within me that I had avoided it until that moment. When it came, it came in a rush. I had always believed that prejudice was a given in our lives and that I was in touch enough with my own "stuff" that it wouldn't interfere with my work. I was wrong.

My supervisor helped during that time, as did my own counseling. I've also come to appreciate the need to continually check on my own attitudes and beliefs and be responsible for my own growth. Even if prejudices really are a given, that doesn't mean I have to be satisfied with my own.

You may believe that you've effectively confronted your prejudices only to be smacked in the face with a nasty reminder of old messages and beliefs that you learned as a child. Facing your prejudices and stereotypes can be painful and can make you feel guilty. If you avoid doing so, however, you're bound to find yourself feeling like Nathaniel: ashamed and disappointed. Take time now, before you enter practicum or internship, to again examine your own beliefs and attitudes about difference. Recognize that guilt is the great silencer, and don't let it stop you from being honest right now.

EXERCISE 10.2 First Thoughts

An Exploratory Exercise

Consider this mix of different people. Read through the following list and write down the first thoughts that come to your head. Don't censor yourself. Just write down your thoughts. Now, imagine what might go through your mind if you were to counsel a member of each group.

Men

_____

_____

Sex Abusers

_____

_____

Elderly

_____

_____

Athletes

_____

_____

Women

_____

_____

Whites

_____

_____

(Continued)

(Continued)

Alcoholics

_____

_____

African Americans

_____

_____

Disabled

_____

_____

Latinos

_____

_____

Rich

_____

_____

Asians

_____

_____

Of course, presenting people as members of groups is always tricky. You run the risk of denying or ignoring individuality for the sake of categorization. Typically, however, you learn your prejudices and stereotypes about groups, not individual people. That's why stereotypes are so specious: They erase your pictures of unique individuals worthy of respect and replace them with faceless images that create fear or contempt.

This exercise is a chance for you to explore how you really feel about yourself and others. Look over what you've written and work to identify your prejudices and stereotypes. Where did these messages originate? How have these beliefs affected you over time? After you've given some time and thought to this exercise, talk with your supervisor and peers about how you approach and accept difference.

We offer one caveat regarding this exercise. You may find that you have to confront—at least in your mind—beloved members of your family. Your Uncle Joey, for instance, who always took you sledding and gave you the most perfect birthday presents year after year, may now appear to you to be a first-class bigot. This realization need not be the end of your relationship with Uncle Joey. It may, however, cause you to evaluate your expectations of others and to consider how you want to handle differing opinions. Furthermore, attempting to understand where Uncle Joey got his ideas and what motivates his clinging to them might be a very illuminating exercise for you. Merely labeling him as a bigot and writing him off is contrary to the values in counseling and therapy. We try our best to understand how everyone sees the world. Good luck in your continued explorations.

Stages in the Journey

The real voyage of discovery lies not in seeking new landscapes but in having new eyes.

—Marcel Proust

Kiser (2011) suggested that internships progress through specific developmental stages that include preplacement, initiation, working, and termination.

Preplacement stage. During your preplacement stage, you work with your professors to decide on internship locations. You spend time carefully matching your needs, along with the program's expectations, to an appropriate site. Activities include writing a resume or introductory letter to potential sites, visiting schools and community agencies, and interviewing. You may be discouraged if you are not able to find a perfect match. However, keep in mind that what you want in an internship may not necessarily be what you need in an internship. It is important to keep an open mind during this stage.

Initiation stage. Once the internship is under way, you begin the initiation stage. During this stage, you meet new people and become familiar with the site's procedures. It is during this time that you begin to develop a trusting relationship with your supervisor. You may "shadow" your site supervisor at this time to help familiarize yourself with your surroundings. This stage of your internship is the "looking" before the "leaping" into counseling on your own. You may be asked to observe procedures, sit in on meetings, and take extensive notes. Remember, this stage does not last forever. Be open and patient. The process *will* unfold.

Working stage. In the working stage, you are focusing your energy on reaching the goals that you developed during the initial preplacement stage. At this stage, you begin to feel more settled and confident. A key element of this stage is taking advantage of learning opportunities that are available at the internship site. Kiser (2011) warned that you should not become too independent and urged that you continue seeking all the supervision, feedback, and teaching opportunities that are available.

The working stage is the time in the journey that you may turn on the car's cruise control. Feeling confident about where you are, where you are headed, and the rate you are traveling, you can relax a little. This is not necessarily a bad thing: Travelers cannot maintain a high level of stress and anxiety throughout such a long journey. But it is important to remember that you are still responsible for keeping the car on the road and headed in the right direction.

Final stage. The final stage of internship is the termination stage. During this time, you begin planning for the completion of the internship, which includes saying goodbye to supervisors, colleagues, and terminating with clients. Don't be surprised if you feel some sadness during this period. Be sure to take time during this hectic period to review your internship, to contemplate on what you have learned, how you have changed, and what you have discovered. And give yourself permission to feel proud of your accomplishments!

Juggling

Once your internship is under way, you may feel overwhelmed at first. You may feel like you have one foot in student life and the other foot in professional life. As classes get under way and supervisor's expectations become clear, you will begin to realize that this is an exciting time. You are given opportunities to try things out while still receiving support and direction from your professors and peers. Once you begin to feel like you are standing on solid ground, take the time to explore. This is your time to ask questions, gather opinions, and formulate your professional identity. If your internship class size is small, take full advantage of the opportunity to use class time to share with your classmates. Although your professional career is only a few months away, you may begin to wonder if you are ready for it, and you may begin to mourn the loss of the community in your training program. Vow to stay in touch with your professors and your colleagues. They will want to know how you are doing, and they will be proud of your future accomplishments.

Making the Most of Your Internship

It is important that you remember to collect postcards along your journey. There are several different types of postcards you can gather to make the most of your internship. Your internship experience is a time for you to acquire as much information as possible from supervisors, peers, clients, professors, and other professionals. Although it is your time to put theory into action, it is also a time for you to make the most of the resources that surround you.

One way to do this is to pick the brains of your colleagues at your site. If you are interning in a school, for example, make a point of setting meetings to learn from educational specialists, classroom teachers, principals, and students. It is important that you develop or maintain a group of professional peers.

It is possible that you will never again have the type of focused, individualized, and invested supervision experiences as you will during your internship and practicum times. Embrace every second of it! Allow yourself to be as open, vulnerable, and transparent as possible. Ask the awkward questions, show your best, most challenging, and not-so-great work, seek multiple perspectives, and soak it all up. Many practicing professionals long for the conversations and connections that happened during their early supervision experiences. Enjoy it and then commit to seeking supervision and consultation as a way of being through the rest of your career. It is not something to outgrow. In fact, it is something to weave right into the fabric of your identity as a professional.

Your internship is also the time to attend as many workshops and conferences as possible. Use these opportunities to see, hear, and talk about techniques, approaches, and interventions that are currently being tried in the field. Take advantage of the cheaper student membership fees and join professional organizations and affiliations! Internship is also a time to meet other professionals and develop a networking system.

A Final Wish

> In the beginner's mind there are many possibilities, in the expert mind there are few.
>
> —Shunryu Suzuki

In Buddhist philosophy, there is a term—*adhikara*. It means "studentship" and is seen as an important core approach to a life well lived. Essentially, adhikara is an invitation to immerse yourself into an always-learning and always-curious approach to your lived experience. This is to embrace a *beginner's mind*. Even when you come to the end of your internship experience, know that you will continue to grow as a professional and that *not* knowing becomes just as important as knowing. Perhaps one of the most amazing things about being a professional helper is the recognition that each person's life is so uniquely different, each situation full of mysterious complexities, and that our willingness to be lifelong learners is the key to becoming the most effective helper and the highest version of ourselves.

Summary

Your practicum and internship experiences are unique opportunities to apply what you have learned. Each experience is your chance to put your knowledge and skills into practice in a supervised setting. With careful planning and consideration, you can learn what it takes personally and professionally to thrive as a professional counselor. When you complete your internship, you will become a professional helper. Along with the opportunities for employment in the field will come many responsibilities. You will be well prepared for your new career, but remember that becoming a successful counselor or therapist is a lifetime pursuit. Commit yourself to be the very best you can be.

Resources

A number of excellent books, which are listed in the References below, can serve as helpful resources for you as you embark on your practicum and internship experiences. The Baird (2014) book is chock-full of detailed and useful information while the Yalom (2009) book is a wonderful invitation for you to engage in self-reflection. Together, the two provide a fine balance of the practical and meaningful.

The book by Barlow (2008) provides you with a great overview of evidence-based practices. The text by Duncan, Miller, Wampold, and Hubble (2010) focuses on the flip side of the coin: how to maximize the counseling relationship in implementing treatment and assessing progress.

As you begin to develop your skills in case conceptualization, you may appreciate the guidance provided in a couple of other books. Halbur and Halbur (2014) offer a quick review of the theories of counseling and psychotherapy and help you identify the theory with which you most align. Sperry and Sperry (2012) provide helpful advice on how to conceptualize cases and develop treatment plans.

American Counseling Association Insurance Programs

5999 Stevenson Avenue

Alexandria, VA 22304–3300

800.347.6647

http://www.counseling.org/membership/membership-benefits

American Psychological Association Insurance Trust

750 First Street, N.E., Suite 605

Washington, DC 20002–4242

800.477.1200

www.apait.org

References

American Counseling Association. (2014). *ACA code of ethics*. Alexandria, VA: Author. Retrieved from http://www.counseling.org/resources/aca-code-of-ethics.pdf

American Psychological Association. (2010). *Ethical principles of psychologists and code of conduct*. Washington, DC: Author. Retrieved from http://www.apa.org/ethics/code/index.aspx

Baird, B. N. (2014). *The internship, practicum, and field placement handbook* (7th ed.). Upper Saddle River, NJ: Prentice Hall.

Barlow, D. H. (Ed.). (2008). *Clinical handbook of psychological disorders* (4th ed.). New York, NY: Guilford.

Chin, E., & Lewis, L. R. (2012). Success in externships and internships. In P. J. Giordano, S. F. Davis, & C. A. Licht (Eds.), *Your graduate training in psychology: Effective strategies for success* (pp.13–22). Thousand Oaks, CA: Sage.

Cohen, E. D., & Cohen, S. P. (1999). *The virtuous therapist: Ethical practice of counseling and psychotherapy*. Belmont, CA: Brooks/Cole.

Cozolino, L. (2010). *The neuroscience of psychotherapy: Healing the social brain* (2nd ed.). New York, NY: Norton.

Duncan, B. L., Miller, S. D., Wampold, B. E., & Hubble, M. A. (Eds.). (2010). *The heart and soul of change: Delivering what works in therapy.* Washington, DC: American Psychological Association.

Halbur, D. A., & Halbur, K. V. (2014). *Developing your theoretical orientation in counseling and psychotherapy* (3rd ed.). Upper Saddle River, NJ: Pearson.

Kiser, P. M. (2011). *Getting the most from your human service internship: Learning from experience* (3rd ed.). Belmont, CA: Brooks/Cole.

Nowell, D., & Spruill, J. (1993). If it's not absolutely confidential, will information be disclosed? *Professional Psychology: Research and Practice, 24,* 367–369.

Pope, K. S., & Brown, L. S. (1996). *Recovered memories of abuse: Assessment, therapy, forensics.* Washington, DC: American Psychological Association.

Sperry, L., & Sperry, J. (2012). *Case conceptualization: Mastering this competency with ease and confidence.* New York, NY: Routledge.

Yalom, I. (2009). *The gift of therapy: An open letter to a new generation of therapists and their patients.* New York, NY: HarperCollins.

11

Launching Your Career

To love what you do and feel that it matters—how could anything be more fun?

—Eileen Nelson

A newspaper cartoon that appeared awhile ago provides a telling commentary on the contemporary employment world. The first frame showed a man working at his desk with a sign hanging prominently behind him: "Seize the Day!" The second frame had the same man sitting in the same position, yet the sign behind him had changed to "Survive the Day!" The caption stated, "Today's corporate philosophy."

Why can't you both love your job *and* thrive each day at work? We believe you can. In this chapter, we discuss how you can forge a passionate and successful career in the field of counseling and therapy. As you prepare to become a professional helper, you will want to consider five specific goals: gaining employment, obtaining licensure or certification, becoming more involved in a professional network, staying creative in your work, and continuing your personal and professional development. This chapter offers you guidelines for designing vigorous job search strategies and participating in successful job interviews. You will learn how to gather information about the different licensure and certification requirements across the United States and explore some of the varied opportunities to participate in professional organizations. You will find out how to stimulate and keep your creativity as a counselor or therapist. Finally, you will explore ways to maintain your professional vitality through a variety of continuing training experiences.

Above all, you will see that your career can be an exciting adventure, another thrilling phase of your journey. You can make a difference through your work—and one way to start is by being opportunistic. Seize this moment to make positive career choices that will make a difference for yourself and others.

Around the Next Corner

Bill's Story

At the age of 36, following 3 years of graduate school and 12 years of experience in one career, why would I make a change? I was in the midst of a promising career and was financially stable. Why would anyone in their right mind leave an annual income of $64,000 for several years of financial worry and stress? (For the record, my average annual income was around $16,000 during 3 of the 5 years of my doctoral program.)

Most of my family and friends thought I was crazy! I thought that of myself a few times. But I wanted to be a counselor and make a difference, and I needed more training and experience to get to the place I wanted to be. For years, I had been doing "counseling" and "crisis intervention" without the expertise, and I was tired of pretending. I needed instruction, more experience, and a sense of personal and professional integrity. So I studied for and took the GRE. I applied for a PhD program and was accepted. I began the journey toward becoming a professional counselor.

Little did I know that along the way, I would have the opportunity to teach counseling and discover my true life's passion—teaching! Now I have the best of all worlds. I am a lifelong learner of the trade I teach, and I have the honor of teaching counseling among some of the brightest minds and most caring people in the world!

My best advice for you as you continue along your career journey is to be prepared for, and open to, the unexpected turns in the road, for around the next corner you may discover a surprising opportunity that may lead you toward discovering your life's passion.

How do you discover your true passion in life? How can you make your career one that is rich in meaning, satisfaction, and fulfillment?

EXERCISE 11.1 Life Span Time Line

Think about all of the career options you have considered pursuing in your life. As a child, you may have fantasized about becoming a professional actor, dancer, or athlete. As an adolescent, you may have seriously explored several other career options. When you became a young adult, you probably experimented by taking a variety of jobs. Now you are at a point in your life at which you are focusing on a few promising career options (Brott, 2001).

Begin by describing your career fantasies, experiences, and plans at different points in the past along your life span time line below. Note the persons, places, or events that influenced your decisions. Look for emerging themes and crucial turning points.

Then do the same exercise, but this time focus specifically on the present. What are your current plans and goals? Note the persons, places, or events that influence your decisions. What messages are you receiving from others? Are these messages helpful or constraining? Again, focus on themes, especially those that seem enduring for you.

Finally, look into the future. Use the time line to explore what you would like to be doing, how you want to be spending your time, in the future. Will additional education be needed? Will you be specializing in a certain area? What type of setting would be ideal for you? How might you, and others, place limits on yourself? How might you, and others, be valuable supporters as you work toward these goals?

How do you move from the present to a successful future?

From Student to Professional

It is good to have an end to journey towards, but it is the journey that matters in the end.

—Ursula K. Le Guin

As you prepare to make the transition from student to professional, you will naturally begin to think more seriously about the specific career path you want to follow. New possibilities and opportunities are constantly developing in the fields of counseling and therapy. Before exploring your options, you can consider your values and family background, your unique interests and abilities, your personality traits, and the needs of others to whom you are committed. You will also want to know where to go to discover the career possibilities open to you. You will need to develop your resume, prepare for interviews, and make plans for the professional writing and correspondence that will be required of you. And finally, you will want to make plans for continuing your personal and professional thriving journey through licensure, certification, and continuing education. Let's address these issues more specifically now.

Exploring Your Values

A great way to start your career development journey is by assessing your values—what you see as truly important—and the unique perspective you bring to life and work. As you gain insight about the role of your values in your career choices, you may feel greater confidence about the choices you are making. Here is an exercise to get you started.

EXERCISE 11.2 What I Truly Want

A Values Exercise

All of us have values and beliefs that govern who we are and the decisions we make in life. Rarely, however, do we take the time to examine these values. The nonprofit organization Foundation for a Better Life includes on its website Values.com an extensive list of values that includes giving back, achievement, hard work, and honesty. These values are inspirational in nature and can certainly provide us with a rewarding sense of commitment and motivation when we're already feeling inspired. However, what about those times when we're simply not sure what in the world we truly want? How do we truly want to live our lives? In order to consider this more fully, look through the following descriptions and determine which are in your top 10 "must have in order to feel fulfilled" list. Then see if you can narrow this list even further. What does your unique list of values suggest to you as you make plans now for your life?
Possible Priorities in Life:

- Working with others who share my interests and skills
- Helping others
- Feeling that I have been successful
- Serving my community
- Obtaining financial security
- Being considered successful by my colleagues
- Working with integrity
- Making decisions for others via supervision and/or administration

- Lifelong learning
- Having good health
- Gaining love and admiration from friends and family
- Freedom
- Feeling self-confident in my work
- Having satisfying relationships with significant others
- Caring for children and family
- Having time to relax
- Working with intensity
- Feeling needed and special
- Being able to work at many different things
- Working for social justice

Exploring Your Roots

Sooner or later, thinking about where you want to go leads you to consider where you have been. As you try to make sense of your career choices, keep in mind that you can best be understood in context and that your context includes the influences of your family of origin. Family can be defined in a number of ways, so don't excuse yourself from this part of the chapter if your caretakers were actually grandparents, foster parents, or older siblings. You can define your family however you like. The important issue to consider at this point is how your heritage affects your career and lifestyle decision making.

Creating a family genogram that includes career paths and values of family members is one way to lay the foundation from which your questions about heritage can be answered. Gibson (2005) illustrated the use of a career family tree through which children and adolescents can plot out the career paths and educational attainments of their families.

My Sacrificing, Adventurous Ancestors

Michele's Story

When I was teaching a career counseling course, I asked my 8-year-old son to complete a career family tree that I could show as an example in class. I was happy to discover that I benefited tremendously from his research because I was able to identify important themes for myself. For example, I recognized that while my great-grandparents were immigrants and lived a

(Continued)

(Continued)

life of servitude (i.e., railroad laborer) in New York City, subsequent generations gained more education, financial freedom, and social privileges and suffered less materially. I was able to see vividly that because of the sacrifices made by my ancestors to create opportunities for their own children, I had lived a relatively privileged life and could focus on higher order needs rather than struggling to put food on the table.

I learned about adventurous tales of second careers (e.g., owning a bar, managing political campaigns, being a professional photographer) that connected with my own sense of adventure. I also recognized that with more social and economic privileges, and the geographic moves that made these options possible, came choices that distanced subsequent generations of my family from our cultural heritage. Unique themes emerged that would not necessarily be accessed via a traditional genogram by creating a career family tree. Try it, and you may also make some exciting discoveries about your roots.

You can begin to answer questions about your own heritage in a number of ways. Think about what you learned from your family about work and career. Were certain jobs considered acceptable and others not? Did your family have different expectations for men and women? Did they value higher education? Finally, are you where you want to be? Give yourself some time to ponder these questions. The answers that arise can be illuminating—and maybe even surprising.

The Legacy of My Parents

Gabe's Story

I grew up in a blue-collar household and was the first member of my family to receive a college degree. As a matter of fact, my pursuit of a doctoral degree was primarily driven by my desire to prove that I could do it. I hadn't really given much thought to the type of lifestyle I would have after I graduated.

In my first job as an assistant professor in a counseling program, I couldn't believe how much my colleagues grumbled about their work. I kept thinking, "These whiners don't realize how lucky they are!" I kept imagining my mother and father and the hard physical work that they had done for years—and continue to do even now! I started to have doubts about my career choice, and I also felt distant from my colleagues.

At first, I felt like an impostor. Deep down, I didn't believe that it was okay for me to have a good-paying job in which I didn't physically exhaust myself. Although my efforts in school had earned my current position, I felt guilty. I also didn't feel comfortable with aspects of my job that required administrative or committee work. I knew I could teach and do research, but the rest of the job seemed like uncharted territory to me. I chose not to participate in many university activities for fear of being rejected, labeled ignorant, or identified as an outsider.

As I continued to think about my family, though, I began to realize a few things about myself. I came to understand that I do work very hard and that I can be proud of my accomplishments. One strength that I now can acknowledge is that I easily empathize with the first-generation college students in my classes. Although I still feel like an outsider at times, I'm working to make a place for myself in my job while honoring the legacy of my parents.

A career genogram can help identify your worldview, perceived barriers, role conflicts, intergenerational patterns, and beliefs about work and roles (Gysbers, Heppner, & Johnston, 2009). Constructing one and reflecting on what you find can be an important step for you in this stage of your journey. Putting yourself in the context of your family, you can explore patterns and influences that have helped and hindered your progress so far. You can then decide what to do with this information in order to make the most of your experiences.

EXERCISE 11.3 Career Genogram

Begin by constructing a genogram of three generations and include occupations for each person. See *Genograms in Family Assessment* by Monica McGoldrick and Randy Gerson (1985) for information on constructing genograms. Now spend some time responding to the questions below.

- Who are you most like?
- What were the dominant values in your family?

(Continued)

(Continued)

- Did any family members have obvious vocational callings?
- What roles did different family members play?
- What values did you learn from your family about work?
- How are love, work, and play balanced?
- What do the vocational patterns that you see suggest to you?
- What did you learn from your family about education?
- If each person were to provide one word about work, what would it be?
- As you notice any patterns, what do you want to do with that information?

Using Your Resources

Many students enter their training programs after working as volunteers or as bachelor's-level mental health providers. These students may have a bit of an advantage in creating a basic network of colleagues and contacts who can ultimately be helpful in securing ideal internships and when they graduate, the perfect jobs to launch their professional careers. Regardless of where you find yourself in this process, however, opportunities do exist for you now to make important connections. One of the best places to start may be with recent graduates of your program. Consider contacting them for specific recommendations regarding how they obtained their current position; they are invaluable resources for learning what employers are seeking, what unique skills are valuable, and what you can be doing right now to enhance your chances of finding the job of your dreams. Then expand your growing network further by engaging in two informational interviews, as described in the exercise below.

EXERCISE 11.4 Interviewing Two Masters

A Journal Exercise

Schedule interviews with two professionals who are well established in the specialized career field you hope to enter. Ask them their reasons for going into this profession to begin with and what keeps them in it. Inquire as to what they like and dislike most about their jobs. You may even want to ask them what they would do differently if they had it to do all over again. Finally, you might ask what they see as future trends in their particular fields.

After each interview, write a reflective entry in your journal about the personal meaning and insight you gained. How did the interview support or challenge your views? How did the interview affect your understanding of the skills you would need in this position? Sometimes it helps to compare or contrast your journey with those of others whom you deeply respect. This exercise may even emerge as the beginning point of a mentor/protégé relationship, as it has for many of our students.

Planning Your Career

Being Intentional

Selecting and pursuing your career goals are obviously important matters that will have a profound effect on your life. Explore your career options thoroughly, not only to improve your chances for eventual employment but also to choose paths that will lead to personal and professional satisfaction (Brown, 2002). Because of their extensive involvement in the field, faculty advisors and other helping professionals are in an excellent position to help you weigh your career alternatives. Rewarding professional experiences seldom happen by chance alone. You will need to carefully consider your options and to be intentional with your plans in order to achieve a happy, fulfilling career. For example, one study about future trends in the profession (Norcross, Pfund, & Prochaska, 2013) predicted that technology-based interventions, such as smartphone applications, online self-help, virtual reality counseling, and social networking interventions, would be commonplace by the year 2022. Although fads often come and go, it appears that you should stay current in your knowledge regarding the uses and ethics of technology as a therapeutic tool.

Spend time now thinking about how to begin viewing yourself as a professional (Peterson & Gonzalez, 2000). Although you are currently a student, very soon you will be entering the profession with endorsements indicating your competence and skill. Other professionals will be evaluating you based on the expectation that you are prepared to take on the responsibility that comes with the degree. For that reason, it may be a good time to conduct your own personal and professional audit.

Start with any social media sites that you use. Does that photo of you on vacation with your arms around your friends speak to your competence? Do your posts reveal wisdom or whining? We don't expect that you will necessarily be "virtual friends" with prospective employers, but remember that others may be able to see the images and pages you have created on social media sites. It is standard practice now for many employers to Google their job applicants. Google yourself and see what emerges! Some employers specifically search Facebook and LinkedIn for information about applicants. Would you want your boss, your clients, or the students you may eventually counsel to see what is out there about you? If you see anything that is remotely questionable, remove it. This advice holds true, of course, once you actually enter the field. We recommend that you avoid posting information about your work site, clients, or students. Social media is not the outlet for this type of information sharing.

In addition to being intentional about your current career path and professional presentation, you might want to consider your personality type and additional career interests in planning for your future. For example, we often ask our students to take the Strong Interest Inventory (SII) (Strong, Donnay, Morris, Schaubhut, & Thompson, 2004) along with the Myers-Briggs Type Indicator (MBTI) (Kaler, 2007). Studies indicate that people thrive in their work environment when there is a good fit between their personality type and the characteristics of the environment. If there is little congruence between an individual's personality and the work environment, dissatisfaction, career instability, and lowered performance may result (Holland, 1996).

Holland's research (1996) produced five main occupational themes or codes. The awareness of one's general occupational themes (GOTs), or Holland codes, along with a greater understanding of your personality type (i.e., via MBTI), can assist you in determining types of work environments, tasks, and conditions for which you are best suited.

Heidi, a graduate student and mother of two young children, took the SII and the MBTI. Her combined report indicated that she is known as an "enthusiastic helper." Specifically, her results on the SII (Strong et al., 2004) indicated that her top three Holland codes (Holland, 1996) were social (highest score), artistic, and investigative. Heidi's MBTI type was E (extraversion), N (intuition), (feeling), and P (perceiving). Her top five interest areas on the SII included counseling and helping, teaching and education, and social sciences. The other two were culinary arts and human resources and training. While Heidi's type seems uniquely suited for her career choice of counseling, it might be that she would eventually want to manage aspects of a community practice or she might want to consider working as a school counselor. If she does not integrate her culinary interest into her work, keeping that interest alive outside of work might enhance her quality of life (Savickas, 2011). Even though you have already chosen your career path, your career may take various shapes and forms along the way and may shift along with other changes in your life.

Becoming Professionally Involved

As you consider your career options after graduation, you may be preparing to seek a position or to continue your education. Regardless of your current intentions, become involved in professional organizations. Kaplan and Gladding (2011) identified principles for unifying and strengthening the counseling profession. Their list includes themes related to portable licensure and embracing the role of advocate. As the profession develops, there will be opportunities to work with various clients and agencies. These organizations, such as the American Counseling Association, American Psychological Association, Association for Counselor Education and Supervision, and their regional, state, and local divisions, offer options limited only by your imagination and initiative. The student membership rates for professional organizations are much cheaper than they are for professional members, so take advantage of this opportunity while you can.

Through professional organization involvement, you can attend conferences, offer presentations, participate in workshops, serve on committees, find a mentor, lobby state and national politicians, keep abreast of current research, or simply meet and socialize with other professionals. Beginning this type of involvement now, while you are a student, will increase your network, perhaps enhance your capability to find an excellent job that matches your interests, and improve the likelihood that you will stay connected and relevant in your own professional development.

When imagining such involvement, some students may immediately ask, "Yes, that sounds good, but how do I get involved?" You may feel intimidated by the idea of approaching strangers and asking if you can join a committee—especially if those strangers are well-known authors or researchers. Encountering a favorite author at a conference can feel like meeting a celebrity! One of the many advantages of being a student is that you can reasonably expect your professors to introduce you to movers and shakers in the field. In fact, you will probably find that your professors and other mentors would love to "show you off."

As you meet people who are involved in professional organizations, ask them if there are ways that you can help. Most conference committees rely on graduate student assistance. Trainees who volunteer to work at national or international conferences usually receive compensation in the form of reduced or waived conference registration fees. They also enjoy the opportunity to see how professional organizations are administered and have the chance to meet colleagues from across the country. Some of these interactions fall into the category of networking—a skill that may seem more appropriate for business and the corporate world. Actually, networking is essential for an active and successful professional in almost any field.

If you want to be more involved in professional organizations, consider the following tips (Huddock, Thompkins, & Enterline, 2000):

- Research organizations by visiting their web pages and then consider joining as a student member.
- E-mail or telephone leaders to see if their committee needs your assistance. Don't be surprised to find that they do. Handle your shyness or nervousness by starting small. Contact local or regional divisions of professional organizations first. Ask a professor to introduce you to a committee chairperson via e-mail or telephone prior to making your first contact.
- Submit a proposal for a state, regional, or national conference. Ask a few peers to present with you. When you attend the conference, participate in the entire experience. Make the most of the opportunities that exist for you to meet people and become involved.
- Don't stop yourself with excuses. Just do it!

Career Possibilities by Degree

Careers With a Master's or EdS

With a master's or educational specialist degree in counseling, you can meet the course work requirements for licensure and can work in a variety of settings, including businesses, hospitals, schools, community mental health centers, and many other public and private institutions. However, these professional opportunities vary considerably and depend to a large extent on the type of training you receive. You may be involved in assessment, providing crisis intervention services, counseling, consultation, in-home counseling, health promotion, vocational rehabilitation, or behavior management.

Licensing and Credentialing. Licensed professional counselors may provide services without supervision by other professionals. Currently, all 50 states and the District of Columbia license professional counselors. Most of those states issue at least a general credential for a licensed professional counselor. All 50 states and the District of Columbia regulate school counseling through their state school boards.

Licensure and credential requirements vary from state to state. Typically, states have course work, supervised experience, and examination requirements for licensure. The course work requirements are generally based on the Council for Accreditation of Counseling and Related Educational Programs (CACREP) accreditation model for a counseling curriculum. The curriculum usually involves 60 semester hours of graduate study in the following areas: human growth and development, social and cultural foundations, helping relationships, group work, career and lifestyle development, appraisal, research and program evaluation, and professional orientation. The supervised experience requirement often involves up to 4,000 hours of work following the completion of your training. The licensing examination requirement typically includes passing the National Counselors Examination or a similar standardized examination. Also, the National Board of Certified Counselors nationally certifies CACREP graduates who successfully complete this examination.

For information on the licensing of professional counselors in your state, look at the state's governmental website. Counseling and related licenses are often located under Department of Health Professions or Board of Counseling web pages. For information regarding your state's regulations for credentialing as a school counselor, contact your state's Department of Education. You can also go to the American Counseling Association website at http://www.counseling.org/knowledge-center/licensure-requirements/state-professional-counselor-licensure-boards and the American School Counselor Association website at http://www.schoolcounselor.org/school-counselors-members/careers-roles/state-certification-requirements for contact information for each state's licensure board.

Other Helping Professions. If you are seeking employment in school psychology, you probably hold an educational specialist degree, which usually requires at least 60 semester hours of graduate study. Most professionals in school psychology work primarily in the schools and are concerned with a variety of psychological and educational issues.

If you are seeking a general, research-oriented degree and you are not planning on pursuing further study at the doctoral level, you may find employment in teaching or research. Without a doctoral degree, however, you may find that your opportunities for employment or advancement in higher education are limited. You may discover that you are seldom able to provide services without supervision.

As a graduate of a professional master's degree program in industrial/organizational psychology, you may find employment opportunities in private businesses and government organizations. You may devote much of your time to the selection and training of employees. You may also focus on human resource development, employee assistance programs, and other programs related to personnel management and employee relations.

Careers With a Doctorate

Counselors, counseling psychologists, and clinical psychologists with doctoral degrees are able to assume many different occupational roles. You may work as a teacher, researcher, mental health service provider, administrator, or consultant. You may be employed in a variety of settings, including universities, elementary and secondary schools, hospitals, human service agencies, private business and industry, and government organizations. In addition, many helping professionals with doctorates maintain independent practices for the provision of counseling and psychological services. The doctoral degree offers you the most professional flexibility and leads to many career opportunities in counseling and psychology.

Obtaining a doctorate requires a deep commitment to academic training. The successful completion of a doctoral program entails at least four or five years of intensive graduate study. You must also pass a set of comprehensive examinations and complete a dissertation research project. If you wish to provide counseling and psychological services, you need to complete a year-long internship plus at least an additional year of supervised practice in a residency experience.

Admission to doctoral programs is highly competitive. The average acceptance rate for doctoral programs is approximately 11%; some programs in clinical psychology accept less than 2% of all applicants. Still, a doctorate in counseling or psychology is a very appealing option for students who are willing to make a substantial personal investment in order to achieve high academic and professional goals.

Counselor education is centered on the goal of training successful counselors who will be prepared to assume leadership roles in the field of counseling. A doctoral degree in counselor education is accredited by CACREP. CACREP emphasizes the training of professional counselor educators and counselors who will have competence in the core areas of counseling, teaching, research, and supervision. Counselor educators often fill multifaceted roles but are most often distinguished as helping professionals who work from a developmental and health perspective.

The majority of counselor educators and counselors who complete the doctoral degree will work in educational settings, such as colleges, universities, public and private schools, technical schools, and a broad spectrum of human service agencies. Professional activities usually include counseling, assessment, diagnosis, casework, consultation, referral, and research.

Conducting Your Search

Organizations such as the American Counseling Association have helpful websites that offer profession-specific information about job hunting and choosing careers. See, for instance, http://www.counseling.org/careers/aca-career-center/job-hunting-tips-resources. These sites include information regarding how to write effective resumes, negotiate salaries, and find jobs that will help you obtain licensure.

Once you have explored these resources, you can begin to seriously consider what job openings are most appealing to you. Use the exercises you have already completed in this chapter to ensure that you are considering not only pragmatic issues such as geographic location and salary but also your unique values and interests. Working intentionally now will help you find positions that are fulfilling to you both personally and professionally.

Where to Look for Jobs

The best way for you to discover an available employment opportunity is still the old-fashioned way—through other people. So it is still vital that you stay connected with your professors, fellow students, professional contacts in the field, and alumni of your program. In many, if not most, helping professions, job opportunities are found through personal contact—through someone you know or people who know you. Maintaining your personal contacts is essential. This does not mean that *what* you know is less important than *who* you know; however, counseling and other helping professions are less likely to advertise positions in more traditional ways, such as through newspapers or websites. You may discover a good job that way, yet we cannot tell you how often we have found our students receiving job opportunities through word of mouth or an e-mail. Keep this in mind.

Local newspapers may still be a good resource for finding specific jobs in your geographic area. Most newspapers now have Internet sites available allowing you access to almost any conceivable job market. Many websites are also maintained simply to provide employers with a means of reaching the largest possible audience of prospective employees. We have listed some of these popular sites at the end of this chapter. There are thousands of jobs available on any given site. Some charge minimal fees for their services, and some are free to the public. Other services, such as resume posting, are also available on many sites.

Professional organizations related to counseling, psychology, and other helping professions also advertise current position openings. The *APA Monitor* and *ACA Counseling Today* are outstanding resources in this regard. Every week, the *Chronicle of Higher Education* posts jobs in academic environments. These professional newspapers also have websites with job listings, and these sites are included at the end of this chapter.

Remember to use your university's alumni office and career center. These centers often maintain websites with thousands of job opportunities that have been targeted for students about to graduate. Networking through professional organizations is also a great way to discover job leads.

Successful Job Interviewing

Some recent graduates find that they are able to move directly from an internship to a professional job at the same site. They are then in the fortunate position to have insider information regarding the culture of the organization, including position expectations and key players. Whether or not this will be true for you, we advise that you consider every job interview as an opportunity to build and enhance your professional reputation. We have found that regardless of the size of the city or town, the network of mental health professionals tends to be a close-knit and connected group. It doesn't take long to build relationships with others, and you never know when those relationships might be helpful in furthering your career goals.

With that in mind, it makes sense to prepare carefully for every interview. We suggest the following:

Before the Interview. Find out all the information you can about your potential employer. Research the history and mission of the company, agency, organization, or institution. These efforts not only demonstrate your personal initiative but also help you determine if this position is a good match for you (Matthews & Matthews, 2012). As a result of your research, you can speak with greater confidence and ask informed questions during your interview. It will be obvious to the employers that you've done your homework. Practice a "mock interview" with a trusted peer or professor before you head out.

At the Interview. Of course, dress appropriately, wearing only business or professional attire. Be prepared to offer several questions to the interview team. Remember that every interview involves finding the best match for a position, so seek to find the answers to your questions about your responsibilities, your potential colleagues, and the work environment.

You may want to bring along the portfolio that you have developed during your training. It can be a great way to showcase your experience, accomplishments, and developing areas of expertise. Finally, make sure you remain energized and focused on the interview. Eliminate any possible distractions by turning off your mobile phone. Above all, be yourself. You will waste your energy and everyone's time by trying to be someone you are not. Trust who you are and the valuable experiences you have had.

After the Interview. Following an interview, write a personal note of appreciation to all key persons who participated in the process, especially those on the search committee. If you are offered the position, in addition to answering with a formal letter providing your response, write notes of appreciation once again—even if you decline the offer. These personal touches will go a long way toward establishing you as a thoughtful person determined to excel in all aspects of the position.

If you are offered the position, be prepared to negotiate salary and benefits. This is often the most difficult part of the hiring process, but it is essential that you prepare yourself for this crucial piece of the process. Also, consider your needs for supervision as you work through any provisional or residency periods associated with eventual licensure or certification. When negotiating, know in advance what you will accept and what you won't (Fisher, Usry, & Patton, 2011). If you are not sure if the position is right for you, ask for 24 hours to consider the offer. Remain confident in your abilities and experiences!

Your Career and Your Life

Lifelong Learning

In our experience, the vast majority of our graduates go on to obtain successful and fulfilling jobs in the field. Those who are ultimately the happiest are those who consider their careers to be one part, albeit an important one, of their life's goals. Even after you land your dream job, consider the importance of continuing your personal and professional growth journey. Keep current with the counseling literature, take additional courses at a nearby university, participate in professional development workshops, and regularly attend conferences. If you are seeking licensure or certification, you will be required to receive additional training after you complete your degree. Enthusiastically embrace these opportunities as they come your way.

Fitting In and Standing Out

> Become aware of what is in you. Announce it, pronounce it, produce
> it, and give birth to it.
>
> —Meister Eckhart

So far, we have offered you advice on how to become a professional in
your chosen field. Of course, in order to belong to any group or organization, you must engage in the behaviors deemed appropriate to qualify you
for membership. To the extent that you can do this successfully, you will be
fitting in. But conforming to the standards and conventions of your field will
also tend to make you ordinary—someone who is just like all the others.

Thriving as a counselor is much more than fitting in—it's standing out.
Lefrancois (2000) asserted that just as not using your intelligence is being
stupid, not using your creativity is being ordinary. So to become extraordinary in your profession, you must exercise your innate creativity. Being creative is simply seeing things in ways that others might miss and coming up
with new ideas that hit you.

E. Paul Torrance (1995) conducted a 22-year longitudinal study of people
in various professions who had been able to maintain their creativity. From
this research, Torrance identified certain important factors and offered a
seven-point "manifesto" to preserve your creativity.

- Fall in love with something and intensely pursue it. Staying fascinated with your work is possible only when you really love what
  you are doing. Of course, your interests will change, and if you are
  not paying attention to yourself, you may not even notice. As a
  result, you may go on doing something that you have long since
  "chewed the flavor out of" and not surprisingly find that it bores
  you. Make sure that what you are doing continues to bring you joy.
  If it doesn't, do something else.
- Know, understand, take pride in, practice, develop, exploit, and enjoy
  your greatest strengths. Sometimes, families seem to divide talents as
  if they were a scarce resource among the children. You've heard people's comments about brothers, such as "John is the shy one, James is
  the confident one." Or they may contrast sisters by asserting, "Jane is
  the artistic one, Jill is the scholarly one." Or they simply slap on a label
  by saying that "Brad is athletic, Bob is bookish." Perhaps because of
  this allocation-of-talent phenomenon in your own family you believe

that there are certain activities you can't do well or domains of endeavor you should avoid. Think again. Try your hand at everything that might interest you. You will be surprised at the many latent talents that you have.

- Learn to free yourself from the expectations of others. Free yourself to play your own game. As we have discussed in Chapter 7, all of us have been reared, to a greater or lesser degree, under what Rogers (1961) called conditions of worth. As children, we received the message that we would be lovable only if we behaved in ways that significant people endorsed. As a result, some of the ways in which you regard yourself are not truly you. Furthermore, you may harbor the belief that in order to preserve your self-esteem you must continue to please teachers, bosses, spouses, and all others who can withhold approval from you. Liberate yourself from the expectations of others. This does not mean that you must become an outlaw and ignore the wishes of people. It simply means that you can't please everyone, so you must first please yourself.

- Find a great teacher or mentor who will help you. Seek out someone who "knows the ropes" in your profession. Only veterans truly understand the many subtle dynamics of counseling that as a novice you are only beginning to grasp. In every setting, there are older people who are in the stage that Erikson (1975) called generativity. They are eager to be helpful to fledgling professionals like you. Search carefully for such a person.

- Don't waste energy trying to be well rounded. Do what you love and can do well. Although you should explore everything that attracts your interest, don't feel that you must know and be able to do everything. In this era of information explosion, it is impossible for anyone to be a complete Renaissance person. Focus on those activities with which you have fallen in love, and refine your abilities in those areas.

- Learn the skills of interdependence. Remember that your professional development is not a journey that you have to take alone. Collaborate and cooperate. Share your talents and borrow talents from others. You will notice, for example, that nine authors wrote this book. We each contributed in the areas of our expertise, wrote the sections with which we were most familiar, and benefited from the contributions of our colleagues. Being a team player has many rewards. Give up the notion that you must be competitive in order to stand out. You will be more respected if you generously give of your creativity and seek the contributions of others in the work that you do.

Think You're Not Creative?

> There is a vitality, a life force, an energy, a quickening that is translated
> through you into action and because there is only one of you translated
> in all time, this expression is unique.

> —Agnes de Mille

Perhaps you are thinking that you are not a creative person. If so, you are either confusing creativity with certain talents, such as painting or playing music, or you have buried your creative spark somewhere along the way. When you were a child, you were constantly creating, inventing new games, allowing yourself to be enchanted by imaginary play, and proposing all sorts of fabulous ideas. But something happens to many children as they grow older and become formally educated. "Many people with the potential for creativity probably never realize it. They believe that creativity is a quality they could never have" (Sternberg & Lubart, 1995, p. vii).

What happens to these creative children? How do they arrive at adulthood having misplaced their potential? What happened to you? In their book *Defying the Crowd,* Sternberg and Lubart (1995) stated that creativity can be developed, but they suggest that one reason we are all not more creative is that creativity is generally undervalued and overlooked in our culture. Critics of our educational system view school as a place that values only certain kinds of learning (Gentry, 2006). The traditional cognitive, convergent, and conforming biases of school make it difficult for students to develop their creative thinking.

Compulsive conformity is the antithesis of creative thinking. Imagination, a precondition for original thought, is often given up as a liability early on. Kim (2011) documented a dramatic slump in creativity from kindergarten to fourth grade. It is at this stage that male and female roles become important, peers become significant evaluators, children are expected to behave in more adultlike ways, and the school curriculum changes. Many elementary teachers prefer conforming and unquestioning students and often consider creative students to be obnoxious (Westby & Dawson, 1995). Even parents are more likely to complain that their highly creative children don't pay attention and get off task. Whether you entered adolescence equipped to preserve your creative thinking depended on whether you were fortunate to have home and school environments that encouraged, supported, and truly valued creativity.

Does any of this sound familiar to you? If you remember yourself being criticized for your daydreaming or off-task behavior, you were probably targeted as someone who needed to be less creative. But the good news is that your creative ability is still *there*, buried under layers of conventional behaviors, and you are past the fourth grade now. You are in a program in which you can once again exercise your creativity. Your professors will appreciate it, and you will feel the exhilaration of rediscovering a part of yourself that you had carefully packed away in elementary school.

Clock-Watchers and Workaholics

Some people work to live, and some live to work. Those who see their work only as a means to an end are the clock-watchers. They live for the time when they are no longer at work. Perceiving their jobs as boring and the time they spend at work as endless, clock-watchers are undercommitted to the work they do.

On the other hand, people who seem to have no time for anything but work are workaholics. Their cell phones and briefcases are their constant companions. Instead of enjoying pleasant midday meals, workaholics "do working lunches." Regarding vacations as merely interruptions of their jobs, they are overcommitted to their work, and their time is experienced as fleeting and frantic.

Both of these extreme attitudes toward work pose dangers. Workaholics tend to burn out, whereas clock-watchers tend to rust out. The philosopher Aristotle (trans. 2013) preached the "golden mean" in all things and was among the first to say that you must find balance in your life. You want to be able to enjoy work and also to enjoy your free time. Unless you are independently wealthy, you must work to live, but don't be a clock-watcher. If you truly enjoy your work, you will live to work, but don't be a workaholic. Be careful to find the proper ratio of work and play for yourself. The only test as to whether you are accomplishing this balance is how you are feeling at the moment. Consult that inner voice.

By the way, if you are a clock-watcher during your counselor training program—marking time until you graduate—you are not getting the most from your classes and practicum experiences. Conversely, if you are a workaholic who is trying to get better grades than anyone else in your program, you need to lighten up and have more fun. See if you can turn your work into play so that it becomes a joy rather than a grind.

Leaving the Nest and Making Mistakes

Do not fear mistakes. There are none.

—Miles Davis

No matter whether your training has been a joy or a grind, as you near graduation, you may be surprised to find that you are approaching it with mixed emotions. You are excited about finally reaching your training goal, but you likely also feel some sadness about what you are leaving behind— and even some dread about what lies ahead. You now have to go out into the real world, leaving behind the safety, familiarity, and comfort of your learning community. Looking for just the right opportunity and interviewing for the "dream job" can lead to disappointment and rejection. However, thinking creatively about this phase of your journey will give you a good start.

Of course, being creative alone will not ensure your success. Creativity may be essential for thriving in your career, but other personal qualities, such as determination and perseverance, are also necessary. John Irving, author of several critically acclaimed novels including *The World According to Garp* and *The Cider House Rules,* described writing as "one-eighth talent and seven-eighths discipline" (Gussow, as cited in Amabile, 2001). That claim brings to mind Thomas Edison, holder of more than one thousand patents and widely described as one of America's true geniuses, who said, "Genius is 1% inspiration and 99% perspiration."

Edison also showed an amazing passion and positive attitude. A reporter once asked him what it felt like to have failed ten thousand times in searching for the right material needed to make a light bulb. Edison replied, "I have not failed. I've just found ten thousand ways that won't work." He was also wonderfully opportunistic because some of his greatest inventions were accidental or resulted from failed experiments (McAuliffe, 1995). For example, when a large supply of chemicals was ruined in storage, Edison stopped all his experiments and used that calamity to invent new techniques for storing and combining chemicals.

No one in your graduate program requires you to write like John Irving or to be as inventive as Edison, but in order to make the most out of your professional career, we offer a few clichéd but important reminders:

- Accept your mistakes as practice.
- Seek clues for success in your failures.
- Consider new efforts as pilot projects.

Summary

In this final chapter, we discussed how you can begin exploring strategies for gaining employment, obtain licensure or certification, become more involved in your professional life, and continue to thrive in your personal and professional development.

One Final Point

Leap, and the net will appear.

—Julia Cameron

Remember the Zeigarnik Effect that we discussed in Chapter 4? It refers to the fact that you are more likely to remember and take with you the lessons that are still ongoing and not fully resolved. We therefore leave you with one final point. Your most important discovery about thriving in your training and throughout your life is an emerging insight, unfolding before you like a velvety, deep red rose on a spring day. You are discovering that thriving is . . .

_____

_____

_____

_____

_____

Resources

Some books we recommend are Bolles's (2014) annual edition of *What Color Is Your Parachute?* and Lamarre's (2006) *Career Focus: A Personal Job Search Guide*. These books provide a wealth of resources, including exercises, questionnaires, and tips for finding your dream job.

American Counseling Association Career Center

http://www.counseling.org/careers/aca-career-center

This is the official employment opportunity site of the American Counseling Association. In addition to position openings, you can also find answers to career-related questions and read suggestions for enhancing your career.

American Psychological Association Online Career Center

http://www.apa.org/careers/psyccareers/

On this site, which is sponsored by the American Psychological Association, you can search for job opportunities for psychologists, read tips on successful interviews, and even post your resume.

Career Magazine

www.careermag.com/

Career Magazine is similar to Monster, just a little less overwhelming. There are often some wonderful articles posted there, as well as the same services listed by Monster.

Chronicle of Higher Education Job Listings

http://chronicle.com/section/Jobs/61/

http://jobs.chronicle.com/section/Home/5

The Chronicle is the primary publication of higher education, so college and university jobs are posted here.

Monster Board

www.monster.com/

Billed as the largest website for career searchers, Monster is a great place to find job openings, post your resume, read career-related articles, research organizations you are interested in, or contact prospective employers. Monster often has nearly half a million job openings posted!

Occupational Outlook Handbook

http://bls.gov/ooh/

The Occupational Outlook Handbook is a nationally recognized source of career information, designed to provide valuable assistance to individuals making decisions about their future work lives. Revised every 2 years, the *Handbook* describes what workers do on the job, working conditions, the training and education needed, earnings, and expected job prospects in a wide range of occupations.

References

Amabile, T. M. (2001). Beyond talent: John Irving and the passionate craft of creativity. *American Psychologist, 56,* 333–336.
Aristotle. (2013). *Eudemian ethics* (B. Inwood & R. Woolf, Trans.). Cambridge, England: Cambridge University Press.

Bolles, R. N. (2014). *What color is your parachute? A practical manual for job-hunters and career-changers.* Berkeley, CA: Ten Speed Press.

Brott, P. E. (2001). The storied approach: A postmodern perspective for career counseling. *Career Development Quarterly, 49,* 304–313.

Brown, D. (2002). *Career choice and development* (4th ed.). New York, NY: Wiley.

Erikson, E. H. (1975). *Life history and the historical moment.* New York, NY: Norton.

Fisher, R., Usry, W., & Patton, B. (2011). *Getting to yes: Negotiating agreement without giving in.* New York, NY: Penguin.

Gentry, M. (2006). No Child Left Behind: Neglecting excellence. *Roeper Review, 29,* 24–27.

Gibson, D. M. (2005). The use of genograms in career counseling with elementary, middle, and high school students. *Career Development Quarterly, 53,* 353–362.

Gysbers, N., Heppner, M. J., & Johnston, J. A. (2009). *Career counseling: Contexts, processes, and techniques* (3rd ed.). Alexandria, VA: American Counseling Association.

Holland, J. L. (1996). Exploring careers with a typology: What we have learned and some new directions. *American Psychologist, 51,* 397–406.

Huddock, T. J., Thompkins, C., & Enterline, C. (2000, May). Counseling students need to get involved in networking, conferences. *Counseling Today, 43,* 16–23.

Kaler, M. (2007). Myers-Briggs Type Indicator. In N. Salkind (Ed.), *Encyclopedia of measurement and statistics* (pp. 676–678). Thousand Oaks, CA: Sage.

Kaplan, D., & Gladding, S. (2011). A vision for the future of counseling: The 20/20 principles for unifying and strengthening the profession. *Journal of Counseling and Development, 89,* 367–372. doi:10.1002/j.1556–6678.2011.tb00101.x

Kim, K. H. (2011). The creativity crisis: The decrease in creative thinking on the Torrance Tests of Creative Thinking. *Creativity Research Journal, 23,* 285–295. Doi:10.101080/10400419.2011.627805

Lamarre, H. M. (2006). *Career focus: A personal job search guide* (3rd ed.). Upper Saddle River, NJ: Prentice Hall.

Lefrancois, G. R. (2000). *Psychology for teaching* (10th ed.). Belmont, CA: Wadsworth.

Matthews, J. R., & Matthews, L. H. (2012). Applying for clinical and other applied positions. In P. J. Giordano, S. F. Davis, & C. A. Licht (Eds.), *Your graduate training in psychology: Effective strategies for success* (pp. 295–306). Thousand Oaks, CA: Sage.

McAuliffe, K. (1995). The undiscovered world of Thomas Edison. *Atlantic Monthly, 276,* 80–93.

McGoldrick, M., & Gerson, R. (1985). *Genograms in family assessment.* New York, NY: Norton.

Norcross, J. C., Pfund, R. A., & Prochaska, J. O. (2013). Psychotherapy in 2022: A Delphi poll on its future. *Professional psychology: Research and practice, 44,* 363–370. doi:10.1037/a0034633

Peterson, N., & Gonzalez, R. C. (2000). *The role of work in people's lives.* Belmont, CA: Wadsworth.

Rogers, C. R. (1961). *On becoming a person.* Boston, MA: Houghton Mifflin.

Savickas, M. (2011). *Career counseling.* Washington, DC: American Psychological Association.

Sternberg, R. J., & Lubart, T. I. (1995). *Defying the crowd: Cultivating creativity in a culture of conformity.* New York, NY: Free Press.

Strong, E. K., Jr., Donnay, D. A. C., Morris, M. L., Schaubhut, N. A., & Thompson, R. C. (2004). *Strong interest inventory* (Rev. ed.). Mountain View, CA: Consulting Psychologists Press.

Torrance, E. P. (1995). *Why fly? A philosophy of creativity.* Norwood, NJ: Ablex.

Westby, E. L., & Dawson, V. L. (1995). Creativity: Asset or burden in the classroom? *Creativity Research Journal, 8,* 1–10.

Index

About Graduate School website, 80
Academic skill development, 82–83
  Birdcage/systematic barriers exercise
    and, 89–90
  Bonnie's story/refreshed academic
    skills and, 83–84
  confusion/cognitive dissonance,
    resolution of, 89
  critical reflection skills, development
    of, 85, 86–87, 92
  emotional arousal state, performance
    effectiveness and, 90–91
  emotional intelligence, engaged
    heart/mind and, 84–86, 87
  flow, immersion in, 88–89, 176
  mindfulness practices and, 86–87, 89
  online resources for, 111–112
  perturbation wave, riding of, 87–90
  presentation skills and, 105–111
  reading skills and, 92–96
  research process and, 96–100
  study skills self-help and, 112
  writing skills and, 101–105
  Zeigarnik Effect, utilization of,
    87, 91–92
  "the zone", full personal engagement
    and, 90–91
  See also Basic needs; Novice trainees
Advisor-trainee meetings, 37, 38
Affect-cognition integration, 216
  brain-to-brain connection,
    therapeutic relationship and,
    219–220
  chronic emotional arousal, warring
    amygdala/hippocampus and,
    218

clinical intuition, right-brain
    processing and, 220
cluelessness, emotionally chaotic
    childhood and, 219
conscious awareness, development
    of, 217
early brain development, growth
    spurts and, 217
emotional memory, amygdala and,
    217, 218
explicit memory, encoding of, 217
explicit memory system and, 217
implicit memory system and, 217
implicit memory, emotional
    associations and, 217, 219–220
infant attachment/bonding
    experiences, imprinting
    of, 217
lateralization of hemispheres,
    implicit memories and, 219
long-term memory, damaged
    anygdala/hippocampus and,
    217–218
memory formation, hippocampus/
    amygdala collaboration and,
    216–219
new learning, consolidation of, 216
nonverbal language, empathic
    understanding of, 220
optimal intensity of stress and,
    214–216, 218
planning process, hippocampus
    and, 216
safety, perception of, 218
stress, corrosive effects of, 218
stress hormones and, 125, 215, 218

trauma, posttraumatic stress
disorder and, 218–219
tuning in/tuning out, hippocampal
functioning and, 218–219
See also Empathic abilities; Neuro-
mindedness; Neuroplasticity
Albery, N., 40
Allen, G., 74
Altruism, 177–178
Amabile, T. M., 308
American Association for Marriage
and Family Therapy, 25
American Counseling Association,
25, 71, 261, 267, 272, 275,
276, 297, 299, 301
American Counseling Association
Career Center, 309
American Counseling Association
Insurance Programs, 285
American Foundation for Suicide
Prevention, 254
American Mental Health Counselors
Association, 26
American Psychological Association,
26, 50, 102, 103, 112, 157,
272, 297
American Psychological Association
Insurance Trust, 285
American Psychological Association
Online Career Center, 309–310
American School Counselor
Association, 26, 299
Amygdala, 204–205, 206, 214,
217–291
Angelou, M., 1, 2, 90, 139
APA Manual, 103
Apprentice trainees, 42
Bill's story/theory-practice
integration and, 43
comprehensive examination,
strategies for, 46–47
disenchantment/resentments,
avoidance of, 45–46
mindfulness practices and, 44
multiplistic thinking and, 42–43
perfectionism, letting go of, 44
portfolios, assembly of, 46
sophomore slump, trainee
disillusionment and, 43–45

Teresa's story/inside-out learning
and, 44–45
time management, necessity
of, 44
trainee-faculty relationships,
development of, 45–46
See also Emergent professionals;
Learning communities; Novice
trainees; Personal growth;
Practica; Training journey
Aristotle, 202, 274, 307
Association for Counselor Education
and Supervision, 297
Attachment phenomenon, 68, 217,
219, 247
Attunement, 208–209
brain-to-brain connections,
therapeutic relationships
and, 219–220
complete connection and, 213
emotional contagion and, 209, 215
Gene's story/attunement
opportunities and, 210
introception, facilitation of, 209
mirror neuron system, empathic
responses and, 211–212
resonance brain circuitry and,
208–209
See also Empathic response;
Neuroplasticity
Authentic Happiness website, 196
Authenticity in relationships, 139, 158,
161, 162

Baird, B. N., 103, 268, 284
Balanced life. *See* Basic needs; Career
launch
Barlow, D. H., 285
Basic needs, 5–7, 54–55
Anne's story/nutritional/exercise
needs and, 77
attachment needs, life span context
and, 68
balance, challenge of, 59, 62
balanced life, creation of, 63–66
Beth's story/greatest fears and, 64
change process, transtheoretical
model of, 75–76
choice, opportunity of, 57

Chris' story/subsidized housing and,
    67–68
community building, emotional
    safety/belonging and, 68–69, 78
Contextualized Needs exercise
    and, 64–65
Dara's story/creating belonging
    and, 69–70
distracting nonessentials, discarding
    of, 58
Ellen's story/challenge of basic needs
    and, 57–58, 59
equifinality construct and, 65
financial assistance sources
    and, 70–74
Guided Fantasy exercise/alternatives
    exploration and, 60
housing concerns and, 66–70
It Takes a Community exercise
    and, 70
Martin's story/physical exercise
    regimens and, 76
Meeting Multiple Needs exercise
    and, 78
Middle Way approach and, 63
needs assessment/inventory, 60–63
online resources and, 80
personal hierarchy of needs and,
    56–58, 59
perspective development, multiple
    needs and, 77–79
Renee's story/needs inventory
    and, 61
Sea Star/balancing exercise
    and, 62–63
self-actualization, fulfillment
    of, 57, 58–60
soul, model of, 56–57, 59
thriving quotient, increase in, 78
values/assumptions, reflection of, 55
wellness, whole-person approach
    and, 74–76, 79
See also Academic skill development;
    Personal growth; Thriving
    principles; Training journey
BASICS factors in risk/resilience, 244
affective factors, 245
assessment, collaborative process
    of, 246–247

behavioral factors, 244–245
cognitive factors, 246
interpersonal factors, 246
resilience assessment questions,
    open-ended/broad form of, 244
risk assessment questions, closed-
    ended/specific form of, 244
somatic factors, 245–246
spiritual factors, 246
See also Suicide; Trauma/crises
Bateson, G., 146
Beginner's mind attitude, 40–41, 284
Begley, S., 224
Behaviorism, 201
Belcastro, A. L., 76
Berra, Y., 190
Boehm, C., 177
Bolles, R. N., 309
Boulanger, N., 4
Brain function. See Neuro-mindedness;
    Neuroplasticity
Brown, L. S., 267
Buber, M., 143, 162
Burnout, 215
Bush, G. H. W., 202

Campbell, J., 8
Cannon, W. B., 121
Capstone experiences, 47, 264–265
Career launch, 287–288
Bill's story/unanticipated
    opportunity and, 288
Career Genogram exercise
    and, 293–294
career goals, selection/pursuing
    of, 295
clock-watching and, 307
counseling/clinical psychologists
    and, 300
creativity, nurturing of,
    304–307, 308
degree type, career possibilities
    and, 298–301
doctorate degrees, career
    opportunities and,
    299, 300–301
emerging insight, harnessing of, 309
family genograms, creation of, 291,
    292–294

Gabe's story/parental legacy and, 292–293
general occupational themes, awareness of, 296–297
golden mean and, 307
human/social resources, network generation and, 294–295, 301
industrial/organizational psychology degree and, 300
intentional career development strategies and, 295–297, 301
interdependent/collaborative practice and, 305
Interviewing Two Masters exercise and, 294–295
job interviews, preparation for, 302–303
job search guidelines and, 301–302
licensing examinations and, 299
life priorities, listing of, 290–291
Life Span Time Line exercise and, 289
lifelong learning and, 303
master's/educational specialist degree in counseling and, 298–300
mentoring relationships and, 305
Michele's story/adventurous ancestors and, 291–292
mistakes, opportunity of, 308
personal values, examination of, 290–291
personality type, additional career interests and, 296–297
professional organizations, involvement in, 297–298, 302
research-oriented degrees and, 299
resources for, 309–310
roots/family of origin context and, 291–293
self-doubt and, 307–308
social media resources and, 296
student-to-professional transition and, 289–294
thriving, fitting in/standing out and, 304–305, 308, 309
What I Truly Want exercise and, 290–291

workaholics and, 307
See also Emergent professionals; Internships; Practica
Career Magazine, 310
Carpentier, G., 183
Carter, A., 66
Castano, E., 9
The Center for Credentialing & Education, Inc. (CCE), 52
Change. See Basic needs; Training journey; Transtheoretical change process
Chi Sigma Iota, 42
Chronicle of Higher Education Job Listings, 310
Churchill, W., 2, 139
Cognition. See Affect-cognition integration; Neuro-mindedness; Neuroplasticity
Cohen, C. P., 225
Communication channels, 36
advisor-trainee meetings and, 37, 38
bulletin boards and, 36
communication skill development and, 13–15
formal assessment procedures, participation in, 37
newsletters and, 36
program committee meetings and, 37
progress reviews and, 37
texts/emails and, 36
Community. See Learning communities
Cone, J. D., 51
Confidentiality concerns, 39, 48, 268, 269–271
Coping styles, 188–190, 247
Council for Accreditation of Counseling and Related Educational Programs (CACREP), 46, 52, 299, 300
Counselor Preparation Comprehensive Examination (CPCE), 46–47
COUNSGRADS listserv, 169
Countertransference phenomenon, 179, 190–192, 250
Cozolino, L., 199

Crap detection, 223–225
Crises. *See* Disaster response;
    Trauma/crises
Critical literature reviews, 50
Critical reflection, 85, 86–87, 100,
    124–125
Csikszentmihalyi, M., 88

Damasio, A., 84, 85
Daritois, J. K., 126
Davidson, R. J., 224
Davis, M., 307
de Mille, A., 306
The Decade of the Brain, 202
Deikman, A. J., 176
Dennett, D. C., 205
Denz-Penhey, H., 130
Depression, 203, 204
Descartes, R., 84, 195, 201, 202,
    203, 204
Dexter-Mazza, E. T., 174
Disaster response, 247
    counselor preparedness for, 249
    disaster response teams and,
        231, 249
    interventions/services and, 247–248
    Lennie's story/post-disaster
        counseling and, 248
    mental health responders,
        sponsoring organizations
        for, 249
    psychological first aid services
        and, 249–250
    resilience of survivors and, 249
    See also Trauma/crises
Dissertations. *See* Research process;
    Research projects
Doctorow, E. L., 101
Donnay, D. A. C., 296
Dopamine, 203–204, 209
Dualistic thinking, 39
Duchenne Smile, 223
Dumas, A., 47
Duncan, B. L., 285

Eckhart, M., 304
Edison, T. A., 308
Einstein, A., 9, 10

Ekelund, V., 92
The Elements of Style, 103
Emergent professionals, 47–48
    capstone experiences and,
        47, 264–265
    cognitive complexity, emergence
        of, 48
    continuous self-improvement
        and, 48
    feedback loops and, 49
    graduation/commencement exercise
        and, 51
    journaling, personal reflections/
        observations and, 48–49
    mastery-level achievement, quality
        inputs and, 49
    mentors/supervisors and, 49
    relativistic thinking and, 48–49
    theoretical approaches, selection
        of, 48
    thesis/dissertation, research
        opportunity of, 49–51
    See also Apprentice trainees;
        Basic needs; Career launch;
        Internships; Learning
        communities; Novice trainees;
        Personal growth; Practica;
        Training journey
Emotional arousal, 90–91, 110,
    208, 213
    chronic state of, 218
    complex emotions, frontal cortex
        organization of, 222
    memory formation and, 214
    optimal/ideal intensity of,
        214–216, 218
    reticular activating system
        and, 220–221
    stress, role of, 214
    Yerkes-Dodson Law, arousal/
        efficiency relationship and,
        214–215, 216
    See also Attunement; Empathic
        abilities; Neuro-mindedness;
        Neuroplasticity; Transformative
        narratives
Emotional contagion, 209, 215
Emotional intelligence, 84–86

Empathic abilities, 9, 104, 124,
    178–179
  brain-to-brain connection,
    therapeutic relationship
    and, 219–220
  clinical intuition, right-brain
    processing and, 220
  communication of empathy
    and, 213
  crap detection and, 225
  cultivation of, 213
  description of, 212–213
  embodied sense of self and, 211
  empathic attunement and,
    207, 211, 213
  I-Thou encounters and, 213
  mirror neuron system, empathic
    responses and, 211–212
  nonverbal language, empathic
    understanding of, 220
  primary empathy and, 213
  self-directed empathy and, 209, 211
  trauma intervention and, 234–236
  See also Affect-cognition integration;
    Attunement; Neuroplasticity
Empedocles, 201
Enrichment experiences, 8–9
Enterline, C., 298
Equifinality construct, 65
ERIC database, 98
Erickson, M. H., 89, 257
Erikson, E. H., 305
Ethics issues:
  ACA Ethical Decision Making
    Model and, 276
  competence, questions of, 267
  confidentiality and, 39, 48, 268,
    269–271, 275
  dual relationships, avoidance of,
    272–273
  Eric's story/HIV status disclosure
    and, 274–276
  ethical dilemmas, resolution of, 274
  ethical practice codes and, 276–277
  ethical worldview and, 274
  informed consent and, 268–269
  personal value construction,
    moral decision making
    and, 273–274

  principled behaviors, adherence to,
    271–277
  virtual dual relationships
    and, 273
Eugenides, J., 199
Exercise regimens, 76, 123
Exercises:
  Birdcage/systematic barriers
    exercise, 89–90
  Breathing exercise, 111
  Career Genogram exercise, 293–294
  Contextualized Needs
    exercise, 64–65
  Critical Reflection exercise, 100
  Detective Work/research practice
    exercise, 100
  Embracing Stress exercise, 132
  Giving/Receiving Feedback
    exercise, 160–161
  Guided Fantasy exercise/alternatives
    exploration, 60
  Hard-Belly Response exercise, 157
  I Am... vs. A Counselor Is...
    exercise, 175
  Imagining Success exercise, 111
  Interviewing Two Masters exercise,
    294–295
  It Takes a Community exercise, 70
  Life Span Time Line exercise, 289
  Magic Mirror exercise, 19
  Meeting Multiple Needs exercise, 78
  Mission Possible Envisioning
    exercise, 133
  Preparing/Practicing Presentations
    exercise, 110
  Reading to Write exercise, 104
  Refreshing Memory/Plotting Course
    exercise, 266
  Saying "No" and "Yes"/stress relief
    exercise, 128–129
  Sea Star/balancing exercise, 62–63
  Sea Star II/thriving in five
    dimensions exercise, 135–136
  Stereotype Examination exercise,
    279–281
  Stress Assessment exercise, 127
  Structured Writing exercise, 105
  Things I Hope My Clients Never Say
    exercise, 179–181

3 Ws attentional strategy exercise, 95
Toward, Against, or Away coping
    styles exercise, 189–190
Traditions reminiscences/planning
    exercise, 33–34
Uncovering Strengths/Resources
    exercise, 134
Visitor from Another Planet
    exercise, 149–150
What I Truly Want exercise,
    290–291
Writing Twice-Told Stories
    exercise, 103
Expert's mind attitude, 41, 187, 284

Facult, F. P., 129
Fariña, M., 55
Fear response. *See* Emotional arousal;
    Neuro-mindedness
Federal Emergency Management
    Agency (FEMA), 239, 253
Field placements, 21
    See also Career launch; Internships;
        Practica
Financial assistance, 70–71
    application process, help with, 74
    comprehensive guide to, 80
    Federal student aid, 73–74, 80
    graduate assistantships and, 71–73
    grants/fellowships and, 71
    Internet resources and, 79–80
    merit-based aid and, 71
    scholarships and, 71
    student loans, 73–74, 80
    See also Basic needs
Flores, L. Y., 98, 108
Flow, 88–89, 176, 252
Foster, S. L., 51
Frankl, V., 114, 116, 139, 140
Free Application for Federal Student
    Aid (FAFSA), 73–74, 80
Freud, S., 11, 191, 217, 225
Fromm, E., 118
Frontal cortex, 202, 205, 222
Frye, M., 89

Gao, J. H., 56
General occupational themes
    (GOTs), 296–297

Genograms, 291, 292–294
Gerson, R., 293
Gibson, D. M., 291
Ginsberg, A., 161
Gladding, S. T., 213, 297
Golden mean, 307
Goldwyn, S., 70
Goleman, D., 87
Gould, L. F., 126
gradPSYCH website, 111–112
Greeley, H., 8
Greenberg, M. T., 126
Griskevicius, V., 56
Groucho paradox, 285–286
Guilt. *See* Imposter phenomenon;
    Self-doubt

Hafifi, B. al, 264
Hakuta, K., 70
Halbur, D. A., 285
Halbur, K. V., 285
Heller, L., 204
Henley, T., 92
Heppner, P. P., 98, 108
Heraclitus, 195
Hergenhahn, B. R., 92, 155
Hero cycle, 163–164
Hierarchy of needs, 56–58, 59
    See also Basic needs
Hippocampus, 216–219
Holdcroft, T. L., 138
Holland, J. L., 296
Horney, K., 188
Hoskins, C. M., 71, 95
Housing concerns, 66–70
Howard, J. K., 98, 108
Hubbard, E., 42
Hubble, M. A., 285
Huddock, T. J., 298
Hughes, L., 124
Humor, 123–124, 235–236
Hurston, Z. N., 96
Hustvedt, S., 223
Huxley, T. H., 262

I-It connections, 162–163
I-Thou connections, 162, 163, 213
Impermanence, 252–253
Imposter phenomenon, 40, 186

Informed consent, 268–269
Internships, 264–265
  beginner's mind attitude, embrace
    of, 284
  capstone experiences and, 264–265
  competence, intellectual/emotional
    facets of, 267
  confidentiality and,
    268, 269–271, 275
  developmental stages of, 281–282
  dual relationships, avoidance
    of, 272–273
  Eric's story/HIV status disclosure
    and, 274–276
  ethics codes and, 276–277
  informed consent and, 268–269
  initiation stage of, 281–282
  internship agreements, writing
    of, 266
  internship classes, professional
    development opportunities
    and, 277, 282
  liability insurance and, 267, 285
  maximized experience of, 283
  Nathaniel's story/personal prejudice
    and, 277–278
  personal value construction,
    moral decision making
    and, 273–276
  prejudice/stereotypes, examination
    of, 278–281
  preplacement stage of, 281
  principled behaviors, adherence
    to, 271–277
  reflective practice and, 277
  Refreshing Memory/Plotting Course
    exercise and, 266
  resources for, 284–285
  self-concept, reframing of, 265
  shadowing phase and, 282
  site selection and, 265
  Stereotype Examination exercise
    and, 279–281
  student life/professional life, balance
    and, 282–283
  supervision sessions and, 277, 282
  termination stage of, 282
  virtual dual relationships and, 273
  working stage of, 282
  See also Career launch; Emergent
    professionals; Practica; Training
    journey
Introception, 209
Irving, J., 308
Ivey, A. E., 209, 222
Ivey, M. B., 209, 222

James Madison University Counseling
  Programs, 32
James, W., 77, 176
Jefferson, T., 271
Johari Window, 160
Jong, E., 157
Journey. See Thriving principles;
  Training journey
Jung, C., 84, 171

Kabat-Zinn, J., 114
Kaplan, D., 297
Keillor, G., 252
Keller, H., 5, 136
Kenrick, D. T., 56
Kent, R., 16
Kenyatta, J., 28
Kernan, A., 131
Kerr, D. R., 51
Kidd, D. C., 9
Kim, K. H., 306
Kimbrough, E., 134
King, M. L., Jr., 86, 133
Kiser, P. M., 265, 281, 282
Kniss, M., 199
Kottler, J. A., 184

Laing, R. D., 176
Lamarre, H. M., 309
Langer, E., 86, 87
Lao Tsu, 35
LaPierre, A., 204
Le Guin, U. K., 289
Leaf, P. J., 126
Learning communities, 143–144
  Antoinette's story/feeling of
    possibility and, 153
  authenticity in relationships and,
    158, 161, 162

collaborative learning environment and, 153–154
diverse frames of reference and, 148–149, 154
effective feedback, guidelines for, 158–159
engaged/vital participation in, 154, 155
feedback, giving/receiving of, 157–161
Giving/Receiving Feedback exercise and, 160–161
hard-belly behaviors and, 156–157
Hard-Belly Response exercise and, 157
hero cycle and, 163–164
honesty/understanding, climate of, 154
I-It encounters/connections and, 162–163
I-Thou encounters/connections and, 162, 163
interpretive categories, meaning-making templates of, 148
Johari Window, self-disclosure and, 160
lifelong learning and, 303
mentors and, 163–165
mutuality/interdependence and, 155, 158
personal growth, relational context for, 151–152
Rebecca's story, process group experience and, 144–146
reflected self, opportunity/impetus for change and, 152–153
relational opportunity of, 144, 146
relational worldviews, interaction styles and, 147–149
resources for, 169
respect/acceptance and, 154
seeming mask, counterfeit connection and, 162–163
self-awareness, interpersonal relationships and, 146–147, 158
significant others and, 166–168
social masks, transparency need and, 161

support staff and, 166
truth, diverse ideas of, 155–156
Visitor from Another Planet exercise and, 149–150
See also Apprentice trainees; Emergent professionals; Novice trainees; Personal growth; Training journey
LeDoux, J., 206, 217
Lefrancois, G. R., 304
Leider, A., 79
Leider, R., 79
Leifer, C., 74
Levin, J. D., 171, 173
Lewin, K., 92
LGBT populations, 157
Liability insurance, 267, 285
Lifelong learning, 303
Lilly, R. L., 98, 108
Limbic system, 204–206, 211, 220, 222
Lindbergh, A. M., 192
Linehan, M. M., 174
Literature reviews, 50, 98
Loving kindness mindfulness, 126
Lubart, T. I., 306
LUVing the survivor strategy, 233
humor, role of, 235–236
listening/concentrated awareness technique and, 233–234
relational linkages, establishment of, 238–239
understanding/empathic encounter technique and, 234–236
validation/acceptance technique and, 236–237
See also Trauma/crises

MacLaine, S., 58
Maroda, K. J., 220
Marx, G., 185
Maslow, A., 56, 57, 59, 68, 143
May, R., 54, 195, 196
McCarthy, M., 131
McClure, F. H., 196
McClure, M., 258
McGoldrick, M., 293
Mead, M., 54

Meditation practice, 57, 120, 124, 126, 145
Memory. *See* Affect-cognition integration; Neuroplasticity; Transformative narratives
Mendelson, T., 126
Menninger, K., 151
Mentors, 163–165
Merton, T., 193
Middle Way approach, 63
Miller, H., 65
Miller, S. D., 285
Mindful schools movement, 126, 140
Mindfulness practices, 7, 16, 44
  beginner's mind attitude and, 40–41, 284
  critical reflection and, 86–87, 89, 124–125
  forms of, 126
  gratitude/loving kindness, cultivation of, 126
  impermanence, experience of, 252–253
  movement-based mindfulness exercises and, 126
  personal turmoil, acceptance/validation of, 174
  reading skills and, 94
  school-based mindfulness interventions and, 126
  self-care strategies and, 250–253
  See also Stress management
Mirror neuron system, 211–212, 220, 224
Miyazawa, K., 230
Monster Board career search site, 310
Montes, S., 200
Moore, T., 79
Morris, M. L., 296
Morrison, T., 19
Mulholland, A. M., 98, 108
Multiplistic thinking, 42–43
Murdoch, J. C., 130
Murray, D., 101
Myers-Briggs Type Indicator (MBTI), 296

National Association of Social Workers, 26
National Board of Certified Counselors, 299
National Child Traumatic Stress Network, 249, 253
National Counselors Examination, 299
Needs. *See* Basic needs
Neimeyer, G., 44
Nelson, E., 287
Neuberg, S. L., 56
Neuro-mindedness, 199–200
  amygdala, stress/threat response and, 204–205, 206, 214, 217–219
  attunement, resonance circuitry and, 208–209
  brain development stages and, 202
  clinical depression, treatment combinations for, 204
  clinical intuition, right-brain processing and, 220
  cortical processing, excessive stress and, 208, 211
  counseling, neural pathway generation and, 199
  crap detection and, 223–225
  cultural biases, amygdala encoding of, 205
  depression, serotonin circuitry and, 203
  emotional arousal, optimal/ideal intensity of, 213–216
  explicit memory system and, 217
  fear response mitigation, "top-down" process and, 205, 206
  fight-or-flight reaction and, 204, 206
  frontal cortex development and, 202, 205
  hippocampus and, 216–219
  implicit memory system and, 217
  Kiara's story/residual fears and, 206–207
  lateralization of hemispheres and, 219–220
  limbic system, emotions and, 204–206, 211, 220, 222

long-term memory impairment,
damaged brain centers and,
217–218
magic, cognition/perception
principles and, 200–201
material brain, function of, 202–204
memory formation, hippocampus/
amygdala collaboration and,
216–219
mind/brain processes,
inderdependence of, 202, 204
mind, physical location of, 203
mirror neuron system and, 211–212,
220, 224
neural pathways, continuous change
in, 202
neurotransmitters, function of,
203, 209
orbitofrontal cortex, deliberate
cognitive processes and,
204, 205, 214
oxytocin, interpersonal trust
and, 222–223
pain, experience of, 211–212
posttraumatic stress disorder
and, 206
quick-response route, "bottom-up"
process and, 204, 205, 206
resources for, 226
secondary emotions, learned
associations/beliefs
and, 205–206
self-care strategies and, 215–216
sense of self, emergence of, 200
smile circuit, basal ganglia and, 223
soul/mind, dual substance belief
and, 201
stress hormones and, 125, 215, 218
thought/mood disorders, excess
dopamine and, 203–204
Yerkes-Dodson Law, arousal/
efficiency relationship
and, 214–215, 216
See also Affect-cognition integration;
Neuroplasticity
Neuroplasticity, 207–208
affect/cognition, integration
of, 216–220

attunement and, 208–213
brain-to-brain connection,
therapeutic relationship
and, 219–220
consolidation/integration processes
and, 208, 209, 216–217
cortical processing, excessive stress
and, 208
counseling experience, power/impact
of, 209, 219
emotional arousal, utility of,
208, 213–216
long-term memory, damaged brain
centers and, 217–218
memory formation, hippocampus/
amygdala collaboration
and, 216–219
mirror neuron system, empathic
response and, 211–212
neural patterning, expressive/mindful
practices and, 208
new learning, consolidation of, 216
perturbations, reorganization
process and, 209
stress, corrosive effects of, 218
transformative narratives,
co-construction of, 220–223
See also Neuro-mindedness
Neurotransmitters, 203, 209
Norcross, J. C., 193
Norris, K., 58
Novice trainees, 31–32
beginner's mind, cultivation
of, 40–41
counseling/therapy, engagement
in, 38
dualistic/right-of-wrong attitude
and, 39
imposter phenomenon and, 40
journaling, personal reflections/
observations and, 38
Juanita's story/selecting counseling
approaches and, 39
opening rituals/orientation
and, 32–33
perfectionism and, 40
personal problems, management
of, 37–38

portfolios, assembly of, 38–39
traditions, reminiscences/planning
    exercise for, 33–34
two-way communication,
    information sharing strategies
    and, 36–37
unlearning assumptions/socialization
    and, 35–36
See also Academic skill development;
    Apprentice trainees; Basic
    needs; Emergent professionals;
    Learning communities; Personal
    growth; Practica; Training
    journey

Occupational Outlook Handbook, 310
Okri, B., 230
Ontological security/insecurity,
    175–176, 177
Oppenheim, J., 55
Owens, J., 177
Oxytocin, 222–223

Parrott, L., III, 184
Pascal, B., 84
Percy, W., 147
Perfectionism, 40, 44
Personal growth, 10, 171
    altruism motivation and, 177–178
    assimilation/accommodation
        and, 186–187
    authentic self, liberation of,
        184–185, 192
    "becoming", primary goal of,
        171–173
    centering, personal stability
        and, 188
    conscientious attention to detail
        and, 188
    coping styles and, 188–190
    counseling/therapy, engagement
        in, 182–183
    countertransference phenomenon
        and, 179, 190–192
    difficult topics, unveiling of,
        179, 192
    Edna's story/personal change process
        and, 172–173

empathic abilities, wounded healer
    role and, 178–179
external affirmation/approval
    and, 188
flow, immersion in, 88–89, 176
I Am experience, discovery of, 195
I Am... vs. A Counselor Is...exercise
    and, 175
identity, continuous evolution of,
    174–175, 195
imposter phenomenon and, 40, 186
Michelle's story/self-understanding
    and, 194
mindfulness practice and, 174
mistakes, growth opportunity
    of, 183–184
moving-against coping style
    and, 189
moving-away coping style and, 189
moving-toward coping style
    and, 189
ontological security and,
    175–176, 177
personal assets, evaluation of,
    184–185
rescue fantasy and, 179
resources for, 196
Robert's story/counselor as client
    and, 182–183
self-acceptance/change and, 174, 188
self-care strategies and, 119–120,
    124, 215–216
self-doubt, Groucho paradox
    and, 185–186
self-examination, accommodating
    uncertainty and, 187–188
self-knowledge/self-understanding,
    cultivation of, 193–195
self-system, "I" awareness/"Me"
    experiences and, 176–177
sense of self and, 173–175, 191–192
Things I Hope My Clients Never Say
    exercise and, 179–181
Toward, Against, or Away
    coping styles exercise
    and, 189–190
unresolved issues/baggage, avoidance
    of, 192–193

value systems, exploration of, 179,
    191–192, 194
    See also Basic needs; Self-
    actualization; Self-care
    strategies; Thriving principles
Piaget, J., 186
Plato, 56, 57, 59
Play therapy, 207
Pope, K. S., 267
Portfolios, 38–39, 46
Positive Psychology Center, 196
Posttraumatic growth (PTG), 231, 252
Posttraumatic stress disorder (PTSD),
    206, 218–219, 231
    See also Trauma/crises
Practica, 257–258
    conceptual framework for practice,
        development of, 260
    Gabrielle's story/questionable virtual
        presence and, 261
    Jerra's story/initial counseling
        experiences and, 259–260
    patience, importance of, 263
    practicum, experience of, 262–264
    professional identity, development
        of, 260–261
    self-doubt and, 258–260
    social media use, professional
        guidelines/ethics codes and, 261
    video recordings, skill refinement
        and, 264
    See also Emergent professionals;
        Internships; Training journey
Presentation skill development, 105
    Breathing exercise and, 111
    class participation and, 106–107
    energy/tension, productive
        presentations and, 110
    Imagining Success exercise and, 111
    improvement guidelines and,
        108–110
    Preparing/Practicing Presentations
        exercise and, 110
    presentation skills, development
        of, 107–108
    presentation skills, need for,
        105–106
    See also Academic skill development

Professional organizations, 25–26, 42,
    52, 297–298, 302
Professionals. *See* Career launch;
    Emergent professionals;
    Internships
Program evaluations, 49
Progress reviews, 37
Proust, M., 281
PSYCGRAD litserv, 169
PsychNet-UK website, 196
Psychological Association, 267
PsycINFO database, 98
Public speaking. *See* Presentation skill
    development
*Publication Manual of the American
    Psychological Association*, 50
Purkey, W., 54

Ramachandran, V. S., 211
Rapport, 123, 252
Reading skill development, 92
    author-reader collaboration and, 94
    Brian's story/approaching reading
        assignments and, 95–96
    concentration, strategies for, 94–95
    graduate school material,
        characteristics of, 93
    mindful reading and, 94
    physical environmental, factors
        in, 93–94
    Reading to Write exercise and, 104
    3 Ws attentional strategy exercise
        and, 95
    time element and, 94
    See also Academic skill development
Reagon, B. J., 175
Relationships. *See* Learning
    communities; Stress management;
    Trauma/crises
Relativistic thinking, 48–49
Rescue fantasy, 179
Research process, 96
    Critical Reflection exercise and, 100
    Detective Work exercise and, 100
    faculty research teams, engagement
        with, 98
    higher order thinking and, 99
    literature reviews and, 98

note taking skills and, 99
online search skills and, 98–99
organizational skills and, 99
personal interests and, 99, 100
research skills, development
of, 97–99
research skills, need for, 96–97
See also Academic skill
development; Research
projects
Research projects, 49
evaluation criteria for, 50–51
faculty committees, selection
of, 50
final drafts, style guidelines
for, 50
final reports, forms of, 49–50
journaling, exploration of ideas/
plans and, 50
See also Emergent professionals;
Research process
Resilience, 123, 130–131, 132, 140,
221, 232–233, 238
See also BASICS factors in risk/
resilience; Disaster response;
Trauma/crises
Rhoades, B. L., 126
Robbins, T., 221
Rogers, C. R., 161, 162, 188, 212,
225, 305
Rooney, S. C., 98, 108
Roosevelt, T., 87
Rossi, E. L., 89
Rossi, S. I., 89
Runbeck, M. L., 63
Russell, D., 60
Rust out, 215

Sarnoff, S., 118
Schaller, M., 56
Schaubhut, N. A., 296
Schizophrenia, 203
Schore, A. N., 220
Scribner, C., Jr., 92
The Secret Life of the Brain
website, 226
Self-actualization, 57, 58–60
See also Personal growth

Self-care strategies, 119–120, 124,
215–216
balanced well-being, maintenance
of, 250
counselor grief experiences,
self-awareness/self-acceptance
and, 251–253
countertransference, hindrance
of, 250
crisis intervention/trauma counseling
and, 250
mindful self-care and, 250–253
personal grief, acknowledgment
of, 251
posttraumatic growth, potential
for, 252–253
rapport/therapeutic alliances,
creation of, 252
wounded healer role and,
178–179, 251
Self-doubt, 185–186, 258–259
career launch and, 307–308
conceptual framework for practice,
development of, 260
Jerra's story/initial counseling
experiences and, 259–260
See also Imposter phenomenon
Seligman, M. E. P., 196
Seng-Chao, 28
Serotonin, 203, 209
Sharp, S., 5
Sherwood, V. R., 225
Siegel, D. J., 209
Smile circuit, 223
Snyder, M., 225
Social masks, 161, 224–225
Social media use, 261, 273
Society for Neuroscience, 226
Soul model, 56–57, 59
Sperry, J., 285
Sperry, L., 285
Stafford, W., 138
Steinbeck, J., 20
Steinem, G., 186
Sternberg, R. J., 306
Stevenson, R. L., 7
Strengths focus, 16, 62, 90, 130, 131,
132, 134, 138–139, 304

Stress, 6–7, 18, 20
  Bill's story/overwhelming stress
    and, 116–117
  character/wisdom development
    and, 136–138
  descriptions of, 117–118, 129–130
  distressing effect of, 115
  emotional contagion and, 215
  eustress and, 115
  meaningful stress, 116, 131,
    137–138
  neurological effects of, 218
  personal transformation and,
    137–138, 139
  strength-building potential
    of, 138–139
  welcoming stress and, 115
  See also Affect-cognition integration;
    Disaster response; Emotional
    arousal; Posttraumatic stress
    disorder (PTSD); Stress
    management; Trauma/crises
Stress management, 114
  Bill's story/managing overwhelming
    stress and, 116–117
  coping mechanisms and, 121–125
  distress symptoms and, 118–119
  Embracing Stress exercise and, 132
  eustress, positive challenge/
    motivation and, 115
  event stressors and, 119–120,
    131–132
  fight/flight/freeze responses and,
    121, 122
  goals, envisioning of, 133
  helping professions, inherent stress
    in, 118
  humor/laughter and, 123–124
  meaningful stress and, 116, 131,
    137–138
  mindfulness practices and,
    114–115, 125–129, 132
  Mission Possible Envisioning
    exercise and, 133
  negative attitudes, attention to, 125
  nutritional moderation/balance
    and, 122–123
  physical exercise regimens and, 123

  positive experiences, cultivation
    of, 126
  professional help for, 124
  Rachel's story/evolving self-care
    and, 119–120
  reflective living and, 124–125
  relationship building/maintenance
    and, 134–135
  resilience under stress and,
    123, 130–131, 132
  resources for, 140
  rest/relaxation and, 122, 124
  Saying "No" and "Yes" stress relief
    exercise and, 128–129
  Sea Star II/thriving in 5 dimensions
    exercise and, 135–136
  self-care strategies and, 120, 124
  strengths, acknowledgment of, 130,
    131, 132, 134, 138–139
  Stress Assessment exercise and, 127
  stress, description of, 117–118,
    129–130
  stress hormones and, 125, 215
  tend/befriend responses and,
    121, 122
  thriving under stress and, 133–136
  time management and, 125
  trainees, resource limitations
    and, 115
  Uncovering Strengths/Resources
    exercise and, 134
  violence and, 122
  writing about stress, cathartic nature
    of, 131–132
  See also Affect-cognition integration;
    Stress; Trauma/crises
Strong, E. K, Jr., 296
Strong Interest Inventory (SII), 296
Strunk, W., 103
Study skills self-help, 112
Suicide, 117, 179
  attachments, development of, 247
  BASICS factors in risk/resilience
    and, 244–246
  client-generated safety plans
    and, 247
  crisis intervention/resolution
    and, 243

empathic/compassionate support
  and, 243
lethal instruments, limited access
  to, 247
listening/concentrated awareness
  technique and, 243
mental health services and, 247
no-suicide contracts and, 247
positive coping alternatives,
  implementation of, 247
prevention interventions and,
  243–247
resilience, promotion of, 247
risk assessment and, 243–244
strengths exploration/enhancement
  and, 244
suicide ideation, inquiry about, 243
voluntary/involuntary commitment
  and, 247
See also Trauma/crises
Survival. *See* Basic needs; Thriving
  principles; Training journey
Suzuki, S., 41, 284
Swan, W. B., 185, 186
Szasz, T., 216

Taormina, R. J., 56
Tarrant, J. M., 98, 108
Taylor, S. E., 121
Teyber, E., 196
Theses. *See* Research process;
  Research projects
Thompkins, C., 298
Thompson, R., 296
Thriving principles, 1–2, 5
  active participatory learning and, 8
  Andrea's story/professor's support
    and, 17–18
  authentic/face-to-face encounters,
    opportunities for, 6
  basic needs, providing for, 5–7
  choice, opportunity of, 57
  collaborative learning, openness
    to, 11–15
  communication skill development
    and, 13–15
  continuous professional
    development and, 9

counseling/therapy, engagement
  in, 7, 38
curiosity, essential quality of, 9–10
destination, misunderstanding
  of, 7–8
empathy, enhancement of, 9
enrichment experiences,
  participation in, 8–9
ethics/values, maintenance of, 23–24
goal setting, clarity in, 18
Jean's story/new trainee and, 2–3
Jen's story/communication failure
  and, 14–15
Journey parable/valuable process
  and, 10–11
learning communities/cohorts,
  supportive environments
  and, 12–13
learning experiences, satisfaction/
  fulfillment and, 2, 9, 20
Lennie's story/supportive
  collaboration and, 21–23
Magic Mirror exercise and, 19
modeling best practices and, 13
personal/professional growth, focus
  on, 5–6, 7, 9–10, 20–21
personal success, formula for, 10
professional organizations and,
  25–26, 42
professors/supervisors, demonstrated
  professionalism and, 13
self-discovery/self-development and,
  15–19, 21
stress, management of, 6–7, 18, 20
stumbling blocks to stepping-stones
  conversion and, 18
therapeutic principles, continuous
  practice of, 7–11
thriving practitioners, fundamental
  qualities of, 18–19
tools/resources, gathering of, 6,
  20–21
trainee-faculty relationships,
  development of, 12
training journey, momentum/
  discoveries in, 19–23
See also Personal growth; Training
  journey

Thurman, H., 31
Time management, 7, 44, 125
Toomer, J., 117
Torrance, E. P., 304
Tourner, P., 15
Training journey, 5, 28
    apprentice trainees and, 42–47
    Cathy's story/trainee evolution
        and, 30–31
    emergent professionals and,
        28–29, 47–51
    milestones in, 29, 46
    novice trainees and, 31–41
    perspectives, developmental stages
        of, 29–31
    self-concept, transformation
        of, 29, 30, 31
    See also Academic skill development;
        Apprentice trainees; Basic
        needs; Career launch; Emergent
        professionals; Internships;
        Learning communities; Novice
        trainees; Personal growth;
        Practica; Thriving principles
Transformative narratives, 220
    co-construction of, 220–221
    complex emotions, frontal cortex
        organization of, 222
    false memory, therapist role in, 221
    memories, reconstruction of, 221
    negative/painful memories,
        acknowledgment of, 221–222
    neural pathways, construction
        of, 221
    oxytocin, interpersonal trust
        and, 222–223
    positive feelings, frontal cortex
        stimulation and, 222
    reticular activating system, selective
        attention and, 221
    See also Affect-cognition integration;
        Neuroplasticity
Transtheoretical change process, 75
    accelerated momentum of change
        and, 76
    action stage and, 76
    contemplation stage and, 75
    maintenance stage and, 76

precontemplation stage and, 75
preparation stage and, 75–76
See also Basic needs
Trauma/crises, 218–219, 230–231
    assessment, collaborative process
        of, 246–247
    BASICS factors in risk/resilience
        and, 244–246
    client-generated safety plans,
        development of, 247
    coping resources for, 253–254
    crisis, definition of, 232
    crisis intervention, purpose of, 232
    crisis intervention techniques
        and, 237–243
    disaster intervention and,
        231, 247–250
    emotional responses, productive
        management of, 240–241
    intervention principles and, 233–237
    listening/concentrated awareness
        approach and, 233–234
    LUVing the survivor strategy
        and, 233–237, 238
    meaning making, shared crisis
        narratives and, 239–240
    mental health services and, 247
    moving on, envisioning new
        possibilities and, 241–243
    posttraumatic growth and, 231
    psychiatric emergency services
        and, 231
    psychological first aid services
        and, 249–250
    referrals to services and, 242–243
    relational linkages, establishment
        of, 238–239
    resilience/growth, psychological
        scaffolding for, 232–233, 238
    resolve, encouragement of, 241
    self-care strategies and, 250–253
    suicide prevention strategies
        and, 243–247
    trauma, definition of, 231
    trauma-informed treatment
        and, 231
    understanding/empathic encounter
        approach and, 234–236

validation/acceptance approach and,
    236–237
See also Affect-cognition integration;
    Posttraumatic stress disorder
    (PTSD)

Validation, 174, 213
Video recordings, 8, 16, 46, 144,
    151, 154, 184, 222, 264
Virtual experiences, 6, 261, 273

Wah, L. M., 156
Wampold, E. B., 285
Washington, B. T., 137
Well-being. *See* Basic needs
White, E. B., 103
Wickett, M., 130
Wilde, O., 91
Wilde, S., 15
Williams, H., 182
Wounded healer role, 178–179, 251
Writing skill development, 101
    case note writing and, 101
    professional correspondence,
        correctness/clarity in, 101,
        102–103

Reading to Write exercise
    and, 104
resources for, 102–103
structural considerations and, 105
Structured Writing exercise
    and, 105
Susan's story/writing skill
    insufficiencies and, 102
treatment summaries/reports
    and, 101
writing skills, development of,
    103–104
writing skills, need for, 101–103
Writing Twice-Told Stories exercise
    and, 104
See also Academic skill
    development

Yalom, I., 284
Yerkes-Dodson Law, 90, 214–215, 216
Yoga practice, 78, 124, 126, 145
Young, M. E., 29

Zalaquett, c. P., 209, 222
Zeigarnik, B., 92
Zeigarnik Effect, 87, 91–92, 309

SAGE researchmethods

The essential online tool for researchers from the world's leading methods publisher

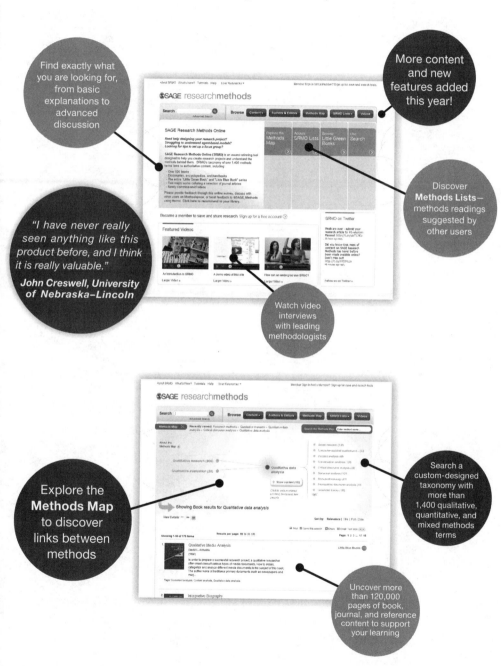

Find exactly what you are looking for, from basic explanations to advanced discussion

More content and new features added this year!

Discover **Methods Lists**—methods readings suggested by other users

"I have never really seen anything like this product before, and I think it is really valuable."
John Creswell, University of Nebraska–Lincoln

Watch video interviews with leading methodologists

Explore the **Methods Map** to discover links between methods

Search a custom-designed taxonomy with more than 1,400 qualitative, quantitative, and mixed methods terms

Uncover more than 120,000 pages of book, journal, and reference content to support your learning

Find out more at
www.sageresearchmethods.com